Recruitment
Handbook

Recruitment Handbook

Third Edition

Editor: Bernard Ungerson

A Gower Handbook

© Gower Publishing Company Limited 1983

First published 1970

Second edition 1975

Third Edition published 1983 by
Gower Publishing Company Limited
Aldershot, Hants, England

British Library Cataloguing in Publication Data
Recruitment handbook.—3rd. ed.
  1. Recruiting of employees
  2. Personnel management
  I. Ungerson, Bernard
  658.3'11   HF5549.R44

ISBN   0-566-02192-7

Printed and bound in Great Britain by
Robert Hartnoll Ltd Bodmin Cornwall

Contents

**PART TWO   RECRUITMENT OF PARTICULAR
CATEGORIES OF EMPLOYEE**

Illustrations

Preface to the Third Edition

Again, every effort has been made to up-date all the material in this book in the light of technical advances, new research findings and, where relevant, social and legal changes.

There are several entirely new chapters. One, on trainability tests by Sylvia Downs, describes a type of technique which has been developed and tested only during the last few years. John Toplis, and a new collaborator, Bernard Stewart, have rewritten the chapter on group selection methods with valuable references to much recent research evidence. Alec Rodger, after a lifetime of experience both as an academic vocational psychologist and as a selector and assessor in industry, commerce and the services, has produced a readable and interesting chapter on using interviews in personnel selection. This eschews a great deal of the usual guidance about how to conduct interviews and has preferred to provide some novel insights into the purpose and problems of interviews and their practical use.

Another new chapter has been necessitated by changes in and additions to the laws on discrimination. This has been jointly written by Baroness Seear and Michael Pearn under the title 'Selection Within the Law'. New legislation also, regarding health and safety, has made necessary an entirely revised chapter by Dr Dennis Malcolm on physical testing. Changes in the organization and methods used in banking have led to another entirely new chapter by David McIlvenna on management trainees in banking.

These major changes, together with the lesser alterations and additions in the rest of the book, should ensure its continued value to all concerned with recruitment.

Two further points should be made. For simplicity many contributors have used masculine pronouns. They all intend these to denote both masculine and feminine and certainly not to suggest any unfair discrimination. Finally, it should be made clear that all authors have expressed their personal views, which are not necessarily those of their organizations.

Bernard Ungerson

Notes on Contributors

Bernard Ungerson CBE, Editor (Introduction: The scientific method in selection) has retired from a distinguished career in industrial psychology and personnel management. The posts and offices he has held include Chief Psychologist at the War Office, Chairman of the Occupational Psychology Section of the British Psychological Society, Chairman of the Staff Management Association, President of the Institute of Personnel Management and Head of Personnel in both national and multinational groups of companies. He is a Fellow of the British Psychological Society and Honorary Life Companion of the Institute of Personnel Management.

Graham Atkinson (Recruitment and the mobility of labour) is Senior Economic Adviser at the Department of Industry. Formerly he was Senior Fellow at the Institute of Manpower Studies, responsible for directing a programme of research on industrial and sector manpower issues. He started his career as a consultant for OECD, followed by economic research at the Department of Education and Science. Mr Atkinson then moved to Canada as a senior research economist in the Department of Manpower of the Federal Government. He holds a first degree in economics and politics, and a Diploma in Education. He is a member of the Manpower Society and has written extensively on manpower issues.

D J Bunter (Supervisors and foremen) is Director of Management Development with The Plessey Company Limited. He joined Plessey as a Management Development Executive with the Electronics Group, moving to become Manpower Resources Executive before taking up his present post. Mr Bunter gained experience in personnel within a number of organizations including Crompton Parkinson Limited, North British Rubber Company and The Thomson Organization Limited.

George Campbell-Johnston (Recruitment of experienced managers) is Managing Director of CJA (management recruitment consultants), the international recruiters of board and senior management personnel. He is Chairman of other companies within the Campbell-Johnston group including Campbell-Johnston Executive Secretaries Limited, Campbell-Johnston Recruitment Advertising Limited, Administrative and Clerical Personnel Limited and Accountancy and Legal Professions Selection Limited.

Prior to forming his own company in 1969 Mr Campbell-Johnston had several years' experience in the industrial bulk products division of Proctor and Gamble followed by five years' experience of personnel management in other companies.

Sylvia Downs (Testing trainability) is an occupational psychologist working for the Industrial Training Research Unit, Cambridge. She is an Honorary Research Fellow of University College London and Chairman of the Occupational Division of the British Psychological Society. Her main concern has been finding practical but validated solutions to problems of individuals in relation to their work in such areas as selection, guidance, training and learning.

T S Duxfield (Sales staff) is a Senior Lecturer and Consultant with the Pirbic Organization Limited, consultants in management and sales training at Sunningdale, Berkshire. Commissioned in 1940, he served for six years in the Royal Artillery. After demobilization he rejoined the timber industry and travelled extensively in Brazil, Ecuador, USA and Canada before becoming Sales Director and later Managing Director of the brokerage firm of Smith and Tyrer Limited. He is co-author of *Management and Training of Technical Salesmen* with A A Jeffries (Gower, 1969).

B J Edwards (Application forms) is an Assistant Personnel Manager in charge of training and development for a large international crop protection company. After reading botany and microbiology at Nottingham University, he joined an electronics company and within three years became Senior Personnel Officer, before moving to Philips Electrical Limited as Personnel Officer (sales). He spent several years with the Industrial Society prior to moving to 3M United Kingdom Limited as Management Training Manager, before taking up his present post.

K G Fordham (Job advertising) joined the advertising department of *The Daily Telegraph* just after the last war and remained with the paper for ten years. After joining Austin Knight Limited in 1958 as an account executive on recruitment advertising, he was appointed to the board in 1962 and became Managing Director in 1970. He is a Fellow of the Institute of Practitioners in Advertising and lectures for the Institute of Personnel Management and management colleges.

John S Gough (Recruitment of graduates at the universities) was for a number of years Head of Staff Appointment and Careers for ICI, following personnel work in The British Council and the BBC. He was Chairman of the Manpower Society in 1970/71. He has served for many years as a member of the Final Selection Board of the Civil Service. He is the author of *Interviewing in 26 Steps* published by BACIE. Since retirement he served for five years as part-time Personnel Adviser to the Department of Health and Social Security.

Derek Gould (Recruitment in local government) is a Senior Organization and Methods Officer for Kent County Council, and a recruitment consultant, participating in training seminars and recruiting typing and secretarial staff. He has been in Local Government for a number of years, holding a variety of accountancy positions before transferring to O & M. Mr Gould is a partially qualified Local Government Accountant and holds a Diploma in Municipal Administration. He has written numerous articles on personnel topics and two books on staff selection.

T M Higham (Choosing the method of recruitment) is Recruitment Manager with Rowntree Mackintosh Limited, which he joined in 1951 as chief industrial psychologist. Prior to this he was an Assistant Lecturer in the Department of Psychology at the University of Liverpool, having received an M.A., and a B.Litt. in psychology from Christ Church, Oxford. Mr Higham is Chairman of the Roffey Park Institute Limited and a Director of the Standing Conference of Employers of Graduates Limited. He is a Fellow of the Institute of Personnel Management and has written many articles for various journals.

Leonard J Holman (Deciding the appointment) retired from the Civil Service in 1967. He joined the Test Agency of the National Foundation for Educational Research as a consultant and later lectured in business statistics at Merton Technical College. Mr Holman started his career as Assistant to the Personnel Manager with David Brown and Sons (Huddersfield) Limited. In 1943 he was commissioned as Psychological Statistician for the War Office and later became Principal Psychologist for the Army in the operational research branch. Mr Holman is a Fellow of the British Psychological Society, a Member of the Operational Research Society, and author of three books on statistics.

J F Jenkins (Management trainees in retailing) is a freelance personnel

consultant. Prior to this he was Manager of the Appointments Department, and later Personnel Manager, at the Head Office of the Littlewoods Retail Organisation. He was responsible for managerial, scientific, technical and executive recruitment and did much research into the selection of management trainees for chain stores. Before the War Mr Jenkins completed an engineering apprenticeship, and in 1945 went to the London School of Economics to study social sciences and personnel management. He is a Member of the Institute of Personnel Management.

Gilbert Jessup (Testing trade skills) was Director of the government's Work Research Unit from 1974 to 1979 and also Chief Psychologist in the Department of Employment. From 1979 to 1981, he acted as an adviser to the Manpower Services Commission on unemployment programmes. He is currently head of the Employment Rehabilitation Research Centre of the MSC.

J G Knollys (Clerical staff) entered the personnel field in 1961 with C & A Modes after seven years in line management. From 1969 to 1980 he was with the British United Provident Association, latterly as Personnel Manager (Hospitals). He also acted as Personnel Adviser to the Nuffield Nursing Homes Trust, and in October 1980 joined the Trust as Personnel Manager. Mr Knollys is a Member of the Institute of Personnel Management.

David McIlvenna (Management trainees in banking) is Recruitment Manager for National Westminster Bank at its city headquarters. He entered the Bank from school at the age of eighteen and joined the Personnel Department some five years later. Since then he has been personal assistant to the Bank's Personnel Director, then Area Personnel Manager in Bristol and more recently a career planning adviser in the Management Development Department in Head Office. Immediately prior to his present appointment he was Assistant Divisional Personnel Manager and has recently assumed his present role where he is in charge of the central Recruitment Department which processes many thousands of recruitment applications annually.

Dr Dennis Malcolm (Physical testing) is group Medical Adviser to the Chloride Group. He graduated with a first degree in Medicine and Surgery at the University of Edinburgh and after serving with the RAMC he gained his Diploma in Industrial Health.

K M Miller (Personality assessment) is Director of the Independent Assessment and Research Centre. He studied at the University of Melbourne and subsequently obtained his doctorate from University College, London, in 1954. During his studies he was a lecturer in psychology at the University of London, followed by a period of five years as a lecturer in psychology at the

University of Tasmania. Dr Miller then became a senior research officer first at University College and later with the National Foundation for Education Research, where he was in charge of research into apprentice selection. He was appointed director of the School Examination Research Unit of the University of London from where he took up his present post.

Richard Mooney (Staff in branches of multiple unit organizations) is General Manager of Accountancy Personnel Senior Appointments. Formerly responsible for selection in a leading audit group AYMM, he also has experience of consultancy and executive search management selection. Before joining them he was a staff manager in The John Lewis Partnership. He has an arts and social sciences degree and is a Fellow of the Institute of Personnel Management and of the Institute of Directors. He is also a careers counsellor for the British Institute of Management and a Member of the Institute of Management Consultants.

Michael Pearn (Selection within the law) is a consultant occupational psychologist with Saville and Holdsworth Limited. He holds degrees in psychology from the Universities of Dublin and London. He has undertaken action research and development projects on selection and training while working at the Industrial Training Research Unit at Cambridge. He has published widely on training, culture-fair selection and the management of equal opportunity. Before taking up his present post he was Deputy Director of the Runnymede Trust and Director of the Runnymede Industrial Unit.

A C Pendlebury (Testing intelligence and aptitude) is Research and Development Officer in the Careers Service in Birmingham. He previously worked as a consultant with HTS Management Consultants Limited, in charge of the company's activities in the personnel selection field. He obtained a first degree in psychology and philosophy at Oriel College, Oxford, followed by a Master's degree in occupational psychology from Birkbeck College, London. He has written extensively on selection and training issues in a wide variety of periodicals.

T E Platt (The job specification) is a Director of Knight Wegenstein Limited, the international management consultants based in Switzerland with offices throughout Europe. Mr Platt is responsible for all executive search and selection activities in the United Kingdom. He was formerly Managing Director of Management Selection Limited and a Director of Judy Farquharson Limited. Before joining MSL as a consultant in 1967, he had been Advertising Manager of William Timpson Limited, shoemakers and retailers, and Advertising Controller of Owen Owen Limited, the department store group.

Clive Purkiss (Recruitment and the mobility of labour) is Director of the Institute of Manpower Studies. Formerly he was in the British Iron and Steel Research Association as Head of the Planning Studies section and then moved to International Systems Research as a senior consultant in business planning. Mr Purkiss holds a first degree in engineering science and a Masters degree in economics. He is a former Council Member of the Manpower Society, a Member of the Operational Research Society and author of many papers and reports on manpower.

Alec Rodger (Interviewing techniques) has recently retired from the positions of Professor of Occupational Psychology in the University of London, and Head of the Department of Occupational Psychology at Birkbeck College. He has been president of the British Psychological Society and of the Psychology Section of the British Association, and a fellow of the American Psychological Association. He studied psychology at Cambridge and then joined the staff of the National Institute of Industrial Psychology. He was the Chief Psychologist at the Admiralty from 1941 to 1948, and part-time adviser to the Ministry of Labour from 1947 to 1968. He was a founder-director of Management Selection Limited and of Manpower Analysis and Planning Limited; and he was the first chairman of the Psychology Board of the Council for National Academic Awards. He edited the journal *Occupational Psychology* from 1948 to 1968.

Nancy Seear (Selection within the law), after a ten-year career in personnel work, spent thirty years as Lecturer and Reader in Personnel Management at the London School of Economics. Recently she has directed research into questions of women's employment and discrimination, at LSE and the City University, where she is now a Visiting Professor. She is a past President of the Institute of Personnel Management.

Bernard J M Stewart (Group selection methods) is currently a Principal Psychologist with British Telecom's Occupational Psychology Division. He heads the Training, Surveys and Special Projects Section, which has responsibility for the design of extended selection interview training courses. He started his Post Office career in 1965 as a technician, left on special leave to read for a degree in psychology and philosophy and joined the unit in 1974.

Humphrey Sturt (Technological staff) is DP Marketing Personnel Manager for IBM United Kingdom Limited. He was a computer specialist in ICT Limited and subsequently developed new selection techniques as joint founder of ASAP, the first computer personnel consultancy in the United Kingdom. While in IBM he has held management positions in manpower planning, salary policy and management development before taking on his present role.

John Toplis (Group selection methods) is Director of the Occupational Psychology Unit at Barking College of Technology. Prior to this he was Head of Diagnostic Studies at the National Institute of Industrial Psychology and responsible for studies of labour turnover, management structure and attitude surveys. Mr Toplis is an Associate of the British Psychological Society and author of a handbook on card punching.

Derek Torrington (Recruiting shop floor personnel) is Lecturer in Personnel Management at the University of Manchester Institute of Science and Technology. Previously he was in industrial relations at Manchester Polytechnic after working as Manager of the Personnel and Training Division of Oldham International Limited. A member of the Institute of Personnel Management, he is also a magistrate. Previous publications include *Successful Personnel Management* (Staples 1969) and *Face to Face* (Gower, 1972).

Part One
Recruitment Methods and Test Procedures

1

Introduction:
The Scientific Method in
Selection

Bernard Ungerson

The general purpose of this book is to bring together the up-to-date views of authoritative writers about the processes of recruitment and selection. The systems and methods described spring in part from tested research findings and in part from the practical experience of managers concerned with personnel recruitment.

Some topics, of course, do not lend themselves to scientific research and, when dealing with these, the writers have brought into play their experience and that of other practitioners and have expressed views as to what are likely to be the most fruitful procedures in modern conditions. The selection process, however, has been dealt with, as far as is reasonably possible in a book of this kind, on the basis of scientific research findings.

The psychological basis

Since the research about these matters has been conducted almost entirely by psychologists, the discussion and the methods recommended are based primarily upon psychology and it therefore seems appropriate to discuss just what this implies.

We should perhaps begin by defining psychology in general terms. Psychology is concerned with the scientific study of human behaviour and, since this is a very wide area indeed, has had to be divided into various subspecialisms. In my view, some of these have stronger claims than others to call themselves scientific and little in the following chapters is based upon the work of those psychologists whose ideas seem to be based upon unsubstantiated dogma rather than upon scientific research. The particular subdivision of psychology upon which much of the content of this book is based is what has come to be called *vocational psychology*, although it is still widely known by its earlier common title of *industrial psychology*.

It should perhaps be stressed that the word 'scientific' is used here in a strict sense. It is quite common for writers to use it when they mean little more than 'systematic', but this is not the intention here. The researches quoted in various chapters and other researches, not quoted but justifying the recommended practices, are, in the true sense, scientific. This means that scientific method has been used by:

1   The formulation of hypotheses.
2   The collection of data either from experimental or from real-life situations.
3   The analysis of that data by appropriate statistical methods.
4   The drawing of conclusions with stated levels of probability.

It is one of the main purposes of this book to suggest, and indeed to stress, that statements about methods of recruitment and selection should be based, as far as is possible in our present state of knowledge, upon findings from researches of this kind.

This is most important because, unless this general principle is observed, it is possible to be grossly misled. There is no shortage, year after year, of published claims for systems of assessing people which inquiries show to have no validity other than the opinions and hopes of their originators. Progress and improvement in selection methods cannot be achieved in this way. It is really quite valueless to write, as an author did recently in a personnel management publication, that 'we think we have found a very good personality test'. A 'good personality test' needs careful definition and can be 'discovered' only by long and arduous statistical analysis of relevant data in a selection situation. Anyone who is familiar with the many years of work which has, for instance, been carried out by Professor Cattell in the formulation of his 16 PF test, in establishing norms and in calculating 'profiles' for a wide variety of jobs will realize that there can be no hope whatsoever of building a sound personality test or questionnaire on the basis of armchair speculation.

There is another very good reason for basing the recommended techniques largely upon the findings of psychologists. A great many of the techniques now widely accepted and used throughout industry and commerce have come to us in the following way. First, theoretical psychologists have investigated psychological problems and found general lines of explanation or solution. Secondly, applied psychologists have considered how to make use of these theoretical findings in solving practical problems in industry and commerce. After that, the techniques developed and used at first by applied psychologists, have come to be adapted to the needs of laymen and applied increasingly widely. Finally the techniques become fully accepted for everyday use. A typical example of this is the development of modern selection boards, described by Higham in Chapter 3 and by Toplis in Chapter 13. These arose from theoretical psychological views about the nature of human personality and the relationship between overt behaviour and personality characteristics. From this, psychologists began to develop practical methods of putting these findings to use in assessing the leadership characteristics of candidates for commissions during the Second World War. After that war, the methods were adapted for use by the Civil Service where, after a long period of operating in parallel with the traditional methods, they have now replaced the latter entirely. During this long period of trial by the Civil Service the methods have been used in a variety of industries although, perhaps, in view of the validity which they have been shown to have for Civil Service selection, not as widely as might have been hoped. However that may be, the development of these boards typifies the normal progression from theoretical psychological research to practical application by laymen.

'Reliability' and 'validity'

Since this matter is touched upon only lightly in the chapters which follow, it may be valuable to describe here the main kinds of research into selection methods which psychologists have carried out and which provide the only sound basis for deciding the practical value of selection methods. The two major concepts have been those known as 'reliability' and 'validity'.

By 'reliability', the psychologist means, in very general terms, the extent to which any assessment procedure—be it examination, interview, practical test, paper test or any other of the many kinds of assessments—will put candidates in the same order if repeated on more than one occasion. This is, of course, very much a definition for laymen and the term covers a number of different research techniques carried out by psychologists which are too complex to fall entirely within this general definition. However, for present purposes, the definition will probably prove adequate.

Clearly, if we find by a 'reliability' experiment that an assessment procedure, when repeated, does not place candidates in a reasonably similar order, we must conclude that the assessment method is not adequate for practical purposes. Many, many tests and other assessment methods have failed to produce satisfactory 'reliabilities' and have, therefore, had to be discarded.

However, it will be quite clear to the reader that 'reliability' is not, of itself, enough. A test or other assessment can be 'reliable' in the statistical sense and yet may not achieve an adequate relationship with some later criterion of performance—which is, of course, what any assessment procedure seeks to achieve. The calculation of the extent to which some form of assessment successfully forecasts later performance, either in training or on the job, is what is known as the calculation of 'validity'.

It is this process of validation which makes for the major distinction between psychologists on the one hand and laymen on the other. The difference between them is not, as is commonly assumed, that laymen use commonsense methods and psychologists use various forms of test. It is, rather, a fundamental difference of attitude. Psychologists come to the problem of selection with a far greater humility than is often shown by laymen. It is the latter who so frequently have overweening confidence in their subjective judgements; it is psychologists who urge that these judgements should be quantified and recorded and that the correlation between them and some reliable criterion of later performance should be calculated in order to find whether the assessments have or, as is more usual, have not any true validity.

It should not be thought that psychologists have concerned themselves only with 'reliability' and 'validity'. Many other, more detailed problems have been studied in particular selection situations, but these two major ones should suffice to establish the major difference in outlook and approach between psychological researchers and others who, often with more confidence than the evidence justifies, advance theories about assessing people.

The fallibility of subjective judgement

The value of a selection technique can never be assessed subjectively. Only proper research can show whether any selection technique achieves, in practice, a reasonable correlation with later performance, or even an adequate reliability. A number of tests which were devised during the Second World War turned out either to be useless or, surprisingly, to forecast success in quite different occupations from those for which they were intended.

A few examples may be of interest.

One was a test of aptitude for learning Morse which was brought to this country from the United States and which proved, when subjected to research, to be of no value because of its low reliability, which was revealed when it was given twice to the same large group of subjects.

Again, a group of sensori-motor tests, which were devised by the psychology department of an English university to select artillery soldiers for the job known as 'operators fire control', proved, when it was studied in detail, to have very low reliability and no correlation whatsoever with success in training for that job.

A pencil and paper test which was designed to help in the selection of women clerks was found to make a substantial contribution to improving the selection of infantry riflemen.

Turning to quite a different field, many people believe that references are of little or no use as selection devices. Such people would be very surprised at the follow-ups of the Civil Service Selection Board which have shown that references written by university tutors can make a real contribution to the validity of the total board selection process.

It has to be borne in mind also that what is felt about the likely value of a selection procedure is no guide to its real value. I remember a discussion with the professor of psychology of a German university who was a devotee of graphology. When asked whether he had conducted any validation studies of his graphological forecasts, he replied: 'No, I have not done that, but I feel in my heart that the forecasts are good.' Unfortunately, only too many such feelings have been proved by proper research to be ill-founded. Assessment procedures cannot be judged subjectively; interviewers who are convinced that they are 'good judges of men', tests which 'look just like the job' and which, to the layman, seem almost certain to plumb the same aptitudes as required by the job—all these must be regarded with scientific scepticism. It is true in this field, as in the physical sciences, that an ounce of empirical research is worth many tons of subjective impressions.

All this may perhaps suggest that psychologists claim to have the answers to all selection problems, but this is far from true. The whole selection process involves forecasting the future performance of that very complex, puzzling and often changing organism, a human being, in a wide variety of equally puzzling and equally changing social settings. It is unlikely that the problem of forecasting performance will ever be solved really satisfactorily, and it would be overconfident to suggest that the views and advice expressed in this book will help those concerned with selection to avoid all errors in future. It is, however, possible that they will help to decrease future failures. There is certainly a great deal of evidence that selection validities can be substantially improved by the use, after proper training, of the techniques recommended in the following chapters.

Individual views within the book

It should be explained that the individual contributors have been allowed, indeed encouraged, to express their own personal views—even if these do not harmonize with those expressed by others. It is inevitable that this should lead to some clashes of opinion, but this is, in my view, quite healthy. There is no value in a symposium in which all participants agree on everything.

I do not propose to discuss these differences or to take sides about them. There is, however, one issue so major that it merits some consideration here: the value of the interview. This issue is clearly and sharply posed by Professor Alec Rodger in Chapter 12.

Nearly everyone who has seen the evidence about the reliability and validity of *unplanned* interviews *carried out by untrained interviewers* will agree that their value is very small indeed, if not entirely negligible. There are, however, two lines of thought about the best way to improve the situation revealed by such researches.

There are those who hold the view that subjective methods of assessing human beings will never prove to be adequately reliable and valid and who therefore turn to objective methods such as personality tests and questionnaires, objectively marked biographical questionnaires, interest questionnaires or other devices, in the hope of improving validities. Others consider that there is hope of substantial improvement if careful job specifications are drawn up and interviewers are thoroughly trained to plan their interviews and carry them out with professional skill and objectivity.

Time alone will show which of these two approaches will prove the more valuable. At this stage, it seems to me (and this is a personal opinion only) that those who work with objective methods are making greater efforts to establish their validity than are the protagonists of improved interviewing techniques. This is, of course, hardly surprising since the first group have objective numerical scores to work with, whereas the latter are concerned primarily with qualitative judgements which are not always easy to quantify. This makes it difficult to conduct research with the same thoroughness, and it is this major difference between the research possibilities of these two approaches that makes it seem likely to me that the objective methods will, perhaps only in fifty years' time or so, ultimately prove superior in assessing personality characteristics.

It would certainly seem foolhardy, at this stage, to come down firmly on one side or the other, and this is the reason for the inclusion in this book of authoritative descriptions of both interviewing methods and objective testing. It remains to be seen whether one of the two approaches emerges as decisively superior and, in the present state of our knowledge, it seems best to be open-minded about this matter, to await further research and, in the meantime, to bear in mind the best established procedures of both kinds, doing what seems to be best in each particular and individual selection situation.

One other point should be made about the interview. However successfully, in the future, objective methods come to assess personality characteristics, *interviews will always be necessary.* They will be needed because they meet the expectations of candidates for human contact with potential employers, because there are some characteristics which can be assessed only by visual and conversational contact, and because information and impressions must flow from the potential employer to the candidate. Other techniques cannot meet these needs.

Interviews will be needed also because, as made clear by Dr Miller in Chapter 10, objective personality tests and questionnaires must be validated in each specific selection situation on samples of adequate size. This is often quite impossible because very few selection situations concern large numbers of recruits for identical jobs in identical conditions. In all other situations, the flexible and universally applicable interview procedure will remain essential.

It will be clear from what has been written about the interview that it has not been possible, in such a difficult matter as the assessment of human beings, to establish and maintain a completely consistent body of theory throughout the book. No apology is made for this. First, many of the matters dealt with and discussed cannot be regarded in a 'black or white' way. As with the interview, many other procedures in selection and recruitment are still wide open to discussion, debate, research and development. It would, therefore, be quite wrong to dogmatize about them. Also, where so many authoritative authors are concerned, it would be just as wrong to seek to restrict them too harshly within imposed guidelines. Every one of the authors has dealt with his main topic and has, where he has thought it necessary, related this to other associated topics. This has inevitably led to a certain amount of overlap and also, as explained above, some conflict of views or at least difference of emphasis. Naturally, an effort has been made to ensure that the same ground is not covered more than once from the same point of view, but the attentive reader will find, from time to time, that an author discusses a topic which is dealt with more fully either earlier or later in the book. It is hoped that the reader will feel that, when this happens, the different discussions will cast light upon the subject from rather different angles and thus succeed in illuminating it more completely.

Structure of the book

The book is divided into two parts. In the first part, there is explanation and discussion of the various techniques which can be brought into play in the total process of recruitment and selection. This discussion includes a chapter which surveys the main methods available and outlines some of the pros and cons which must be taken into account in deciding what method or selection of methods to employ. After the chapters dealing with the various testing techniques comes a final chapter which suggests ways in which the various assessments made during a total selection procedure can be synthesized into a final decision.

The second part of the book consists of descriptions, by practical men with relevant experience, of the problems met in recruiting and selecting for various different specific fields. It is hoped that their views, based for the most part on everyday company experience, will help to fill out the picture presented in the first part of the book by those who have described techniques without reference to specific selection areas.

Finally, it is hoped that readers will find, in these two divisions, a useful summary of theory and practice in the field of recruitment and selection, arranged in a way which will be found interesting, informative and, upon occasions, provocative and challenging.

2

Recruitment and Mobility of Labour

Graham Atkinson and Clive Purkiss

The nature of labour mobility

The reasons for studying mobility

Recruitment policies in firms, if they are to be sensibly planned, must take account of the availability of suitable supplies of labour, both in the local labour markets where their plants operate and, for certain types of skills, in the national and possibly international labour markets. This might seem a simple enough statement—perhaps tending towards the obvious—but experience in meeting firms and discussing recruitment problems has shown that many firms exist on a day-to-day basis of notifying vacancies and simply hiring casual callers to staff their positions. Increased awareness in firms, however, of the importance of adequately skilled and trained labour has drawn attention to the planning of recruitment and this, in turn, demands a better understanding of the operation of the labour market and the mobility of labour.

Many factors condition supplies of labour to different markets; for example, the type of educational system through which prospective employees pass, and the attractiveness of the working environment offered by employers relative to those offered in other areas or in other firms. Relative wages are clearly important, although there is not a great deal of evidence for the proposition that higher relative wages will induce transfer of labour from areas of abundant supply to areas where labour is scarce. Some firms are fortunate enough to operate in areas where the interaction of these factors provides plentiful supplies of labour with the right skills and experience, located at the right place and available at the right price. But, as the market 'tightens', management has to search further afield for people, and it is in this situation that the importance of the relative mobility of labour becomes apparent.

The recruiter needs to know what kinds of people, with what training and what experience, are physically and mentally able to cope with the job offered. He must know what will attract a man or woman to do a certain type of job, to enter a new firm or even industry, or to uproot his family to move to another part of the country. It helps him also to know the extent to which such movement is prevalent among different occupations in order to ensure that his recruitment strategy is realistic and relevant.

Internal and external mobility

Mobility can take two forms: it can involve a change of job within an existing firm (this is normally referred to as 'internal mobility') or it can involve a complete change of job ('external mobility'). Both types of mobility are important to the recruiter. As far as the first type is concerned, the job structure within the firm and opportunities for promotion clearly affect the extent to which the recruiter has to look outside the firm for additional labour. The extent to which manpower planning has been developed in the firm will greatly determine the extent of internal mobility—whether it is positively encouraged or whether it just happens. More significant to the recruiter, however, is the second type of mobility, namely external mobility. This normally involves a change of occupation, industry or area of work, and possibly a combination of all three. Since this is more important to the recruiter, we shall limit most of our discussion of labour mobility to external mobility for the remainder of this chapter.

The facts about external mobility

Previous studies of job changes show that labour is less static than is often assumed. In the UK, some one-third of the labour force change jobs in the course of a year, frequently involving a change in industry, area or occupation as well as a change of employer[1]. For example, a study in South-east England[2] found that one-third of all job changes involved a change of area or industry, and of occupation; one-half of the job changes involved changes in occupation, whilst three-quarters involved a change in industry.

Thus external mobility can be geographical, occupational or industrial, or these can be interrelated. The Government Social Survey, which investigated labour mobility in Britain between 1953 and 1963[1] found that almost half the people surveyed had lived at their present address for ten or more years, whilst one-quarter had lived at their present address for twenty years or more. More recently, another government survey of households in Great Britain[3] has brought these mobility figures up to date, and these are shown in Figure 2.1.

Length of residence (years)	GHS 1971(%)	Survey 1963 (%)
Under 1	8.8	7.6
1 but under 2	6.1	5.2
2 but under 3	7.9	7.2
3 but under 4	6.7	6.4
4 but under 5	6.2	5.2
5 but under 6	4.5	
6–10	18.6	21.0
11–20	23.4	22.5
21–30	8.0	15.0
31–40	6.8	5.9
over 40	3.0	4.0
Sample size (base = 100%)	25 823	19 924

Source: Adapted from reference 3, table 5.49.

Figure 2.1   Length of residence of persons aged 15 and over in 1971 and 1963; all members of household (aged 15+) in Great Britain

The 1971 Household Survey shows, for example, that 35.7% of the population aged 15 or over had moved within the previous five years[3], and between 1958 and 1963 about 31.6% had done so. There was little significant difference between the findings of the two surveys. A further comparison can be made with earlier housing surveys. A 1960 housing survey estimated the annual rate of movement of households living within England and Wales at 8%, and a 1964 housing survey at between 7% and 8%. These figures ignored multiple moves by some households and revealed no difference between London and the rest of England and Wales. The 1971 survey found the annual rates of movement to be 11% for Greater London and 8% for the rest of England and Wales.

By contrast, interindustry mobility is even greater. For example, as much as three-quarters of those leaving a job in commerce move to another industry[1]. But no systematic patterns seem to occur in the movements between industries.

As far as movement between occupations is concerned, many studies have shown occupational mobility and skill to be inversely related, occupational change becoming less frequent the higher the qualification level of the occupation group.

The benefits of movement

The simple result of labour movement should be to shift a person from one job to another where productive performance will be higher and satisfaction greater. For the economy as a whole, if knowledge about individual capabilities and job opportunities is good, the net result will be a gain. But, the pay-off for the employer and employee can differ with the circumstances.

The main benefit to the employer is that he can maintain a flexible labour force which can be adapted to the needs of the moment. With skilful manpower planning he can adjust the size of his work force to a change in the demand for his products or to changes in the technology he uses. If the age structure of his staff is no longer likely to provide him with a stable pattern of career development he may alter it by replacing those who leave with people in the right age bands. Less frequently, but as important, he can relocate his factory or offices to where critical resources or good communications are more readily available, yet still draw to himself the skills he needs.

Against this, the employer must set his costs of recruitment, relocation, induction and training. Rapid turnover can upset the social cohesion of work groups. An inability to retain the younger worker can worsen rather than repair the damage to his age balances.

The employee sees things differently. If he is escaping from a poor position, he is seeking to meet his basic needs: adequate earnings, relief from overstress, good working relations. More positively, movement may mean the furtherance of career aspirations, the possibility of developing new skills or the chance of establishing himself in a location where job opportunities are more plentiful. Against this he must weigh up any loss of job security consequent on his established position in the hierarchy, losses of pension benefits, the need to establish himself with new colleagues, and the problems of housing and schooling. The recruiter will need to help the potential recruit to make a fair judgement of the balance, if he is to retain as well as to recruit him.

Characteristics of the mobile person

We now consider what kind of people change jobs in the population and whether there are any differences between people in respect of occupations and locations which will tend to make them more mobile. We shall draw on two main sources of information for this [1,4] and we shall look at the main factors involved.

Age

This is probably the most important factor affecting mobility. The pattern for the younger age groups follows that for the middle age groups, as younger people living with their parents will share their experience of house-moving. This is shown in Figure 2.2.

In contrast to the lower mobility of the very young and the middle age groups, only one-third in the 20–24 age group and as little as one-seventh in the 25–30 age group had not moved. In general, the age pattern of mobility shows high mobility in the ages 20–24, after which the number of moves falls off rapidly.

Age group	Had not moved (%)	1 move only (%)	2 or more moves (%)	No. on which % based
15 – 19	52.9	30.6	16.5	1 890
20 – 24	33.8	30.3	35.9	1 474
25 – 30	13.9	34.8	51.3	1 846
31 – 44	30.5	39.3	30.2	5 063
45 – 54	58.0	29.8	12.2	3 603
55 – 59	65.8	25.0	9.2	1 641
60 – 64	70.2	23.1	6.7	1 422
65 and over	66.9	25.5	7.6	3 016
All ages	47.5	31.2	21.3	19 955[1]

[1]Excludes 20 people not giving age.

Source: Reference 1, table 10.

Figure 2.2   Number of moves between 1953 and 1963 for different age groups

Education level

The higher the level of education, the higher the proportion of people who are likely to move[1]. Amongst those educated in the UK, the people with the most moves are those who attended university; about one-third of movers were found to have moved three times or more. Grammar and public school leavers showed a slightly higher degree of mobility than those leaving commercial or technical schools. The least mobile were those who last attended comprehensive or pre-1947 central schools.

Confirming these facts, the Government Social Survey[1] showed that people with academic, technical or commercial qualifications are among those most likely to be willing to move. Over 60% of men with degrees or similar qualifications said they would move compared with 50% of men who are skilled. Men who had no skills or qualifications were the least likely to be willing to move.

Marital status

The government survey also investigated the characteristics of those who would not move compared with those who could be encouraged to move. Two of the most frequently quoted characteristics can be highlighted: first, marital status and, second, type of housing possessed. Figure 2.3 shows the willingness of males and females to move, according to marital status.

It is clear that, if anything, a slightly higher proportion of married men say they would move if conditions were suitable. Married women and widows, on the other hand, are less likely to be willing to move than single women.

Marital status	Males		Females	
	% willing to move	No. on which % based	% willing to move	No. on which % based
married	53.1	5 653	19.2	2 044
single	49.9	1 789	34.4	1 466
widowed	33.5	173	22.2	342
All informants	51.9	7 615[1]	25.3	3 852[1]

[1] Excludes 12 men and 2 women whose marital status not given.

Source: Reference 1, table 26.

Figure 2.3 Marital status of men and women workers who could be encouraged to move

Housing

The government survey also showed that the least likely to move according to type of housing were local authority tenants, followed closely by those in controlled rent dwellings. Owner–occupiers were more willing to move but the highest proportion of possible movers was found among those renting accommodation from private landlords, or living rent free.

Regions

Analysis of national patterns of interregional mobility show that certain regions are more popular than others. Some difference can be observed between industrial and nonindustrial areas and, in general, nonindustrial areas are more favoured than industrial areas. The area most favoured as a place to move to is Southwest England, as is indicated by Figure 2.4. The next preferred areas are London, together with the nonindustrial part of the Midlands.

Percentage willing to move (men only) at present living in

Area to which men willing to move	North	Northeast	North Midlands	East	London and Southeast	South	Southwest	Wales	Midlands	Northwest	Scotland	All regions
London	33.6	39.5	36.6	36.6	37.7	29.9	28.7	49.3	40.7	41.3	48.2	39.3
Industrial area in—												
Southwest	59.5	60.8	66.9	66.7	74.2	71.8	65.4	64.8	75.3	63.9	55.4	66.9
Midlands	38.0	33.3	44.4	30.3	27.7	30.3	26.3	41.7	xxx	36.7	50.7	34.6
Northwest	34.7	31.1	22.2	19.9	22.5	19.4	19.5	42.7	29.0	xxx	43.4	28.3
Northeast	xxx	33.5	23.8	20.7	21.6	22.2	20.6	33.3	25.5	26.6	45.3	26.9
South Wales	23.2	22.5	22.4	23.6	29.6	24.6	28.4	xxx	38.1	31.1	34.6	28.9
Scotland	32.6	25.7	23.9	23.7	25.5	23.1	22.2	27.6	30.0	31.4	58.7	27.9
Northern Ireland	18.2	19.4	14.6	20.3	21.3	14.6	20.2	22.1	25.2	22.3	29.9	21.3
Non-industrial area in—												
Southwest	63.4	69.4	73.3	78.9	83.0	90.6	xxx	67.8	77.7	71.2	56.4	73.8
Midlands	37.1	39.4	55.9	37.4	35.2	42.4	35.8	47.7	59.9	42.8	47.3	41.4
Northwest	34.3	36.2	33.5	23.4	27.9	26.4	26.5	42.6	35.2	67.6	42.0	35.0
Northeast	xxx	37.3	31.4	24.2	26.4	25.9	25.5	33.5	26.7	31.2	42.1	30.6
South Wales	22.2	27.8	27.9	28.6	32.2	32.5	32.8	xxx	40.4	32.8	33.5	32.2
Scotland	36.1	28.1	27.3	30.8	29.2	31.1	28.6	32.0	33.8	32.9	57.4	31.9
Northern Ireland	16.7	21.9	17.7	24.8	22.3	19.8	22.8	23.4	25.8	23.5	28.8	22.8
Number of men on which percentage based	245	358	273	272	936	217	200	207	383	523	376	3 990

xxx   Numbers too small on which to base percentage.

Source: Reference 1, table 31.

Figure 2.4   The willingness of men living in different regions to move to certain specified areas—subject to satisfactory work and housing

Managers

A special study has been made of the mobility of British managers[4]. They exhibit certain behaviour patterns which are of particular interest to the recruiter of management staff. This study concluded that the mobility of managers, both geographically and between employers, had doubled in the last 30 years; specifically it found that younger managers are more mobile than those of previous generations. One-third of managers had never moved region, whilst 15% had moved region four times or more during their careers; confirming the results of the previously mentioned surveys, those with qualifications were more likely to move around. The study also confirmed that managers attached importance to the same kind of social and economic factors as other professional workers in deciding on whether or not to move. The particular characteristics they are looking for in a new job are complex and cover such features as self-expression, creativity and job interest as well as the more basic considerations of pay and security.

Attitudes to mobility

The reasons for people moving

A large proportion of recruits are those men and women moving from one firm to another. The government survey[1] found that half of all those who had moved had a job to go to before leaving their old jobs. Bowey[5] has written a useful summary of the reasons why people leave a job and these illustrate the kinds of motivation which the potential recruit will have when applying for a post. Under the positive factors which attract a person to a company are included higher earnings, career development or a wider range of job opportunities within the firm or in its locality. At the other extreme are the stresses from which a man or woman may be withdrawing. These can be due to interpersonal conflict, early recognition of a bad choice of firm or job, overwork, changes in working requirements or a redundant job. The recruiter must identify the prime motivations of the potential recruit in order to ensure that these will not continue to be a barrier to satisfactory employment.

The Government Social Survey[1] investigated the reasons which would encourage workers under retirement age to move away from their areas of residence to other work. Figure 2.5 gives a list of these factors, together with the percentage of those asked who responded positively.

Prominent in the list are pay, promotion prospects, housing and job security. Very little mention is made of other factors relative to these. Higher pay, improved prospects and so on are clearly positive inducements to people to move, but we also know, from the same survey, the conditions that need to be satisfactory before people will decide to move, whatever the financial

Encouraged to move by	Men (%)	Women (%)	All workers (%)
nothing at all—would not move	46.5 ⎫	60.5 ⎫	51.2 ⎫
would only move out of UK	1.4 ⎬ 48.1	1.0 ⎬ 74.7	1.3 ⎬ 57.1
would only move if spouse/another member of h/d moved	0.2 ⎭	13.2 ⎭	4.6 ⎭
secure, regular work	7.2	1.7	5.3
pay, promotion, prospects	36.8	12.9	28.8
other conditions of work	5.7	3.5	5.0
move of present employer	1.8	0.5	1.4
accommodation and housing good	10.6	6.2	9.2
prospects for children (including schools)	1.2	0.9	1.1
climate and weather	1.9	0.7	1.5
other physical characteristics of locality	4.3	3.3	4.0
social amenities, sports, etc.	1.1	1.5	1.2
close to friends	0.3	0.5	0.3
bereavements, changes in domestic status	0.6	1.6	1.0
miscellaneous reasons	0.6	0.8	0.7
No. of workers on which percentage based[1]	7 627	3 854	11 481

[1] Percentages add to more than 100, as many people gave more than one reason.

Source: Reference 1, table 25.

Figure 2.5 Factors which would encourage workers under retirement age to move

inducement they are offered. The single factor of concern to most people is housing, with over 80% of people mentioning this as a condition, and, when prompted, 95% agreeing it to be important. Of importance to fewer people, but still a major concern, is the security of the job, the attractiveness of the surroundings and the availability of good schools. In general, men tended to attach more importance to these conditions in their employment than women. Manual workers were slightly more concerned about security than others; professional and managerial people specified more often than others the importance of good schools and amenable surroundings.

Implications for recruitment and selection policy

The arguments for recruitment versus retention

It is too easy to assume that every vacancy must be filled by a recruit; it is also too often thought that labour turnover cannot be controlled at all. The recruiter's job could more aptly be described as resourcing; he can draw on the skills of people already within the firm as well as without. No recruitment decision should be *ad hoc*; each should if possible be made with reference to other parts of corporate and manpower policy in the firm.

The recruiter needs to know, too, what is happening to those he recruits—are they leaving a short time after recruitment? Are the vacancies arising in the same jobs time and time again? The proper analysis of labour wastage requires that the rates of loss of people recruited at different times into each type of job are constantly monitored. If the loss rate is high for any particular group, then the cause needs investigation. Although mobility between firms may be characterized by general statements of the kind discussed previously, labour wastage from an individual firm is much more subject to local peculiarities.

Job and man specifications

To link up with available knowledge about potential movement of people to a firm, job specifications need to be expressed in terms relevant to the labour market in general. They should also relate to other jobs in the firm so that a shortlist of internal candidates with relevant experience can be drawn up. Terms like 'manager', 'supervisor' or 'clerical worker', used in many surveys of employment in firms, are simply not informative enough or used consistently. A good job classification needs to be able to identify the work to be done, its complexity, the authority held and the kind and level of knowledge required[6]. It is a basis for the man specification, but separate from it; ideally a classified file of all jobs should be held.

The man specification, in addition to what it normally includes, needs to bring out any characteristic which will limit the sources of recruitment: age, problems of travel to work outside of normal hours, the areas of the country for which the costs of relocation are likely to be unreasonable.

Identifying recruitment sources

Many jobs are normally filled by people living locally. The Employment Services Agency (ESA) has carried out experiments in parts of the country to identify and bring together the kinds of information which the recruiter needs to have in order to assess the potential local labour supply: information on school leavers, female participation, housing, principal travel routes, new business developments, redundancies pending and so on. Some agencies have introduced a newsletter; most are worth approaching for advice. Otherwise the recruiter will need to build up his own picture. Further information for certain areas and occupations, on wage rates, labour wastage and other manpower statistics, can be got from the Census and the various surveys organized by the Department of the Environment, CBI, BIM, IPM, Industrial Society, Institute of Manpower Studies and other specialist bodies.

We have shown that managers and professional people move more easily than others from one part of the country, or from one industry, to another. The reports already mentioned give limited but dated information on this. Again, up-to-date information on the potential labour supply outside one's immediate area is most likely to be got through the ESA and the Professional and Executive Recruitment Service (PER).

Once a potential labour market has been chosen, the need is to identify what kind of man or woman is most likely to move. We have described the characteristics of the mobile person. Briefly, we know that in general a worker who is in the 25-30 age group, married and well qualified is more likely to move than one who is not. The recruiter must know in his own situation which factors are likely to be most critical.

Costs as a limiting factor on recruitment

It can easily cost £10 000 or more to recruit a senior executive. The recruiter needs to work through a complete checklist if he is to evaluate properly his policy, the costs of prerecruitment, search, evaluation and selection, training and relocation. A list of over 30 items under these heads has been prepared by the Manpower Society[7]. Relocation costs, involving hotel charges, disturbance allowances, premiums, travel subsidies and so on, can be large and limit the range of locations from which labour can be attracted.

Making the job attractive

The factors which, if not satisfied, cause a man to leave one job and those which attract him to another have been described. The recruiter must ensure that the pay and security of the job are clear to the potential recruit. Where relevant, he should explain the prospects for promotion. If he is aiming to move a man from one location to another he should be prepared to provide information about housing, schooling (particularly for recruits in the 30-50 age group), public transport and possibly even shopping facilities and social amenities. For manual occupations he may need to emphasize the security of the job, and for professional and managerial occupations schooling and social amenities as well. If a person is married, he or she may move more readily if aware that employment opportunities for their wife or husband are plentiful.

Wider implications

Some locations simply do not have and cannot attract enough people to work in them. In certain occupations there is a general shortage of skilled and qualified people. In these, labour wastage may be high, the working population mobile and retention difficult. The employer needs to be able to recognize whether his problems are unique to himself or more general. He needs benchmarks. Is he getting a fair proportion of school leavers with 'O' and 'A' level qualifications? What is his success rate with offers to graduate recruits? How does his age structure compare with others? Is he losing people more readily than his competitors in certain jobs, age groups, locations or after a certain length of time has elapsed since recruitment? If his recruitment position has deteriorated, has it done so relative to that of his competitors? Government statistics can provide a good indication of what is happening in the economy at large. But, they are too broad-based to give a proper understanding of these problems. Many companies exchange information with colleagues in local firms on an *ad hoc* basis; others have come together to organize an exchange in a more comprehensive and systematic way[8].

If the problem is low retention relative to others, internal policies need to be reexamined; if it is more general, different tactics must be employed. Possibilities include restructuring and deskilling jobs, training unskilled people or retraining existing workers; proposals for more concerted action by government or central agencies can be put forward—for more relevant training in government training centres, by industrial training boards and professional institutions, for resettlement allowances, for the provision of suitable housing and so on.

Positive steps

Once they have settled down with a satisfactory employer, people do not readily move from one employer to another if they have a skill or professional knowledge. Mobility between one region and another is even more limited, so the market for potential recruits needs careful analysis. The steps to be taken can be summarized as follows:

1 Analyse internal and external labour situation.
2 Prepare job and man specifications, and include labour market factors.
3 Search internally for suitable candidates.
4 Review local labour market.
5 Review other potential recruitment sources.
6 Calculate costs of relocation and induction for each potential source.
7 Identify important factors in making the job attractive to potential recruits.
8 Examine, where necessary, wider implications of shortages of suitable people.

Acknowledgement

The figures in this chapter are reproduced with the kind permission of the Controller of Her Majesty's Stationery Office.

References

1 Government Social Survey (A. I. Harris and R. Clausen), *Labour Mobility in Great Britain 1953–1963,* HMSO, London, 1966.
2 M. Jefferys, *Mobility in the Labour Market,* Routledge and Kegan Paul, London, 1954.
3 Office of Population Censuses and Surveys, *The General Household Survey—Introductory Report,* HMSO, London, 1973.
4 S. Birch and B. Macmillan, *Managers on the Move: A Study of British Managerial Mobility, BIM Management Survey Report No. 7,* 1971.
5 A. M. Bowey, *A Guide to Manpower Planning,* Macmillan, London, 1974.
6 D. J. Bell, *Planning Corporate Manpower,* Longman, London, 1974.
7 D. York and C. C. Dooley, 'Checking the manpower costs', *Personnel Management,* June 1970.
8 *Manpower Survey: Aims and Scope,* Institute of Manpower Studies, London, 1974.

3

Choosing the Method of Recruitment

T M Higham

A large firm may, in a single year, recruit craftsmen for its workshops, clerks for its offices, graduates as trainees, and accountants, buyers, chemists, computer programmers, engineers, salesmen, systems analysts, work study engineers and various other skilled staff. A small firm over the same period may need to recruit only a few factory and office staff and perhaps a salesman or an accountant. But, whether the demand is large or small, the same strategy applies in both situations, even if the tactics to be used vary greatly.

Principles of systematic selection

The strategy of recruitment refers to the principles underlying systematic selection which are (following Rodger[1]) as follows:

1 The methods used must be technically sound. For example, if tests are used, they should be those that measure what they purport to measure. Interviews should be aimed at finding out facts about candidates that have a bearing on the job to be filled; the job itself must be properly described (in terms of what is done) and analysed (in terms of what is needed to do it effectively).
2 The method must be administratively convenient. It must not be so short that judgements are superficial or candidates not given the chance to show their worth. Nor should it be so long or arduous that candidates and staff are worn out by the end of it.
3 The method used must be, and must be seen to be, as fair as possible, so

that every candidate feels that he has been judged on his merits, and not that his selection or rejection has been based on favouritism, irrelevancies or luck.

These principles apply equally to the selection of an office junior or a company secretary. The methods to be used will differ but, whether simple or complex, they should be sound, convenient and fair. It would be a waste of effort and time to use group selection methods or an elaborate testing procedure for a routine factory job; but they might well be the best methods of selecting a graduate for the marketing department.

Although the principle of technical soundness is probably the most important of the three, they are interdependent. For example, it could be that the best technical method of selection is by administering a battery of ability, aptitude and personality tests—and nothing else. This could take a whole day to administer, and perhaps as much again to score. Even if the time and convenience are discounted, the feelings of the candidate cannot be. He could well believe that he was denied a (to him) vital opportunity of showing his merits in an interview; he could feel that his qualifications were enough to show their worth without having to submit to tests of whose value he was sceptical—and so on. It always pays to explain about a selection procedure beforehand, and to be prepared to discuss it afterwards, in an interview.

Tactics of systematic selection

Each of the methods of recruitment and selection will be examined against these principles, and their use will be discussed for different varieties of candidates.

But, before doing so, the general tactics of systematic selection need further explanation. If selection is to be systematic it must follow a pattern—one adaptable for all vacancies, and capable of being expanded or contracted as necessary. The term 'systematic' is used rather than 'scientific', because inevitably human judgement is fallible; but, by using a regular pattern or system, the more obvious and common mistakes can be avoided.

Selection could only be called scientific if its probability of success was considerably higher than it is likely to be at present; and that is unlikely to happen for a long time yet. A systematic approach is the nearest we can get to full technical soundness at present; the results of it, in both industry and the services, are enough to validate its claim to be reasonably effective. Systematic selection calls for four distinct phases, most of which are described in detail in other chapters. They are summarized here for convenience but also because they are inseparable from the method of recruitment:

1   The study of the job, and of the qualities needed to perform it well. This covers both the specification of the job, and of the man to fill it. It is dealt

with in detail in Chapter 4. One very necessary aspect of it is the study of what Alec Rodger has termed the difficulties and distates of the job. It is far easier to say why people do not succeed in a job than it is to lay down criteria for success in it—not least because the latter tend to be lists of abstract nouns (loyalty, initiative, drive) which are usually impossible to assess accurately. In one of the earliest studies carried out by the National Institute of Industrial Psychology, it was found that the candidates who later proved successful on the job had little in common 'except their freedom from marked failure characteristics'. This is where the Institute's seven-point plan (covering physical make-up, attainments, intelligence, aptitudes, interests, disposition, circumstances and background) is particularly useful in that the headings provide a basis for specifying the candidate sought, in the light of his success or failure under each of the seven headings.

2   The study of the candidates to see how far each one measures up to the demands of the job. This can be done by use of the following:

(a)   *Application forms* (see Chapter 6). These normally include sections covering *identification* (name, address, age, dependents and so on), *education* (primary, secondary, university or professional), *occupation* (jobs, whether full or part time, and including time in the services) and *recreation* (interests, hobbies, and general social activities).

(b)   *Tests* (see Chapters 7–11). These may be of *general intelligence* or of *aptitudes* and *interests* or of *personality factors.* Many tests can be given to groups of candidates, all at one time, or to candidates individually. Some tests can be given only individually. This term is also sometimes used to describe group discussions and leaderless discussions which are usually used in group selection procedures, even though they do not conform to the normal methods of test construction and standardization. They are tests of social characteristics but their assessment is subjective—that is, it is based on the views of the observers of the group, and not set against standard criteria.

(c)   *Interviews* (see Chapter 12). One purpose of the interview is to gather together the information provided by application forms and tests and to explore in greater detail around pointers thrown up by them. The interview has, of course, other functions as well, but at the end of it the interviewer should be able to say: 'In the light of all the information I have now gathered, from the application form, test results and interview findings, I can decide how far this candidate matches up to the demands of the job', which leads to *(d)*.

(d)   *Group selection procedures.* These are methods of studying candidates in groups, with a view to improving the assessments of their personal characteristics. These methods are discussed in

Chapter 13.

3 The comparison of what each candidate has to offer against the specification of the job and of the man needed to fill it (see Chapter 4). This is the selection proper—the separation of the sheep from the goats. It may be carried out by one man or by a panel; its essential element is the assessment of each man against previously set criteria.

4 *The follow-up.* This is very important but is the most neglected aspect of all. An appointment must be followed up at some stage, to see whether the individual who has been selected is doing the job well and, if not, why not. It is an essential check on the three previous steps, and the only way of improving selection in the future.

Once we are sure of the value of the main strategy and the general tactics to use we can see how far, and to what depth, the tactics need to be used to fill different vacancies.

Design and use of application forms

It is, of course, possible to interview without an application form, and either to record all the necessary details under the four headings given in 2*(a)* above, as the interview progresses, or to use a letter of application (provided it gives appropriate details) instead. But application forms have the great merit of recording standard information in a systematic way. By that means, candidates can be compared on an equal footing beforehand, and this may be necessary for shortlisting purposes.

Applying form design to job level

A single application form cannot be used for all types and levels of job. Obviously it is simpler and cheaper to have a single form rather than several, but the details that can be given by a fifteen-year-old secondary modern school leaver and by a professional man with several years' experience are so widely different that separate forms are necessary. The form to be used, while covering the four main areas already described, should be simple or elaborate, depending on the type of applicant sought. The one feature common to all forms should be a wide margin 50–75 mm (2–3 in) in which the interviewer can write his notes. There should always be enough room, under each section, to accommodate comfortably the most exuberant handwriting.

For juniors and factory staff, there is less need for space for educational attainments; but for office staff more room is needed, while for graduates and professional people, enough space should be left for full details of GCE 'O' level and 'A' level passes attempted and obtained, degree subjects, specialization and class, and professional examinations passed or attempted.

With school leavers, it is often advisable to list the main school subjects and ask applicants to tick those they liked and place a cross against those they disliked. This information can then be expanded in the interview.

Similarly the amount of space given to the work record should be adapted to the type of candidate. A useful device, especially on forms for use with factory staff, is to ask for short details of the last job and for how long it was held. Below this a space is left blank, in which the interviewer can list all previous jobs and the relevant dates. Alternatively, applicants can be asked to list all their jobs themselves. The former method has the advantage of greater accuracy in the interview.

With managers and professional staff, it is often preferable to ask for a list of previous appointments (and salaries) but to leave space for the present job to be described in detail. Such a section might ask for particulars of the main duties and responsibilities, the type of authority exercised and over what or whom. It gives the candidate space and scope to enlarge on his job in the way he thinks most fit.

Some people find it hard to fill in a section devoted to hobbies or interests—and this is especially true of schoolchildren who may have a wide range of interests and no absorbing hobby. This difficulty can be got over by providing a list of interests—artistic or cultural, constructive, physically active and social—against which the applicant can put a tick or a cross depending on the degree of his interest. With older, or better educated candidates, all that is needed is space in which to describe what they do in their free time, and to give details of clubs and societies to which they belong.

Avoiding misuse of application forms

The application form should be designed as an aid to the interview—a skeleton, upon which the interview puts the flesh. That is why the use of wide margins is emphasized and why, for certain types of information, the use of checklists is desirable. The margins allow the interviewer to add details that are brought out in conversation, the checklists provide starting points for discussion.

Unfortunately, application forms are often used later for other purposes, and there is a temptation to ask for other information which may not always be necessary, but which an interviewer may easily forget. The personnel department may need to keep records of next of kin and of the number of children; so details of these are requested on the form. Some company pension schemes for widows take into account how long a man had been married; so he is asked to put in the date of his wedding. This may make it easier for the personnel department but its effect on candidates may be to make them ask why such questions are necessary. One form asks not only for the date of marriage but also for the birth dates of all children. Quite apart from its impertinence (literally) the form might fall into wrong hands and provoke gossip. (At this point it should be emphasized that application forms, being personal documents, must always be kept in locked files.) If questions asked on an application form are too personal, or too ambiguous, they often provoke frivolous replies, or the questions are ignored. Such responses *may* tell something about the author, but they more properly reveal shortcomings in the form itself.

Some application forms are more akin to projective personality tests. They ask the applicant to describe himself as seen by a friend or by an enemy; or to write a short essay on what he wants in life. These forms, to quote Dr R. B. Buzzard of the NIIP, are 'attempts to get at underlying motives or traits of personality. *Get at* is the right term and the people who don't feel they're being got at may be too stupid to be of use to you.' There is no evidence that such forms lead to better selection, but there is considerable danger that answers will be given which have been contrived to give an acceptable impression, or which are the product of collusion.

Danger of form-based preselection

Such forms are sometimes used to preselect candidates—usually at graduate level or above. Very often shortlisting can only be done on the basis of application forms, which is why a proper job specification is necessary—at least those with inadequate qualifications or job experience can be rejected. But it is far less easy to sort out and shortlist undergraduates who have not yet got degrees, and who have not had any but vacation jobs. It has been suggested that projective application forms will help in that, but there is no evidence to prove it. Shortlisting undergraduates on the basis of application forms alone has about the same chance of success as pricking names with a pin. A further consideration is that, if someone has taken the trouble to apply and to fill in an application form, it is only courtesy to see him unless there is real evidence that he lacks some essential qualification.

Preselection can sometimes work, but only if there is additional information, such as test scores. For example, it was possible to predict on paper, with a 60 to 70% chance of success, which new Royal Marine recruits would make section leaders. But the recruits had all taken a test, and the norms for section leaders were known. The other criteria for paper selection were education, job record and experience of taking charge at school or elsewhere. But to test large numbers of undergraduates would be as time-consuming as to interview them all.

To summarize: application forms help to make selection systematic. The form should be adapted to the type of candidate sought and should give enough space for him to answer in detail. Checklists of preferred school subjects and of interests can be incorporated at lower levels. Information should be sought only on relevant aspects, and projective type forms should be avoided.

Nature and suitability of test procedures

A test implies a comparison with a standard. The difficulty with tests is usually the objectivity of the standard. An essay can be a test, but marking it is subjective. A series of problems in simple arithmetic is a test, but as the answers are right or wrong, the marking is objective. But the setting of pass marks—or cut-off scores—is less easy. Sometimes they seem to be arbitrarily established—40, 50, 60% and so on.

With a standard intelligence test there are usually norms—the range of scores attained by the top 10, next 20, middle 40, next 20 and bottom 10% of candidates taking the test. There may be norms for candidates for different jobs or for candidates of different educational levels. This means that anyone's score can be compared against the scores of similar candidates. If, as a result of follow-up, one knows that most successful clerks or salesmen tend to get scores above X or Y, then when a candidate is tested one at least knows whether he has the intelligence to make a good clerk or a good salesman.

Of course, intelligence is not the only factor, but at least on that one aspect of the candidate one has some objective information. Its relevance appears in its relation to other objective evidence—such as where poor school or university attainments are combined with a high intelligence test score or a good degree with a low score. One reason for the interview is that all such findings can be related and evaluated as a result of discussion with the candidate.

Technical soundness and validation of test

The principle of 'comparison against a standard' applies to all tests—whether of intelligence (or general ability), aptitudes (such as clerical, manual dexterity), attainments (such as mathematics) or even of 'personality' factors and attitudes. In every case the score is—or should be—expressed in terms of the 'norms' for the test. To quote a 'raw score' is meaningless; to express that score as a percentage is no better. It must be possible to compare the score of the individual with the norms derived from testing a large sample of the population. Without norms, it is little use giving tests and basing assessments on the scores obtained.

Any test used must be 'reliable'. It is therefore given with standard instructions, in a standard time in standard conditions. To check reliability, the test is given twice over a short period to make sure that its results are consistent, and that scores do not vary from one occasion to the next.

The test must be 'validated'—that is, the results must be compared with some criterion of performance, such as success in examinations, measures of output or (less objective) assessments of performance. In this way it can be seen whether the test can predict achievement—whether high scores go with high achievement, low scores with low. The pattern is rarely clear cut; the most frequent result is that the majority of high scorers, and a minority of low scorers do well on the job, while a minority of high scorers, and a majority of low scorers do badly. This leaves a proportion for whom the results do not predict well. The degree of agreement between test and later performance is commonly expressed as a 'correlation coefficient' and the decision whether to use a test should depend upon this being shown to be adequately high.

A test which is reliable and which predicts performance is a useful instrument in the right hands—namely, those of someone who is trained to administer and interpret test results. In unskilled hands it is of little use. Unfortunately, many firms regard tests as a cure-all for selection ills and imagine that, if only they can find the right test, their troubles will be over. Some tests are put on the market without proper standardization; some firms even make up tests which are then used without ever having been standardized or validated at all. Proper standardization and validation takes a long time—mainly because of the difficulties of finding enough subjects to test, and of waiting to get evidence against which to compare the test results.

There is very little point in giving a test to a candidate if there is no one who is trained to interpret the test. But the full interpretation of the test must also rely, to a large extent, on interview findings, eg a high test score but poor school attainment might be the result of a number of factors: these would have to be carefully explored during the interview. It follows that tests should not be used in isolation. They are a part of the whole procedure and without a subsequent interview cannot be properly interpreted.

Rowntree Mackintosh Limited have over fifty years' experience of using selection tests almost all of which have been validated on their own staff. Other firms have sometimes asked for copies of the test to use on their staff, but this has always been refused and, quite rightly, because the tests were validated on Rowntree staff doing Rowntree jobs. If they were to be used elsewhere, they would have to be revalidated on the user's staff.

Assuming that a properly validated test is used (whether validation has been carried out internally, or the test is a reputable one supplied by an outside agency which insists on training in test administration and interpretation before its tests are issued) it can be either an individual test or a group test. An individual test is given by the tester to one candidate alone. A group test (which can, of course, be administered the same way) is normally given to a group of people together. Individual tests, such as form boards, blocks and varieties of personality tests, may take a fairly long time to give to single individuals; group tests, normally paper and pencil ones, may take ten, twenty, forty minutes or even longer—but, of course, a lot of people can take them at the same time.

Administrative convenience of test procedure

If there are twenty people to test, and the test takes half an hour, a group test will be over in just half an hour. The individual test, however, will occupy six hundred minutes or ten hours of testing time. So, when considering the test from the administrative convenience standpoint, the group test is the more suitable.

Acceptability of test to candidates

Most school leavers will have taken tests at various times and probably take well to the notion of being tested for a job. Undergraduates, on the whole, do not object to taking tests, provided their purpose is explained, and it is made clear that no one is accepted or rejected on test scores alone. Some may quibble, on the grounds that their academic record is proof enough of their ability, but others regard tests as an indication that a firm or employer takes selection seriously. Older applications may be rather less approving but, if the purpose is explained, objections are soon overcome. No one should be forced to take a test.

Test results like application forms are personal documents and must be treated as confidential. Nor should a test score be disclosed to anyone who has neither training nor experience in interpreting them; if an indication of performance in the test is called for, then it should be given in terms of norms or percentiles, eg 'this test score places him in the middle 40% of factory applicants' or 'this test score suggests that he is better than 80% of the graduates seen here'. Such information can then be qualified or expanded as necessary.

Reactions vary according to the type of test used. Qualified engineers would probably object to taking a test of mechanical comprehension, designed for apprentice candidates. There is likely to be even more objection to personality tests, and to some tests of attitudes, particularly if they do not appear to be relevant to the appointment. Suspicion of such tests is natural, even if at times irrational.

Group selection procedures

One method of gaining insight into personality factors has been to collect a group of candidates, and observe their behaviour in performing a task. The method was developed by the British War Office, and later adapted for civilian use by the Civil Service and by industry. By seeing candidates for a day and a half or two days instead of the forty or sixty minutes of an interview, it is felt that more accurate assessment is possible, particularly if they are observed doing something. Practical exercises of the assault course kind are usually impracticable, although some firms have used them. Instead, the task the group is given is one they must discuss among themselves.

Sometimes such groups operate without a chairman, sometimes they are left to elect their own, or not, as they please; or candidates are allotted roles which they have to play. The subject to be discussed may be a problem requiring study and the assimilation of evidence—such as the siting of a new branch factory; or one of a series of general topics—perhaps a letter to *The Times*. Very occasionally the group is asked to decide what they want to discuss, and then to discuss it.

Technical soundness of group discussion method

By itself, a group discussion is valueless; it is almost as subjective as the essay. At best it reveals clues—how well someone can put a case, stand up for it, modify or stick to it; how he stands up to attack or ridicule; whether he makes intelligent contributions, or none at all; and what his relations seem to be to other members of the group. At worst, it has a spurious face validity, prompting the unwary to favour or reject candidates on the basis of a few remarks or none at all. It can be made more effective by use of a rating scale, but the evidence seems to suggest that a general grading (on a scale with three, four or five points) is equally suitable. As so often, the general grading is often a better measure if it has been reached after rating on individual contributions or characteristics first.

Group procedures of this kind are only a part of the total selection programme. Like tests, they provide clues about people, which should be investigated more fully in the interview. Group discussions throw some light on how a man behaves in the company of his colleagues, and that is about all. For example, an undergraduate seen at his university may seem alert, with wide interests, hardworking and intelligent, and may show some signs that he has been used to taking authority. In a group discussion he may also show that he can be intolerant, aggressive, and even a bore—clues which the interview alone would not have elicited. So the evidence from group discussions must be considered, with that provided by tests, in the final assessment.

A full group procedure includes tests, interviews, and possibly a formal meal, although some prefer to leave candidates to make their own arrangements outside the formal session times. The formal meal gives an opportunity for an informal question-and-answer session about the vacancy, the firm and so on. It rarely adds much to the selection procedure, unless some emphasis needs to be put on table manners, social ease and the capacity for food and drink.

Administrative convenience of group procedure

The obvious advantages are that six or eight people can be observed and interviewed in a day and a half. Not all the observers are required for all that period; the key figures (the manager with the vacancy, and the recruitment staff) may need to devote one working day and perhaps part of the preceding evening to a group procedure. This concentrates into a comparatively short period the efforts of a limited number of executives, and is more economical than seeing the same number of people for an hour, with interviews spread over several days or even weeks. Offers can be made, or candidates turned down within a very short period, instead of deferring the final selection until all the candidates have been seen.

On the other hand, the procedure makes demands on both candidates and observers. If a series of group procedures is being held over a short period, the strain on the recruitment staff is all the greater—not least because other work is apt to suffer. This suggests that a close season (perhaps the Easter vacation) is best reserved for holding a series of such tests, and other selection work arranged accordingly.

Acceptability of group methods to candidates

Group procedures are generally accepted by candidates, who can usually see that there is a purpose behind them, but their acceptance is subject to four conditions:

1 The matters to be discussed must be appropriate to the level of the appointment.
2 There must be the right number of candidates in the group—six to eight is ideal, four is too few, ten is too many.
3 The procedure must not be too long, nor so short that it hardly gives anyone a chance to show his worth, or gives an inadequate sampling of the candidates' behaviour.
4 The procedure must be appropriate to the type of appointment.

If a problem is to be discussed (rather than, say, a general topic), it should be one that can have a number of possible solutions, none of which is ideal. A typical problem might be the siting of a new factory: details can be given in the brief supplied to each candidate of a wide range of factors which need to be considered—labour supply, access to railheads or motorways, costs, and so on. These details can be expanded for some groups (such as labour supply and trade-union influence for personnel candidates) and not for others. If the group has a choice in this way, it is almost certain that there will be disagreement among its members on the best one to make! The problem, however, must be appropriate to the general level of the candidates—as indeed must be any general discussion topics that may be used instead of or to supplement discussion of a problem.

The best combination is a group problem (one hour to study and one hour to discuss) followed by three shorter unprepared topics, usually based on newspaper articles or letters. The shorter topics often bring a response from candidates who were silent or hesitant on the main problem. By allowing only a few minutes for each topic, some premium is put on the ability to switch quickly from one topic to another.

The ideal number for a group is six, seven or eight. This gives enough points of view to guarantee discussion; a group of only four is likely to be too harmonious. If the number in the group exceeds nine, it is difficult for it to remain as a group; it tends to split into two subgroups.

Acceptability of the procedure is influenced by the time it takes. The most acceptable (and for that matter the most technically sound) programme follows a timetable such as the following:

Monday
19 00   Candidates arrive at local hotel.
19 30   Dinner, with manager and personnel staff or hosts. After dinner, the manager explains about the job, its setting in the company's structure, and answers any questions about it. The personnel staff deal with questions about the company. After this, the group discussion problem is distributed and the hosts withdraw.

Tuesday
08 30   Candidates arrive at the company's headquarters and spend the next hour studying the problem.
09 30   Observers arrive (manager and personnel staff). Candidates discuss problem.
10 30   Coffee.
10 45   Candidates discuss topics.
11 15   Tests.
12 30   Lunch. (The hosts are graduates who joined the company the previous year; they have no part in the selection procedure.)
14 00   Interviews (each candidate has two—one with the manager, one with a member of the personnel staff).
17 00   Candidates depart.

The procedure could certainly be lengthened—perhaps by including a tour of the factory, or of a particular department—but for this particular category of candidate, it has proved satisfactory in its present form. Much shorter procedures have been used for selecting salesmen—taking half a day, beginning with luncheon—but this proved less satisfactory.

The nature of the vacancy affects acceptability in the sense that group procedures are more satisfactory for undergraduates and professional men in their early or mid twenties. Older and better qualified or experienced people sense the artificiality of the procedure more keenly, and feel that their experience is more important than their verbal skills. There may well be a reluctance to participate as a result. It does not seem appropriate, either, with internal applicants, possibly because they are naturally hesitant to put forward their own views when their managers are present. No matter how fair and objective a manager may be, a junior member of his staff can feel he is sticking his neck out unduly by discussing a problem or topic under his very eyes and ears. As a result, discussion takes some time to get going, and tends to be spasmodic and unilluminating.

The interview: core of the recruitment procedure

From what has already been said, it will be clear that the interview holds a central place in any recruitment procedure. This is not to deny its unreliability as a selection method. It is perhaps unfortunate that critics of interviewing usually pick on evidence forty years old—Hollingworth's study of the interview ratings given independently by twelve sales managers of fifty-seven salesmen candidates. There is other more recent evidence which needs to be studied, and which is dealt with in Chapter 12. For our purposes, in this chapter, it must be enough to say that the interview serves four functions:

1 A means of gathering together information provided by application forms, tests, group procedures, and of going into more detail about points thrown up by them.
2 A means of checking information given on the application form.
3 The opportunity to answer questions about the job, and the company.
4 The opportunity to put across to the candidate a positive impression of the company.

The first two functions relate to the selection aspect of interviewing, the last two to its public relations aspects.

Technical soundness of interview method

Leaving aside matters more properly considered in Chapter 12, the interview is only likely to prove a sound method if the interviewer has been properly trained and if he has carried out his preparatory work thoroughly.

The evidence given by Sidney and Brown[2] in *The Skills of Interviewing* suggests that interviewers can be helped by training. It seems that 'the more carefully their objectives are defined, the more practice they have, and the more standard their procedures, the more closely they can agree'. But, as they rightly point out, training and practice alone will not turn anyone into a competent interviewer. Some people are naturally better interviewers than others—but even they improve with training. Vernon and Parry[3] in *Personnel Selection in the British Forces* summarize the findings of research workers on the characteristics of a good interviewer:

The main qualities of a good interviewer, and the main factors leading to good rapport, are thorough knowledge of the job or other matters with which the interviewee is concerned, and of topics in which he is interested, emotional maturity or a well-adjusted personality such that the interviewer is not shocked by anything the interviewee says, and a reputation amongst previous interviewees for sincerity, sympathy and sensitiveness. Good health and freedom from fatigue or strain are also valuable.

The interviewer must know what he is looking for so he must have studied the job, and possibly—indeed preferably—carried out of the job description and specification himself. Few things are worse than not being able to answer elementary questions about the job, or even about the company—even when a candidate is perhaps to be interviewed later by a specialist with the appropriate knowledge. Lacking the information about what sort of person is needed—or should be avoided—the interviewer can only formulate vague general impressions which have little technical soundness.

The interviewer serves a public relations function as well. Interviewers sometimes forget that to a candidate they represent the company. The impressions they gain from the interviewer—as both a person and a member of the firm—seem to be among the factors which prompt them to accept or reject any subsequent offer of a job. The interviewer is very much 'on stage', and should not forget it—but there is no need to overact. If the best advice to candidates is that once found in an Admiralty waiting room: 'Endeavour to create above all an impression of frank sincerity'; it is equally good advice for the interviewer to remember when he swivels round in his chair and says to the candidate: 'Is there anything you would care to ask me?'

Administrative convenience of interview procedure

The interview scores heavily here: most people can fit in an hour in the day to see a candidate—but the vital preparatory work, of course, takes longer. If candidates have to be seen by a number of people, as well as the personnel or recruitment staff, it is wise—as well as courteous—to tell them beforehand how long the selection procedure will last; they can then make their travel arrangements more easily. But it also pays to consider how long each interview should take, and to draw up a suitable time-table which should be kept to as far as possible.

In general, allow each candidate enough time to do himself justice. With less well-qualified or experienced applicants, twenty minutes may be adequate; with those with more education and experience, forty minutes is probably necessary. Allow at least an hour for the main interview with graduates and professional men—remembering that nearly half of it will be given over to answering their questions. For example, when seeing school leavers for factory work, a personnel officer might need half an hour, and the works manager twenty minutes. But, with an engineer, the personnel manager may want at least an hour, and the chief engineer an equal period.

Acceptability of procedure to interviewee

Candidates expect interviews, so they rate high on acceptability. But how acceptable they are will depend very much on the way the interview is conducted. When talking about interviews at universities, we are often asked about 'stress' methods of interviewing. These are anathema to those who take interviewing seriously. It is sometimes assumed that by subjecting a candidate to stress—such as rudeness and hostility—in an interview you can somehow get an indication of how he will stand up to stress on the job. There is, of course, no evidence to support this view: the two situations are entirely different, and the causes of stress on the job include many other frustrations besides those of someone in a superior position being deliberately discourteous. It is perfectly legitimate for the interviewer to say to a candidate: 'For the sake of argument, I am going to take an opposing view', thus making it plain that he is not assaulting his personality, but testing his powers of discussion. But, in general, anything savouring of stress should be avoided in the selection interview. Equally some interviewers intersperse questions with long periods of silence, as some form of test of nerves. Others ask fantasy questions: 'What would you do if you won the Pools?' or produce an object and ask you to sell it to them. With such mistaken, if not ridiculous, techniques, there is every excuse for candidates replying (or not replying) as they think fit. But what they think of the firm which allow its interviewers to use such methods is a different matter. It is, mercifully, not unusual for candidates subjected to such methods to decline to continue the interview. Such 'alienation from interaction' as it has, inevitably, been called is a healthy measure of the unacceptability of such unsystematic recruitment methods.

The whole point of the directed conversation which forms the basis of an interview, is to get the candidate talking freely about himself and his achievements, hopes and interests; and to give him, in return, a good picture of the job for which he has applied, in its setting in the organization. There is enough stress inherent in the interview situation without adding to it.

Undergraduates who, in the course of seeking jobs, attend many interviews, talk freely to each other, and sometimes even to recruiting staff, about their experiences with other companies. 'They were very fair', 'I had a good run for my money', 'He was very helpful' are comments which show that acceptability was not only high, but a factor which weighed heavily with them. Indeed, the employer is often being interviewed as much as interviewing, and candidates will judge the firm from the impression they get before, during and after the interview—from those small but significant clues which suggest whether they are to be treated as human beings or not.

Making the choice of recruitment method

The choice of method depends on the vacancy to be filled, but the elements of studying the job and the applicants, comparing what each has to offer against the demands of the job, and subsequently following up the selection, are common to all methods. Selection should not be a matter of seeing how much applicants will take—this can be wasteful of time and resources: the aim should be to use systematically as many or as few supplementary aids as will give the information sought. Tests, if properly standardized, can help; so can group selection procedures, in certain situations. Whatever aids are employed, they must be technically sound, easy and not over long to administer, and be accepted by those on whom they are used. These three criteria, if constantly referred to, not only help to improve recruitment; they also give a name among applicants for fair and straightforward recruitment.

References

1   A. Rodger, *The Seven-Point Plan,* Paper No. 1, National Institute of Industrial Psychology, London, 1952.
2   E. Sidney and M. Brown, *The Skills of Interviewing,* Tavistock, London, 1961.
3   P. E. Vernon and J. B. Parry, *Personnel Selection in the British Forces,* University of London Press, London, 1949.

Further reading

Anstey, E. and Mercer, E. O. (1956): *Interviewing for the Selection of Staff.* London: Allen and Unwin.
Higham, T. M. (1952): 'Some recent work with group selection techniques', *Occupational Psychology,* **26,** 169–75.
Higham, T. M. (1971): 'Graduate selection—a new approach?', *Occupational Psychology,* **45,** 209–16.
Higham, T. M. (1979): *The ABC of Interviewing,* London: Institute of Personnel Management.
Macrae, A. (1967): *Group Selection Procedures.* Paper No. 5, London: National Institute of Industrial Psychology.
Plumbley, P. R. (1974): *Recruitment and Selection.* London: Institute of Personnel Management.
Plumbley, P. R. and Wiliams, R. (1973): *The Person for the Job.* London: BBC Publications.
Reeves, J. W. and Wilson, V. W. (1951): *Studying Work.* Paper No. 2, London: National Institute of Industrial Psychology.
Roff, H. E. and Watson, T. E. (1961): *Job Analysis.* London: Institute of Personnel Management.
Vernon, P. E. (1960): *Intelligence and Attainment Tests.* London: University of London Press.

4

The Job Specification

T E Platt

The job specification is the blueprint for any recruitment exercise. Its purpose is to set out clearly the reasons why the job exists, what there is to do, how it is to be done, and finally—as a deduction from these factors—the man best suited to do it within the context of the employer's existing and developing requirement. It is clear therefore that anyone embarking on a recruitment programme must ascertain clearly, at the start of the assignment, all the essential facts of the situation, otherwise any deficiencies will become apparent either during the subsequent interview programme or, even worse, after the appointment has been made.

Job specification and the personnel specialist

The personnel specialist, whose task it is to prepare and undertake the recruitment, must work closely with the line manager, with whom the final decision on the appointment must rest. Yet so often he will be requested to find a man for such and such a job, with the comment: 'You know what I want!' Investment in manpower is as expensive as investment in machines and equipment, yet rarely does one find the same quality of judgement and analytical assessment devoted to the former as to the latter.

Besides recruitment, the job specification can fulfil other incidental but equally important purposes for the personnel specialist. These include the following:

1   *Training and development.* Simply stated, a man's training needs can be
    derived from comparing his performance with the requirements detailed

in his job description. If it is regular practice to review individual job objectives and standards in this way, it then becomes possible to identify the need for training and the skills or knowledge that are absent.

2 *Organization review.* Job descriptions within an organization, appropriately summarized and abstracted, can provide the following patterns:
(a)   Relationships.
(b)   Accountability for results.
(c)   Related decision controls and communication.
(d)   Activities.
(e)   Aims and short-term objectives.

3 *Salaries.* All job descriptions have salary structure implications and form the basis of systematic salary administration. The salary level of any job should be the value attributed to it in relation to other jobs within the same organization, taking relevant market rates into account.

The need for detailed information

Every job is unique. Even two jobs seemingly identical in title and function must differ substantially if their phsyical environments (ie the company, the organization structure, the people in it—and possibly the products, problems and priorities) are different, because all of these factors will impinge in significant ways upon the job to be done and the choice of person to do it.

The first requirement is therefore to gather such essential background information. This can often be gained from balance sheets or sales literature but should certainly cover the following:

1   A brief outline of the history of the organization, its development and growth.
2   Its products—and the volume in relation to the industry and its competitors.
3   The markets for the products and the methods of distribution.
4   Finance available, sales turnover (and whether this is divided into export sales and home sales), the profitability of the organization and whether or not there have been any mergers or takeover bids.
5   Centres of operation, plant locations, methods of production and the numbers of people employed both in total and within the division, unit, department or function concerned.

As well as establishing such factual information, it is equally important to uncover or make judgements about the 'intangibles' of an organization—which may include such factors as its style of management, the degree of delegation (or nondelegation) of authority practised, the existence of 'power groups', the personality of the chief or senior executives, the influence of family ownership and so on.

The next important requirement is to establish why the job exists. In order to do this, it is necessary to know the structure of the organization into which the job will fit. One of the easiest ways of doing this is to examine the relevant organization charts (if they exist) which should give a picture of either a well-defined mechanistic or possibly organic structure. Many questions may be needed at this stage to establish that the job requirement is genuine—it sometimes is not. The 'nonjob' generally shows up during an attempt to replace an unusual individual. 'The accommodation of an individual's strengths' may be a euphemism for creating a job for a mediocrity, or may be an accurate description of how a man's unusual talents, or willingness, have been exploited. Personnel specialists, by virtue of their ability to analyse jobs and to assess alternatives, are in a position to make creative suggestions to line managers about effective employment of their staff.

It must be ascertained, early on in any recruitment exercise, whether or not there are any internal candidates, and if so why they should not be considered. If the job is a new one, the recruiter will gain much from discussing the requirements not only with the person to whom the job holder will report but also with other executives or managers with whom the new job holder will have important working relationships. If the job description is for the purpose not of recruitment, but of an organizational review, the discussions will be with the job holder and also with his superior (either together or separately) in order to establish the performance and relationship parameters of the job in question. It may be important, or valuable, to visit locations so as to observe their working, processes and surroundings, if these are relevant.

The third stage in the job specification is the obvious one of establishing the actual job role and its accompanying purpose and responsibilities, namely what the job holder will be expected to do, how he will do it and the results that will be expected to flow from this. While this stage may appear straightforward it is still essential, when engaged in it, to use analysis and judgement in assessing not only the job content, but its dimensions, its 'size' or seniority, its critical accountabilities or objectives, the authority that it needs or carries and, not least, the resources in terms of staff or facilities (or sometimes financial or management backing) that will be essential for its successful performance. Such factors will be apparent in the following section.

Writing the job specification

Once the detailed information has been established, the task becomes one of translating that information into specific terms. A written job specification generally follows an established formal pattern, although the details of lay-out within it will vary from company to company:

1 *Job title.* This should describe accurately the job and its function. If it does not do so, then it will be advisable to change it if only because—if the job is to be advertised—the accuracy of the description will affect the response.

2 *Purpose.* This should be a straightforward, simple statement of what needs to be done and the objectives to be achieved. Thus a product manager may have a definition as follows: 'He will be responsible for obtaining a realistic share of the market which he handles. This will involve originating the marketing plan, the preparation of the marketing budget, sales forecasting, promotion planning and product development.'

3 *Relationships.* The main reporting and working relationships for effective job performance should be indicated. These will cover internal and external contacts, committees, boards and subordinate roles.

4 *Dimensions.* What often determines the size or seniority of the job are the dimensions conferred upon it within this section—such relevant data as the number of people reporting to the job holder, the size of the budgets he will control and the volume of business and profitability that he will be expected to produce. At the same time, if the job holder will sit on boards or committees or will be the company's representative on outside bodies, then this also gives an indication of the size and nature of the job. If he is expected to travel abroad, then the expected number of days he will be travelling in the course of his duties should be indicated.

5 *Accountabilities.* This should describe the job holder's tasks and indicate the areas in which he has sole responsibility or accountability for results. It will include his own key results stated and ranked with quantified or concrete standards and a time scale where possible, and also those of his subordinates. The main decisions taken by him or delegated by him or regularly referred elsewhere will also be recorded in this section. If he has a sales function for example, what authority has he on pricing, product change, marketing methods, etc? Will he have any authority for capital expenditure, in the setting of salaries, or for hiring and firing? Finally, the controls and communications relating directly to the job holder's key results should be indicated, listing their importance and effectiveness, volume, method and frequency.

6 *Attainment of objectives.* The job analyst should define the principal objectives to be achieved and set out priorities and time-tables. Note should be made of the resources required and the support necessary from superiors or colleagues to achieve these objectives. They should be quantifiable if possible, certainly positive and hence recognizable. For a man with profit responsibility, obvious areas of importance are the components of profit performance. For a man who does not have this responsibility, objectives can range from performance targets which have an effect on short-term profitability to those of cash flow or cost control. This statement and analysis should also establish whether it is necessary, for example, for the job holder to have the same degree of technical

expertise as his subordinates or whether his role will be more one of man management, in which case the human relation skills stipulated in the job will have a high influence in its success or otherwise.

7   *Salary*. If the job has been analysed fully, the salary will reflect both its content and its importance and should bear a direct relationship with other jobs within the organization and to relevant market rates. Without a good job description defining know-how, problem solving and accountability, the exercise of measuring it in money terms becomes hit and miss.

The job specification does not exist in isolation. The job, the job environment, the salary that will be appropriate and, finally, the right man for the job are all interrelated parts of the whole recruitment 'piece'. The 'man specification' will be dealt with next.

The man specification

The man specification is the translation of the job specification into human terms, without which the recruiter cannot effectively establish the type of man he is looking for. It requires just as much detailed attention and should reflect not only the demands contained in the job description but also those of the man's superior and of the job analyser.

Before commiting oneself to paper, it is advisable to list what are in effect the essential criteria. There is always a tendency to write a man specification for the Archangel Gabriel and it is seldom, if ever, that one meets the person who can match all the criteria specified, some of which have no relation to the job! The criteria should therefore be realistic and such that, without them, the job cannot be performed to the standard required. It is equally important to record those factors which would exclude a candidate (an airline pilot would never be employed if he were colour blind!) although one should guard at the same time against 'exclusions' that are not valid but simply prejudices of the employer.

The market for potential candidates must also be taken into consideration at this stage, particularly where there is known to be a shortage of candidates of the kind specified. The requirements of the man specification—particularly in regard to age, qualifications and length of experience—may have to sensibly modified by taking into account the likely response to an advertisement of the job in question.

As with the job, the man specification generally follows a standard pattern:

1   *Age*. This is normally prescribed by the company's structure and by the real demands of the job. A man aged fifty may not fit easily into a young team of thirty-year-olds, but equally a man of thirty is unlikely to have the

experience necessary to run a factory employing five thousand people, with all the skills of human relations that such a job requires.

2 *Background.* The early upbringing, schooling and employment pattern of a person can be relevant in so far as they may have shaped subsequent interests and behaviour. The importance of such varies as much with the characteristics and background of the company as with the actual requirements in the job.

3 *Education.* This section should specify the level of educational and academic attainment—and possibly also the type of schooling—which is considered desirable or essential.

4 *Qualifications.* This should define any technical, academic or professional qualifications required for the task and should be clearly related to the job requirements. Thus, a legal executive in a large corporation would almost certainly need to be a lawyer or solicitor but not an MBA as well, even though that might be useful or advantageous.

5 *Experience.* This is an important area which the job analyser will need to analyse carefully and define clearly. There is always a tendency to demand a higher or broader order of experience than the job will actually require, but the key factors are those which define the nature and length of a candidate's previous experience and his success or failure during this period.

6 *Appearance, manner and speech.* Outward impressions sometimes—but not always—indicate the possession of physical or mental attributes. Where particular attributes are of importance—and obviously they are likely to be so in areas such as sales, negotiating and public relations, where the candidate will be representing the company—they should be set down, as an interviewing guide.

7 *Intelligence.* Intelligence should preferably be expressed in terms related to a defined section of the population and is discussed later in Chapter 8. In simple terms it should define the analytical and critical requirements needed in problem solving. The latter will of course depend on the job requirement and the nature and perplexity of the problems to be solved.

8 *Self-expression.* Again, this should be related to actual job needs. Some jobs may call for a high degree of articulate expression and communication; while in others this is relatively unimportant. Where there is a requirement for the former (perhaps entailing public speaking) it is essential that this should be specified.

9 *Disposition.* Although a person's disposition (in itself a rather nebulous term) is not always easy to interpret at interview, one should attempt to define particular characteristics that a job will require. A man with rather timid traits would not be the man to lead men of similar tendencies into the jungle; nor would an aggressive extrovert suit a situation requiring tact, modesty and diplomacy. In completing this section one should try to provide indications rather than attempt to lay down hard and fast criteria,

which a lay interviewer may not, in the event, prove capable of interpreting.

The final analysis

To sum up, the job specification should be written in three parts: first, the background to the job which gives the details and data on why the job exists, second the job specification which gives in precise terms the tasks to be carried out, and finally the man specification which defines the man most suited to the job. Specifications should, naturally be, wherever possible, written specifically rather than generally—and of course, with clarity rather than ambiguity.

The particular skills which all job analysers should develop to help them succeed in their job are as follows:

1 *Observation.* The ability to see quickly if an operation is working smoothly, whether the shopfloor is disorganized or efficient, how people respond to management, initiative and authority, etc.
2 *Listening.* It is important to piece together the real picture—often from a mass of ill-presented information—and not simply to make assumptions or superimpose one's own viewpoints or solutions.
3 *Appraisal.* The ability to see the wood from the trees, to analyse the factors and problems and to weigh the arguments, and possibly the vested interests of the line manager, in order to produce and define a meaningful solution.

5

Job Advertising

K G Fordham

Cost effectiveness, AB profiles, cost per 1000 readers, corporate images and so on have become accepted as part of the recruitment officer's dialogue. Against a possible charge of breaking into unnecessary jargon, it is desirable to trace the modern recruitment officer's position as a buyer in his own right. Hitherto, the purchasing power of the recruitment specialist has been overlooked or brushed aside. He is, however, concerned with direct and indirect expenditure and has a duty to his company to buy wisely. Failure to do so may result in manpower stagnation; his inability to recruit may limit his company's growth or he may mismanage his departmental budget by frittering away thousands of pounds on abortive advertising.

The role of the theoretician or, in this industry, the consultant is that of advising, with all the protective clothing that the title suggests. Practical application is an extension of this theory for consideration and implementation by the buyer. The recruitment problems of 1972–4 and 1977–9 confounded many professionals. During trade recessions substantial lay-offs occur and many leading as well as medium-sized concerns cut back or stop altogether the recruitment of graduates, school leavers and management trainees. When trade improves they can be found wanting in these categories and the total manpower requirements produce massive problems which hold back many concerns. Who is to say what will happen now because, as this chapter is written, we have entered into what may yet prove to be the most severe trade recession this country has ever experienced. During the last twenty-five years, recruitment has always proved more difficult when trade expands again and each new era of growth produces greater problems and shortages of all types of manpower. Recruitment problems will undoubtedly multiply again in future years, company expenditure will increase and so will responsibility for the improvement of existing methods and the development of new techniques.

Scale of recruitment advertising

Recruitment advertising is today very big business but it has not always been like this. Thirty years ago, the national press was dominated by one newspaper which carried approximately six columns of appointments advertisements each day. The revenue derived was a mere pittance compared with that taken today. Few practitioners realized that in the short space of a few decades many media owners would be fighting for survival with the vigorous exploitation of a buoyant recruitment advertising market.

Marketing has in most companies been developed into a highly scientific function. While its application may not guarantee success, it can go a long way to avoiding failure. Despite condemnation of management in the newspaper industry, some of their classified advertising forces have attacked the recruitment market with quite devastating results. They alone in many enterprises have assured their masters of continuation in business. Telephone sales girls, an extra column to the page, three insertions for the price of two and specialized features are all part of their sophisticated armoury. Success has come to them and a current national expenditure in excess of £150 million is a target for their unrelenting assault forces.

£m 1975	1976	1977	1978	1979
75	79	100	151	173

Figure 5.1 Newspaper* recruitment advertising by type

*Based on national dailies and Sundays, regional dailies, evenings and Sundays and on weekly newspapers, but excluding free sheets.

Source: Advertising Association.

Sales pressure can be resisted for much of the time but everybody weakens occasionally. Why? It is not because the seeker of labour thus gains any material benefit. Often it is simply a case of uninspired work, applied under extreme pressure and against some of the fiercest competition ever faced for labour. It is surprising to recall that recruitment advertising was once an embarrassment to media owners and particularly to advertisement directors. Not so very long ago they would have gladly abandoned it and concentrated on the consumer advertising plums. These pickings did not last, however.

Independent television saw to that and, within a short space of time, many publications were placed in jeopardy by their losses. Indeed many disappeared from the bookstalls, never to see the light of day again. Radio has now been added to the competition.

Full employment was, oddly enough, the saviour of a large sector of the newspaper industry. Enlightened sales managers soon took advantage of the nation's labour shortage. Studies were made of North American techniques. Many have since been applied in the UK and their use, together with the engagement of different types of personnel by publishers, has achieved a dramatic breakthrough for some media owners. Whilst Figure 5.2 shows only the steady growth of the *Daily Telegraph's* volume, many other newspapers also broke into the market and established a worthwhile foothold.

Currently our national press is beset by further problems, industrial and technological. These problems concern the workforce and their fears about jobs because of the need to introduce new technology. The need for change is not in dispute but the methods are. Whilst the negotiations smoulder on, production breakdowns, distribution problems and disputes have caused losses and frustrations for advertisers. 1978/79 could have been prosperous years for the national press, with larger papers and more advertising. Instead long delays, frequent omissions, continuous uncertainties and a long stoppage of Times Newspapers occurred.

Recruitment market in terms of people and skills

The recruitment market varies according to specific requirements. For explanatory purposes it may be assumed that the following sectors are of most importance to the majority of employers. These four groups of people provide

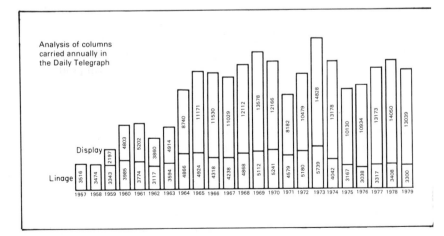

Figure 5.2   Growth of situations vacant advertising

the major recruitment problems. You may ask: 'What about salesmen?' or 'What about research staff?'. It can be admitted that they also create tantalizing situations but they are generally obtainable with less difficulty. In the selling field, selection is the main problem; in the research field, job satisfaction.

Technical and professional staff

This group provides undoubtedly the greatest challenge of all in recruitment advertising. From designers to draughtsmen to all categories of engineers, from accountants to computer staff, the shortage is universal. Advertising budgets have risen faster in these fields than in any other. In engineering, enormous contracts have hung in the balance through the inability of contractors to recruit technical staff. Industries running down or reputed to suffer from government interference are hardly likely to attract ambitious men. Yet they must employ these people, so their problems become increasingly acute. A shortage of candidates often results in companies paying more to fill vacancies but this leads to dissatisfaction with the work and turnover in the job.

Clerical staff, secretaries, shorthand-typists

For many organizations this group presents the most hazards. Much of the work is routine; office bureaux have almost a monopoly on the supply of labour and an offer of higher pay is a frequent cause of departure. The lure of temporary work with shorter hours and more money reduces the size of the direct recruitment market and consequently ensures that the employment gap may never be closed.

Many companies have failed to appreciate the tactics required for this kind of recruitment. Girls looking for alternative positions collect one of the free sheets, buy an evening paper or a weekly local publication, select four or five likely jobs and telephone for appointments. Their selection is normally made from the classified columns and from advertisements arousing some special interest, fairly brief but inviting immediate action. The company which interviews a girl first and can offer all the desirable things she may be looking for in her job will probably obtain her services. The others she has telephoned for an appointment may never hear from her again. Failure to attend for interview is a common occurrence. *The Times* still enjoys the monopoly for top secretarial posts.

Trainees

Only a few years ago this category, apart from the graduate round, presented moderate difficulties and those were largely the image of the employer,

Figure 5.3 Example of a newspaper advertisement for both technical and overseas

prospects, pay and agreed need. After the cutback of these programmes in the early seventies the demand rose so dramatically that few organizations reaped their projected requirement in numbers or quality. The category covers school leavers with 'A' levels to those having graduated. Employers range from government to industry, retailing, banking and the Armed Forces. In the 1970s some of the largest companies were forced to advertise continuously in an attempt to reach their manning targets. Research carried out amongst prospective candidates showed that 'A' level students wanted training, status, money and prospects and 'graduates' sought good on-the-job training and needed to feel wanted and respected. Companies stressed most of these requirements and candidates had a splendid choice and whether they responded to Woolworth's or Sainsbury's, Barclays or Lloyds, GEC or Plessey, may have been a matter of image, career selling, ability or a parent's preference. Most employers appeared to be offering similar conditions and opportunity and so creative advertising became more important. Currently, with another recession, there is a surplus of candidates for most requirements and another cutback because of cost.

Overseas

In the 1970s overseas postings became an important category of recruitment advertising. Industrial and military investment in the Middle East and throughout Africa has brought about a constant demand for specialists in many disciplines. At the outset recruitment was relatively easy. Conditions in the UK, high income tax, poor industrial relations, political disenchantment, erosion of differentials and increasing bureaucracy made working abroad attractive to many. However after the early build-up, when those who were very keen had been hired, the market began to harden. By the end of the decade many categories, radar technicians and computer personnel for example, became difficult and some countries, Nigeria, Saudi Arabia and South Africa for example became less attractive. The pressure on overseas recruitment has helped some media considerably.

Economic aspects of effective advertising

Regrettably, the aim of a company's recruitment advertising is rarely considered. For selling consumer perishables or durables, a clear plan is laid down. The task in hand is plainly understood. By advertising, point of sale or test marketing, the model is to create awareness, to nurture acceptance, to establish a liking and to arouse the interest to provoke action. A simple model perhaps with 1001 interpretations is to sell and establish a product range.

How far does recruitment advertising really differ? Are the same ingredients used? One can perhaps be rather more specific in identifying the basic aim: it is to recruit at economical cost. To achieve this, four compounds should be remembered at all times:

1 Advertising must set out to communicate with an appropriate audience.
2 The advertisement should produce an adequate number of replies.
3 The advertisement must also minimize the number of wasted replies and the consequential unfruitful time spent on the administration of unsuitable applications.
4 It is highly desirable that advertising should seek to build a continuing image of the company as an employer, for long-term purposes.

It is worth taking a little time to analyse these four components in a little more detail.

Making the advertisement communicate

This entails an accurate appraisal of the labour requirements in relation to the media coverage to ensure that the right audience is addressed.

Producing sufficient replies

For one appointment, the attraction of 100 replies is surely a mark of failure to communicate properly. An accurate assessment of the market is an essential element of a company's recruitment advertising. An adequate and select number of replies is sought for shortlist purposes.

Minimizing unsuitable applicants

Waste replies mean extra work; minimization results not only in a more satisfactory solution for the selection officer, but also reduces the number of disappointed and irritated applicants who merit only an early rejection.

Building a continuing image

Recruitment becomes tougher as every year goes by. No opportunity should be missed to promote an organization as a progressive and desirable employer. To this end, every advertisement can project a long-term recruitment image. If well done, advertisements will inevitably attract some applicants to make contact without waiting for a specific job advertisement to appear.

There are some important differences between product and recruitment advertising. Most staff requirements are urgent, advertisements having to be placed tomorrow. Yet tomorrow may be the worst day of the week; so the task of keeping the line manager quiet frequently results in the personnel manager taking the easy and most expensive way out. The time allowed for the reception of replies is normally quite short and it may be known within seventy-two hours by the quality of the replies whether or not success has been achieved. One positive advantage, however, is that the results of recruitment advertising can be measured and all companies can therefore work on the basis of knowledge and statistics built up over a period of time.

Assessing the state of the labour market

As in all job functions, the ability to prepare the facts and to plan ahead increases the chance of success. Following the study of a job analysis, job and man specification, it can be useful to assess the overall market under the headings of demand, value, appeal and prospects:

1   What is the demand like for this particular category? If it is limited and the supply is plentiful, the advertisement copy can be more specific and thereby minimize the number of unsuitable applicants. Alternatively, if there is a substantial shortage of people within this category, perhaps the specification and subsequently the advertising copy should be slackened to improve the chances of success.
2   Will the salary offered be competitive for this type of person? If not, is it worth the time, cost and consequential delay in changing the specification? Many concerns spend several hundred pounds to confirm what should have been proved by simple research.
3   Does the job have appeal? If it does not by its title alone but may when carefully put over at interview, the copy approach should be planned to counteract the disadvantage. In this way, the opportunity to interview candidates may be real, whereas failure to recognize the unattractiveness of the job by definition will probably result in no applicants at all.
4   In the light of the above assessment, what are the chances of success? Additionally, does the company have a good reputation? Will this man be a 'foreign' specialist in the organization, the only one or perhaps one of a select few? If so, this may evoke a hostile reaction because of his desire to work with a group of similarly qualified people.

Although a requirement will seldom satisfactorily withstand the above scrutiny, the information that emerges can provide the basis for a revised and perhaps refreshing approach to the advertisement. Without scrutiny, such revision may be overlooked. On the other hand, the market assessment may convince management that their requirement may not be recruited at a price it is prepared to pay. The department concerned may therefore have to be reorganized or the job redefined.

Elements of copywriting

Recruitment advertising can be an outlet for two separate but coordinated creative talents: copywriting and visualizing. As every advertisement has to be written, whilst only a few are visualized, copywriting must be the major consideration.

Different people do not write with identical style, meaning or impact, and it would be unwise to lay down a tight formula. Nevertheless, some guidance is desirable, for advertising copy is one of the most positive links in the recruitment chain. It is the interpretive link between specification and selection. One without the other can mean disaster or simply hit or miss.

Advertising is essentially a form of communication and its prime objective is to inform its public. It has to set out to satisfy a need. Without this, a competitor's advertisement can have a distinct advantage. As well as being informative, it must also be comprehensive, logical, not too long-winded, understandable and relevant to the level it is intended to address. The primary purpose is to recruit and the copy must not, therefore, be written to please the personnel man or his director.

Preselective copy can go far towards achieving a select and useful set of applications. The advertisement that generalizes is likely to produce 90% plus waste replies. Intelligent copywriting should seek to reverse this. It must also achieve several other objectives, all of which fall within the four essentials of all advertising copy: attention, interest, desire and action.

Capturing the reader's attention

The headline must catch the reader's eye. It must be meaningful and clearly identify the audience at which it is beamed. If it does not, the title should be replaced by a suitable subject heading as an adequate alternative. Subject subheadings are also a useful addition and may include a specific industry, if not apparent by the main title. The incentive or the location should be indicated in the subheading. Employer's names should rarely be used in headlines—few, if any, companies can recruit today on their name alone.

Arousing interest in the company

Next it is necessary to give details of the company or organization, the job and the requirement. With the competition faced in the advertising columns, the inclusion of company data may make all the difference to results. Depending on the merits of the situation, this information may include what the company does, its size and, perhaps, structure, achievements and market position, growth and prospects. The job information may embrace, for example, the reason for the appointment, the position held by the person to whom the successful candidate will be responsible, the duties to be undertaken (and the project stage if relevant) and details of support management and/or subordinates. The requirements may cover the age range, education and qualifications, experience, mobility and special factors.

The other extreme, of course, is to use a box number. Does anyone need to respond to a box number today? Not unless there are some unique or highly interesting facts to persuade him. Most companies at some stage or other use box numbers, perhaps for reasons of product or development security, a desire to state an attractive salary without disclosing it to existing employees, or because of a plan to remove an unsuitable employee. The box number is unlikely to succeed unless it creates one or more advantages which could not otherwise be achieved over an agency or company name.

Desire: salary, benefits and prospects

The copywriter must try to assess the relative importance of the incentives and the likely reasons why a candidate will wish to apply. Pay is nearly always of prime importance. The inclusion of a figure or scale must result in eliminating some unsuitable applicants on this count alone, thereby minimizing waste. References to 'attractive salary' or 'salary according to age, qualifications and experience' are meaningless and just a waste of space. Opinions on what constitutes a suitable salary for a particular post can vary enormously and pay haggling rarely creates a calm understanding.

On the other hand, when salaries are secret, and scales not announced to all employees, they should not be quoted in advertisements. If they are, it will probably lead to industrial relations difficulties which could well have been avoided. Benefits may vary from post to post but can cover commission, bonus, car and pensions.

Job satisfaction is frequently an important motivator and for many young people, the experience that jobs offer them may be of considerable advantage in developing their careers. The working conditions and equipment may warrant a mention and most people are interested in their promotion prospects. In an era of training and management development, information about this sphere of an employer's activity may also provide a desirable element of interest to the reader.

Inciting the reader to action

While perhaps the simplest to meet of the four essentials, the call for action on the part of the reader is, incomprehensibly, often neglected. No advertiser should publish his wares or wants without being equipped or ready to respond. If the line manager is ill-prepared to deal with applications or about to embark on some prearranged tour which will keep him out of the office for several weeks, it is quite wrong to advertise. If applicants are kept waiting, they will assuredly be lost to the more efficient organization which displays speed of action, courtesy and enthusiasm. The company that ignores this precept may be left with the unemployables and the need to readvertise, which delays the appointment and more than doubles the cost.

Action should be invited in accordance with the probable habits of the type of applicant required. If unskilled workers are sought, they would probably prefer to call in at the labour office. Technical or professional people would rather write or perhaps telephone. Job seekers now have a more favourable attitude towards application forms than was once the case. They may, however, be irritated if a request for letters giving full details is followed up by the dispatch of a company application form. Many concerns transfer given details from a letter to an application form; this certainly impresses applicants who are then more than ready to supply the missing data.

For important technical and EDP (electronic data processing) posts inquiries can be invited by telephone. On such occasions, a technical member of the staff should ideally receive these inquiries. With his knowledge he is able to lead the suitable applicant towards an early interview. When this method is adopted, the member of staff chosen must have the necessary personality to deal effectively with people by telephone. It is an added advantage if he is favourably known within the industry.

If the post has to be advertised anonymously the use of a reputable agent's name is preferable, provided the candidates are processed in an acceptable manner.

For mass recruitment, particularly through the popular press, coupons can be effectively used. The inquiry rate increases and this provides a useful number of likely candidates. On occasions, the coupon can be enlarged to ask certain questions relevant to the requirement or the manner of the job and thus enable some form of preselection to take place at the coupon stage. There is little evidence to suggest that the addition of a *reply paid* coupon increases the return. It does, however, seriously increase the amount of space required in order that the advertisement may fold up into an envelope.

Informal hotel interviewing can also be exploited when reasonable numbers of technical staff are required, but there are hotels that do not approve of such arrangements being advertised. The advertiser's intention must be made clear and the manager's approval obtained, preferably in writing; otherwise the usual newspaper check for authenticity will undo the arrangements. This method of recruitment normally increases the number of applicants handled. However, because of its simplicity, whereby candidates may call without an appointment and without any prescreening, the normal conversion rate may not apply. It is most likely that there will be two or even three times as many applicants to handle as is desired, but the method may speed up recruitment and, in the long run, reduce the cost.

Laws and codes of practice

It is important to realise that the law has extended into recruitment and in particular recruitment advertising. Racial discrimination — advertising specifically for a white or black person, a British or West Indian subject — is not permitted. Exceptions are few and there have been hardly any instances of abuse.

Discrimination by sex is also not permissible unless falling within prescribed exceptions. Sadly there have been a minority who have closed their eyes to this Act and have on occasions deliberately tried to provoke trouble. This has brought a reaction from media who are also liable under the Act, and many now reserve the right to insert 'male or female' or to change the copy without recourse to the agent or advertiser ie it has become a condition of acceptance. The EOC's guide-lines are worth reading and compliance with them will avoid problems.

Advertising codes of practice have been developed to avoid the need for further legislation, and accuracy, care over illustrative matter and the fast checking of any complaints can all help to reduce the risk of legal action.

Selecting the advertisement media

Media selection, while easier to conduct in the recruitment field than for, say, detergents, has been based on hunch for far too long. Basically, the choice often lies between, in the provinces, morning and evening newspapers and, nationally, the daily. or Sunday popular or serious publications and the technical and professional press. Statistics are circulated by many different bodies and the results of surveys are frequently quoted, but until recently there has been little or no scientific study.

Most publications provide details of their readership compared with their competitors. They all manage to reveal just how superb this readership is but without any evidence of their pulling power in relation to recruitment. Media owners often couple research figures with the phrase 'continuing use of our columns must surely be evidence of our pulling power'. However, this may be entirely due to effective selling rather than to good results. Until more scientific information is available, advertisers will have to rely on their historical information, properly maintained and analysed. Specialist agency advice can be invaluable and even hunch decisions may still prove to be adequate.

Where the job seekers look

Job seekers usually turn to certain publications, depending on their level of understanding or reading habits. The socioeconomic groupings give some indications here, but again these are produced for different forms of media selection.

Locally, the selection of newspapers is fairly straightforward unless there is

% Readership in Social Class

	Recruitment advertising % Jan–March 1980	Circulation (millions) Jan–June 1980	Men				Women			
			A Class		B Class		A Class		B Class	
			Profile	Universe	Profile	Universe	Profile	Universe	Profile	Universe
Daily Mail	11.5	1.98	5	17	18	17	4	16	17	16
Daily Telegraph	35	1.44	14	38	35	24	14	29	36	20
The Times	7	0.315	20	15	38	7	22	9	36	4
The Guardian	10	0.375	8	9	38	10	11	8	40	7
Financial Times	6	0.197	25	19	36	7	8	2	23	2
Daily Express	15	2.32	3	14	15	19	4	14	15	16
Sunday Times	11	1.41	13	37	34	25	12	31	32	21
The Observer	3	1.01	11	24	29	16	8	16	33	17
Sunday Telegraph	1.5	1.03	10	21	28	15	12	24	28	15
TOTAL =	100%									

Universe:
Men Class A   666 000
Men Class B   2 852 000
Women Class A   705 000
Women Class B   2 841 000

(Aged 15+)

Figure 5.4 Leading newspapers' share of recruitment advertising

a choice between weekly and daily publications. Unskilled, semiskilled and skilled men, and clerical staff would normally be expected to respond to either the weekly press or the evening paper if one circulates in the district. Some clerical workers, particularly secretaries, may respond to the morning press and to the quality dailies. In addition there is a wide choice of free sheets depending on location. Certainly media selection for these categories is not very difficult. It is in the technical and professional areas that more skill and a little luck is desirable.

Analysis of national newspapers

Currently, the national choice largely centres around the *Daily Telegraph* and *The Sunday Times*. Figure 5.4 makes interesting reading. It sets out the leading papers' shares of all recruitment advertisements in the national daily and Sunday newspapers for the first quarter of 1980. Also given are their circulation figures, together with their A and B profiles for men and women.

In fairly simple terms it is often a question of quantity or quality. For decades the Sunday press was not regarded as the hunting ground for jobs: the *Daily Telegraph* virtually controlled the market. Through its complacency it let in the Sunday press. In this way, the response pattern has certainly changed. While the job hunters still resort to the *Daily Telegraph* and for orthodox recruitment this paper still dominates the scene, when quality is of paramount importance, the Sunday press frequently carries the day. It is sometimes necessary to restrict the choice to the Sunday press and gamble for quality at the expense of quantity; this may, however, result in no replies at all.

In recent years, the emergence of the popular press as recruitment media has changed the pattern for many categories. The *Sun* is most effective for mass or national recruitment of artisans and even young people with five 'O' levels. The *Daily Express* and *Daily Mail*, one grade higher, are also proving to be most effective. However, by raising the grade of requirement, the quality of applicants frequently falls short of the standard sought. Regional purchase is possible in some popular papers, which for northern or Scottish employers means an attractive buy although national advertisers take priority and may freeze out those not taking full coverage.

Some papers, particularly regional mornings, do have certain days when recruitment advertisements are concentrated together and clearly the results are more impressive when this occurs. It is therefore important to specify the day required and to refuse insertion on any other. At the time of writing, for example, the position is as shown in Figure 5.5.

Supporting role of technical press

The technical and professional press, while an attractive proposition, remains to a large extent an enigma. A few journals, particularly those published by professional or technical institutes, can be used effectively. Timing is critical because press dates have to be met and internal distribution schemes slow up readership and consequently the receipt of replies.

Whatever market place is chosen, competition is continually evident. The choice is between saturation of the market, involving a spread of five papers, or concentration on perhaps two of the five. The latter course, which may mean one national newspaper supported by the most appropriate technical or professional journal, can offer the best of both worlds. It provides outlets in the mass market and in the compact technical field. Additionally, by not

Daily Express	Monday and Friday Wednesday Thursday	Overseas Sales and Management Computers
Daily Mail	Monday Tuesday	Computacareer Equal opportunities (clerical jobs in the south) Opportunities in the North
	Wednesday Thursday Friday	Engineering and overseas Sales and management Local government
The Guardian	Monday	Secretarial Creative and Media
	Tuesday Wednesday	Education Guardian Public appointments (including the Health Service)
	Thursday	Futures (science and technology) Commercial appointments
Financial Times	Tuesday Thursday	Appointments editorial Popular day
Glasgow Herald	Monday Wednesday Friday	Situations vacant
Scotsman	Friday	Popular day
Bristol Evening Post	Thursday and Friday	Premium rate charged
Birmingham Evening Mail	Tuesday and Thursday	Popular days
Manchester Evening News	Thursday	Popular day

Figure 5.5   **Feature days for recruitment advertising**

excessively dispersing available resources. it provides for a little more domination in the chosen two.

Bank holidays, budget days and sensational news days may affect readership adversely. Where these are known, or can be predicted, the information should be acted upon or the advertiser will pay the penalty for his neglect.

Techniques of visual presentation

Twenty years of displayed recruitment advertising have seen many changes. The visual presentation has now entered a more sophisticated stage with more creative designs, corporate house styles and expensive production. Yet it must not be overlooked that recruitment advertising often starts in the classified columns. Many types of people look no further. Therefore it is important to consider the target and ascertain his likely reading habits before selecting any one of three forms.

Run-on or undisplayed advertising should still have attention value and the first few words can be crucial. If an accountant is wanted, the advertisement should start with that title and not with: 'Well-known company requires ....' That would be classified under the letter W and readers would have to read through the whole column or columns to find it. In a semi displayed advertisement, however, the job title automatically is in more prominent type. This may mean that the anonymous introduction will not detract from the effect of the advertisement, even though the job title may appear in the middle.

Displayed advertisements demand greater skill by the selection and balance of typefaces. A combination of headline type, bold and light typefaces can project the headline and penetrate a wider readership. Taste in typeface and size, and the economics of space buying, are largely responsible for the final appearance. Prominent headings are highly desirable, but the width of the advertisement across one, two or more columns controls the size.

Type is measured by its depth in points—there are seventy-two points to an inch. Most headlines range between 14 point and 30 point, that is to say, from less than a quarter of an inch to almost half an inch in depth. The text matter normally varies from 6 point, which is fairly small but readable, to 8 point. The text of this handbook is set in 10 point. Book type with serifs is usually more reliable for printing and reading, but this modern era has produced a range of popular sans serif faces for advertisers to promote up-to-date images. Examples can be seen on the motorway signboards. Company logos can help display advertisements provided they do not overdominate. They should not conflict or confuse the main heading and for most advertisements are probably more satisfactorily placed at the base. Having expressed this in inches it is important to remember that space is now purchased in centimetres, usually with a minimum of three.

Form recording advertising effectiveness

Order number _____
Date of order _____
Other reference _____

Job title. _____
Total males/females required ____ ; Salary/scale envisaged £ _____

Job category _____
Was post previously advertised? Yes/No
Does ad reveal salary or scale? Yes/No
Company named/box number/ _____

Key	Publication	Insertion dates	Space size and setting	Cost		Replies number	Interview		Offers made	Number of starters	Starting salaries
				Per insert	Total		Number invited	Number attending			

Production costs
Grand totals

Copy of advertisement attached
Other comments

Number internally promoted

Figure 5.6 Form recording advertising effectiveness

The object is to obtain continuity and consistency of style and thereby gain immediate recognition coupled with dominance. The reasons for employing new corporate designs are well founded, but their use must not be carried to extremes for recruitment advertising purposes. Many companies insist on special type-faces being used for all advertising and publicity matter and this usually means the purchase of blocks which add to the recruitment advertising costs. Corporate images must ideally be flexible and not interfere with the purpose of recruitment advertising.

Analysing the response to advertisement

Analysis of response provides a record of present action and guidance for the future. Two sets of factors affect response, one outside the advertiser's control and the other completely within it.

External, the day of the week, the news of the day, the make-up of the paper, the position of the advertisement and the competition all contribute in some small way to success or failure. On the advertiser's score card, the job, the requirement, the way these are written up, the company's image, the inducement, the location and the action requested may all affect a reader's reaction.

With the short life of a recruitment advertisement and the normal progressing of applicants, it is possible to evaluate results and to predict and determine a budget for many recruitment categories. It is in the interests of every advertiser to maintain accurate records and to analyse them. Failure to do so can only result in using ineffective newspapers, a lack of basic information and, more seriously, a rapid increase in advertising expenditure.

The work of recording and analysing response to advertisements falls into three parts:

1   Noting information known in advance—such as media employed, type of setting and so on.
2   Recording each applicant's progress.
3   Analysing points 1 and 2 above.

The specimen form shown in Figure 5.6 sets out a typical progress chart, completed and ready for comparison on a quarterly basis by job category. A chore, maybe, but without it can one really be satisfied with the advertising formula, its results and the expenditure for tomorrow?

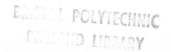

6

Application Forms

B J Edwards

Manpower planning, written job specifications and an advertising policy which promotes both the company and its vacancies are all of great value to an organization in establishing an effective recruitment programme. This value is lost, however, when companies fail to carry through the analysis of job and company requirements to the development of clear application forms, which a potential employee is able to complete easily, and at the same time put all the relevant facts about himself to the recruitment officer.

Purposes of the application form

To be completely effective, application forms should be designed with the following main purposes in mind:

1 To aid the selection of candidates for interview.
2 To provide a framework on which the interview can be built.
3 To become part of the permanent personnel record.
4 To form the basis of a 'future vacancies' file.
5 To be of use for labour market analysis.
6 To identify the most successful advertising media and recruitment sources.
7 To assist in the establishment of better public relations.

Selecting candidates for interview

The application form is a fundamental part of any selection interviewing technique. The applicant should be able to record on the form all the details about himself that are relevant to the job, and in such a way that the potential employer has an ordered, comprehensive picture of each individual.

Compilation of a shortlist of candidates is considerably easier and more rational if the employer is able to compare applications on the same basis. Wading through a pile of application letters, many of which may be comparatively illegible, takes considerable time. Where speed in filling a vacancy is paramount, written applications which contain a *curriculum vitae* are a great help.

Should an employer decide to send out an application form to all applicants and, for many technical jobs this is advantageous, the advertisement should clearly state: 'Please write or telephone for an application form quoting job reference number . . . .' This avoids antagonizing potential employees and saves time. (See Chapter 5.)

A framework for the interview

Analysis of the completed application form shows areas of weakness and highlights facts needing elucidation. Provided the form has been laid out logically, the interviewer is able to mark those areas requiring attention and deal with them logically at the interview.

Permanent personnel records

Some application forms contain additional items concerned with the engagement of staff, such as medical examination, terms of engagement and so on. These items are for the use of the personnel department and need careful delineation.

Future vacancies file

Many companies find that applicants may be suitable for one or more jobs and, although shortlisted, they were not appointed to the first job they applied for. Agreement with the candidate to put him on a future vacancies file speeds up recruitment for potentially difficult jobs.

Labour market analysis

A personnel officer new to an area will find it helpful, in assessing the type of labour available, to retain the application forms of rejected candidates for a period and then to analyse them in simple categories.

Identify the most successful recruitment sources

Although the more progressive advertising agencies are very well informed as to the best national or trade press for advertising various jobs, they are often not as aware of the impact of local papers and 'give-aways'. A simple question on an application form, such as: 'Where, or from whom, did you learn of our vacancy?' enables a quick, effective analysis to be completed when a recruitment programme is reviewed.

Assisting better public relations

Poor quality paper, printing and lay-out of an application form often have a bad effect on the public image of a company. A well-designed and well-presented form continues the image building which began in the job advertisement.

Contents of the application form

There have been few studies of the content of application forms. However, the Industrial Society analysed fifty application forms and found that, of the seventy questions listed, no firm asked more than fifty questions and most had a good deal fewer than fifty. Apart from the name of the firm and the date, the applicant's name came first in forty-five cases. The analysis showed the following results.

Information required	Number of firms
Identification	
Full name	15
Surname and forenames	35
Maiden name (or surname at birth, if different)	2
Marital status (or single/engaged/married/widow/er)	45
Male/female	2
Address (immediately after name)	50
Alternative address (permanent/temporary)	5
Telephone number	9
Date of birth	48
Age	25
Nationality	29
Place of birth	7
National Insurance Number	10
Children (number and ages under 18)	32
Next of kin (or whom should we contact in emergency?)	14
What relatives have you here?	20
Member of a trade union	7
Type of work required	22
Rate required	10

Willing to work nights/shifts/overtime? 17
Date free to commence 19
Registered under the Disabled Persons (Employment) Act 1944 }
Details of disability } 26
Number of DP 21 certificate and date of expiry
State of health 22
Doctor's name and address 8
Height and weight 11
Section for medical officer's comments 9
Driving licence 2

Education
School and further education (primary school, secondary
    school, university, dates, examination passes) 33
Membership of professional and scientific bodies 13
Apprenticeship 6
Indentures, trade and so on 6

Occupation
Military service 27
Liability for service in reserves 2
Previous employment 50
Most recent job only 6
Start at most recent job and work back to give complete history 24
Dates of employment 50
Reasons for leaving 50
Have you worked here before? 32
Have you applied to work here before? 3

Recreation
Hobbies and interests }
Sports and clubs } 14

Miscellaneous
Names and addresses of referees 6
Where did you learn of our vacancy? 2
Signature 25
Date 34
Space for office use 29
Space for interviewer's comments/test results 14
Agreement (brief condition of service) 9

More recently companies have included the following questions.

Identification
Aliens Work Permit Number
Aliens Registration Number
Work telephone number (if we may contact you there)
House owner
Are you willing to work anywhere in the United Kingdom/Europe/overseas?
Preferred work locations
Space for passport size photograph

Education
Current studies
Languages ability giving level attained/practised

Occupation
Fringe benefits (holidays, holiday bonus, contributory/non-contributory
    pension, etc)
Précis of job history
Personal objectives for the future

Recreation
Any form of social service

These lists are intended as prompters, rather than a series of compulsory items
for inclusion in an application form. However, many organizations are taking
a longer view of their human resource requirements, promoting and
transferring increasingly from within the company. Successful career
planning, training and development programmes require detailed data if they
are to be effective.

Design of the application form

Many organizations find it practicable to include on an application form
sections for which other companies raise separate forms. The list below gives
possible alternatives for combination depending on the procedure adopted
within a company.

Type of form	Main purpose
Application form	Data about applicant
Interview assessment form	Test results and interviewer's opinion

Medical examination form	Medical examination result stating fitness for job only
Engagement form (office use only)	National Insurance number, Tax Form P 45, birth certificate checked, references checked
Deduction slips	Sports Club/charities/trade unions/ sick club/pension contributions
Contract of employment Receipt of employee handbook }	Both need employee's signature as confirmation

In designing a company application form, the whole range of jobs within a firm must be kept in mind. There is a wide variation in the information required from a school leaver, a labourer, a skilled craftsman, a clerk, a technologist or a manager. The information asked for therefore varies considerably in detail, and so does the design and lay-out of the application form.

Checklist on design

The following checklist can be of help in designing various types of application form:

1 *Adopt clear and concise wording.*
2 Avoid underlining headings and titles—a larger clear type-face is more effective.
3 Check used existing forms for spaces rarely or never used.
4 *Arrange layouts for speed and accuracy of entry,* and extraction of details.
5 Design the form to cater for slightly more than the average number of entries, not the maximum, and allow for exuberant handwriting.
6 Whenever possible make the form do two or more jobs.
7 *Provide ample space for writing* (at least one-third of an inch between horizontal lines, as in typewriter double spacing).
8 Give printed alternatives for ticking or deleting to save writing time.
9 When using perforation, arrange for long slits rather than round holes.
10 If the torn-off portion is to be filed, allow a filing margin.
11 Prepunch forms at time of printing, if they are to be filed in a ring binder.
12 *Standardize form sizes as far as possible.*
13 For redesigned or new forms, obtain a pilot run, duplicated rather than printed, to see whether there are any snags and whether the forms efficiently serve their purpose. Line managers are often a constructive source of comment.
14 Choose paper of suitable surface and thickness for method of form completion, such as ink, type, pencil.
15 If the same forms are to be dealt with all day, choose a light buff or a

lightly coloured paper: it reflects less light than white and so is less glaring.

16   See that the printer follows your instructions precisely.

17   Order quantities related to possibilities of revision. In most cases a six months' run will disclose possibilities for further improvements. The true cost of a procedure or a form is often the *clerical cost of using the form, not the production cost.*

18   Maintain a file of specimen forms and a brief breakdown of how each is used.

Lay-out of the form and grouping of questions

The name of the company should be clearly stated—preferably in the company's house style at the head of the form. The type of application form—such as manual employees, clerical or management—should also be shown.

Each question should be challenged to see if it will screen, select or identify the candidate and whether the information is needed at the form completion stage, or if it would be better obtained at an interview once rapport has been established. Some personal questions may be resented on an application form but a carefully phrased inquiry at an interview will frequently achieve more than a basic reply. One company includes the following introductory sentences on its application forms.

> The information called for will help us to assess your suitability for a post. *If there are any questions you prefer not to answer in writing, you are under no obligation to do so.*

There are four categories of questions that will be required to appear on most application forms:

1   Identification: to identify the candidate.
2   Education: to further determine the candidate's qualifications.
3   Occupation: to fill the vacancy.
4   Recreation.

So that the applicant is able to fill the form in with the least confusion, each section of the form should be carefully identified. (N.B. The following specimen sections are much reduced in size.)

Identifying the candidate

Job applied for

This section can be completed either by the candidate or by the potential employer. In large organizations, space for a job reference should be included (Figure 6.1).

Application for position of	Job reference number
Source of application. Name of newspaper; through professional association; personal contact, etc	

Figure 6.1 Specimen form: job reference

Personal particulars

Basic personal details should be grouped together in a block. The order shown in Figure 6.2 is the most usual format; notice that there is sufficient space for an alternative address. The order in which this section is laid out will largely be determined by the main company personnel record. Records clerks find transference of details very much easier if the same pattern is adopted on the main records and source documents.

Personal particulars			
Surname Block capitals	Forenames		
Address		Telephone number	
Age in years	Date of birth	Place of birth	Nationality
Marital status		Sex Age Children Sex Age	
		1	3
		2	4

Figure 6.2 Specimen form: personal particulars

Medical history

Many industries have stringent requirements for employees' health and the application form may include questions on specific illnesses. An example is shown in Figure 6.3

Medical history
Please state with dates, any serious illnesses, operations, or disabilities
Are you on the disabled register?   If so please give details of your green card
Yes/No   Registration details   Expiry date

Figure 6.3   Specimen form: medical history

Statements of educational attainments

Basically, there are two ways in which the statement of educational attainments can be treated.

1   As a list which the candidate completes (see Figures 6.4, 6.5 and 6.6).
2   Use of check-off system (Figure 6.7).

The former case is useful for manual and clerical vacancies. The form should state clearly whether primary education is of interest to the employer or not.

General education			
Please give details of your <u>full-time schooling</u> only in this section. University education, technical courses, part-time studies, correspondence courses, etc, go in next sections			
Age From To	Name of school or college	Type of school primary, secondary, grammar, public, etc	Examinations taken, prizes or scholarships won, etc Give all subjects taken in these examinations and indicate results obtained

Figure 6.4   Specimen form: general education

University education (if any)			
Dates	Name of college, etc	Subjects studied	Examinations taken with results, giving class of pass, awards, scholarships, prizes, etc
From / To			

Figure 6.5 Specimen form: university education

Technical, professional or occupational training (including apprenticeship, articleship, etc and correspondence courses)				
Dates	Firm, college, institute, etc	Type of training apprenticeship, articles course of study, etc	Subjects studied	Qualifications gained, Membership of Professional Associations, etc
From / To				

Figure 6.6 Specimen form: technical training

Many candidates express dissatisfaction at having to give complete educational history which is not pursued at the interview and which is not relevant to the job. Technical training should be included in this section because in many cases it is an extension of the general education (Figure 6.6). Space is the most important feature when dealing with education; lists of GCE passes written badly and in a cramped space are not at all easy to read. The checklist offers an alternative method of presentation (Figure 6.7). Where separate forms are to be used for various grades of staff it should be remembered that young people and scientific staff require extra space for detailing their educational attainments.

| Education | | Total: |

"O" levels (tick off)

☐ Biology   ☐ Greek   ☐ Scripture
☐ Chemistry   ☐ History   ☐ Spanish
☐ English Language ☐ Latin   ☐
☐ English Literature ☐ Maths   ☐
☐ French   ☐ Maths (Additional) ☐
☐ Geography   ☐ Physics   ☐
☐ Geology   ☐ Physics and Chemistry ☐
☐ German   ☐ Russian   ☐

Total:

"A" levels (tick off and grade)   Arts   Science

☐ English   ☐   ☐ Biology   ☐ Physics
☐ French   ☐   ☐ Chemistry   ☐
☐ German   ☐   ☐ Geography   ☐
☐ History   ☐   ☐ Maths (Applied) ☐
☐ Latin   ☐   ☐ Maths (Pure)   ☐

Figure 6.7   Specimen form: education checklist

Special abilities

Some companies may require specific abilities such as Scandinavian languages, and a section concerned with this is a useful addition. Some attempt should be made to establish the degree of fluency in the languages (Figure 6.8). Salesmen and representatives need space to give details of their driving record.

Languages							
(If fluent mark "A", if working knowledge mark "B")							
Language	Speak	Read	Write	Language	Speak	Read	Write

Figure 6.8   Specimen form: languages

Occupation: employment history and experience

The main problem again in this section is to provide sufficient space for the applicant to give relevant details of his career (many companies allow one side of a foolscap sheet for job history alone). Clear instructions should be given as to the amount of detail required, and the chronological order preferred.

Figures 6.9 to 6.13 are taken from application forms for various grades of staff.

| Particulars of vacation work (or previous employment) | | Dates | | Salary |
Employer	Appointments held and responsibilities	From	To	

Figure 6.9   Specimen form: graduate job history

| Employment history Including part-time, vacation work, and military service | | | |
| Dates | | Employer's name and address (Last firm first) | Type of work |
From	To		

Figure 6.10   Specimen form: graduate/trainee job history

Previous experience					
Please give details of all positions held in your last four employments, starting with your present and last employer and working backwards					
Name and address of employer	Dates		Position held	Salary or wage	Reasons for leaving
	From	To			
(1)					
(2)					
(3)					
(4)					

Figure 6.11   Specimen form: general job history

Previous employment (Including service in HM Forces) Please give your present or most recent job first and work back from there							
Name and address of employer	Type of industry	From	To	Salary		Position held and duties	Reason for leaving
				Starting	Leaving		

Figure 6.12   Specimen form: general staff job history

Employment history						
Please state in order, from first job to present day, positions held since leaving school, including vacation work. Indicate your period of service with the armed services, if any, at the appropriate dates but the details of your service career go on the next page						
Dates		Employer's name, address and nature of business	Approximate number of employees	Positions held and duties. Number of people of whom you were in charge	Salary	Reasons for leaving
From	To					

Figure 6.13   Specimen form: manager's job history

Service with the forces

Although National Service has been discontinued many applicants will need to give details of their military career (Figure 6.14).

Service with Armed Forces or with Civil Defence	RN RAF Army CD	From	To	Rank	Are you required for annual training?
	Duties performed				

National service

Please give details of your service career, or reasons for exemption from National Service

Arm or branch of service	

Date of entry	Date of release

Rank	Dates	Typical duties and responsibilities, appointments, campaigns, awards, decorations and other details of service

Military service

(including N F S, Civil Defence or Police Forces during or since 1939–45 war)

The name and branch of the service	Name	Branch
Your period of service	From	To
Your service trade or occupation		
Please give details of any trade or other qualifications you gained, including training courses taken		
Your rank on discharge		

Figure 6.14   Specimen form: military service

Leisure interests, hobbies, games played, etc
Are you a member of any clubs, societies, professional associations, etc? Please give details, including offices held at present, or in the past. Include positions held at school or college
Do you play any sports or games? Have you won any prizes, colours, etc?
What other leisure interests and hobbies do you have?

Activities and interests			
	School	University/college	Elsewhere
Activities and interests			
Positions and offices held			
Social and sporting activities at school and university/college (Mention positions of responsibility)			
Activities and interests outside school and university/college (Mention positions of responsibility)			

Figure 6.15   Specimen form: leisure interests

Recreation: leisure activities and interests

This section is of particular value in giving points of contact to develop when interviewing young people as well as more senior staff. Some examples are shown in Figure 6.15. Space should be allocated for the candidate to give any further details he considers of interest and relevant to his application, as well as giving room for his signature and date of application.

Additional items to help the interviewer

The application form should be designed so that there is plenty of space for the interviewer to make pencilled notes for follow-up at the interview. This can be done as follows:

1 Print the form so that part of every page is blank except for a heading: 'For company use only' (Figure 6.16).
2 Insert a slip of paper when the form is stapled together (Figure 6.17).
3 Use wide margins, say 50–75 mm (2–3 in) in width.

An interview assessment form based on the seven-point plan (Figures 6.18, 6.19) is a useful reminder in recalling a candidate, and as a means of comparing candidates. It is usually printed separately from the application form and slipped on to the form before the interview. An alternative is to provide a space for the comments of interviewers.

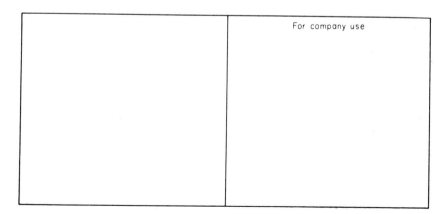

Figure 6.16   Specimen form: for company use, section

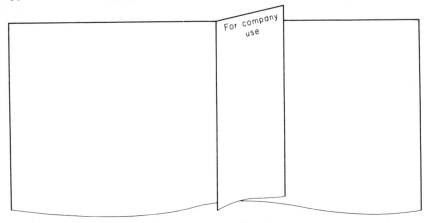

Figure 6.17   Specimen form: for company use, insert

	A	B	C	D	E	Comments

1 Physique, appearance and manner
  Physique
  Appearance
  Manner						

2 Attainments and previous experience
  General education
  Specialized training
  Relevant experience						

3 General intelligence
  (Consider way he/she answers
  questions, grasps ideas,
  his/her sense of purpose,
  and general outlook)						

4 Special aptitudes
  (Mechanical, manual, speech,
  writing, figures, ideas, etc)						

5 Leisure interests and activities
  Active
  Well–chosen
  Social
  Leadership						

6 Disposition
  Evidence of:
      Dependability
      Persistency
      Sociability
      Self–reliance						

7 General background
  Consider whether family
  background and environment
  (if known) are likely to be
  an advantage or not						

Overall assessment						

"A"= very good, "B"= good, "C"= average, "D"= fair, "E"= poor
+ and − signs may be used for finer ratings

Figure 6.18   Specimen form: interview assessment

Staff selection—Evaluation summary
Accounts/Trainee/Clerical

Applicant's name_____

Vacancy for_____

A   General appearance   5   4   3   2   I   O
     (Manner, speech, health, energy)

B   Character traits   5   4   3   2   I   O
     (Stability, industry, perseverance, loyalty,
     compatability, self-reliance, leadership)

C   Intelligence, ability   5   4   3   2   I   O

D   Relevant experience and/or knowledge   5   4   3   2   I   O

E   Powers of expression   5   4   3   2   I   O

F   Education   5   4   3   2   I   O
     (In relation to minimum requirements
     for this opening)

G   Aptitude, interests   5   4   3   2   I   O
     (The extent to which these make applicant
     suitable material for the objective of
     this opening)

H   Suitability for immediate position   5   4   3   2   I   O

I   General suitability   5   4   3   2   I   O
     (In relation to the company's future needs)

Notes: Availability
         Salary
         Housing
         References
         Holidays

Overall recommendations:

                 Signed_____

                 Date_____

Figure 6.19   Specimen form: evaluation summary

Contents of 'for company use' section

The personnel department may include the following details in a block headed 'for company use':

Medical examination—with sufficient space for doctor's comments on fitness to do the job.
Engagement details.
Starting date.
Department.
Job title.
Grade.
Salary and review period.
Hours.
Name and address of bank—bank code.
Department head signature.
Personnel department approval.
Recruitment statistics for vacancy analysis.

Acknowledgements

I acknowledge the cooperation of the following companies in reproducing sections of their application forms: William Dolan Limited; Philips Industries Limited; Western Mail & Echo Limited; Wiggins Teape Limited.

Further reading

Dyer, B. (1979): *Personnel Systems and Records*. 3rd edition. Aldershot: Gower (in association with The Industrial Society).

7

Physical Testing

Dr Dennis Malcolm

Statutory medical examinations in industry were first started in the days when children were employed in the mines and cotton mills and labour was often obtained from the workhouses. The purpose of these examinations was to certify that the child appeared to be above the minimum age of nine years required by law[1] before he or she started work. Under the Appointed Factory Doctor scheme, statutory examination continued until 1972 when the position of Appointed Factory Doctor was abolished by the Employment Medical Advisory Service Act.

Today the examination of young persons is selective, based on the vetting of the Y9 report from the careers office which is sent to the Employment Medical Adviser (EMA). The careers office is informed of the employment of young persons aged 16–18 when the employer submits a form 2404. The EMA selects individuals on the basis of the information of past health problems indicated on the Y9, which does not indicate the degree to which any medical diagnosis may affect performance.

In practice, information as to health problems at school is not always available and would in any case be available only from State schools. The lack of quantitative information makes effective selection of cases difficult. This scheme should be carefully reviewed to determine how much really effective action is resulting from it, and how many individuals who may require advice or help with placement are not receiving it.

Medical examinations were started in the armed forces in the last century in an attempt to improve the physical standard of recruits. In the early part of this century, it was said that 33% of the nation were unfit for military service.

Purpose of medical examinations

A few industries at the beginning of this century had started medical services and the practice increased during the First World War. In the early days, the purpose of such examinations was to try to employ only the healthiest section of the population with the aim of avoiding excessive absence, minimizing labour turnover, protecting the pensions fund (if one existed), keeping down accidents and avoiding false or excessive claims under workmen's compensation or common law. Not surprisingly, such practices were often resisted by trade unions. Too often, management felt that by employing a doctor they had discharged their duty to maintain the health of their employees.

Attitudes towards preemployment medical examinations slowly changed and, with the manpower problems during the Second World War, the aim became to make the best use of every available man and woman. This need contributed considerably in showing the value of proper placement based on medical advice. The further expansion of occupational medical services after 1945 and the Disabled Persons (Employment) Act of 1944 made the preemployment medical examination more compatible with the doctors' professional outlook. This change made these examinations more acceptable to the patient and the trade unions and was in the interests of the enlightened employer.

Placing the employee in suitable work

Medical examinations became directed towards suitable placement, with the objective of safeguarding the health of the individual by placing him in work which would not adversely affect his health nor his ability to make the best contribution he could towards the aims of the organization. In the long term, this outlook was in the company's interests as well as in the employee's. It also helped to create a better climate between employer and employee.

In the 1940s, much attention was paid to the employment of disabled persons. This was linked to the Disabled Persons (Employment) Act of 1944 by which at least 3% of the workforce of any firm with over 20 employees must be registered disabled persons.

Reasons for carrying out preemployment medical examinations

Today most potential employees welcome the chance for a full check-up with the doctor. On the other hand, there are people such as epileptics who often find it difficult to obtain and keep employment. They will avoid examinations when possible and, for obvious reasons, may conceal their disability, as do people with an alcoholic problem.

The main reasons for preemployment medical examinations are as follows:

1   To record health information about the individual as a base line from which any change can be measured. This is important when the health of persons exposed to potentially toxic materials or physically hazardous work is concerned. It is important when examining people prior to exposure to hazards, to determine whether they have any condition which might be aggravated by exposure to such hazards.

2   To protect the health of vulnerable groups. Today, as a group, young people are the healthiest in the community. Handicapped individuals or those with certain diseases such as epilepsy, diabetes or respiratory illness, may require special placement to avoid further aggravating their condition and, so far as possible, to avoid difficulties which might arise because of their handicap.

3   To safeguard the health of other employees and the public. While the risk from infectious diseases is today very much reduced, especially with tuberculosis, care to ensure that food handlers are not carriers of disease which might be transmitted by food handling remains important. It is also important to ensure that people with conditions which might be a risk to the public are not employed as drivers or pilots in public transport.

4   To advise where treatment is required for any existing health problems, particularly when the problem might affect work performance.

5   To ensure suitable job placement so far as possible, where this may help the individual with physical or health problems. It is recognized that suitable placement may depend on the availability of suitable work.

What the doctor needs to know

Norman[2] says that at every examination the doctor should consider: Why am I examining this particular applicant? The answer leads to the second question, namely: What do I need to know about this individual?

In order to carry out this function successfully, the doctor should have a good knowledge of the types of work for which he is examining the patient, and which is best acquired, when possible, by actually doing the job. He should also know the social and psychological climate of the organization, particularly in respect of the more responsible appointments.

Today, fitness to join a pension fund is not normally considered. Actually, the risk is calculated on the average population and in any case, unless there is a large death grant or widow's pension, a pension fund does not suffer in the same way as life insurance funds from early death or incapacity. Where the cost of death grants or widows' pensions is high, then consideration should be given to the need for medical examination prior to entry into the pensions scheme.

Substitutes for preemployment medical examination

Many doctors working in industry have come to regard routine preemployment medical examinations as time-wasting unless there is a sound reason as listed above for the doctor to be involved in carrying out a full medical examination.

This view has given rise to the practice of using a questionnaire to select individuals requiring more detailed investigation. Thompson, reporting on the large scale use of a health questionnaire compared with medical examinations, in the Civil Service, has shown that detection of significant health problems was similar in number and nature, whichever method was used. What this paper does not show, and where objective evidence is lacking, is the real benefit to the individual or the employer of medical examination or questionnaire.

D'Souza[3] (1979), reviewing the evidence for routine medical examinations, concludes that there is at present inadequate evidence to show that periodic examinations or screening have any real benefit to the health of individuals, although some screening procedures have changed the distribution of causes of death.

Scientific evidence for the value of preemployment and routine medical examinations is urgently needed in view of various pressures which may lead to a considerable increase in this practice for all employed people.

One of these pressures may come from the harmonization of EEC laws on health and safety at work. As is well known, the French law already requires all employees to be medically examined each year. The TUC at their annual conference in 1977, also passed a resolution urging the British Government to require a general health check for all workers.

In my own experience, either after medical examination or screening by questionnaire, very few people have been rejected for medical reasons. One of the major difficulties in carrying out scientific research in this field is the difficulty of showing that anyone not accepted would have had a real problem, or more important, that all those rejected would have caused a greater problem than comparable groups of people accepted.

How nursing staff can help

Where nursing staff are available, it is useful for applicants, not only those who fill in a questionnaire, but also those who may require suitable medical examination, to be seen by a nurse.

Checking of urine, haemoglobin, blood pressure, height, weight and eyesight can all be done by properly trained nursing staff. Also by discussion and a look through the questionnaire, the nurse can decide whether any complaint is trivial and will not affect general health or work, or whether it is necessary to arrange for further investigation and advice by the doctor.

Health hazards associated with certain types of work

Ideally, any significant hazard to health or wellbeing should be prevented by the employer. However, this is not always fully practicable, even if the technology to achieve such conditions has been developed. In practice, it is desirable to have a medical examination or a suitable screening procedure for all employees where there is any significant risk of toxic or physical harm to health or where the health and safety of other employees or the public may be at risk. There are still many industries with such hazards where there are no statutory requirements for medical examination and where the employers make no provision for such examinations. The real need in such areas has not been adequately assessed.

Where medical examinations are carried out, these should be arranged before the commencement of employment whenever this is possible. Any change in placement or in fitness recommended after commencement of employment, creates difficulties within the organization.

The doctor must understand fully the type of work and the nature of the toxic hazard in the industry for which he is carrying out the examination. For instance, at one time it was thought necessary to reject from lead work anyone with a history of nephritis or any albuminuria or hypertension. Today, in a well controlled industry it may be justifiable to take on such people. It was once automatic to exclude nail biters from battery manufacture, but today many of the men wear gloves and so never get lead on their hands.

It is advisable to exclude from most toxic industries anyone whose personal cleanliness or habits are unsatisfactory because they will usually be a risk to themselves and to others.

Certainly, no one with chronic bronchitis or even a history of frequent bronchitis in childhood should be allowed to work in dust or irritant fumes. In any potentially toxic industry, particularly those involving exposure to harmful dusts, it is essential to have a record of previous exposure to toxic materials or dusts, and in the latter case, a history of smoking habits.

Any history of severe renal disease or persistent albuminuria should lead to exclusion from work with mercury or cadmium, especially if cases of proteinuria are still occurring in the industry. The reason for such exclusion is not only that a damaged kidney may be more susceptible to further damage by exposure to nephrotoxins, but if kidney damage increases, it may be impossible to tell whether this is due to previous disease or toxic damage, or both.

As O'Dwyer[4] points out, the preemployment medical examination with proper and adequate recording of the essential facts is the baseline against which changes are measured.

Safeguarding the health of the worker

Statutory examinations

Regulations require preemployment medical examinations in a number of industries. These at present include some lead-using industries, but proposed revision of the lead regulations will apply to all lead-using industries. Other industries such as chrome plating, exposure to carcinogenic substances, diving and compressed air work, India rubber work and ionizing radiation exposure, require statutory preemployment and periodic medical examinations.

Surprisingly, work with dusts causing fibrosis of the lungs does not require preemployment or periodic medical examinations. A research project set up under the Employment Medical Advisory Service in effect has screened most asbestos workers who spent more than six months in the industry since 1969.

Toxic hazards

Where the toxicology of the process is well understood, the task of the doctor is to answer the question: Is there anything about the health or history of this patient which might make him more liable than a normal man to suffer any departure from his normal health because of working in this industry?

In making this assessment, the doctor must take into account the standards of safety achieved in that particular process or factory. He should also assess the capacity of the individual to look after himself properly. Has he adequate intelligence and a reasonable attitude to safe working practices? Are his personal cleanliness and general habits adequate to enable him to work safely in this hazard?

Physical hazards

Under this heading, the doctor may have to decide whether the man is physically strong enough for the job. Some years ago, a man of forty-five who had on occasion to lift battery cells up to a weight of 60 kg suffered a back injury and requested help with lifting for some time afterwards. His manager asked if he was malingering. The man was 1.7 m tall and weighed 55 kg. The doctor who carried out his preemployment medical had found him perfectly fit, but had known nothing of the type of work for which he was being engaged.

Similarly, it is no use putting a man who cannot stand high temperatures on repairing a steel furnace or working in a mine rescue team or casting metals, unless the job can be made comfortable.

Skin hazards

Those entering work which involves skin hazards should be told about the drill for the care of personal health. They should also be warned about the temporary itch which occurs when working with fibre glass and told to report back if this persists for longer than two or three weeks.

A history of allergies is important and could be a reason for rejection. Skin patch testing may be helpful.

Radiation

Excessive exposure to radiation might affect any part of the body, so a good general standard of health is important where there is any real risk. Intelligence should be adequate to comply with the safety regulations. Suitable records should be made of the necessary blood examination for reference against periodic checks. Those with other than slight abnormalities of the blood are probably best rejected for work in radiation hazards.

Dust and fume hazards

Anyone with a history of recurrent attacks of bronchitis, even in childhood, should be excluded from occupations where there is still a hazard from dust or fumes. To a large extent, chronic bronchitis could be a preventable disease, but too many men with a tendency to this disease are employed in dusty industries. The risk is certainly compounded by the habit of smoking.

There are records of six or seven patients who were removed from dusty work such as french chalk or packing with straw in the 1930s and labelled as chronic bronchitics. Over twenty years later, the disease had not progressed in this group. Unfortunately, this is too small a group for epidemiological study.

Chest X-rays before employment in asbestos and silica industries are essential. Under present legal arrangements, chest X-rays may be taken at the request of the Pneumoconiosis or Asbestosis Board either early or much later in the period of employment in these industries. If they are not taken before or at the beginning of employment in these industries, no basic standard exists against which to measure change.

Overseas work

When sending employees overseas for tours of duty of several years, it is important to know, so far as possible, that the individual is not unduly likely to suffer from ill health during the tour. A thorough check, incuding chest X-ray is desirable and an assessment should be made of his ability to stand up to climatic conditions. A stable, mature personality is important, particularly where local conditions may impose a strain on his health or personality.

It is also advisable to see the wife and family. In about 70% of cases where employees return from overseas assignments for health reasons, the cause is the wife's inability to adapt to being away from her family or to the very different type of life in another country. It is however not easy to predict how people will adapt, but evidence of previous adaptation is useful.

Groups particularly vulnerable to medical hazards

Young persons

Routine examination of all young persons working in factories was abolished by the Employment Medical Advisory Service Act 1972. Routine examination of those working in shops and offices had never been statutory. Most of these young people are healthier and better educated than ever before.

Herford[5] takes the view that this is a vitally important transition stage when young people are receptive to advice and often require disinterested help to learn good health habits and to obtain suitable work. If school health records are available to the appointed factory doctor, he is able to follow on where the school medical officer finished. Undoubtedly useful work can be done in this field, but perhaps too few doctors have sufficient training and interest to offer real help to this important group. Employers might take more interest in the effects that dead-end and degrading types of work can have on young people. While there is a good deal of opinion, we have very little scientific knowledge of the effects of such work on the psychological health of people.

Disabled persons

The Disabled Persons (Employment) Act 1944 was designed to help people who had a substantial handicap in obtaining employment in competition with fit persons. Most industries must employ a minimum of 3% registered disabled persons. Because of full employment, this group have not found too much difficulty in obtaining suitable work and many who could be registered have not bothered to do so. Some take the view that to be registered is a handicap in obtaining work. Preemployment medical examination should be aimed at placing disabled persons in jobs where their disability is not a handicap. In this way, most of them compete well with their normal colleagues. Their earning power is increased and their morale kept high.

Hanman[6] in America did a great deal of work in analysing jobs and disabilities so as to arrange a suitable match. Although these studies did much to show the abilities of handicapped people, it has proved very difficult to keep job analyses up to date with constant change. Also, whatever a man's disability, if he really wants to do a job, he will usually find a way. The psychological make-up of the disabled person is often the most important factor in placing him. It is in this respect that help will give the best results. With current trends to higher unemployment, protection of the disabled will require to be strengthened.

Psychologically handicapped persons

With modern treatment, many more people who are psychologically handicapped or have had psychiatric treatment are now fit enough to find suitable employment and are being encouraged to do so. For many of them, work is therapeutically beneficial. Here, cooperation with psychiatric social workers and the patient's doctor can often be most helpful in obtaining a full history of the patient's difficulties and also his abilities.

Placement requires great care for not only must the company be willing to help such people but the work must be suited to the individual's needs. It is equally important that the person's immediate boss has an understanding of his difficulties and that fellow workers are considerate. Creating the right climate for these people is all part of the doctor's work in following up preemployment examinations of such patients.

Epileptics

Many epileptics are so well controlled that employer and often the company doctor are unaware of their disability. As this group often have considerable difficulty in obtaining employment, they may try to conceal their illness.

Medical examination should be directed towards finding how well they are controlled and what abilities they have, and advising on job placement accordingly. It is most important for the doctor to know the work thoroughly. Sensible rules for employing epileptics are the following:

1 They should not be a risk to themselves or others should they have an attack at work.
2 The immediate supervisor, and, where necessary, a workmate, should, with the patient's permission, know that the person has epilepsy and exactly what to do if he should have an attack. This prevents the panic that usually occurs in a work place if an attack occurs without anyone knowing of the possibility.
3 Apart from the above reservations, epileptics should be treated as normal people.

General rules for handling disabled persons

With most types of disability, the rule can be applied of using the abilities and avoiding the handicaps by suitable placement. Such placement at present usually means waiting for a suitable vacancy. Particularly with manual work, there are usually many light or suitable jobs being done by perfectly fit people. In order to help handicapped people to make the fullest contribution and to get the most out of their work, management and unions should work out an agreed system of flexibility to help them.

Generally, chronic bronchitics and advanced cardiac cases are more handicapped than those who have lost limbs. On the other hand, they tend to get less sympathy. The most handicapped are those with a poor attitude to work but even some of these can be helped by advice, encouragement and proper placement. A good supervisor can often do more than the doctor in this respect.

Avoiding danger to other personnel

Driving

To obtain a driving licence, applicants are required to declare that they are not suffering from prescribed diseases such as epilepsy, giddiness or fainting and that they can read a car number plate from 25 yards in good light, wearing spectacles if required. From June 1971 a licence may be granted[7] to an epileptic who has been free from attacks for three years.

To drive a public service vehicle (PSV) or a heavy goods vehicle (HGV), the prescribed form must be signed by a medical practitioner on first application. A medical certificate is required to renew a HGV licence after the age of 60, and, for a PSV, periodically after the age of 50.

Evidence at present available suggests that only a few accidents are caused by reason of medical conditions. The real problem is not only one of medical fitness, but of overall suitability to drive a vehicle. Some firms also send potential drivers for a driving test and this practice is probably an even better test of suitability and safety for the majority of applicants than a medical examination. With train driving and flying, such tests are automatic as part of the training and follow up.

Crane drivers, in particular should have good eyesight and there should be no history of fits or any condition likely to make them lose control.

Handling food

Applicants should be free from chronic septic conditions, of clean habits, and free from any disease which might be communicated by food. Their training should also include awareness of their responsibility to report at once, any newly acquired infection, however slight it may seem.

Tuberculosis

This disease is now comparatively rare in the UK, but some immigrants come from countries where the rate of tuberculosis is very high. Particular attention should be paid to this group, especially if they are to live in hostels. Evidence of recent satisfactory chest X-rays is important.

All school teachers should have a chest film taken before undertaking teaching, and, in fact, a full medical examination is given prior to their training.

Cardiac conditions

Patients should be advised not to drive within three months after clinical recovery from coronary thrombosis as there is a danger of anginal attacks while driving. When they are fit to drive, they should avoid becoming fatigued.

Hypertension without complications is not a reason for advising against driving. Heart conditions liable to cause syncope or faintness under driving conditions, however, should exclude driving.

Stricter standards are necessary for drivers of public service vehicles and heavy goods vehicles.

Diabetics

Only diabetics who are not well controlled should normally be discouraged or prevented from driving and similar tasks. Proper understanding of how to control their disease is essential.

Central nervous system

Many conditions of the central nervous system may interfere with driving ability. Any condition interfering with consciousness, awareness or judgement of the continually changing pattern of traffic should prevent driving and similar occupations, as should any condition affecting coordination and control of movement, if chronic. This also applies to such conditions as persistent Meniere's syndrome.

Drugs

Judging by the published figure for barbiturates and tranquillizers prescribed, a great many people must be driving while regularly taking drugs which affect the central nervous system.

Under the Road Traffic Act 1962, driving under the influence of drugs is an offence which leads to automatic disqualification. Is a patient whose depression is removed by tryptazine under the influence of drugs?

The nature of the conditon for which the drugs are being given must also be taken into account. At present, far too little is known about the complex problem of the effects of drugs and the illnesses for which they are being given. In such cases, doctors have a high degree of responsibility to determine whether the individual who is taking drugs should be passed as fit to drive a bus or train or to fly an aeroplane. Where public safety of passengers and other road users is concerned, risks cannot be justified.

Special health hazards of senior executives

The question may well be asked why senior people in industry should be treated differently from anyone else. If there is a reason, it is because their fitness for the job, in the widest sense, may affect the well-being of a large number of people. It is therefore important not only that those responsible for the selection of such staff should have an adequate job description, but that the doctor concerned should also have this information so that he knows for what job the candidate has to be fit.

Too little is known about all the complex factors which cause success or failure in top jobs, but considerable mental energy is required and any condition which interferes significantly with a man's energy might well exclude him from senior responsibility. It would be inadvisable, for instance, to promote a man to a busy senior position if he was suffering from generalized arteriosclerosis with signs of mental rigidity developing, whatever his past record.

Many men, however, continue to perform well after moderately severe coronary thrombosis and in some cases the frustration of lack of promotion could be more stressful to the patient than carrying a senior job, especially if the executive is well supported.

Alcoholics or problem drinkers should not be promoted to jobs which increase their burden. The extent of this problem is usually underestimated. It is very common for senior management to turn a blind eye to drinking problems because they do not know what to do about them. In many cases, a great deal can be done if the problem is tackled early on sound medical advice.

In considering the fitness of executives, judgements are often very complex and there are many unknowns. It is not justifiable to interfere with a man's ambitions and promotions unless there are very sound reasons for deciding that he will be unable to do the job or that the job will have a serious effect on his health.

The individual should, wherever possible, be told why he is considered unfit for the job. After full discussion of all the facts, some senior executives will decide to withdraw their application, if there are clear indications that extra strain or work would impose a significant burden on their health.

Prevention of excessive absence

Apart from certain obvious conditions, such as chronic bronchitis, chronic rheumatic conditions, persistent anxiety states and other chronic diseases, health and absence from work do not correlate very highly. For people with chronic conditions, there has to be an acceptable course between excessive absence and the individual's right to work and the skills he can bring to the organization. Many organizations which have no preemployment medical examinations do not find their proportion of chronic sick a real embarrassment. Those which employ a doctor may get some help in proper placement and advice to the patient on how best to control his illness.

Some people who have been found quite fit at preemployment medical examinations lose more time from work than the chronic sick. The present view is that absence from work depends more on the attitude towards work of the employees and this is determined by the interest of the job and the general morale of the organization, both being a reflection of management's skill in managing.

Some years ago, the author carried out a review of absence and labour turnover related to preemployment examinations. There was no correlation between absence and physical fitness, except for the registered disabled and those who were eligible for registration. With careful placement, the absence and labour turnover among this group was significantly lower than other groups.

An attempt was also made to grade psychological stability on a three point scale. Again there was no correlation between absence habits of the first two groups, but those in the third group, who had had three or more jobs per year in the previous two years, were unlikely to stay long and also had a high absence rate.

References

1   Factories Act 1833.

2   L. Norman, *Modern Trends in Occupational Health*, (Ed. R.S.F. Schilling), Butterworth, London, 1960.

'3   D'Souza, Chapter 22, *Current Approaches to Occupational Medicine*, (Ed. A. Ward Gardner), Wright, Bristol, 1979.

4   J. J. O'Dwyer, *Mental Health and Human Relations in Industry*, (Ed. T. M. Ling), H. K. Lewis & Co., London, 1954.

5   M. E. Herford, *Youth at Work*, Max Parrish & Co., London, 1957.

6   B. Hanman, *Physical Capabilities and Job Placement*, Stockholm, 1951.

7   Medical Commission on Accident Prevention, *Medical Aspects of Fitness to Drive*, Royal College of Surgeons of England, Lincoln's Inn Fields, London WC2A 3PN, 1971.

8

Testing
Intelligence and Aptitude

A C Pendlebury

People differ from one another in many ways. They differ according to their age, sex, physique, appearance, working experience, attainments (skills and knowledge acquired formally or informally), intelligence, aptitudes, interests, personality, background circumstances and career intentions. It is important to recognize the many ways in which people differ. Tests, when rightly used, can provide a useful indication of whether applicants for a particular job have the appropriate attainments, intelligence and aptitudes. However they do not provide all the information needed. An applicant may have the appropriate attainments, intelligence and aptitudes for a job and yet be in other ways unsuitable for it and will therefore correctly be rejected on other grounds. It must be admitted that this can happen. The person who pins his faith in tests as the panacea for all his selection problems is as mistaken in his view as the person who spurns their use entirely.

Distinction between attainments, aptitudes and intelligence

A test of attainment (or achievement) measures the extent to which a person possesses skills and knowledge acquired either on a formal training or education course or informally at work or elsewhere. The schoolboy sitting 'O' level chemistry, the craft apprentice producing a test piece on a lathe and the commercial trainee completing the post-test of a programmed text on accountancy are all taking attainment tests. They are indicating what they have learnt.

A test of an aptitude (or ability) provides a measure of a person's general facility with questions or items of a particular kind, for example numerical or verbal items.

Influence of recent experience

The distinction between a test of an aptitude and a test of attainment can best be illustrated by reference to two numerical tests. Most people would probably perform fairly poorly on a trigonometry test. For many their last experience of questions on trigonometry will have been many years ago when they took 'O' level mathematics or some similar examination. A trigonometry test would be an attainment test and would be done badly by those without recent experience of trigonometry. These same people might nevertheless have a high degree of numerical aptitude or in other words be generally quick and fluent at questions involving figures. A test such as a numerical series test or a numerical matrices test might reveal this aptitude.

Tendency for intelligence to be broad-based

When a group of people, randomly selected from the population as a whole, take a range of tests of different kinds of aptitude, there is a tendency for the same people to do better on all the different tests. The person who did best on the numerical test would probably do well, if not the best, on the other tests. It would be most unusual for anybody to come very near the top on one test and near the bottom on another. This indicates that there is some general mental ability or 'intelligence' which people possess to a greater or lesser degree.

Effect of experience and environment on intelligence

People's scores on tests of intelligence and of aptitudes are more stable than their scores on tests of attainment, which reflect recent experience more. But it would be wrong to believe that intelligence and aptitudes are static and unaffected by experience and environment. Several illustrations will emphasize this point:

1   On average, people perform better on intelligence and aptitude tests until their late teens and progressively less well on them after the age of twenty. But among brighter people, possibly because they enjoy a more stimulating working and leisure environment, there is less of a decrease in scores with increasing age.
2   The intercorrelations between tests of different aptitudes become smaller with the increase in age of the tested groups, a reflection of the fact that people tend to specialize more as they grow older and thus are likely to use some of their aptitudes, while others lie dormant.

3   On average there is less of a decrease in scores with age on tests measuring vocabulary span than there is on tests of any other type, an indication that, whatever other aptitudes people manage to do without, they still continue to use words in communicating with one another.

Classification of available aptitude tests

Different research workers into the nature of ability have produced different classifications of aptitudes. The following classification does not reflect any one piece of research but is rather a reflection of the availability of different types of test in the UK at the present time.

Tests of numerical ability

Some arithmetic tests measure simply the speed and accuracy with which a person can add, subtract, multiply and divide whole numbers. These tests are not very difficult. They are often given not as individual tests but as one of a battery of tests in which other abilities such as verbal ability and clerical ability are also measured.

Other arithmetic tests also require a testee to be familiar with decimals, fractions, percentages and so on to complete them successfully. These tests may be measuring numerical attainment as well as aptitude.

Tests in which testees are given a series of six numbers and have to write down the number which comes next in the series are common. The questions in these tests are arranged so that the easy questions come at the beginning of the test and the more difficult questions come at the end. Take for example the following two items:

$$6, \quad 9, \ 12, \ 15, \ 18, \ 21, \ \_$$
$$76, 38, \ 36, \ 18, \ 16, \quad 8, \ \_$$

It is much easier to see that the next number in the first series is 24 than it is to see that the next number in the second series is 6.

Numerical problems tests often consist of numerical questions set in a verbal framework. An example of such a question might be: 'A man spent one eighth of his money on postcards and twice as much on writing paper and then had £2.00 left. How much money did he have at first?' In these questions the actual numerical calculations involved are often straightforward. What is important is that the testee carefully reads the question before he makes his calculation. Such questions would require more time than the simpler examples given previously, and research might show that they measured verbal ability as well as arithmetic aptitude.

Tests of verbal ability

A vocabulary test is probably the best single indicator of verbal ability. Vocabulary tests can include such items as this:
CONNECT

accident	join
lace	bean
flint	field

The testee has to indicate which of the six words below the word in capitals has the same meaning as it.

Below are some of the items which might appear in a test of verbal ability.

1   Uncle — Nephew: Aunt — Brother   Sister   Niece   Cousin

Which of the four words on the right has the same relation to aunt as nephew has to uncle?

2   Re-arrange the words below to form a sentence.

a battle in racket very tennis useful is

3   Which one of the five words on the right bears a similar relation to each of the two words on the left?

Loud   Hard   Noisy   Brittle   Soft   Difficult   Inaudible

Tests of verbal or logical reasoning provide an indicator of clarity of thought and expression, which is especially valuable in work where communication of information is involved as well as in many other kinds of work situation.

The ability to spell correctly seems to be a fairly distinct ability which correlates less highly with all the other tests of verbal ability than they intercorrelate with one another. Obviously it is necessary for people in the secretarial field to be good at spelling.

Tests of clerical ability

People who do well on clerical ability tests can do routine things well. It may be useful to possess this ability not only for the performance of routine clerical work but also for the performance of other elementary activities, where speed and accuracy but not depth of thinking is required. The most widely known tests of clerical ability are number checking and name checking tests. In these tests the testee is faced with many pairs of numbers and names and, working at speed, has to indicate whether the two numbers or names in each pair are the same or different. Examples of test items are shown below.

Number checking: 3856—3586
                       600301—600301
Name checking: Ascot, Berks—Ascot, Berks
                   Wigan, Lancs—Wigan, Lincs

Usually on these tests testees are given two scores, one for accuracy and one for speed.

Tests of spatial ability

Spatial ability is a capacity to manipulate shapes mentally in two or three dimensions. A test of spatial ability is shown in Figure 8.1.

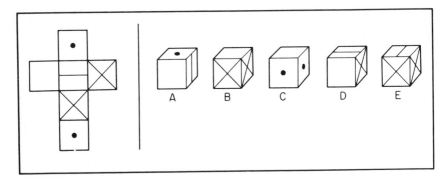

Figure 8.1   Test of spatial ability

   In this test the testee has to decide, by visualizing, which of the five cubes on the right can be made from the figure on the left.
   Spatial ability tests have been found useful in the selection of draughtsmen, inspectors, watch repairers and work study personnel.

Tests of nonverbal or abstract reasoning

An example of a nonverbal reasoning test is given in Figure 8.2.
   In this test the testee has to decide which of the five shapes on the right follows the sequence of shapes on the left.
   Both spatial and abstract reasoning tests involve the use of shapes. However they differ in that the testee must apply different thought processes in arriving at his answer. With spatial tests he is visualizing. With abstract reasoning tests he is reasoning logically.
   It was once thought that abstract reasoning tests provided a culture-fair indication of intelligence, as contrasted with intelligence scores obtained

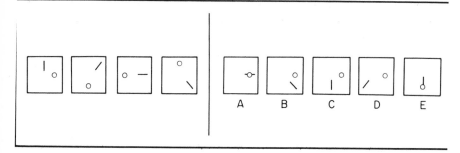

Figure 8.2   Test of abstract reasoning

through predominately verbal and numerical items. We are now aware that performance on any test is influenced to some degree by the culture or environment in which the testee has been brought up. In general, people on the science side do better on abstract reasoning tests than people on the arts side. These tests have been found useful in the selection of apprentices, higher scientific and technical staff and computer personnel.

Tests of mechanical aptitude

In tests of mechanical aptitude the testee is usually presented with a series of pictures and he has to answer questions to indicate his comprehension of physical and mechanical principles. These tests have been found helpful in the selection of craft apprentices in the engineering industry. They can also be used in electrical and other practical trades.

Tests of manual dexterity

A number of tests of manual dexterity are still available. However it is important to recognize that, with the changes in the ways in which things are made, many people in production do not need the manual dexterity they once did. A skills analysis should be carried out on a job to make sure that the ability which the manual dexterity test measures is relevant to the job under review.

Tests of creativity

In all the ability tests discussed in this chapter the items have been so designed that there has been one and only one correct answer to them. It has been alleged that these tests do not allow testees to be imaginative and original in producing their answers. Attempts at measuring creativity were therefore designed and have been in use since 1950, but they have not proved particularly successful. It is possible that people differ in the extent to which they are creative because of differences in their personality rather than differences in their abilities.

Other ways of classifying tests

Tests so far have been classified according to their content. They can be classified in two other ways.

1　A test may be an individual test in that it can be administered to only one person at once or it may be a group test, which can be administered to many people simultaneously. Almost all the tests used in industry are group tests.
2　Most tests seek to discriminate among the general population as a whole, although with these tests there is always the danger that those of high ability will find them too easy while those of low ability will find them too hard. Some tests are high-level tests in that they are designed to discriminate among people in the top 10 or 20% for intelligence or a given aptitude.

Characteristics of a good test

Some tests are good while others are poor. The criteria for deciding whether or not a test is good may be placed under three broad categories, viz., technical, practical and specific.

Technical considerations

Reliability.　If a test is to be used in selection, it must provide a reliable or accurate measure of an aptitude or attainment. One way in which test constructors determine the reliability of a test is by giving it on two occasions to a group of people and correlating the scores obtained on the first occasion with scores obtained on the second occasion. Another way is to give a group of people parallel or equivalent forms of the same test and to correlate the two sets of scores obtained. The statistic used to indicate the reliability of a test is the product-moment correlation coefficient. A correlation coefficient can vary in size from 1 (perfect positive correlation) through 0 to −1 (perfect negative correlation). The reliability of a test, as reported in the manual for that test, should equal at least 0.8.

Test norms.　A test manual should contain adequate norms, which show how various groups of people such as randomly selected members of the population, or those with a certain level of education, or applicants for a particular type of work, have performed on the test. Without such norms there is no way of deciding how the score of an individual on the test compares with those of the total population, or alternatively, with a defined group of people.

Level of difficulty. It is usual for items in a test to be in ascending order of difficulty so that the easy items come at the beginning of the test and the hard items at the end. This does not apply to tests of clerical ability, where the ability being tested is one of being able to cope speedily and accurately with easy routine items.

Practical considerations

Test administration. It is preferable to have a test for which the administrative instructions are straightforward. The way in which testees tackle a test can be influenced by the manner in which the test is presented and this is more likely to vary if the administration of the test is difficult.

Test practice. Before the test there are usually some test practice items through which the testees can become aware of the sort of items they will be meeting in the test. This has benefits both in increased reliability and, to some extent, evening out differences due to some testees having more test experience than others.

Ease of scoring. A test should preferably be able to be scored easily, quickly and objectively. Often during a selection procedure test scores need to be obtained quickly, and inaccuracies of marking can occur if the marker is unduly pressed to produce the results of tests.

Length of test. The cost of test materials is usually not excessive. The cost of paying a person to administer tests can however be expensive. If two tests are likely to achieve more or less the same results, the one which takes a shorter time to administer is clearly preferable.

Specific considerations

Predictive validity. No test is of universal applicability. In examining a test manual a personnel selector would hope to see evidence that the test had been used successfully to predict the performance of members of an occupational group similar to the one in which he is interested. Such evidence might suggest that the test is valid for the occupational group. As already explained in Chapter 1, however, it must be proved that this validity holds in the particular situation. The predictive validity of a test (like the reliability of a test) is usually given in the form of a product-moment correlation coefficient indicating the relationship between test score and job performance.

Face validity.   If a test has face validity, this means that it looks a good test for the selection of members of a particular occupation. It is possible for a test to have predictive validity and no face validity or vice versa. A test without face validity might offend applicants to the extent that they turn down a subsequent offer of a job in the organisation. But it must be remembered that a test with face validity is not necessarily a good predictor.

Differences between men and women on aptitude tests

It has already been pointed out that people tend to do better on tests until they are about twenty and that their performance on tests thereafter becomes less good. It is also well established that, on average, men do better on some tests while, on average, women do better on other tests. If a random sample of men and women were taken and given a battery of tests, it would be found that while some men and some women did well and badly on all tests the mean or average of the scores on some tests would be higher for men and on other tests higher for women.

Women have a tendency to do better on clerical tests than men. Men have a tendency to do better on spatial tests than women. They also tend to do better on mechanical tests. This difference could be explained partly by the fact that in their childhood boys are encouraged to develop mechanical interests more than girls and because of their wider experience they are subsequently able to tackle more effectively tests with mechanical items.

It used to be thought that men did better on numerical tests while women did better on verbal tests. It is possible that these differences between men and women are not as great as they used to be.

In the test manuals of some tests the norms show both how men and women have performed on the test.

The 'normal distribution' of abilities and intelligence

Test manuals usually give not only the mean of the scores of groups of people on the test but also the standard deviation of their scores. This is a measure of the dispersion of scores and is of great value in interpreting test scores. If we were to measure the heights and weights of a large random sample of adult British males, we would find that there were a lot more men of about average height and weight than there were men who were very tall, very small, very heavy or very light. Similarly with tests of aptitudes and intelligence more people obtain about average scores on tests than score very high or very low. Tests like height and weight are normally distributed and Figure 8.3 shows the relationship between the normal distribution and the standard deviation, which expresses statistically the extent to which measures are scattered or

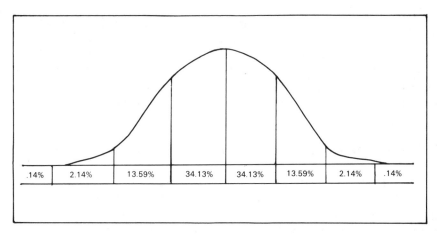

Figure 8.3 The normal distribution

dispersed. It can be seen that approximately a third of people obtain scores between the mean and one standard deviation above the mean and approximately a third of people obtain scores between the mean and one standard deviation below the mean. Approximately 95% of people obtain scores between two standard deviations below, and two standard deviations above, the mean. Very few obtain scores lower than three standard deviations below the mean and higher than three standard deviations above the mean. If we know both the mean and the standard deviation of the scores of a group of people on a test, we are in a much better position to see how a particular person has done on the test than we would have been if we had been given the mean only.

Because aptitudes and intelligence are normally distributed, it is the practice in test manuals to show the scores which split off people in the top 10% of a group, the next 20%, the middle 40%, the next 20% and the bottom 10%. These scores help, in a simple way, to relate the score of any individual to the test population as a whole—or, where appropriate, to those of a particular occupational group, of a certain minimum educational standard, or applying for a particular kind of job.

Using tests in selection

There are two situations in which tests are used in selection. One may be selecting a person for a unique position in an organization. If this is the case it is very important to draw up a detailed job description of the post first and assess what are the aptitudes required to carry out the job successfully.

Often in large organizations many people are being selected for the same type of job eg secretaries, typists, operators, apprentices and other trainees. In such a situation it would probably be worthwhile to do some applied research first to be sure of using a combination of tests which, as part of the total selection procedure, provided the best overall forecast of success. In selecting draughtsmen, for example, the job description and man specification might suggest that tests of general intelligence, abstract reasoning, spatial ability, numerical ability and mechanical ability would be suitable.

Further research could be conducted as follows:

1 Obtain a sample of draughtsmen in the company or, as would be more practical, trainee draughtsmen nearing the end of their training.
2 Obtain an assessment of the job or training performance of all the members of the sample.
3 Give all of them tests of the five types suggested above.
4 Correlate test scores with job or training performance.

The results might indicate that three tests only, say the spatial, numerical and mechanical tests, would distinguish the better from the poorer draughtsmen to a degree which was not substantially improved by using additional tests. These tests could then be incorporated into the selection procedure. At a later date it should be ascertained whether the tests were as predictive as the research study had suggested.

Some would argue that tests should never be used in selection without statistical evidence of their predictive validity. They say that applicants should be given a battery of tests at selection first and that no account should be taken of their test scores in making selection decisions. These scores should be stored until an adequate measure of job performance was obtained for those applicants who were selected. If it was then found that some of the tests would have been good predictors of success, they could be used with greater consequence. The difficulty of this approach is that it may be some years before adequate measures of job performance can be obtained. If it appears that a selection procedure requires improvement and that the use of tests might improve it, it is undesirable and impractical to wait several years before doing anything about it. This more cautious approach, although technically sounder, is consequently often rendered impracticable.

Validation of tests in selection

The usual method of validating a selection test is to correlate test scores with performance scores for a given group of people by means of a product-moment correlation coefficient. Ideally the correlation between a test (or a score derived from scores on all the tests used at selection) and job performance would be 1.0 (perfect positive correlation) so that the better a person's test score, the better his job performance. In practice, correlations between test scores and measures of job performance are nothing like as high. The following are some of the factors which can reduce the size of the correlation.

1   *Other characteristics of the applicants.*   Other factors about a person, especially his interests and personality, affect his job performance. Some of the applicants could have the right ability for the job but have inappropriate interests and/or be of the wrong personality for it. Therefore the correlation between the test scores and job performance would be reduced.

2   *Other abilities important on the job.* It may be that other abilities than those measured by the tests used are needed on the job. If the wrong tests are used, the correlations are lower. Also the wrong weightings can be given to the different tests in the battery.

3   *Restriction of range.* If the members of the group on whom the validation study is carried out are very similar in aptitude or job performance, the correlation between test score and job performance is likely to be less than if there is a wide range of test and job performance scores.

4   *Inadequate measures of performance.* It is well known how difficult it often is to obtain fully reliable measures of job performance. When these measures of performance are not reliable, the size of the correlation between test score and job performance is reduced.

5   *Environmental factors.* The reasons for success and failure at work cannot be attributed solely to the strengths and weaknesses of the people themselves. Factors outside them also affect their performance. These include the quality of their training, the quality of the managers for whom they work and the morale of the group in which they work. If, in the time between selection and the subsequent assessment of job performance, all the members of a group were subjected to a similar quality of training, a similar quality of management and so on, the correlation between test scores and job performance measures would be higher than it would be if some of the group, regardless of their test scores, had experienced training programmes and managers vastly different in quality.

When it is recognized how many factors affect performance, it is no surprise that correlation coefficients obtained in a validation exercise are usually, at best, of the following order:

1	Between score on one test and job performance.	0.4
2	Between a prediction based on scores on all the tests in the battery and job performance.	0.55
3	Between a prediction based on evidence from the whole selection procedure and job performance.	0.7

It must be noted that validation exercises can only involve the applicants who were accepted. Many are normally rejected and this restricts the range of scores of those chosen. This, in turn, tends to lower the validation correlations.

Effect of practice on test performance

A criticism often levelled against aptitude tests is that people can, with practice, improve their performance on tests. Thus, it is argued, an applicant who had recently taken a similar aptitude test at another selection procedure might be at an unfair advantage over another applicant who had not had such a recent experience of testing.

In reply to such an argument it should be stressed that practice effects apply in the case of all selection procedures. An applicant can learn how to write his initial letter of application for employment, how to fill in his application form tactfully, how to answer questions in interviews, how to behave in a group discussion and so on. Practice effects are probably of less importance in aptitude testing than in any other selection technique.

Some of the improvement with practice can be taken account of if a short practice run on a test or practice examples precedes the test proper. One obvious reason why people improve with practice is because they learn to employ a better test strategy over the whole test. They feel better equipped to cope with a test if they have taken one before than if they are being confronted with a test for the first time. If, in the test administration preceding the test, all testees are made to feel at ease, if they are all clearly informed about the nature of the test, if they all know how much time is allowed for the test and if they are all put in the right spirit to tackle the test, it is more likely that those who do best on the test have the superior aptitude rather than a superior test strategy.

Dangers of recording test scores

In practice, people are tested to help in making a decision about them. The decision may be to accept, reject, transfer or promote a person. Test scores are usually recorded, one reason being that they offer a check at a later date on the effectiveness of the selection procedure. As soon as test scores are recorded, there is the danger that they may be used by somebody ignorant of the nature of human aptitudes to make a decision about people several months or even years after they were tested. This is undesirable. If another personnel decision has to be made about a person some months after the initial testing and this decision requires knowledge of his aptitudes, he should be retested. The aptitudes of people can change and these changes may sometimes be for better, sometimes for worse.

Testing problem occupational groups

The claim of some highly qualified people with sound academic and professional qualifications is that their qualifications should be sufficient evidence of their ability and therefore aptitude tests are not required. Such a claim would be valid in some professions such as dentistry where professional work is closely related to professional training. However, in large industries and organizations, people move into positions where abilities are needed whose presence cannot be assumed from their qualifications. For example a technical person with low verbal ability might not adequately fill a technical management position where verbal skills were essential in communicating information. A non-technical graduate in manufacturing industry, whose numerical and mechanical aptitudes are low, might be of little value despite his first class honours degree in some arts subject. Again, some people do relatively badly in examinations at university because they felt there were better things to do during their years as a student than toil for academic success. Such people may, at interview, seem to have a greater interest in working in industry than they had in an academic course of study. A high-level test of intelligence, on which such an applicant did well, might be used to dispel any lingering doubts about his ability from his academic qualifications. Conversely, other people, having struggled to obtain high qualifications, fail to achieve much afterwards. Perhaps a test would provide evidence that their abilities were not as high as might have been thought and suggest they would be better in less demanding work.

If older applicants are applying for posts, where they will be using skills and knowledge applied in previous jobs, an assessment of their attainments may be more relevant than measures of their aptitudes. If, however, they are moving into a slightly different field, where they will be using aptitudes which they have not recently been using, a test may provide useful additional evidence of their potential. With older applicants it is important to use tests which have high face validity and it is preferable to use tests which call for depth as opposed to speed of thinking.

Managers and foremen are often promoted internally and therefore it should be possible to obtain evidence about them which is not available about external applicants. Again the main question to ask is what additional aptitudes a person needs in his new job which cannot be assumed from his recent past experience. Consider a highly competent craftsman, well respected by his fellow craftsmen and by people in higher positions in his company, who seems to be a possible candidate for a foreman's position. His lack of the necessary verbal, clerical or numerical ability for the foreman's job may not be detected without the use of tests. In general it does not follow that somebody who has competently performed one job will be equally competent at the next level up the hierarchical ladder.

Considerable skill and understanding is required by testers when some of the groups which they are testing are immigrants, or the children of immigrants although they were born in Great Britain. As has been indicated earlier culture-fair tests do not exist and while it is more obvious that people from overseas would find tests of verbal ability more difficult than those born in this country do, they could also find other tests more difficult to carry out. The tests would be administered in English which might not be their first language. Many from other cultures have not had the experience of working at that extra and unnatural speed often demanded in speed tests. They have not had the similar experience of working in short bursts to a time limit. They often have not had the experience common to all in developed societies of seeing from early childhood pictures and drawings of three dimensional material. This may reduce their skill at tests of abstract reasoning, mechanical and spatial ability. Those who are new to a country could find the testing experience emotionally disturbing and without a highly competent tester may fail to participate effectively.

The importance of training in testing

Readers of this chapter will have recognized that before they give aptitude and intelligence tests it is important that they receive sound training in testing. Such training involves learning about the nature of human intelligence and aptitudes, the skills of test administration and the interpretation of test scores. The main distributor of tests in Great Britain is the Test Department of NFER Publishing Company Ltd, Darville House, 2 Oxford Road East, Windsor, SL4 1DF. Only qualified people are able to purchase tests from the NFER and a qualification is usually acquired through successful attendance at a training course on aptitude testing. The NFER itself does not run courses on testing. However it will advise on and give details of approved courses. An organization interested in the use of testing should have at least one member of its staff attend such a training course before it uses tests. A catalogue of tests for industry is available from the NFER Publishing Company.

Further reading

The book by Kline (1976) gives an introduction to the measurement not only of intelligence and ability but also of interest and personality. Four good books dealing solely with testing are those by Anastasi (1968), Anstey (1966), Cronbach (1970) and Butcher (1968). For those who want a clearer picture of the characteristics of a good test the book by Wood (1960) is recommended. It is possible to gain a good short introduction to statistics from Miller (1975) while Guilford and Frutcher (1973) provide readers with a much more detailed knowledge of relevant statistics. Ghiselli (1966) shows the extent to which success on different tests relates to success in many different jobs.

Anastasi, A. (1968): *Psychological Testing,* 3rd edition. New York: Collier-Macmillan.

Anstey, E. (1966): *Psychological Tests.* London: Nelson.

Butcher, H. J. (1968): *Human Intelligence, its Nature and Assessment.* Methuen's Manual of Modern Psychology, London: Methuen.

Cronbach, L. J. (1970): *Essentials of Psychological Testing.* 3rd edition, New York: Harper and Row.

Ghiselli, E. E. (1966): *The Validity of Occupational Tests,* New York: Wiley.

Guilford, J. P. and Frutcher, B. (1973): *Fundamental Statistics in Psychology and Education,* New York: McGraw-Hill.

Kline, P. (1976): *Psychological Testing,* Malaby Press Limited.

Miller, S. (1975): *Experimental Design and Statistics,* London: Methuen.

Wood, D. A. (1960): *Test Construction,* Columbus, Ohio: Merill.

9

Testing Trainability

Sylvia Downs

Selection problems can be placed on a continuum; from assessing an experienced, trained applicant's knowledge, skill and general suitability, to measuring the capacity of a complete novice to master a skill and perform well in the job. Aptitude testing becomes more relevant towards this latter end of the continuum, while various forms of 'trade' testing, wrapped up, in some cases, as an interview, can usually cope at the other end.

Often, however, a job does not yield easily to analysis in terms of 'aptitudes'. All too often the careful job study ends up with the same old recommendation: a general reasoning ability test, a mechanical aptitude test, a spatial ability test, an arithmetic test etc, etc. These usually do a fair job of prediction, but apart from missing out some of the distinctive flavour of the job there are many applicants, especially those who left education early, who don't react too positively to pencil and paper testing.

The selection interview can be supported by a more objective analysis of biographical information. For example, people who have kept their minds active by pursuing hobbies which demand mental flexibility usually have an advantage when retraining is necessary. As with aptitude tests, however, there is always the problem of measuring and predicting from clues one or two steps removed from the job in question.

This difficulty is sometimes overcome by using training as a secondary selection device. In Government Skillcentres, for example, the first three weeks of training are a probationary period during which assessments are made of the trainees' likelihood of success, according to which training may be terminated.

While this has been shown to be an effective method of selection, it is obviously costly to an organization; it may be disruptive to the group under training; and it is distressing to those individuals who are prevented from continuing the training course.

All these problems led the Industrial Training Research Unit, in 1965, to consider new approaches to predicting, at the selection stage, the likelihood of successfully completing training. If the assessment made during the probationary training period could be first condensed and secondly transferred to the selection stage then it would retain the advantages of this method and avoid some of its disadvantages. This form of prediction became known as a 'trainability test', and the rest of this chapter describes what these are, how they were developed, their uses, advantages and disadvantages.

What is a trainability test?

A trainability test involves giving job applicants a short, highly structured, period of training in skills crucial to that job, and then asking the applicants to carry out the task in the way in which they have just been taught. Trainability is assessed by careful observation of errors of technique, and where it is appropriate, an assessment of any workpiece produced.

The test therefore has to be designed by following a number of procedures. First, the crucial elements or skills in the job have to be identified. This is done by finding out where the poorer trainees have the most difficulties. The next step is to choose a workpiece or task which has the following attributes:

1 It is related both to the job, and the most serious learning difficulties.
2 It is complex enough to allow a broad range of errors to be made.
3 It can both be taught and carried out in a reasonable length of time.
4 It allows close observation of techniques and procedures.
5 It does not require any previous experience.

Once the workpiece has been decided upon, comprehensive and systematic instructions have to be scripted or formalized. This is because, human nature being what it is, if there is no such script the instructors giving the test will be likely to change its format, simplify or introduce new topics to it, and generally invalidate the test.

The final stage is to list all the possible errors, and describe general performance, which becomes the error check list and overall rating. It is important that the check list should be presented in a negative form as this focusses the assessor's attention on important factors and reduces the amount of recording needed.

These steps are described more fully later on, and once they have been completed, the trainability test can be tried. Its form is always the same:

1 It is given by an instructor who must first be trained in the use of the test,

and also must have at least six months experience in teaching the particular job for which the applicant is being selected.

2   It is given in an environment as similar as possible to that in which the applicant will train and work.

3   The procedure is carefully explained to the applicants by the instructor who tells them that they will be taught how to do something which is part of the training for the job. During the learning period they will be encouraged to ask questions and receive help, following which they will be expected to perform the task unaided.

4   The teaching method and content is closely defined so that every applicant has an equal opportunity to learn and subsequently perform the task. Instruction is always given as clearly and simply as possible, emphasising what the applicant needs to know, and weeding out vigorously that which it is merely nice to know.

   It has already been mentioned that a script is desirable. This can be in written form, as in the sewing test described below or, as in dentistry, the script can be tape recorded. In this latter form, the tutors demonstrate in time to the tape, stopping it as and when necessary.

   Again, in some craft jobs, instructors have found a script inhibiting, and in that case a good procedural job breakdown and the high-lighting of key facts has been used and found sufficient, provided the instructors always clearly stated the key facts.

5   The applicant is asked to perform the task without help, and the only interjection is, first and foremost, if the applicant is putting himself or others into danger, or, much less frequently, to encourage an applicant to continue.

6   The instructor observes carefully and marks down any errors made by the applicant on a standardized error check list, either as the errors are made, or, if that is not possible, as soon afterwards as practicable.

7   Immediately after the test, the instructor rates the applicant. This subjective assessment is, of course, strongly influenced by the errors noted, as it includes memory of procedures, ability to note errors and correct them, and evidence of relevant manual and perceptual skills. At the same time, instructors are encouraged to use their expertise to take into account such factors as nervousness, speed of work, confidence and interest.

The overlock sewing test is included to illustrate these principles (Figure 9.1).

Figure 9.1   Example of instructor's script for a trainability test
INSTRUCTIONS FOR OVERLOCK MACHINE

*Before the assessment
starts each applicant should
be provided with:*

1   *A completed bag.*

2   *A pile of pieces for
making the bags.*

3   *An overlock machine–
threaded.*

*The following instructions
are given while the applicant
is sitting at the machine
(Figure A).*

For an inexperienced applicant

1   *I understand that you
would like to be trained
as a skilled machinist.*

2   *I am going to teach you
how to make a bag,
(show completed bag)
like this, using all the
correct movements of
your hands and feet and
the right order of doing
things. While I am
teaching you how to
make the bag you may
ask as many questions as
you like and I will do all
I can to help you.*

3   *Then I will ask you to
make three just like it,
using the same methods
as you have been shown.
While you do this I
cannot give you any help
so make sure that you
know what you have to
do before you start.*

Figure A

For an experienced applicant

1   *I know you have had some
experience of machining but
I am going to ask you to do a
simple task like this (show
completed bag).*

2   *I know you may be used to
using the machine differently,
but for this task would you do
exactly what I ask you to do.*

3   *I will tell you how to make
the first bag; then when you
are ready I would like you to
make three more by yourself.*

THE TEST

Introduction to the machine

(Make sure the applicant is sitting comfortably. If at any stage she does not seem to understand, the assessor must help her as much as possible.)

First of all we will see how the machine works. Underneath the table you can see two pedals, a large one on the left and a small one on the right. (These instructions will have to be amended for knee controls.)

Press the small pedal with your right foot and look at the machine to see what happens. (Do not tell the applicant but let her find out for herself.) The part which goes up and down is called the foot of the machine.

*Press the large pedal on the left with both feet and see what happens. When machining you will **always** use both feet on the large pedal. When you are using the small pedal to lift the machine foot, you leave your other foot on the large pedal. **Never** press both pedals at once.*

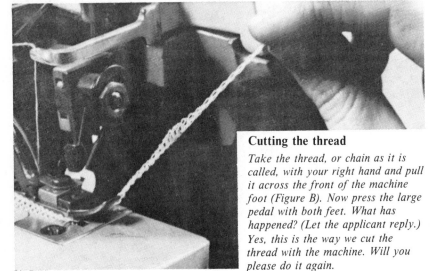

Cutting the thread

Take the thread, or chain as it is called, with your right hand and pull it across the front of the machine foot (Figure B). Now press the large pedal with both feet. What has happened? (Let the applicant reply.) Yes, this is the way we cut the thread with the machine. Will you please do it again.

Figure B

Instructions for the first seam

Pick up two pieces of cloth and line up the pointed corners.

Press the small pedal to lift the foot and put the material under the foot for about ½ inch.

Now get the edge of the material level with the edge of the plate (Figure C). (Show the applicant what is meant by the plate.)

Hold the tail end of the pieces of cloth in your right hand, putting your

thumb underneath and your fingers on top, and make sure the ends are together.

Put your left hand to the left of the foot and rest it lightly so that it can help to guide the cloth.

Now you are ready to sew. Put both feet on the big pedal and sew the seam in one burst of the machine. (Allow the trainee to do this.)

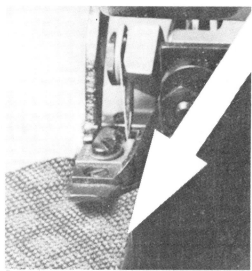

Figure C

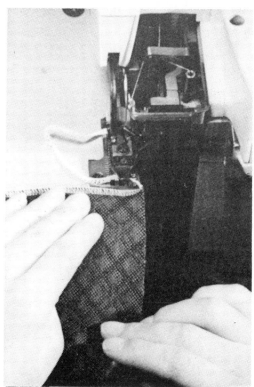

Figure D

Run off the end for about two inches so that you have a chain (Figure D). This will enable you to turn the cloth.

Instructions for the second seam

Turn the bag and position it under the foot, making sure that the edge of the material is level with the edge of the plate.

Hold the tail end of the pieces of cloth in your right hand, putting your thumb underneath and your fingers on top, and make sure the pieces are together.

Put your left hand to the left of the foot and rest it lightly on the cloth.

Put both your feet on the big pedal and sew the seam in one burst of the machine.

Run on for two inches for turning.

Instructions for the third seam

Turn the bag and put it under the foot, making sure that the edge of the material is level with the edge of the plate.

Hold the tail end of the pieces of cloth in your right hand, putting your thumb underneath and your fingers on top, and make sure that the pieces are together.

Put your left hand to the left of the foot and rest it lightly on the cloth.

Put both your feet on the big pedal and sew the seam in one burst of the machine, running off for two inches and cutting the thread.

Final instructions

(The applicant is allowed and encouraged to ask any questions at this stage. She is then asked to make three bags using the method she has been shown.'

OVERLOCK TRAINABILITY ASSESSMENT FORM

Factory ....   *Assessor* ....

Name ....   *Age* .... *Date* ....

Country of Birth ....   *Experienced/Inexperienced* ....

	Seam 1 Bag 1	Seam 1 Bag 2	Seam 1 Bag 3
Aligns wrong seam first			
Presents incorrect corner			
Forgets to position cloth correctly			
Forgets to align seam			
Puts thumb on top			
Does not use fingers of left hand correctly			
Does not use fingers of right hand correctly			
Seam not completed in one sew			
Does not remember cutting method *on last seam*			

Other errors (please describe)...

Total errors........................

Overall ratings

Positioning of hands good: Always.....generally.....sometimes.....rarely.....
Positioning of feet good: Always.....generally.....sometimes.....rarely.....
Notices errors and subsequently corrects:
                Always.....generally.....sometimes.....rarely.....

Please circle appropriate letter.

A Extremely good. The assessor would expect her to become a very good machinist in a short time.

B Fairly good without being outstanding. The assessor would expect her to reach 100 performances in a reasonable time.

C Good enough for simple work. The assessor would expect her to become a steady worker on a simple machine, or task.

D Would have difficulty in training. The assessor would expect her to take longer training, and to perform a simple task.

E Would not be trainable. Even with a great deal of attention she would not make the grade, even on an easy operation.

Figure 9.2   The assessment form

Early work on trainability tests

The first research on trainability tests was carried out in Government Skillcentres, or Government Training Centres as they were then called. It focussed on the problem of selecting older applicants for training, and showed that this practical approach was both acceptable to the older recruits and predictive of their likelihood of passing the course. The first study in industry was carried out in clothing companies to help in the selection of sewing machinists. At that time, the pinboard and formboard were widely used as selection tests, but confidence in them had been somewhat shaken by the Hosiery and Allied Trades Research Association whose research had shown that there was no significant relationship between job performance and these aptitude test results.

The industry was also faced with a change in its traditional labour market. There were many factors, including the raising of the school-leaving age, which had caused a labour shortage in the traditional age group for recruitment, and the industry had to think about recruiting older women. It therefore wanted to be sure that its selection methods were applicable to a wide range of age groups, and were related to ability to learn the necessary skills.

Pilot studies on the trainability test involved 80 trainees in four factories in the Pasold group, whose main products were children's clothing. Subsequent research with a further 73 trainees was conducted in four factories in Northern Ireland which made men's suits, shirts and night wear.

Following the promising results of these researches the Knitwear, Lace and Net Industry Training Board mounted a study involving over 50 factories and 1134 applicants. All the companies were asked to use their existing methods of selection and trainability tests were given in parallel. In no case were the trainability tests used for selection at this stage, and the results were collected and compared with success during training and later, competence at doing the job. Following these successful validation studies the tests were introduced to many hundreds of factories.

Trainability tests have been devised and implemented in a variety of other industries. A trainability test for the selection of fork lift truck operators was carried out at three training establishments and validated by comparing results with the competence test recommended by the Fork Lift Truck Training Joint Committee of Industrial Training Boards.

A large electronics firm found that the memory and speed tests that they used in selecting electronic assemblers bore little relationship to the work done in the factory, and shop floor supervisors were complaining about the competence of new staff. The company consulted the Industrial Training Research Unit, which devised a trainability test. This was found useful for predicting end-of-training attitude, quality of performance and on-the-job speed of performance.

In dentistry, 'A' level results were found to be unpredictive of the operative skills required later in the course, and a pilot study was carried out at the University of Bristol Dental School. The results led to the conclusion that the trainability test should be tried out on a national scale.

All the tests described have been validated, and there are many other trainability tests in a variety of industries which are in course of validation. The Industrial Training Research Unit in Cambridge has a 'library' of available tests and will be able to give up to date information.

Reliability and validity

The reliability of a measure is the confidence one can have that if it is used more than once, it will give the same, or a similar result. Many tests, such as those which measure aptitudes, can be given twice over a period of time to establish reliability, because experience has little or no effect on the qualities being measured.

The trainability test, however, cannot be assessed for reliability in this way, because any intervening training given in the time between the tests would affect the test results.

This problem could be overcome in the clothing industry because there were two different machine tests involved, namely the overlock and lockstitch, both involving the same crucial skills of cloth handling and hand-eye-foot coordination.

The results shown in Figure 9.3 demonstrate the reliability of this trainability test.

T T measure	Correlation	Significance level	Number of people tested
Errors	.64	$p < .001$	91
Rating	.89	$p < .001$	91

Figure 9.3   Correlation coefficient between the lockstitch and overlock trainability test

Chapter 1 discusses the significance of both reliability and validity to any test. The important measure of validity for the trainability test is the degree of similarity between the initial predition of the trainability test and the eventual outcome in terms of performance as measured by independent criteria, and over a sufficient number of results. The predictive validity of a number of trainability tests is shown in Figure 9.4. It must be remembered that throughout these researches the trainability tests were not used for selection, but were given to applicants who had been selected using the existing methods within each organization. Only when the trainability tests had been validated

Job	Test piece	Criterion	Follow up period	No. in study	Significance of correlation coefficients between TT and criterion	
					Error	Rating
Sewing machining	1 Joining 2 pieces to make an open bag. Three identical bags. Overlock machine	Training success.	6 w	82	**	***
Sewing machining	2 Joining 2 pieces to make an open bag. Three identical bags. Lockstitch machine	Training success. On-the-job success. On-the-job success.	4 w 13 w 26 w	73 65 55	** ** n.s.	*** *** ***
Sewing machining	3 Joining pieces of cloth. Lockstitch machine Overlock machine Linking machine	Assessment of speed, quality adaptability & attitude.	4 w 4 w 4 w	46 77 38	not compared	** *** ***
Fork truck operating	Drive truck round a drum and pick up a pallet; place pallet in a marked area & reverse truck back round drum to start. Reach truck. Counterbalance truck.	Error score on operating test at end of training.	3/5 days	84 32	*** ***	*** ***
Electronic assembling	Soldering joints of 3 types.	End of training: attitude, quality, speed On the job: speed. quality. versatility.	2 weeks 6 weeks	57 57	n.s. n.s. n.s. n.s. n.s.	** n.s ** n.s. **

** p<.01
*** p<.001
n.s. not significant

Figure 9.4 Validity of trainability tests

could a decision be made whether or not to use them within the total selection procedure.

It will be apparent that there are many important differences between trainability tests and the conventional tests of reasoning, aptitudes etc. These can be summarized as follows:

Trainability tests	*Reasoning and aptitude tests*
1 Job specific.	1 General applicability.
2 Measure trainability for specific job.	2 Measure the aptitudes and abilities hypothesised as underlying trainability.
3 Practical.	3 Written, pencil and paper.
4 Given in realistic work surroundings, normally the training school.	4 Given in the personnel department.
5 Given by instructors working as testers.	5 Given by personnel staff.
6 Instructors trained to give test.	6 Personnel staff trained to give test.
7 Applicant's previous experience of the skill has an acceptable influence on performance in the task.	7 Applicant's previous experience of the tests can given an unfair advantage in performance in the test.
8 Applicants can ask questions during the learning period, about how to do the task.	8 Applicants can ask questions during the test instruction period, but not about solutions to problems in the test.
9 Applicants tested only on what has been taught.	9 Applicant tested on new problem material.
10 No timing.	10 Strict timing.
11 Scoring by recording of errors during test and a subjective rating.	11 Scoring made after the test by objective measures.
12 Task normally completed but errors are expected.	12 Test not normally completed in time.
13 Given individually or to small groups.	13 Can easily be given to large groups.

Disadvantages and advantages of trainability tests

The major disadvantages of trainability tests are inherent in the fact that they are job-specific. This means first, that new tests have to be designed wherever the crucial elements of a job differ. For example, sewing machinists can be tested on either an overlock or lockstitch machine because the crucial elements of the required skill are the same. On the other hand, three trainability tests involving metal using, fitting and electrical work were given at the start of training to a number of apprentices in the Shipbuilding Industry. As they progressed, phase tests in these trades were given, and it was found that each trainability test was significantly related to its corresponding trade phase test, but not to the others.

Secondly, because a trainability test involves assessing the way each person carries out a task, the test is time-consuming and therefore costly. The tests are normally given individually and involve instructors who have had to be trained in their use, and often machinery and materials.

Thirdly, it is essential that the instructional part of the test should not deviate from the form in which it has been validated, and therefore regular supervision is necessary to ensure this.

Bearing all this in mind, where standard psychometric tests have been shown to be valid, it is obviously both cheaper and more convenient to use them.

The advantages of trainability tests include, first and foremost, the provision of a selection device in circumstances where other forms of selection have been undependable or not valid. Apart from this, the trainability test allows applicants to experience the type of work, visit the training school and meet the instructors. Although the acquaintance may be brief, it gives the test a realism and application to the job which is not present in most other selection devices, and allows a greater degree of two way assessment: the company of the applicant and the applicant of the company and the job. This latter possibility can be very important, as in the following examples.

A graduate applicant to a building society was given a trainability test which involved training in conducting a mortgage interview. His response was that if that was the sort of thing he would have to do, then he would rather not get the job, and he withdrew his application.

The effect of the sewing trainability test on the applicant's perception of the job was shown well in the Knitting Lace and Net ITB research. Whilst all the 1134 applicants who took the trainability test had been offered the job on the basis of other selection criteria, the number who eventually turned up for training was related to how well the instructors had rated them. Although the applicants had not been told their test results, they had seen for themselves how fitted they were to picking up the necessary skills.

Similarly, a woman applied for a plumbing course, and was offered a training place on the basis of a trainability test. She declined the place because the test made her realize that plumbing was a very physically-demanding job.

The examples given are all negative, in that the applicants realized that the job would not suit them. But it must be remembered that training places are expensive; for example, one estimate gave a cost of £160 a week for sewing machinists; so that the perceptions gained as a result of the trainability test may well have saved a large training investment by identifying those applicants who would be most likely to withdraw or be found unsatisfactory during or after training.

A more positive example occurred in a Skillcentre, when an older man was persuaded to try an electric arc welding test. He did well, found to his surprise that he liked it, and after successfully completing the course, returned six months later to thank the instructor for introducing him to a trade he had thought he would not want to do.

Another advantage lies in the fact that the trainability test is concerned with doing part of the eventual job. Some applicants may feel frustrated by their inability to communicate, or to deal with written tests, particularly where they can see little relevance to the job in the questions asked or the tests given. Applicants often feel happier when they have something in their hands so that they can show what they can do. The pertinence of the trainability test to the eventual job also gives applicants confidence in the fact that they can cope with training, and be successful.

The trainability test also engenders more involvement, not only on the part of applicants, who feel they have been carefully considered as individuals and that time, thought and effort have been put into the selection decision; but also as far as the instructors are concerned. There is often a rift between selectors and instructors, with the latter complaining about the standard or type of people sent to them for training. Whilst the personnel department must be involved in the final decision on selection, because trainability is only one of the factors to be considered, the fact that the training department is involved leads not only to better relationships between personnel and training, but also to more training commitment on the part of those trainers who have taken part in the initial selection.

The skills for which trainability tests are suited

Semi-skilled manual jobs

Early tests were developed and validated where a real need had presented itself because either existing tests had not proved valid, as in the clothing and electronic industries or where, in the past, tests had not been used and selection had been based mainly on an interview, as in stentering and the forestry industry. The jobs which were the subject of these trainability tests are normally classified as semi-skilled and the training period may last between one week and several months. These occupations all involve a large component of manual and perceptual skills, remembering procedures and the recognition and correction of errors. They do not involve much theoretical learning, diagnostic skill or social skills.

Skilled manual jobs

On the face of it the test for dentistry students may appear to be tackling a higher level occupation, but in fact this test was developed to try to predict for the manual and perceptual skills which are tested during the second year of the course when the students start their practical work. 'A' level results and written psychometric tests, although related to theoretical papers, did not predict the manual skills so important to dentistry.

The use of trainability tests for selecting for craft training has great face validity, which has been backed up by predictive validity where tests have been tried on six month training courses run in Skillcentres. Where tests have been tried in apprentice selection in the construction and shipbuilding trades the results have been less impressive. They predicted the results of tests early in the training, but not final City and Guilds examination results. One possible reason for this is that the trainability test results seemed to be related to apprentice turnover, in that the poorer performers on the tests were more likely to leave during training than better applicants. This means that better trainees are retained and significant correlations between the trainability test scores and criteria scores is less likely to occur. However this is not the whole story; as the trainability tests were designed to assess memory of procedures, recognition and correction of mistakes, and relevant manual and perceptual abilities, they did not assess the basic intellectual abilities which should be related to planning and diagnostic skills. As the craftsman moves into the higher levels of his trade, the manual and perceptual skills become subservient to the higher level skills. Where manual, perceptual and intellectual components are all involved it is important to use a corresponding variety of tests.

One large electrical contracting firm has successfully used a range of tests for some years in its apprentice selection. After assessing suitability from the application forms, selected applicants are given a number of psychometric tests (IQ, arithmetic, spatial relations and craft knowledge/mechanical comprehension). Those who score above an established cut-off point on all the tests take a trainability test. Unfortunately each part of the total system has not been validated separately, but the overall effect of introducing this procedure was markedly to improve performance in City and Guilds examinations. Comparing recent results with historical data, 90% now pass as against 45%, with 60% passing at the advanced level as against 10%. Another effect of the improved selection system is a lowering of the drop-out rate in the first two years from 25% to 5% and after four years, turnover is now 10% compared with a previous 50%. From these results it is suggested that, for apprentice selection, trainability tests should be given together with psychometric tests.

Supervisors, instructors and managers

The feasibility of using the trainability approach for jobs where rather more elusive skills have to be learned is now being tackled. The need to improve our ability to select for middle management is clear, but the training given can be diffuse and training objectives are often obscure. Perhaps this is because management training frequently involves a complex structure of knowledge, skills, attitudes and interpersonal behaviour. Given this, it is extremely difficult to establish criteria on which to validate any tests, let alone the difficulty of designing the tests in the first place.

In general terms we have evidence that a trainability test is effective where the training and subsequent job are mainly concerned with manual and perceptional skills. As diagnostic and interpersonal skills become increasingly important in successfully carrying out a job, then the effectiveness of trainability tests may well diminish, but there is, as yet, comparatively little evidence in this area.

Suitability of the tests for different applicants

Since selection methods have been subjected to increased scrutiny it has become apparent that some tend to discriminate against certain types of applicants, whose poorer showing on the tests may not be reflected in poorer ability to do the job. For example, as people get older they tend to concentrate on accuracy rather than speed. Older persons may, as a result, obtain lower scores than they merit on some tests because they concentrate too much on getting early test items correct irrespective of the time this takes, rather than passing quickly on to later items that they may find easier. In verbal tests, where the nuances of words are important, those who are not fluent in the language will inevitably be discriminated against.

At one time it was thought that this problem could be overcome by concentrating on tests which involve reasoning using symbols rather than words, but even the use of symbols and drawings did not result in culture-free tests. For example, some cultures rarely represent three dimensional objects in two dimensional drawings and therefore an individual's difficulty in dealing with these problems may not have the same significance as the difficulty of someone brought up in a Western culture. Tests which have been well designed and validated in the Western world may not be transferable to other cultures. If they are transferred without being well validated then applicants could be unjustifiably rejected. There was clearly a need for research into the value of trainability tests in avoiding such discrimination and some such work has already been carried out.

The effect of age on trainability tests

During the validation of four of the trainability tests, for carpentry, welding, sewing and fork-truck operating, it was possible to look at the effect of age related to scores on the tests and on subsequent training results. In all cases the tests predicted significantly for both younger and older age groups. The carpentry and welding tests in fact predicted better for men of over forty years than for younger men. In the fork-truck operating research it was found that there was no significant relationship between the age of the trainees and their performance on either the trainability test or the criterion test drive when they were operating counterbalance trucks. When the vehicle was a reach truck, older trainees did less well than their younger colleagues on both the trainability test and the competence test, because of transfer problems not present in the counterbalance truck. All the available evidence indicates that trainability tests are predictive over the working age range, and difficulties experienced by older applicants in the test will be mirrored in training, so that poorer test performance by older candidates may well indicate that training methods need adapting to their needs.

It is known that many older applicants are nervous of, or resistant to, doing psychometric tests. They may have been in manual work and away from school for many years and thus find the relevance of such tests hard to fathom, whereas the realism of a trainability test makes more sense to them.

Trainability tests for immigrants

Only in the sewing researches were large numbers of tests given to immigrants but the results indicated that the tests were as predictive for them as for the native UK population. The main problem occurs both in the test and subsequent training when the language is not understood and no interpreter is available.

The fact that the test is a microcosm of the training should ensure that differences of sex, age and cultural background are minimized except where they are reflected in training problems. Some recent research in the United States, designed to assess the effect of racial bias on the use of work samples for personnel selection showed that where a highly specific behavioural recording form was used there was no racial bias. They conclude that 'by using careful work sample development procedures and by assisting subjects in focussing on and recording relevant behaviour, the potential for bias in the use of work samples appears small'.

Conditions under which it is worth using a trainability test

Certain questions are posed below, and if the personnel department finds it is answering 'Yes' to one or more then it is worth while considering the use of an appropriate validated trainability test:

1   Is there a high drop-out or failure rate in training?
2   Are some trainees taking too long to reach an acceptable standard?
3   Could the present selection methods discriminate against an applicant on the basis of age, sex or culture, rather than ability to learn the necessary skills to do the job?
4   Is there a crucial element of the skill taught at a late stage in training which some trainees cannot master?
5   Is there a need to consider retraining the present work force?

There are two further requirements, the first being that systematic training exists within the company, as there is otherwise little point in assessing trainability; indeed, it would be impossible to begin to design a suitable trainability test.

Second, that instructors who will give the test are properly trained to do so. Appropriate training courses are available within some of the Industrial Training Boards, Fielden House Productivity Centre, Manchester, and Fork Truck Training, Hampshire.

Design of trainability tests

Ideally it is best to consult a trained designer or to attend a trainability test designer's course. The Industrial Training Research Unit, Cambridge can give information on designers in the Training Boards, approved consultancy organizations and available training courses. If it is not possible to consult an expert then a small handbook *Trainability Tests, A Practitioner's Guide*, can be obtained from ITRU, and this gives step by step instructions on designing, validating and administering a test.

In brief the procedure is as follows:

1   Interview as many instructors as possible, and ask them to describe in specific behavioural terms the problems of poor trainees, such as:
    (a) Actual procedures which were forgotten
    (b) Faults which were not noticed or corrected
    (c) Manual problems encountered in the way they controlled tools or materials
    (d) Perceptual problems
    (e) Faults which were found in workpieces (if these were produced).
    From these interviews identify the crucial elements in learning the skill.
2   Select a workpiece or task which incorporates these skills and operations.
3   Write a check-list of errors which are liable to be made during the performance of the task. Check that the errors relate to the crucial elements identified in stage 1. The check-list is always written negatively.
4   Decide on the range of ratings to be used, and give behavioural

descriptions of the expectations, eg **A**: Would expect this applicant to be trained to a high standard in the shortest possible period of time, **E**: Would expect this applicant to be untrainable.

5   Design and write the instructor's script.

When designing the test the following factors must be remembered.

(a) The test will be given to novices, as well as applicants with some experience so no previous experience should be assumed.

(b) The test task should be part of the job.

(c) The test task should incorporate, if possible, all the crucial aspects of the job.

(d) The test task should be sufficiently complex to enable errors of many different types to be made.

(e) The test must not take too long, although the length of the test will relate to the complexity of the training. Tests designed so far range from 10 minutes for sewing machinists to 90 minutes for electrical contracting apprentices.

When the outlined test has been produced it must be tried out with an instructor who has not been involved in developing it to ensure that the script is accurate and that the error check list is clear and does not include ambiguities. It must then be given to a range of individuals, to give the instructor practice in using the test and the error check list. This also enables the test designer to see if the test is discriminating adequately among the various levels of ability to perform the task, in that some people make a great many errors and some very few, with most making an average number. If few make errors, or no-one can do the task, then the test has to be redesigned. However, if only minor amendments are necessary then the test is ready for thorough validation which can be done in a number of ways. The best is to give the test to all successful applicants, with the selection decision being made in the same way as in the past. The test results are then kept until they can be compared with an appropriate criterion measure. This could be a practical test at the end of training, or subjective assessments made by the training officer and supervisors on the shop floor. If subjective ratings are used, and often they are the only practical measures, they can be made more reliable by using descriptions of behaviour rather than a numerical scale. To guard against a 'halo effect', that is, a tendency to score a good trainee highly on everything and a poor trainee low on everything, the behavioural descriptions can be put in a random order. An example of this form of assessment is shown in Figure 9.5. When a number of trainees have completed training, their results can be compared with their trainability error score and ratings.

Unfortunately it is not always possible to use this ideal approach. Where the company has good records, the test can be used for a trial period, and the results of the new applicants can be compared with previous recruits. For example, a trainability test for circuit board wiring, introduced at a firm which

NAME OF OPERATIVE   . . . .   TIME IN FACTORY   . . . .
JOB   . . . .   TIME IN JOB   . . . .
DATE   . . . .   ASSESSOR'S NAME

Please tick one statement from each category which best describes the trainee at the moment. Allowance must be made for problems outside his or her responsibility such as work shortages, machine breakdowns and difficult tasks.

1 QUALITY OF WORK	Usually produces work to a high standard ☐	Often produces poor quality work ☐	Produces work of satisfactory quality ☐	Consistently produces high quality work ☐	Sometimes produces poor quality work ☐
2 SPEED OF WORK	Works at a rather slow pace ☐	Consistently fast worker ☐	Very slow worker ☐	Usually maintains a good speed ☐	Works at an average pace ☐
3 ADAPTABILITY TO NEW WORK	Tackles any new work confidently and quickly ☐	Is very slow to adapt to new work ☐	Finds some difficulty in adapting to new work ☐	Can adapt to new work in reasonable time ☐	Adapts well to new work ☐

Figure 9.5   Sample performance assessment sheet

had previously selected trainees on the basis of their application forms and interviews raised the training pass rate from 27% (of 21) to 83% (of 62). One must ensure, of course, that the improved results are not due to a change in type of applicant or better training methods. If all else fails, the test can be used to select, but with a low cut-off point so that only the very worst applicants are rejected. It can then be validated by comparing the results of those accepted with the independent criteria measures. If those with high ratings and low error scores prove to be the best trainees and those with low ratings and high error scores poor trainees then the selection cut off can be raised.

The *Practitioner's Guide*, referred to previously, gives full information on test design and validation together with suggestions on methods of statistical analysis.

The effect of previous experience on test results

All the tests devised until now have been validated with applicants with no previous experience of the skill. In some circumstances the tests were also given to applicants who claimed previous experience. As might be expected, those with previous experience tended to be rated higher and have fewer mistakes, but then in training they also did better. When their test and criterion scores were compared statistically they were significantly correlated. It must be remembered that the tests are not claiming to measure a fundamental ability such as intelligence, but the ability to learn the specific job. Good *relevant* experience is important; there is a problem that is found in some industries where applicants claim, in good faith, experience which they assume to be relevant but which may not be. For example home dressmakers may not appreciate how different are the machines and skills used in industry from those which they have used. Men who have done some carpentry at home may have developed habits and methods not acceptable in the trade and hard to unlearn. For these reasons many companies prefer to give tests to all applicants. Where there is no ambiguity about the form or extent of the applicant's previous experience it is obviously better to give a straightforward trade test.

Summary

Trainability tests involve giving applicants a short, highly structured period of training in skills crucial to the trade and then asking them to carry out the task in the way in which they have been taught. Trainability is assessed by careful observation of errors of technique and, where appropriate, assessment of the workpieces produced. The tests are given by trained instructors in an environment as closely as possible resembling that in which the trainee will train and work. Where valid, they have the additional advantages of enabling the applicant to experience a microcosm of the training scheme and job, and the instructor to take a part in the selection procedure. Their validity does not appear to be affected by age, sex or previous experience.

They are costly in terms of instructor time and have to be carefully designed, validated and monitored. At present their main use is in semi-skilled trades, but the boundary country is being explored.

Further reading

Trainability Tests: A Practitioner's Guide. ITRU Publication SL2. Obtainable from ITRU Ltd., Lloyds Bank Chambers, Hobson Street, Cambridge, CB1 1NL.

10

Personality Assessment

K M Miller

Psychological tests are customarily divided into two categories—those that are designed to obtain assessments of maximum performance and those that elicit typical performance. Tests of aptitudes and abilities constitute the first group and have been discussed in Chapter 8. Tests of personal or motivational characteristics make up the second group. Technically these are not tests as they do not have objectively correct answers. So it is more usual to refer to questionnaires, blanks, records or inventories. From such measures a unique pattern of responses is obtained for an individual and this is taken to represent the typical pattern of behaviour, that is, the preferred way of responding, for him.

The meaning of 'personality'

Some psychologists use the term *personality* to cover the full range of an individual's make-up, including his abilities and aptitudes. They consider that the way a person functions in everyday life depends on the interaction of the whole person with his environment. Other psychologists restrict the term personality to motivational factors and these can be further divided. Some would include interests, values and personality traits whilst others would see interests and values as separate.

For assessment purposes, abilities and aptitudes are frequently treated on their own because tests used to measure them have been developed more extensively and with greater reliability and validity than is the case with measures of personal characteristics.

The present chapter is concerned with all types of personal characteristics and treats interests, values and personality traits as falling along a continuum. At the one end we have interest measures dealing with expressed preferences which do not always tell us the degree of importance they have for the individual. Values are of more importance, while personality traits, at the other end of the continuum, have direct implications for the individual's everyday behaviour.

Function of interests, values and personality traits

While it is convenient to keep these three aspects separate when it comes to considering measuring devices, in fact they often overlap. Guion describes them all as measures of motivational variables. The personnel officer, in considering aspects of typical performance, is seeking to obtain information about how an individual is likely to use his aptitudes and abilities. Knowledge of motivational aspects of a person can help to predict how he will perform. At the simplest level, interests may be regarded as attitudes towards activities; those interests strongly held are likely to motivate an individual to action, because, on the whole, people do what their interests suggest. The assessment of interests has been extensively used in the field of counselling and guidance and to a lesser, but effective, extent in personnel selection and classification.

The assessment of values, or basic motivational patterns, involves investigation at a somewhat deeper level than is the case with interests. A person's value system influences, consciously or unconsciously, his immediate decisions or long-term goals. His personal satisfaction depends to a large extent on how extensively his value system can find expression in everyday life. The presence of strong but incompatible values in a person, or conflict between his values and those of colleagues, could affect his efficiency.

Theories of personality

When reference is made to the personality of an individual it may be that his behavioural traits or style are being considered. On the other hand, a more inclusive concept that encompasses basic theoretical ideas, such as needs, defence mechanisms or emotional states may be considered. A further alternative is Ghiselli's definition:

> Personality refers to those traits of the individual or those aspects of his behaviour that have emotional, social, motivational or moral connotations such as stability, extroversion, perseverance and honesty.

Since the nineteenth century various attempts have been made to classify aspects of personality and to develop theories of personality. Some of these attempts have been based on clinical observation (Freud, Jung, Kretschmer), while others have relied on statistical procedures and logical analysis (Cattell,

Eysenck, Gordon, Gough, Guilford). Of the latter group Cattell has conducted the most extensive theoretical and research work to develop a measure of personality.

Briefly, his approach was to examine the 4500 words in the English language which describe mental traits. Many of these are very similar and Cattell was able to identify 160 words which were completely distinct from one another. The next step was to make a comprehensive survey of previous research and relevant literature and then to proceed to a statistical study by means of 'factor analysis'—a process which analyses the intercorrelations between a number of measures or assessments and elicits the basic factors which lie behind them.

From these studies, Cattell found that personality can be described in terms of sixteen primary traits or dimensions. He also shows that a simpler presentation can be made by combining certain of the primary traits into four second-order traits. These findings formed the basis of his well-known 16PF questionnaire.

Three other psychologists who have made extensive contributions to personality theory over the past thirty years have pursued similar approaches. Guilford's work has led him to describe personality in terms of ten factors while Eysenck finds that three broad factors are sufficient: extroversion, neuroticism, psychoticism. Gordon, who has made the most recent contribution in this field, also using factor analysis, has defined eight dimensions.

The logical-statistical approach is more to be accepted and encouraged than any without such an empirical basis. An example of a less-sound approach is that of a researcher who decides that sociability is important and who puts together a series of statements intended to measure this trait.

One theory of values that has had a long-term effect in psychology is *types of men* put forward by Spranger. As will be seen below, the Allport–Vernon Study of Values, based on this theory has been used, with periodic revisions, for over thirty years. At various times it has had some prominence in the personnel field.

The existence of different theories of personality, values and interests may suggest that little can be gained from trying to assess any dimensions of typical performance. While admitting that the lack of firm definition in the personality area has been one of the reasons for the slower utilization of systematic assessment—compared with abilities and aptitudes—there are strong reasons for heeding the point made by Ghiselli that, while theoretical classification is useful, the personnel problem can be attacked without delaying to consider such matters.

Approaches to measurement of motivational aspects

Three main approaches are available to those wishing to assess motivational

aspects of an individual. They are as follows:
1   The projective technique.
2   The questionnaire.
3   The objective approach.

The first and last of these might be grouped together as approaches where the assessor is able to disguise his purpose, while the second is one where the aim of the exercise is more or less apparent to the person completing the questionnaire. Psychological statisticians have developed techniques for countering any anticipation that might seem natural on the part of the candidate.

Projective approach

The underlying principle is that an individual will interpret ambiguous stimuli, whether visual or auditory, in a way that is reflective of his own personality. Most people have heard of the 'inkblot' test. This is an example of the type of projective technique which has been used by clinical psychologists to obtain data to assist in diagnosing mental disturbance. Some companies have used the approach with certain categories of staff, particularly sales and managerial. However, as the use of such techniques requires a fully qualified and experienced clinical psychologist to interpret the information, no further reference will be made to it in this chapter.

Questionnaire approach

Basically a questionnaire contains a number of items through which the individual is asked to report on himself. The method of reporting is either by rating or on a forced-choice basis. The rating approach is the older and more common.
    The individual has to rate a question in terms of some evaluative judgement. For example, he might be given a list of questions or statements about activities and have to indicate the following:

1   Whether he would like to perform the activity.
2   Whether he would not like to carry out the activity.
3   Whether he is uncertain about it or indifferent to it.

    In another situation he might be asked to read a statement and answer 'true' or 'false' or 'uncertain', depending upon which answer was most often the case for him.
    As a result of certain criticisms of this type of approach, such as persons giving a socially acceptable rather than a genuine response, a forced choice approach has been developed. In this situation the candidate is faced with, for

example, two statements which are equally acceptable socially (would you prefer a long shopping spree or a weekend in Paris?) or equally unacceptable (waiting for the dentist or waiting for an examination to start). He is then asked to select one statement which best describes his behaviour and one which least describes him. By systematic variation of the questions it is possible to counter the criticisms of the other type of inventory. It will be shown that the criticisms were not necessarily true in all or even a majority of cases.

Objective approach

The person taking this type of test finds it without direct meaning although the situation is clearly structured for the person administering it. The type of situation which is presented to the subject is clear. For example, visual stimuli are presented to the person who is asked to respond as soon as the stimulus is perceived, as by pressing one key for a green light and another for a red. In this situation the more cautious the individual the slower the reaction, thus providing a measure of restraint.

This approach has two main limitations: the development of appropriate situations can take a considerable time while the actual testing time can be longer than with printed tests. However, after many years the public edition of Cattell's Objective/Analytic Personality Battery has recently been issued: this is somewhat shorter than the trial editions. In the UK an objective test of personal 'steadiness' is being developed by Randell; early studies suggest that it could be particularly applicable to people of low literacy levels. Morrisby's Differential Test Battery includes four objective tests; the patterns of responses to these provide indicators of temperament.

Dealing with faking and distortion

When an individual has to give an answer to the type of question that appears in the rating type of inventory it is possible that he will succumb to one of the two types of distortion or, if he is in a competitive situation, such as applying for a job, he may attempt to fake by answering in the way he thinks would make a good impression.

Two types of distortion

The first type of distortion has been mentioned above—that of social desirability or acceptability, whereby an individual is likely to select an alternative because he recognizes it as one that is more acceptable to his fellows and because he realizes that selecting the other alternative would reveal a socially undesirable trait. Choosing the acceptable response may not be deliberate but an unconscious move on the part of the individual to put up a good front. The inclusion of neutral items of social desirability in scales and other techniques have been used to overcome the tendency to respond in this way.

The second type of distortion is sometimes described as personal preference or as *response style* and means that an individual may be more inclined to answer 'yes' or 'no'. Psychologists involved in making questionnaires have used various devices to overcome this tendency, such as reversing the direction of the question so that a 'no' response is sometimes the appropriate one. When attention was first focused on the social and personal desirability aspects, considerable concern was expressed that true information was being concealed. Then came a period when it was considered that the response style of an individual was an important personality characteristic in its own right. The most recent summing up on response styles has come from Anastasi, who points out that the controversy over these may have been a storm in a teacup but at the same time it has probably led to a better appreciation of methodological problems and to a considerable refinement in the construction of personality inventories. She admits the possibility that personal style may be a valid predictor of occupational success in some cases but maintains that it is not as useful as the content aspects of personality questionnaires.

The forced-choice approach discussed above has been the main alternative to the rating approach and it clearly has a number of advantages. It has been suggested that it may have lower reliability than the other approaches and choice is made more difficult. However, scrutiny of the technical manuals for a number of forced-choice instruments reveals reliabilities above 0.80—a level seldom exceeded by rating type questionnaires.

Nature and aims of faking

Faking is sometimes seen as partly due to social desirability distortion and partly as an attempt to produce a pattern thought to be appropriate to the job being tested. In clinical type tests, a lie scale or distortion scale is sometimes included.

One form of Cattell's 16PF Questionnaire has a motivational distortion (lie) scale which the psychologist may use 'to conclude, in an extreme case, that the noncooperation is so great as to justify rejecting all a person's scores'. The practice of excluding the scores of fakers has some obvious limitations, because it removes a rather eccentric type of person from the sample.

Recently another form of the 16PF Questionnaire was analysed, using American data, to identify some items which together seem to indicate that respondents may have been 'faking good' or 'faking bad'; and a procedure was devised for 'correcting' scores for apparent distortion. This should be used with some caution, as the items used to identify distortion also contribute to the scores on various personality factors.

In the case of someone trying to produce a pattern he thinks will give him an advantage, such as a salesman always responding with the socializing response, there are two main points. First, with current carefully developed inventories, it is difficult for an individual to select all the appropriate answers. Second, and more important, if the reason for applying the test is carefully explained to the applicant and he sees that it is to his advantage to be as truthful as possible in his responses, there is but a slender chance that he will fake his responses. Both Cattell and Ghiselli have discussed this topic.

Types of assessment instrument

There are a great many individual assessment devices available on the test market: some have been used widely in many countries, others may have been used by very few people anywhere. The more frequently used are evaluated carefully in standard textbooks such as those by Anastasi, Cronbach or Guion. All are reviewed in the *Mental Measurement Year Books.*

In this section it is proposed to mention one or two of each main type to illustrate the points made above and to give an idea of the range available.

Vocational interests

Two main approaches to the assessment of vocational interests have been available for many years. The first, an inventory approach, was used by Strong in developing the Strong Vocational Interest Blank, which was first published in the 1920s. It has been revised from time to time, the last revision being in 1966. It is based on the principle that a prticular pattern of response can be isolated for a specific occupation. At present there are scales for 59 male occupations and 34 female.

The other approach is to ascertain a person's order of preference for particular fields of work. The number of fields may vary according to the principles on which the author is basing his instrument. Among examples of this type of record are the Kuder Preference Record (vocational), the Connolly Occupational Interests Questionnaire and the Rothwell–Miller Interest Blank, which assess ten, seven and twelve fields respectively. The last two have been prepared for British use while the Kuder is of American origin and was used quite extensively in the UK before a British revision was published in 1973. The fields covered by the Rothwell–Miller are outdoor, mechanical, computational, scientific, persuasive, aesthetic, literary, musical, social service, clerical, practical and medical.

In order to overcome some of the problems associated with the completion of self-report devices the Rothwell-Miller Interest Blank requires that job titles, one representing each field, be ranked in order of preference. There are nine such groups. The Kuder employs a type of forced choice asking the respondent to select from a triad of statements the one he would most like to do and the one he would least like.

Interests are the first stage on the continuum of personal or motivational characteristics. The assessment of them is more effectively carried out for school leavers and young dults. The more work experience a man has had, the more difficult it frequently is for him to provide information uncoloured by his experience.

Measures of values

The one measure of values that to date has been extensively used in the UK has been the Allport–Vernon Study of Values. Although developed as an UK–USA enterprise in Harvard and used, with revision, in the UK, there is now an English edition produced by Richardson. The same six values are included: theoretical, economic, aesthetic, social, political and religious. In some recent work Randell has shown the study to be useful in the selection of salesmen. The first part of the assessment is designed to overcome self-report problems by having the respondent assign values to each item in a group. In the second part the respondent has to rank the attitudes which follow a statement.

Two other scales much used in the USA are now being increasingly used in the UK, particularly for selection and counselling purposes. These are Gordon's Survey of Personal Values and his Survey of Interpersonal Values. Several major studies in the UK have shown their usefulness in contributing information to the selection process. Both surveys are in forced-choice format. The personal values are practical mindedness, achievement, variety, decisiveness, orderliness and goal orientation. The interpersonal values are support, conformity, recognition, independence, benevolence and leadership. By providing two instruments, Gordon allows the user flexibility to employ the one most suitable for his purposes or to use both if this is more appropriate. The surveys are relatively short and of quite high reliability.

The most recent extensive and comprehensive research into the nature of values has been conducted by Rokeach whose work is presented in *The Nature of Human Values* published in 1973. The Rokeach value study has potential for use in the personnel field.

Personality questionnaires

These fall into two main groups, those primarily developed to assess personality disturbance and those designed to describe normal personality. Only the latter type are illustrated here. As indicated above Cattell, Eysenck and Guilford have been major contributors to both theory and practice.

Before the various personality factors are discussed, one important warning must be given. These factors are often given titles which are words in common use. They are, however, used by the constructors of questionnaires and other devices in technical senses based upon statistical research. Laymen should, therefore, resist any temptation to interpret them in the light of the everyday use of these words.

Eysenck's questionnaire is the simplest, because it gives scores for only three factors of very wide coverage.

Cattell has put forward a more detailed classification of personality factors, distinguishing between primary and second-order factors. In Cattell's terms, Eysenck's neuroticism is a second-order factor (called anxiety) made up of five constituent factors of anxiety: instability, insecurity, unreliability, tenseness and suspiciousness. The other secondary factors are extroversion, tough mindedness, conservatism, independent mindedness and morality.

In addition to an intelligence scale Cattell uses fifteen primary factors:

1 *Anxiety factors.* Self-discipline versus unreliability; stability versus instability, tenseness versus relaxedness, insecurity versus security, suspiciousness versus broadmindedness.
2 *Extroversion factors.* Unreservedness versus shyness, friendliness versus aloofness, dominance versus submissiveness, liveliness versus reticence, group dependence versus independence.
3 *Tough mindedness factors.* Sensitivity versus insensitivity, shrewdness versus unaffectedness.
4 *Conservatism factors.* Liberalism versus traditionalism, unconventionality versus conventionality.
5 *Morality factor.* Moral attitudes versus expediency.

Cattell has also derived some indicators based on reference or criterion groups. These enable the user to gain some idea of the similarity of a record with groups showing, eg high leadership, high creativity, success in professional level type jobs and potential for academic success or quickly learning to cope with new situations.

Guilford has published several personality scales. A derivative of these, produced in association with Zimmerman, covers ten factors, some of which are similar to certain of the primary factors in the Cattell scales. The Guilford–Zimmerman factors are activity/energy, restraint/seriousness, ascendance/social boldness, sociability, emotional stability, objectivity, agreeableness, thoughtfulness/reflectiveness, cooperativeness and masculinity.

The questionnaires of the three authors mentioned above are all to some extent prone to the response set and other problems. Forced-choice approaches have again been developed by Gordon who in his Personal Inventory assesses cautiousness, original thinking, personal relations and vigour. The Gordon Personal Profile assesses ascendancy, responsibility, emotional stability and sociability. As in the case of his value surveys, these can be used independently or in concert as required.

The above presentation has been purely descriptive. No instrument for assessing any aspect of personal characteristics is perfect, though all have been shown to be very useful in some circumstances. If it is seriously intended to introduce personality testing then it is essential to study the test manuals and the findings of research studies before proceeding further and to discuss the best ways of implementing these with someone who is well experienced in the field.

Ghiselli has recently published his work on a self-descriptive index and Fineman in Sheffield has been working on variations of approach for British industry, in particular on a selected form of the achievement scale in the self-descriptive index.

Selected attributes

Psychologists have also given attention to personality measures for particular purposes—sales attitudes and supervisory attitudes. Very often they are too strongly based in the culture of origin to be useful in the UK without modification. One that does not seem to suffer from this problem is the leadership opinion questionnaire of Fleishman. This assesses the dimensions of 'concern' and 'structure'.

Another approach is that of Sweney who has developed two complementary scales. One assesses supervisory style in three broad areas — controlling, delegating and being permissive — while the other elicits subordinate style — independent, cooperative and conforming.

Although not a 'test' in the conventional sense the repertory grid technique is being more often used as a device for gaining information about personality.

Standardizing the scores

It is not practicable to use the raw scores on different tests or questionnaires or even on subsections of a single test or questionnaire. This is due to differences in the average scores and also to the fact that the spread of scores around each average differs from one to another.

It is, therefore, necessary to standardize the scores in some way and two main methods have been developed.

Percentile method

The first is by means of *percentiles*. When a test or questionnaire is being developed, it is given to a large sample of the population or some specific section of the population (if that is more relevant to the particular assessment problem). The spread of scores is then divided up into *percentile ranges*, such as the bottom 10% or, say, the upper quarter. It then becomes possible to compare the score of any individual with the norms and say how far up the scale his score places him. If this is done with all tests, subtests or questionnaires, scores can be compared on a rational basis.

Standard deviation method

The second common method of standardizing scores is in terms of the *standard deviation*. This is a measure of the dispersion of the scores around the average and its calculation is described in all statistical textbooks. If the score of an individual is divided by the standard deviation of the scores of a large sample of testees, it is standardized and can then be directly compared with scores on other tests or questionnaires which have been similarly standardized in terms of their standard deviations. A familiar version of this method of standardization is the use of *stanine* or *sten* scores, which are based on the standard deviation and divide up the total range into nine and ten grades respectively. It should be noted that each grade does *not* contain the same percentage of all scores (because scores are not equally frequent throughout the range but are more heavily concentrated near the average). Thus, only $2\frac{1}{2}\%$ of all scores fall in sten 1 (or sten 10), $4\frac{1}{2}\%$ in sten 2 (or sten 9). The two central stens (5 and 6) each include 19% of all scores.

One of the main advantages of the relatively small number of grades is the elimination of the overinterpretation of small differences which was rife when more detailed values were commonly used.

Ipsative method

Another approach that is becoming more common is the method of *ipsative scoring* whereby a person's score on one dimension is compared with his own score on another.

Making allowance for errors

No matter which method of presentation is used, it is necessary to remember that, in the measurement of human behaviour attributes, there is always an error of measurement to consider. As the instrument that is used cannot be perfectly reliable (all possible questions could not be included) and the individuals being assessed are not static organisms, a degree of tolerance must be associated with any particular score.

In the case of ability and aptitude tests the authors usually report the error of measurement in points of raw score. In the case of measures of typical performance the error value is less frequently given. However, the user of any assessment tool must be aware that the score obtained is not fixed and immutable and be cautious in using the information obtained.

Ethical considerations

All psychological testing is governed by ethical considerations. In Australia and the United States the professional bodies have codified the ethical standards expected of users of pscyhological tests. In the UK the same professional standards are expected and all divisions of the British Psychological Society have produced codes of conduct.

It has been suggested that personality assessment is immoral. I do not agree with this, although I recognize that information gained by such assessment could be used to the disadvantage of the person tested.

Some of the criticisms of personality assessment have referred to the creation of adverse social consequences and the violation of personal integrity. Without going into details of the allegations and the specificity of the counter arguments, one can state that extensive and appropriate rebuttals have been made.

One point raised is that individuals reveal themselves in the way they answer questions and that the information may be read by personnel officers or even their secretaries. This overlooks the fact that most of the questionnaires in use have the responses entered on a separate answer sheet. Even if a testing clerk scores the answers the test booklets should not be available to her, nor to a personnel officer unless specifically trained and aware of the ethics involved.

Using the results in personnel work

Psychologists who develop measures of typical performance, as those who develop aptitude and ability tests, provide as much information as they can about the technical aspects of their instruments. The test user encounters more difficulties with the results of measures of personal characteristics than with optimum performance tests, in that it is more difficult to validate the former. To establish the minimum score required on an intelligence test in order to achieve a reasonable chance of success in a particular post is comparatively straightforward. However, to determine whether a certain level of emotional maturity or of tough mindedness is required is more difficult.

In a measure like the 16PF questionnaire the user has to consider sixteen factors, some of which tend to modify each other. For this reason it may be preferable for the less experienced user to start with a measure using fewer factors, such as the Gordon personal inventory or personal profile, or to confine himself to the second-order factors on the 16PF.

Use to determine unsuitability

The most direct way of using the information from a personality measure is as a negative screen. For example, it might be shown that persons scoring low on the conscientiousness factor are unlikely to be successful in a civil service setting; that persons scoring low on emotional maturity are unlikely to stand up well to pressure; that someone with a low score on the independence second-order factor is unlikely to be well placed in a situation where he has to take considerable initiative and make decisions without the support of colleagues or superiors.

It is less easy to show, for example, that a successful salesman must have a particular score on extroversion, because research has now shown that a wide range of personality characteristics can be associated with a sales career. The important modifying variables are the type of product being sold and the nature of the company's business.

Deriving a standard profile

There is a strong demand from personnel officers, or their managing directors, not just for some salient personal characteristics but for a profile involving all of the traits assessed by the questionnaire. It is possible to test, say,. one hundred systems analysts and obtain an average score on each variable and so construct a profile. However, when the variation around the average value is considered (usually of the order of plus or minus two or more points on a ten-point scale) it becomes clear that the profile cannot be used in a simple fashion such as appointing only those whose profile matches the standard one. Cattell has provided an index of profile matching which over the whole set of dimensions indicates the degree of discrepancy. However, even this does not indicate whether the discrepancy is found mainly on a few variables or on all.

Even though successful employees may vary around the average established for a particular occupation, there is still real value to be obtained from deriving a profile for the occupation in a firm. Such a profile provides information about the traits which are high and those which are low in that company. Departure from these by more than a standard deviation would then be of significance.

Establishing prediction equations for each location

Another way of using the personality information is to establish a prediction equation. This requires the user to have tested an adequate number of individuals in a particular occupational category and to obtain performance assessments for them. By means of appropriate statistical techniques it is possible to determine which variables are most important and what weight should be assigned to each.

The author of the 16 PF provides such an equation for certain occupational categories. While this gives a good general guide, it is desirable for it to be checked out in each company. The need was demonstrated in a UK study of systems analysts. Two establishments of the same organization using the 16 PF, one near London and the other in the North, were studied. The factors which were most associated with success in the London location were different from those associated with success in the North, even though the tasks carried out were similar. A suggested reason for the difference was the pressure placed on the group nearer to headquarters.

The implication is very clearly that each firm must develop its own prediction equations. This should not be confined only to personality information because the contribution of aptitude and ability data in association with motivational data will almost certainly yield the best information.

Systematic description

The results of a comprehensive personality questionnaire which obtains information on a number of dimensions provide a more systematic description of an individual than can be obtained by most interviewers. Descriptions of several persons being considered for one position enable the selection or promotion committee to make more meaningful comparisons.

Checking the usefulness of personality assessments

In any validation situation two factors are involved: the scores, and the criteria against which they are being evaluated. The validation process assesses the degree of association between prediction and performance. The checking of psychological information seeks to establish the strength of the contribution being made and not whether there is some absolute truth or perfection that might be achieved.

Choosing the relevant criteria

Deciding which criteria are relevant for validating personality assessments is crucial. It is not likely that personality information will predict production performance; it is more likely to predict production consistency, which is, in part, likely to be a function of motivation or attitude. Personality information has been shown to predict turnover and job level achieved. The latter is possibly an outcome of ambition and this in turn is a function of personal motivation or perhaps of vocational interests. Interests have been shown to relate to job satisfaction, while accident rates have been shown to correlate with assertiveness and speed of decision.

Provided that what is being predicted is some form of behaviour that is influenced by attitudes, motives or general preferences for doing things in certain ways, there is some chance that personality, value or interests measures will succeed. As Guion says: 'They should not be damned for failure to predict other kinds of criteria'.

Dangers of 'faith' validity

Clearly, the main problem is to obtain appropriate criterion measures. However, there is much evidence that personnel managers in search of measures of motivational variables tend to ignore the need for evidence of this kind and place reliance on what is known as 'faith' validity. This obtains when the personnel manager takes a 'test' and considers that it has predicted his own personality perfectly. On this evidence he then decrees that this device is the answer to the company's problems.

The unreliability of this approach has been demonstrated by Stagner who convinced a number of personnel managers that a personality questionnaire had described their personalities well. All had been given the same generalized description—and the tests had not even been scored. Stagner warns that:

> The personnel manager should avoid being seduced by the flattering report on his own fine qualities into purchasing a test which is worthless when evaluated scientifically.

Limitation of current employee criteria

Testing present employees and correlating results with present performance is a commonly used short cut. It is reasonably effective with tests of ability and aptitude but less so with interests and personality, because these aspects of a person are more liable to change in specific circumstances. Moreover, there is always the problem that present employees may not approach the testing situation in the same way as applicants do. It appears that responses to personality and interest measures are most subject to variation; consequently any findings from a concurrent study should be taken as broad guides only. The aim should always be for predictive validity.

When validating personality measures, each should be checked against several criteria. It has been shown that sometimes a measure is positively correlated with one criterion but negatively with another. For example, in a study of the selection of engineers using measures of interest, it was found that high scores were related to staying in the job, while low scores were associated with high output.

The statistical properties of the distribution of the scores may be very important. Therefore, in addition to looking at averages, the degree of variability and the amount of skewness should be considered.

Sometimes it may be important to include in the validation study, as well as the personality measures, certain organizational variables, such as type of management, size of department and the like, to see whether they are moderating the relationship between the predictor information and the criterion.

When deciding whether to introduce personality measures into the personnel function (selection or career development) it is quite a sound procedure to include the chosen measure for a year or even two without using the information in the decision-making process. When criterion data become available, the check can be made and knowledge gained of the probable improvement had the information been used.

Hazards of untrained testing

In concluding this section it is not the intention to suggest that personality testing should not be introduced. It is necessary, however, to restate that this aspect of psychological measurement is more hazardous than others. The issues have been summed up by Guion:

> Clearly, if personality testing is to be done without danger to the organization doing the testing, or to the people tested, the preliminary research must explore many avenues. It must be thoroughly and competently done. It is no job for the untrained do-it-yourself amateur.

It follows that anyone considering introducing personality tests or questionnaires needs expert advice, which is available in the UK, from certain organizations and from qualified psychologists with specific experience in this field.

The supply of personality tests and questionnaires, as explained at the end of Chapter 8, is principally in the hands of the National Foundation for Educational Research.

Further reading

Anastasi, A. (1976): *Psychological Testing.* 4th edition. New York: Macmillan.

Cattell, R. B., Ghiselli, E. E., Baxter, B. and Drenth, P. (1969): *Assessing Personality,* London: Independent Assessment and Research Centre.

Cronbach, L. (1970): *Essentials of Psychological Testing.* New York: Harper & Row.

Fleishman, E. (1969): *Manual for the Leadership Opinion Questionnaire.* Chicago: SRA.

Ghiselli, E. E. (1971): *Explorations in Managerial Talent.* California: Goodyear.

Guion, R. M. (1965): *Personnel Testing.* New York: McGraw-Hill.

Rokeach, M. (1973): *The Nature of Human Values.* New York: Free Press.

11

Testing Trade Skills

Gilbert Jessup

There is sometimes a requirement to assess whether a candidate possesses certain skills or knowledge on entry to a job as distinct from whether he has the potential or personality to succeed. For example, a requirement for a secretarial job might be shorthand and typing at certain speeds. Trade tests are also commonly employed at the end of an introductory training course to determine whether trainees have acquired the required standard. Some readers may have had little first-hand experience of trade tests of this type. Nevertheless, they will probably be familiar with the standard driving test which provides an example of the assessment of skilled performance.

Considerable confusion exists between the objectives of intelligence and aptitude tests on the one hand and measures of achievement, knowledge and skill on the other. Educational examinations of the kind taken at school and university form a third category of cognitive tests. Understanding how these measures differ will help to get trade testing into perspective.

Nature of tests and examinations

An intelligence test is designed to measure a person's basic capacity to process information, that is to reason and to learn. It is in theory unrelated to the specific knowledge a person has acquired. Assessments of intelligence are often used in selection for jobs, both because the more intelligent person is likely to be successful in learning the job and also because he is more likely to be able to cope with new problems and adjust to new situations. A person's level of intelligence sets rough limits to his level of achievement, particularly in intellectual pursuits. Intelligence tests in practice often assume a certain low level of knowledge in the numerical and verbal domains. Nevertheless, an analysis of the operations required to solve intelligence test items normally reveals the processes of inductive and deductive reasoning in a fairly pure form. Special aptitudes are in the same class as intelligence, which may be thought of as a general aptitude. Aptitude tests measure potential in specific areas. Examples are numerical aptitude (the ability to process numerical information), mechanical aptitude and musical aptitude.

Achievement tests or tests of proficiency measure knowledge and/or acquired skills. They are often set at the end of training to assess whether a man has acquired the knowledge and skills taught on the course. Ideally, of course, the test would measure the knowledge and skills required to perform the job for which a man is being trained. The techniques for assessing knowledge acquired are different from those for assessing practical skills.

Difference between eduction and training

Educational examinations such as the General Certificate of Education ('O' and 'A' level) and university degrees are primarily tests of achievement. But they differ from trade tests in that they attempt to measure something far less specific. A trade test rates performance in relation to a certain range of tasks (such as those involved in carpentry) or a particular task (such as driving) but an examination such as GCE 'O' level history is set without any job in mind.

This brings out the basic difference between education and training. Training is job related while education is the pursuit of knowledge for its own sake or at least with no clear objective in mind. The distinction has implications in the form each type of test takes.

In educational examinations the candidate typically has a good deal of choice in the questions he answers. This suggests that it does not matter what the candidate knows so long as he knows some part of the subject examined and can answer a few questions in depth. It is possible to get through such examinations, having skipped vast chunks of the syllabus, with a little luck and a fair knowledge of the remaining areas.

In a typical trade test no choice of questions is allowed; all questions must be answered or all tasks attempted. In the driving test, for example, the candidate does not have a choice between demonstrating clutch control or steering. Both are clearly essential aspects of driving a car and the candidate must demonstrate competence in both these skills plus many others.

A further difference between education and trade examinations is in the manner in which the questions are posed. Whereas the questions in trade examinations are normally quite straightforward, in educational examinations they often attempt to elicit information in a novel way. One example is the sort of question where the examinee is asked to compare and contrast two areas of knowledge which he may never have thought of in relation to one another before. By posing questions in an oblique way, educational examinations measure intelligence and possibly some specific exam-taking skills in addition to the subject matter of the examination.

Methods of job analysis

Before a trade test or a course of trade training can be devised, an analysis of the job or trade is required. This may seem obvious but carrying out a systematic analysis of the job to find out what men actually do would come as a novel idea to many firms in the United Kingdom, even today. The main aim of the job analysis is to answer the following questions:

1 What are the component tasks that make up the total job or trade?
2 How frequently is the tradesman required to perform each task?
3 How difficult is each task to perform?
4 How critical is it that the task is performed correctly? In other words, what is the cost of an error or substandard performance?

Job analysis can be performed at many different levels, from the detailing of each minute activity (lifting hammer, banging head of nail) or each mental process (discriminating between different screws to select one of the appropriate size) to major elements of the job (constructing a bookcase). The following example illustrates the way in which a job may be divided into four hierarchical levels:

1 The trade, such as motor mechanic.
2 Tasks or duties, such as wheel changing, engine overhauls, diagnosis of faults.
3 Task elements, such as removing the hub cap, loosening the wheel nuts, using jack to raise the vehicle.
4 Cues and responses, which is probably the lowest level into which the job can be conveniently divided. In the wheel-changing example, the feel of a tightened nut is the cue, and the mechanic's response is to cease tightening the nut.

Figure 11.1 shows how a job can be divided into these four levels. Each task divides into a number of task elements, and each of these is in turn divided into a series of cues and responses. The diagram shows only a few completed items for the purpose of illustration.

Where facilities are available it is worth performing a detailed analysis down to level three or four. Level four is more relevant to the determination of training techniques than to trade testing. An analysis of the job requirements is essential to training as well as trade testing. It is also valuable in the organization of work. A job analysis often reveals that certain tasks which are being carried out by one group of tradesmen could be more effectively performed by others. Job analysis is also being used in determining wage rates.

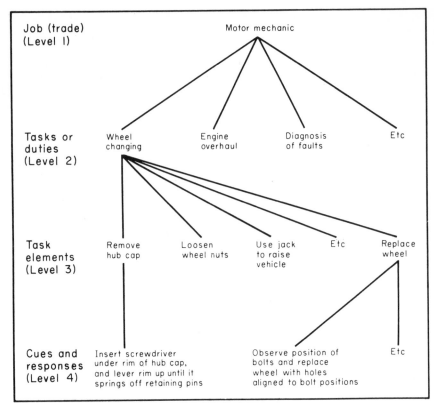

Figure 11.1   Division of job into four hierarchical levels

Determining the difficulties of a task

Job analysis must normally be performed by observing men actually carrying out the task and by interviewing them to obtain information on difficulty, frequency and so on. This should be supplemented by interviews with supervisors and managers, particularly to determine difficulty and criticality of tasks. Interviews with supervisors and managers alone are never sufficient. A good deal of expertise is now available on techniques of job analysis and some relevant references are given at the end of the chapter.

Apart from asking tradesmen, the difficulty of a task can be assessed by such indices as the variability of performance on the task. If some men are able to perform a task much more quickly than others or to a much higher standard than others it suggests that the task is difficult. The difficult tasks can be expected to sort out the more able workers from the less competent. Easier tasks may be well within the scope of all workers. A large number of errors in any particular task indicates, of course, that tradesmen find that task difficult. The number of times men seek assistance from supervisors is another possible index of difficulty.

Selecting the tasks for testing

It is clear from the range of tasks which make up a job such as that of motor mechanic that it would not be feasible to examine a man, in a formal test situation, on all the tasks which make up the job. Only a sample of the tasks and knowledge required for the job can be included in the test and often this is but a small fraction of the total trade. It therefore becomes particularly important how the elements of the test are selected. For this reason the test should concentrate on tasks which are difficult and occur frequently in the tradesman's job. It must also include critical tasks where mistakes could be dangerous or costly. Tasks which are easy, whether frequent or not, are less important because most men can perform these tasks or at least learn them quickly on the job.

The difficult but infrequent tasks pose a problem. It might be argued that it is particularly important that these tasks are mastered in that the tradesman will not have much opportunity to practise them on the job. This would certainly be true if the tasks were critical in the above sense. Where tradesmen work together in groups it might be argued that it is uneconomic to train and test all the men on a difficult task when one man, perhaps the supervisor, could cope with the task each time it came up. It could then be left out of the job requirements of the other tradesmen. If tradesmen are likely to work alone then the difficult infrequent tasks should certainly be included in the trade test.

Having limited the field to the categories of task suggested above, it is usually still necessary to select a sample of these tasks for any one test. The sample should, as far as possible, be representative of the total trade. It should consist of a heterogeneous group of tasks calling upon as widely differing skills as exist in the trade. There is of course the further consideration that some tasks lend themselves much more readily to the test situation than others. Those which are relatively short and capable of being objectively scored are obvious choices. But they must be important tasks within the job.

Validity of the chosen test

If we are to adopt a scientific approach to trade assessments we must look upon the trade test as a measuring instrument. As with other measuring instruments it must conform to certain technical requirements. One is that it should be reliable. That is to say, repeated measures of the same characteristic of a person (such as height, weight, trade knowledge) must produce the same reading or score. If different testers examine the same characteristic they should also obtain the same reading of score. Reliability is, in fact, never perfect but close agreement between testers or the same tester at different times should be expected.

Reliability can be expressed statistically in terms of the correlation between scores obtained on different occasions or awarded by different markers. While most physical measuring instruments have almost perfect reliability, properly designed trade tests would normally fall in the 80 to 90% reliability range.

High reliability indicates that the test is an accurate measuring instrument. It does not indicate whether the relevant characteristics are being measured. The relevance of the measured characteristics determines the validity of the test. Trade tests are normally designed to assess whether people are capable of performing a job. In this instance the validity of the test could be determined by comparing test scores with some later measure of job performance. This index could also be expressed as a correlation coefficient. Validity, like reliability, is a matter of degree. The validity of a test cannot be assumed. Experience shows that a set of seemingly relevant questions often does not predict future job behaviour very accurately.

The validity of a test is ultimately the only thing that matters. Other characteristics are important only inasmuch as they contribute to high validity.

Forms of trade test

Trade examinations can take the form of a paper and pencil test or a practical test, or both. The term 'practical' is used rather loosely to include any manipulative exercise. In general, knowledge can be adequately measured in a paper and pencil test while the assessment of the acquisition of skills requires demonstration, which normally means a practical test. The performance of a skill usually involves some motor activity of the body (such as typing, driving, bricklaying) but the word is also used to cover other behaviours such as managerial skills, social skills, or verbal skills, where situations rather than things are handled. Certain skills, such as some verbal and clerical skills, can be measured in a paper and pencil test.

Paper and pencil tests

The rather cumbersome term 'paper and pencil' is used rather than 'written tests' because the more effective forms of paper and pencil test are those using objective type questions where no writing is required. By far the most popular form of objectively scorable question is the multiple choice, which might take the following form:

To temper a screwdriver blade, heat until it is:
1 Blue.
2 Straw.
3 Dull red.
4 Silver.

One of the main advantages of this type of item is that it can be marked simply and accurately. Similar questions requiring a written answer often produce answers which cannot be marked unambiguously right or wrong. One examiner might mark an answer right while a second might mark the same answer wrong. This clearly reduces the reliability of the test.

Design and use of multiple-choice questions

Considerable skill and ingenuity is required in designing effective multiple-choice items. Unless particular care is taken it is very easy to provide candidates with clues to the correct answer. It is important to ensure that the distractors (the answers other than the correct one) are plausible answers to the questions. They should be the more common wrong answers that candidates would give if the question had been posed as an open question. All answers to a question should be similar in form (length, part of speech and so on). The position of the correct answer should vary at random from question to question throughout a multiple-choice test. There are many rules for designing multiple-choice items which are dealt with in detail in references at the end of the chapter[1,2].

Where circumstances permit, questions should be tried out on a sample of tradesmen before they are used in a trade test. The results of the trial can be analysed to check the difficulty of each item, whether it discriminates between tradesmen (do the capable people tend to get it right while the less competent get it wrong?) and also whether all the distractors are attracting a significant proportion of the candidates. A great deal can be learned from the experimental trial of items. Following the trial, poor items can be dropped or improved before the final test is put together. If items are reused in future examinations the experience gained in one examination can be used to improve future tests. The design and statistical analysis of multiple-choice items has reached a high degree of technical sophistication.

Multiple-choice tests are used extensively in the United States throughout the educational system as well as in trade examinations. Their use in the UK in education is limited but they are used by some organizations for trade-testing purposes. Probably the best example of their use in a large-scale trade testing system is in the forces as described by Jessup, Knight and Laslett[2]. Multiple-choice tests are most effectively employed in large-scale examination systems.

Another characteristic of multiple-choice questions is that they are short and can be answered quickly. This means that a relatively large number of questions can be used in an examination of an hour or so. It is thus possible to sample quite effectively from a wide range of knowledge. This is another way in which multiple-choice tests have the advantage over traditional essay examinations.

One criticism often levelled at the multiple-choice form of question is that it is possible to get the correct answer by guessing. This is of course true but the overall chance element in a test made up of a large number of questions is small. The good luck and bad luck cancel each other out. The chance element inflates the scores of all candidates somewhat and their relative positions in the order of merit are only slightly affected.

The multiple-choice form of question is not limited to the measurement of factual material. With some ingenuity it is possible to pose quite complex problems. It is possible to assess a candidate's comprehension and whether he can apply what he knows to solving a problem. For example, the following item tests the ability to apply Ohm's law:

The current through a resistor of 8 ohms when the potential difference across it is 20 volts is:

1   160 amperes.
2   0.4 amperes.
3   28 amperes.
4   2.5 amperes.

It is also possible to pose problems which require the analysis and synthesis of information or the evaluation of propositions in multiple-choice form. For examples of such items see Vernon[3].

There are other objective type question forms but they are mainly variants of the multiple-choice item. One is the question requiring an endorsement of true or false. This is in effect a multiple-choice item with two alternative answers. Matching questions are another more complex variant of the multiple-choice form. For example, a problem might be to match a list of capital towns against a list of countries, or colours against their resistor values in resistor colour code. These question forms may be particularly appropriate to certain types of material but overall they are of limited value in trade testing.

Forms of open-ended questions

Open-ended questions can be used effectively in trade tests provided the questions can be structured to produce answers that are unambiguously right or wrong. This restriction normally limits open-ended questions to those requiring an answer in the form of a numeral or one or two words. Numerical problems are an obvious example. A marking schedule showing which answers are acceptable and which are not should be drawn up at the same time as the question is constructed.

The problems of producing an entirely objective marking scheme for open-ended questions is greater than at first seems apparent. Questions are often interpreted in ways which had not been considered by the examiner. The skill in writing short answer items, when the question to be asked has been decided, is in anticipating all the possible ways in which the item might be construed. Then the unintended, but nevertheless correct answers that may be produced can be anticipated. Finally, the question can be restated or qualified in order to eliminate such answers.

For example the initial question may be: State Ohm's law. This would involve a very complex marking schedule because the law could be produced as a verbal statement in a variety of ways, the formula could be supplied in words: $current = \dfrac{voltage}{resistance}$, or symbols: $V = IR$, with various permutations.

The question could be improved if it were asked in the form: State the formula for Ohm's law. The easiest to mark would be: Ohm's law states that $... \times Resistance = ...$

This last form of question does not measure precisely the same thing as the first but it may measure knowledge which is equally useful.

To decide whether the final form of the question is acceptable the examiner should ask himself why he is asking the question at all. In what circumstances is the candidate likely to require the knowledge? In what form will he be required to use the knowledge? This should help to decide whether the item meets its intended purpose.

Open-ended questions should be short and a test should incorporate a large number of questions to provide an adequate sample to represent the trade requirements. Open-ended questions have the advantage over multiple-choice of being a more natural form of question and the element of luck in obtaining the correct answer is removed. On the other hand the restrictions necessary to provide reliable marking make them less versatile than multiple-choice questions.

Unreliability of essay questions

Essay questions or questions requiring long written answers are still quite commonly used in trade tests but their use is seldom justified. The marks produced by such tests tend to be of low reliability, as is demonstrated by the fact that different examiners often allot widely varying marks to the same answer. Apart from the question of reliability, they tend to be of low validity because the form of question places too much weight on verbal skills which are possibly quite irrelevant to the trade. Also, essay examinations typically consist of a few long questions which do not adequately represent the subject matter.

It may be argued that the essay is the only form of question in which the candidate has the opportunity to express his ideas and demonstrate originality or creativity. This may be so but there is seldom a requirement for such measures in trade tests and it is very doubtful whether an examiner can mark an essay on the basis of its originality or creativity. If, despite these considerations, essay questions are used, their effectiveness can be somewhat improved by structuring the questions to make clear what form the answer should take. This suggestion follows the principle discussed above of reducing the ambiguity of the question in order to limit the range of acceptable answers.

Practical tests

It is difficult to generalize on the setting of practical examinations. Certain skills, such as typing and Morse transmission, can be assessed in terms of speed and accuracy over a standard passage. But in most trades the skills are more varied and less well defined. This is first a problem for job analysis as discussed earlier. There is also the problem of sampling the skills for examination in trades with a wide variety of skills.

It may be artificial to perform the task under test conditions outside the normal work setting, as is clearly the case with certain managerial and social skills. In fact, practical tests are commonly so artificial that it becomes difficult for the examiner to attach much importance to them. In addition, the criterion of successful performance in many tasks is a subjective assessment (as, for example, in cooking) which reduces the reliability of the marks awarded for the test.

An attempt to produce a rating of performance for the practical exercise of frying an egg is shown below as an illustration. Eight relevant dimensions of a well-cooked egg are each rated on a three-point scale.

Rating scale for eggs (fried)			
1	2	3	Score
Appearance of white			
1 dull		soft lustre	1 ...
2 spread out and irregular		thick with rounded outline	2 ...
3 greasy		no excess fat	3 ...
Appearance of yolk			
4 broken		whole	4 ...
5 not coated with white		coated with white	5 ...

Consistency of white			
	6 watery or very solid	uniformly coagulated	6 ...
Tenderness of white			
	7 leathery or crisp and hard	tender	7 ...
Taste and flavour			
	8 stale, flat, salty, or unpleasant fat flavour	fresh, well seasoned	8 ...
		Total score ...	

The tasks selected for a practical test should be primarily the more difficult and frequently occurring tasks. They must also be relatively quick to perform, convenient to administer and scorable. Standardization of the procedure is essential, as in all tests, and presents particular difficulties in practical tests. The test instructions, the equipment, the timing and the system of marking must all be specified in advance and rigidly adhered to. Practical tests require close supervision and often individual supervision as in the driving test. They often require a good deal of preparation of equipment prior to each administration. For these reasons they are costly and must be kept short.

Another problem experienced in practical tests is that it is administratively difficult to produce a series of tests consisting of different samples of tasks of equal difficulty. As a result practical tests tend to be the same for examinations occurring over a period of years. The candidate thus has a good idea of the skills which are going to be tested and preparation for the test naturally concentrates on those to the exclusion of others. This tends to invalidate the testing procedure unless the practical test is comprehensive and includes all the important skills of the trade.

The driving test is an example of a practical test which covers most of the basic skills in driving in the space of thirty minutes. Driving instruction is based almost entirely on preparing pupils for the test. Certain skills, like parking the car in a small space and handling a skid, which are not part of the test, are almost entirely neglected in training.

The assessment of performance in the driving test is largely subjective but agreement between examiners on whether a person has passed or failed would probably be quite high. A second and perhaps more important source of unreliability is the variability in human performance from one day to another. In addition, owing to nervousness, performance in the test situation may be unrepresentative of normal performance.

An example of a task with similarities to that of driving a car is operating a fork-lift truck. The construction of a practical test for fork-lift truck operators which aims at objectivity is presented in Hurley, Jackson and Rodger[4]. Part of the test consists of driving the truck down an aisle only 12 inches wider than the truck without touching the sides, halting within 6 inches of a point, picking up a load with no more than 2 inches in 2 feet sideways tilt and so on. An error does not necessarily result in failure but a candidate is required to operate successfully within the tolerance limits stated, nine times out of ten, on most elements of the task. This practical test was, of course, based upon a detailed job analysis.

In order to provide adequate coverage of the knowledge and skills required, a trade examination should generally include both a practical and a paper and pencil test. The paper and pencil test should examine required knowledge, particularly the application of knowledge, while the practical test should examine the relevant skills.

References

1 Dorothy C. Adkins Wood, *Test Construction: Development and Interpretation of Achievement Tests*, Charles E. Merrill Books Inc, Columbus, Ohio, 1961.

2 Gilbert Jessup, M. A. G. Knight and R. E. Laslett, *A Manual of Trade Proficiency Testing (Royal Air Force)*, Ministry of Defence, London, 1970.

3 P. E. Vernon, *The Certificate of Secondary Education: An Introduction to Objective Type Examinations*, Secondary Schools Examinations Council, HMSO, London, 1964.

4 P. Hurley, P. Jackson and A. Rodger, *Selection and Training of Fork Truck Drivers*, British Industrial Truck Association, 1968.

Further reading

Bloom, B.S. (Ed.) (1956): *Taxonomy of Educational Objectives, Handbook I: The Cognitive Domain*. New York: Mackay.

Ebel, R. L. (1965): *Measuring Educational Achievement*. New York: Prentice Hall.

Rust, W. Bonney (1973): *Objective Testing in Education and Training*. Pitman Education Library, London: Pitman.

Singha, H. S. (1974): *Modern Educational Testing*. New Delhi: Sterling Publishers PVT Ltd.

Thyne, J. M. (1974): *Principles of Examining*. London: University of London Press.

Tyler, L. E. (1973): *Tests and Measurements*. 2nd edition. London: The Open University Press, Prentice Hall.

12

Using Interviews
in Personnel Selection

Alec Rodger

The selection interviewer's first task is to appreciate the demands of the jobs he has on offer. His second is to sum up his applicants. His third is to reach conclusions on how well the applicants 'match' the jobs. It makes no difference whether he is operating solo or as a member of a team: these three tasks are inescapable. He can tackle the first two by finding and filling gaps in the information he already possesses about the jobs and about the applicants. His job information is not likely to be as up-to-date as he would like, especially when he reflects on such changeable factors as the state of the labour market and the introduction of new work processes and equipments. His information about the applicants is almost certain to be inadequate, even though they may all have coped with application forms, and perhaps with tests and questionnaires of some of the kinds dealt with in earlier chapters. This chapter is primarily about the use of interviewing in assessing job demands and in assessing applicants. However, it is concerned also with the matching to which these assessments lead, and indeed with which they interact in ping-pong fashion. Such distinctions can help us to think straight, if they are used sensibly. In fact, the selection interviewer must be ready to seize on possibly relevant information, about jobs and people and matches between them, whenever and wherever he spots it.

Appreciating the demands of jobs

In the previous edition of this handbook, this chapter ended with a short account of an incident which, some have suggested, deserved fuller treatment. It concerned a selection panel, of which the author was one of three members, set up to interview six applicants for a temporary psychological appointment in a certain government department. The programme said we would have thirty minutes in which to interview each applicant and make up our minds about him. The chairman arrived fifteen minutes late, at 2.15, full of apologies about his lunch having been delayed by a long morning meeting. With further apologies, he explained that an unexpected meeting, later in the day, would make it necessary for him to be away by 4.30. We would therefore have to hurry, he said, as he pressed the bell-button on the baize-covered table.

The first applicant he greeted by the wrong name, so there were more apologies. Having found the right application form, he did what many unprepared chairmen do. Despite the fact that his two colleagues on the panel had photocopies of the document, he spent half the available time, now reduced to twenty minutes, reading out the man's date of birth, place of birth, family particulars, schools attended, GCE results and university record. The applicant said 'yes' at each point, and his anwers were pronounced 'good'. The chairman then remarked that, as time was short, he wondered whether there were any really urgent questions the applicant himself would like to ask, adding that so far his answers had been so clear that perhaps his own colleagues on the panel would not wish to pursue any of them. The applicant, as it turned out, did have some questions to ask. The first was, 'Sir, what exactly *is* this job?' The chairman held up a closely-printed two-page handout. 'Did you not have a copy of this sent to you with the application form?' 'Yes, Sir, and I read it very carefully. It told me a lot about the conditions of employment, the pay, the hours and so on; but it said nothing about what I would actually have to *do*.' The chairman shrugged his shoulders a little. He was afraid he could not answer that question himself. 'I am only from the Establishments Branch.' However, he added, Mr X, his colleague on his left, to whom the successful applicant would be responsible, would no doubt be glad to tell him — briefly, of course — what he wanted to know. Mr X quickly reminded the chairman that he himself had been 'in post' only two weeks: he had not yet got round to finding out what his psychologists did. Then perhaps Professor Rodger could help, suggested the chairman. Professor Rodger, who had had some of the Department's psychologists as postgraduate students, did what he could in the three minutes left. As the door closed on the young man, his potential boss said, testily, 'He'll find out soon enough what he has to do.' Alas, he did not find out. Though he was judged the 'best' of the six applicants seen that afternoon, he declined the appointment when it was offered to him.

Let us forget the discourtesy with which the interview was handled. The chief fault in it was the failure of the 'inside' members of the panel to recognise that a selection interview is not merely an occasion for passing judgment on an applicant. It should be used thoughtfully to feed him with job information which will help him to play his part in the decision-making process. Many other interviewers have failed, and continue to fail, in the same way. It is not simply that they do not know enough about the jobs they are selecting people for: often they think their ignorance does not matter.

The main remedy for stupidity of this sort lies in the training of selection interviewers to build up their own 'pictures' of what happens from day to day in the jobs with which they are dealing. In many organizations job descriptions (whether they go by that name or some other) are available and should be used. But they are rarely enough as they stand. They need to have flesh put on them by being related to real people. More important still, the pictures of a job an interviewer puts together, in a kind of 'episodic film-strip' in his mind's eye, must be selective. They should represent what have been called 'crucial activities and situations', highlighting the pitfalls, stumbling-blocks and hazards commonly encountered in the job. If this sounds a rather negative approach to picture-building, let us remind ourselves that modern preventive and curative medicine has its main foundation in pathology, the study of disease. A vivid example may relieve the hint of gloom.

Acting in an advisory capacity to the managing director of a national daily newspaper company, the present writer found a ready response to his suggestion that an urgently-needed survey of managerial jobs in the company should be tackled from this standpoint. A trial run was agreed. It turned out that the head printer of the paper was due to retire soon, but that no one had yet been appointed to succeed him, because it had been assumed that a replacement could quickly be found among the head printers of various weekly and monthly magazines published by the group. The retiring head printer proved willing to be questioned closely about his job, in the presence of his managing director, a man who had spent most of his life 'in the print', not only as a journalist and editor but also, recently, as 'director of production and personnel'. (This very unusual title sprang from the belief that if, in a strike-prone industry, you can find somebody with hands big enough and strong enough to look after both production and personnel, let him get on with it.)

The description of the head printer's job in the company's file was made available to the interviewer. The single sheet of paper on which it was typed was obviously as clean and unsullied as it had been on the day it was put into the filing-cabinet, which according to the date at the foot of it had been four years earlier. That was perhaps the fate it deserved. Like many good conventional job descriptions it was concise, clear, and up to a point comprehensive. But it said not a word about the pitfalls, stumbling-blocks and hazards of the job, its 'crucial activities and situations'. The interviewer kept it beside him during the subsequent discussion, sharing it with the head printer, who had helped in the original drafting of the statement.

At an early stage a question was asked which led quickly to highly relevant disclosures. 'What do you think you will be most glad to get away from, Mr Y, when you retire at the end of December?' Mr Y paused and smiled. 'Two lots of people, the journalists and my compositors.' Invited to say more, he began with the journalists and expressed firmly the view that these so-and-sos had no sense of urgency. They all had instructions about the delivery of 'copy' to the head printer's desk. Certain kinds were expected by 6pm, other kinds by 6.30, 7, 7.30, 8, 8.30, but nothing — repeat, nothing — after 9, unless there was a risk of another paper scooping a big story. But night after night stuff came in 2 or 3 hours late; and, as much of it had to be vetted by the legal department to check that it was not actionable, every night was like a bad dream. Suddenly Mr Y stopped, aware that his managing director and his interviewer were both listening intently. Then he said quietly but almost fiercely, 'You can imagine what this has meant to me, professor, when I tell you that in the seventeen years I have been head printer on this daily paper, these so-and-sos have been up to time on two nights.' He repeated the 'two nights' with colourful emphasis.

At this point the interviewer picked up the job description. Pausing momentarily for effect, he read out the solitary item which dealt with the head printer's relations with the journalists. All it said was: 'To liaise with the editorial department.' There was not the slightest hint of any 'crucial' activity or situation.

'And what about the others, your compositors?' The head printer, with a gesture of helplessness, explained that they had him in the hollow of their hands. For reasons widely accepted at that time in the field of tabloid journalism, they were paid partly on a sort of piece-rate basis. As soon as a compositor had done a page, he took it up to the head printer, who had to give him a price for it. This was a regular exercise every night, six nights a week, and every time it could be crucial. Both were well aware that, if the price did not seem fair to the compositor, tomorrow's paper might not appear at all. Everyone in the place knew that the vans were lined up in the basement, waiting to take the night's output to the trains and the planes. They knew, too, that the trains and planes would not wait while 'an industrial dispute' was being settled.

Again the interviewer consulted the job description. He read out the single item which covered the head printer's relations with his compositors. It said: 'To supervise the work of the compositors.' Still there was no hint of nightly agonies. Like the previous declaration about his relations with the journalists, it was concise; it was, in a way, clear; and it was, in a way, comprehensive. But neither of them contributed anything to the planning of the recruitment, selection or training of a head printer of a daily paper with a massive circulation; nor did either give any leads in the matter of reviewing his methods of work or its organization. As for any contribution they might make to the evaluation of the job (that is, in estimating its worth to the company), there was, we might say, 'nothing to report'. Nowhere is the study of crucial activities and situations more needed than in job evaluation, and it is to the credit of specialists in this field that they are among the few who accept the fact. Whether they stick to conventional schemes and base their findings on the demands a job makes on 'skill, effort, responsibility, and the toleration of danger and dirt', or adopt a more sophisticated system of the 'know-how, problem-solving and accountability' kind, they are the people who make the best use of the approach to the study of jobs outlined and advocated in this chapter. It is applicable to the study of jobs for *all* the usual purposes — guidance, selection, training and development, methods and organization of work, equipment design, and the arrangement of working conditions and rewards.

The story has two tail-pieces. The first is that the managing director said later that he would have to think again about his hope of replacing Mr Y quickly from the pool of head printers of his company's weekly and monthly periodicals. Though they all had the same job-title, and though their jobs might be describable in the same general terms, it now seemed clear that their appropriate skills and attitudes, judged by the crucial activities and situations involved in each of their jobs, might vary considerably. Secondly, as an example of a crucial element in his own job as managing director, he gave two facts from a memorandum his company had recently submitted to the Royal Commission on the Press. In 1939, the production of a 40-page issue of the daily paper called for the employment of just over 200 men in what is designated 'the publishing room'. In 1964, twenty-five years later, a 40-page issue required the presence of just over 800 men. 'That', he remarked with restraint, 'is what we call overmanning.'

Let us now develop further the idea that selection interviewers should be trained to build up their own supply of 'episodic film-strips' of the jobs they need to know about. They should aim at packing each of them tight with information of the 'crucial activities and situations' sorts. The mental picture of a job put together in this way can be invaluable, as we shall see later, as a backdrop for interviews with applicants. As the picture moves from episode to episode, the interviewer will ask himself, 'Can I see him performing this activity, or coping with that situation?' But whether he puts the question in that way, making a distinction between 'activity' and 'situation' which is often useful but never essential, or sticks to the simpler form, 'Can I see him doing *that?*', there is in fact a more important distinction to be made. The point is that the last question needs two prongs. It has to become: 'Can I see him doing that *well?*' and, separately, 'Can I see him *liking* it?'

Down the centuries, pairs of words have been used to express the distinction adopted here. In our own language, we tend to carry on with contrasts of ability and interest, talent and temperament, aptitude and preference, capacity and inclination, and of course skill and attitude. All these are devices for acknowledging the distinction between being *good* at something and *liking* it. We are not always good at things we like doing; nor are we always keen on things we happen to be good at. Teenagers are often better at seeing the point than adults. 'What do you like most at school?' asked a trainee careers officer. 'English, miss.' 'Oh, you're good at English, are you?' 'I didn't say I was good at it, I said I liked it.' Neglect of the difference is at the root of much faulty guidance and selection. Too frequently is it assumed that, because Bloggs appears to be enthusiastic about something, he will turn out to be good — or good enough — at it. He may; he may not. Disparities between ability and interest in leisure pursuits do not worry most people, but they can lead to disaster when they become occupationally manifest. Adult misfits are commonly people who took up an occupation in which they found, too late, that their abilities were far below the level of their interest.

In tracking down a job's crucial activities and situations, we soon discover that they can be sorted usefully into two separate heaps — those which give rise to *difficulty*, and those which give rise to *distaste*. Activities and situations which many people *find hard to do well* present difficulties which may be overcome by the cultivation of appropriate *skills*. Activities or situations which many people *find irksome* give rise to distastes which may be removed, or at least reduced, by the cultivation of appropriate *attitudes*, especially of tolerance. Of course, difficulties and distastes often go together: indeed, an activity may be distasteful to us just because we find it difficult. But this is not always so. Some difficult tasks we enjoy, so we label them 'challenging'. Some easy tasks we dislike, so we call them disparagingly 'part of the dull routine'. In short, the words 'difficulty' and 'distaste' are not meant to be synonyms, and they should not be used interchangeably. Any job activity or situation in which things tend to go wrong should be looked at from *both* standpoints. It may produce difficulty *or* distaste *or* both.

In gathering insights of these kinds, we must always be eager to have the help of people who have knowledge of the job, through having done it, or taught it, or supervised workers in it; or who have collaborated with others in designing it, or organizing it, or planning or choosing equipment for it, or arranging working conditions or payment for it. The level and type of questions to be asked will clearly depend a great deal on the interviewer and the sophistication and fluency of those he interviews. However, it has been found that even workers in simple assembly and operating jobs can produce useful answers to the two basic questions: Are there some parts of this job that you find more *difficult* than other parts to do really well? (Which are they?) Are there some parts that you *dislike* more than other parts? (And which are they?)

Summing up the applicants

A well-designed application form is, for all jobs except the simplest, the selection interviewer's most desirable springboard. The chapter on application forms provides a wealth of realistic comment on the subject, not least in its plea for margins wide enough for an interviewer's notes. But the form must have been completed properly, if it is to serve the purposes of both the applicant and the interviewer; and many forms are not. How many applicants fail to reach the short-list by their own neglect? In these times of redundancy and unemployment, the need for thought is greater than ever, for the proportion of applicants who never see an interviewer probably grows daily. Some let themselves down through despair. The present writer, helping in the clear-out of old 'personal history forms' in a management agency of which he was a director, studied a large batch of forms sent in by people who had tackled the standard form on at least six occasions; that is, in applying on different occasions for at least six different jobs. In many cases, the deterioration in content and presentation was both clear and sad. The message of the applicants seemed increasingly to be: What's the use? Some firms using standard application forms find that it encourages applicants, and helps those who have to prepare a list of those apparently worth interviewing, if a short supplementary form, manifestly related to the appointment advertised, is provided too. Another firm of consultants, after reviewing its own recruitment procedures, decided to introduce a series of supplementary forms covering each of its main divisions — finance, production, marketing, personnel — and later concluded that it had improved and expedited its short-listing by inviting applicants to make fairly specific claims about their relevant experience, knowledge and skills. The questions in the supplements were based on studies of 'crucial activities and situations' in each kind of consultancy work, and on the 'episodic film-strip' approach outlined earlier.

However, it is clearly not enough that an interviewer, in building up his picture of an applicant, should focus his attention merely on conventional 'particulars' eked out by specific claims to relevant experience, knowledge and skills. He should aim at a fuller and more rounded picture. Various frameworks have been suggested. They are essentially lists of headings under which it has been found useful and convenient to assemble facts and opinions about an individual. The 'seven point plan' produced by the present writer for the now-defunct National Institute of Industrial Psychology is one of them. Munro Fraser's five-fold grading is another. It matters little what plan we use. The important thing is to get into the habit of using *some* plan that encourages comprehensive, clear-headed and methodical summing up. Some years ago a survey of selection procedures carried out by the British Institute of Management indicated that 30% of the member-firms covered in the survey used the NIIP 7PP (as it has been called), whose headings are: physical characteristics; attainments; general intelligence; specialized aptitudes; interests; disposition; and circumstances.

Oldfield, who later became professor of psychology at Oxford, researched for the NIIP on interviewing. He argued that the user of such a framework in assessing others was in effect creating, in his mind's eye, a working-model of a person. As the model gradually took shape through the accumulation of data on the seven points, he could pitch it, in his imagination, into various activities and situations, and guess how it might function. In the study of an applicant, the working-model (Oldfield's *homunculus* or 'little man') has the scene set for it by the episodic film-strip that depicts a series of important features of the job for which application is being made. In short, the working-model and the episodic film-strip provide the selection interviewer with what he needs for the matching process that emerges from their interaction. We shall look at that matching process, and what it entails, in the next part of this chapter. In the meantime let us face some common problems in the mechanics of the selection interview. In doing so, let us hold tenaciously in mind the fact that the purpose of the exercise is to enable the interviewer's gradually-evolving working model of the applicant to 'do its own thing' in his gradually-evolving episodic film-strip of the job under consideration.

Before a selection interview starts, thoughtful preparation is always needed. The receptionist should not have to search for an applicant's name on her list. Her conversation with her colleagues should stop as soon as he arrives. Her manner should be immediately welcoming. The interviewer himself should have studied the application form and made notes in the margins on points to be clarified, especially gaps in the educational or employment record. He should have looked carefully for signs of topics that may need delicate handling, incuding family misfortunes. If the event is to be a board interview, the chairman should indicate the pecking order before the applicant comes in. He should then introduce his colleagues, and himself, by name and function, pausing long enough to give the applicant a chance to nod to them all. If any of the board know they have met the candidate before, the chairman himself should acknowledge the fact at the outset. Each member of the board should make it clear, by his demeanour, that he is ready to listen and learn, with that combination of empathy and detachment that is essential, if justice is to be done and is later felt by the applicant to have been done.

Particularly for the 'occasional' interviewer (a departmental head, for example) and for the interviewer-in-training, there is much to be said for a chronological progression, provided it is not of the truly deplorable kind outlined in the anecdote at the start of this chapter. A step-by-step approach is easier for both inexperienced interviewers and applicants than a series of unrelated questions. Sir Frederic Bartlett, FRS, the first professor of experimental psychology at Cambridge, once defined a skill as 'a smooth, well-timed performance'; and interviewing skill provides a good example of Bartlett's aphorism. It may be that for some purposes catch questions and 'stress' interviews have their uses; but unless our job is to pick 'moles' they are perhaps better left off our list of techniques.

But a smooth, well-timed interview should never be a hurried interview. Pauses are needed by both applicants and interviewers; and perhaps some of the most effective interviewers (not only in the field of personnel selection) are people who know how to pause, and how to glance at an applicant with a slightly-raised eyebrow and a fetching smile. Equally valuable can be verbal but ungrammatical prods of the 'What about marketing?' kind. No less useful are double-prods of the 'Are you more inclined to marketing than to finance, or....?' However, as soon as we get away from the openended simplicity of the single-prod, we run the risk of importing voice modulations which give the question a bias. Even the single-prod, when time pressures operate, can become a dangerous leading question of the common-or-garden sort. 'I don't suppose you'd like marketing?' is bad enough: far worse is 'I don't suppose you'd like marketing, would you?' It takes what used to be called a strong character to reply: 'As a matter of fact, I think I would.' Once that happens, even a normally passable interviewer may slide into a bout of counter-productive argument, and we come near disaster. All it needs then is for the interviewee to show a little 'aggro' by weighing in with a rather vehement, 'But *surely* . . .' or to say, with ill-concealed disagreement, 'But, Sir, with all respect . . .'

These, of course, are all matters of interview technique or style. But inseparable from them are the hazards of risky topics. We touched on two in our remarks on the need to be ready for unexplained gaps or hints for family misfortunes. One of the riskiest is an applicant's background — economic, social, educational, occupational. Information about it may turn out to be important in forming a judgment of ways in which, and the extent to which, an applicant's capacities and inclinations may have developed despite handicaps imposed by adverse circumstances. But the manner of raising the topic can produce trouble. 'What's that got to do with it? *I'm* your candidate, not my father'. The interviewer's mistake on that occasion came not from a badly-worded question but from bad timing. If he had raised the matter in the context of the applicant's declared interest in the job under consideration, and had gently enquired whether any other members of the family had gone in for that kind of thing, the brush might have been avoided. (In the event the situation was saved by the superior interviewing skill of the chairman.)

Nowadays, of course, complications often arise through fears of bias in matters of sex, race and religion. In spite of advances made in recent years against the use of discriminatory practices, they still flourish quietly. The present writer, taking part in a management selection assignment, eventually found himself discussing three possible applicants with the chairman and managing director of the client company. His agreed task had been to submit three names, and so say, in effect, 'We do not think you would go far wrong with any of them, but the choice must be yours, because you are going to work with the man and pay him.' After a pause, the chairman and MD looked at each other, and the former declared, rather glumly, 'Of these three, it would have to be C.' Why, he was asked, would it *have* to be C?. The chairman's reply, offered with some embarrassment, was: 'Let us be quite frank. A is a Jew and B is a Roman Catholic.' 'Why did you not bring these points up at an earlier stage?' 'Well, of course we saw clear signs of them on the application forms. We just hoped these two men would not have to be discussed.'

The chairman and the MD were at least aware of their bias and reluctantly ready to acknowledge it. Greater problems arise in selection, and in careers guidance too, through an interviewer's unrecognized prejudice. The present writer worked full-time for ten years giving careers guidance to the sons of fairly well-to-do parents, many of them in the professions. It was not until he had settled down later as the chief psychologist in one of the defence departments that he realised that not once had he advised a boy to think about becoming an officer in one of the Services. His blinkers fell suddenly when he was consulted by an exceptionally able and rapidly-promoted young regular officer, recently awarded a medal for bravery, who had decided that he was at heart, in spite of it all, a conscientious objector. He wanted advice on civilian jobs he might go for 'when the battle is over and I am able to retire'. Later we agreed that we had both been discovering unsuspected prejudices.

The 'subjectivity' of interview judgements is now widely recognized. There is general acceptance of the view that, if we continue to use interviews (as we must, if we accept their value in giving and discussing job information), we should do our best to give them 'shape', by seeking agreement on what we are looking for in summing-up our applicants; by being methodical in our note-taking (even to the extent of using marginal quotation-marks to distinguish words he actually used from our own observations or comments): and, if we can bear it, by disciplining ourselves by the use of rating-scales.

Matching applicants and jobs

It will be assumed in this section of the chapter that the reader has become familiar with the terms used in it. To the four main ones — episodic film-strip, crucial activities and situations, difficulties and distastes, and working-model —a fifth (the term rating-scale) will now be added. All five have their place in using interviews in personnel selection. The idea of the interview as 'having a talk' is undoubtedly attractive to the fearful, but here we have more serious and more specific purposes in mind; particularly when we consider interviews which may affect a person's plans for the next fifty years of his life. Most of what we are saying now applies not only to selection interviewing but also to careers guidance interviewing, including the sort now often arranged for adults who have reached the condition known crudely as 'redundancy' but who hope that something called 'counselling' will remove some of the unpleasantness. In activity of all these kinds there is a clear need for improvement in the knowledge of jobs and their 'requirements'; and an equally clear need for improvement in the assessment of people who apply for jobs or who seek help in deciding what to apply for. This, of course, is where the need for 'matching' comes in, and where the need for it will increase.

It may seem odd to write about 'rating-scales' in this context. They vary greatly in their complexity, but some of the simplest seem to be the most useful. At the National Institute of Industrial Psychology, applicants for careers guidance were presented with a list of paired adjectives (sociable–solitary; frank–reserved; talkative–quiet; pushful–retiring; confident–anxious; and so on). They were asked to underline the word in each pair which they thought described them best, using two lines for emphasis and putting a question mark between any pair on which they had no firm opinion. The device was intended mainly as a basis for discussion. In what ways are you inclined to be solitary? In what ways would you call yourself pushful? What was in your mind when you underlined 'anxious'? As a short-cut to revealing conversation, it was invaluable. Whether the self-judgments made were fairly accurate could be doubted, although they frequently tallied closely with those of parents and teachers. However, a striking point came up when a large group of 'cases' was 'followed.up' thirty years later by one of the present writer's PhD students. One of the questionnaires they were asked to complete contained several identical pairs of adjectives. The consistency of self-judgment over the thirty years varied, as might be expected, but statistically-sophisticated readers of this chaper may like to know that for the three items deliberate, retiring and impulsive, $p < .001$.

Rating-scales are, of course, most commonly used in recording assessments made of applicants or learners of some kind. A main reason for introducing the topic here is to draw the attention of selectors, advisers and trainers of all sorts to the proved worth of a type of rating-scale which has come to be known as 'paired statements'. Instead of having single words, as in the NIIP self-assessment form, there are pairs of statements, often with the more favourable and less favourable facing each other, with a five-point space in between to enable the assessor to indicate clearly where his preference lies. Extensive use of such forms in the Service led to their adoption after the war by the Civil Service Department and the Ministry of Labour. In the reading list there are mentions of relevant work by Anstey, Cavanagh, and Sneath, White and Randell. The paper by the three last authors is strongly recommended to the attention of trainers.

The adoption by various Civil Service bodies of report-forms of the paired-statements kind is, in the writer's view, an important reason for giving them attention here, not least because they can be of particular value in helping a selector (working alone or as a member of a board) to handle the final 'matching' process satisfactorily. Paired-statement report-forms could be used in obtaining reports from referees, teachers, employers and others, to an extent which has obviously not yet received adequate consideration. They helped the Navy greatly in seeking help from schools; and they could help in a similar way bodies like the Careers Service. Their style and content can be 'made-to-measure'. The flavour of a practical, down-to-earth form can be gained from these extracts from Cavanagh's industrial rehabilitation unit form (bearing in mind that there was provision for five grades between the two blocks of statements:

he is very good with his hands	versus	he is clumsy and awkward
he takes any amount of trouble	v.	his work is a bit slapdash
his work is always well turned out	v.	he has no eye for finish
he grasps instructions quickly	v.	you have to give him very simple instructions
he has plenty of go in him	v.	he is a limp sort of chap
he always finishes his job	v.	he leaves his work half done
he can be relied on to get on by himself	v.	he needs constant supervision
the others took to him quickly	v.	he doesn't fit in easily
he takes a prominent part in things	v.	he hangs back and lets others take the lead
he has a sensible attitude to authority	v.	he is a bit of a troublemaker
he is making good use of his time here	v.	he is not making much headway
Were I an employer, I would be very willing to take him on	v.	Were I an employer, I would prefer not to take him on

In this case, use was made of phrases commonly used by the supervisor in their conversations and at staff conference. Also, space was provided for additional comments anyone wanted to make. The Sneath, White and Randell paper already mentioned provides evidence of some high correlations between workshop assessments and the scores obtained earlier by the men concerned in certain 'aptitude' tests which the Royal Navy allowed the Ministry of Labour to use in its industrial rehabilitation units.

This section of our chapter has stressed the usefulness, in 'matching applicants and jobs', of certain concepts and devices which can help in the matching process, particularly by encouraging selectors (individually and collectively) to agree on what they are trying to do and on how they are trying to do it. But however hard we try, with our episodic film-strip pictures of the jobs we want to fill, and our accumulated knowledge of their difficulties and distastes arising from their crucial activities and situations, and our gradually-improving 'mind's eye' model of each candidate, and the aid we can call in through paired-statements about the people we are dealing with — however hard we try in all these ways, we must recognize that our overall aim is to reduce the errors which will creep into our assessments because of our problem in striving for impartiality and detachment.

Types of interview

Criticism is often levelled at the whole practice of interviewing, as if there were only one type of interview. It is unwise to take a subject out of context in this manner. Nevertheless there are good and bad interviews. Some of the distinguishing characteristics have already been mentioned: time-wasting irrelevance, sometimes defended because it allegedly helps to put the candidate at his ease, is the worst of all features of the bad interview; but a closely allied fault is lack of balance in the topics raised. The interviewer who knows little or nothing about the job for which he is selecting candidates is prone to stick closely to a man's occupational record, but not because he is keeping a lookout for points relevant to the present application.

Selection board or individual

There is the question of whether selection should be by board or individual. It is not easy to offer a generalization. For many purposes an individual interview (or a series of individual interviews) is to be preferred to a board interview. Individual interviews may seem to involve greater expenditure of time and money, and they sometimes do; but they often lead to a more thorough scrutiny of a candidate's capacities and inclinations, and they frequently reduce the problems that arise in planning selection timetables and in keeping to them.

The usefulness of a board interview may depend a good deal on the competence of the chairman, and on the good sense of board members. A promising board interview can easily be ruined by a member who does not appreciate the line of questioning being pursued by one of his fellow-members and who interrupts with irrelevancies.

Doubtful value of the stress interview

What place is there for stress interviews, in which the interviewer speaks or behaves provocatively? If the aim is to simulate conditions in which the candidate, if selected, may later find himself, there may indeed be something in the idea. The American Office of Strategic Services has reported its use of stressful situations of various kinds. This did not give much information about the predictive validity of such interviews but the OSS seemed satisfied with them. No doubt there were advantages from their standpoint but the technique is unlikely to commend itself to young entrants to industry and the public services.

Selector's use of notes

Much has been written and said about the need for friendliness in the interview, about the need for pleasant surroundings and suchlike. Certainly, there should not be unfriendliness or unpleasant surroundings, but these are really minor matters. The chief need is that the interviewer should know what it is he is trying to find out, and should so conduct the interview that he will find it out in a businesslike fashion.

He will probably find it useful to make notes, if only because (as research on short-term memory suggests) it is not easy for an interviewer to form adequate judgements without them, particularly in circumstances in which he has to remember seven or eight candidates in order to join in sensible discussion of them at the end of a day. He is worse off still if he has to remember a bunch of candidates for several weeks.

Note taking is an art to be cultivated. Nothing is so destructive of an interview than laboriousness in the recording of notes. For this reason, if for no other, it is very desirable that application forms (and any other questionnaires used) should be provided with a margin wide enough to enable the interviewer to make notes in the right places at the right times. It is a good plan to develop a habit of putting the candidate's more important phrases in quotes, to distinguish them from words the interviewer himself jots down in recording his impressions as the interview proceeds.

Validity of interviews

As a means of judging applicants for an appointment or a training course, the interview has often been attacked. Critics have pointed to 'experiments' which, they maintain, have shown it to be worthless. One study widely used for this destructive purpose was reported by Kelly and Fiske[1]. These two eminent American psychologists provided a wealth of detail about the agreement, or lack of it, between various 'predictors' (including interview assessments, test scores and questionnaire data) and various 'criteria' (including reports on progress in training and on later performance on the job). Their guinea-pigs were 700 male graduates in psychology who were aiming at becoming specialists in the field of clinical psychology. It appeared from the evidence collected that assessments made on the basis of two interviews with each of the 700 graduates did not agree at all well with subsequent reports on training progress and job performance.

Flaws in the argument

Critics who have used this argument have been either disingenuous or careless in their reading of the Kelly and Fiske report, which makes it clear that the whole exercise was highly artificial. The 700 who went through a 'selection' procedure consisting of interviews, tests and questionnaires knew perfectly well before they started that they were home and dry. They had all been told of their acceptance for the course in clinical psychology. Apart from the fact that competitiveness had been removed from the situation, the procedures they had to endure were clearly unacceptable to many of them. Kelly and Fiske made no bones about it. They said, for example:

> Since the students knew that the evaluation would have no direct effect on their professional careers, many were less than enthusiastic in their participation. The majority were as cooperative as could be expected in the trying conditions imposed upon them.

They went on to report a circumstance of an equally damaging kind:

> Similarly, although the staff members applied themselves to their assessment tasks with a concentration of energy which was 'above and beyond the call of duty', it became increasingly apparent that our earlier assessment plans underestimated the demands imposed . . . and overestimated the energy capacity of the staff.

To use a study of the Kelly and Fiske kind to 'show' that interview judgements are not worth having is indefensible[2]. Dr Kelly told the writer of this chapter that he was surprised that the report had been used by psychologists in Britain, especially by Professor H.J. Eysenck, as providing evidence against the use of the interview for selection purposes.

Contrary evidence

There is admittedly a dearth of evidence in favour of the interview. One of the chief causes of the scarcity is the difficulty researchers commonly have in persuading senior people in an organization to commit themselves to a firm judgement that Mr A has done better than Mr B. It is usually much easier to arrange these things in the public services than in the private sector of the economy. In fact, the defence services have on the whole done far more than anyone else in this field. Unfortunately, however, it is rare for the publication of results to be permitted. In one unpublished study in which I participated, comparisons were made between the predictive value, in the selection of naval officer candidates, of three 'instruments'. The first was a normal selection board consisting of senior naval officers. The second was an occupational psychologist, interviewing the candidates by himself. The third was a short (45-minute) series of written tests of intelligence, mechanical comprehension and elementary mathematics. The selection board had in front of them, at their interview, the candidate's test results and a report on his progress in the ship in which he had already served. The psychologist had the test results but no report. When the judgements of the three instruments were compared with the eventual passing-out marks of the accepted candidates, at the end of their officer training, it was clear that the occupational psychologist, aided by the test results, had achieved the best predictions. The test results by themselves came second. The selection board, despite its knowledge of the test results and the sea-report, came third.

An Israeli study

Recent work of considerable importance has been carried out by Reeb[3] for the Israeli defence services. In interviews lasting 15 to 25 minutes, carried out individually by nonpsychologists with only a few months of relevant training, assessments were made of a man's capacity to adjust to the demands of military service. The main characteristics studied were designated 'masculine (military) pride', 'sociability', 'independence', and 'sense of duty'. The number of men interviewed was large. The results showed very clearly that the assessments contributed usefully to the prediction of success, even when the men's educational records and intelligence-test results had been taken into account.

Variations between interviewers

Although it now seems clear that 'the interview' is not as useless as some would have us believe, it is also clear that much depends on who the interviewer is. Studies in the British defence services have shown that some interviewers (for example, among nonpsychologist personnel selection officers) are better than others at spotting good applicants, even if all the interviewers have had the same kind of training and supervision. A military study of 3000 officer candidates, traced backwards, showed that there were significant variations in the soundness of the judgements of the personnel selection officers who had spotted them in the first instance. This is not surprising, but it suggests that perhaps our attention should be directed as much to 'the interviewer' as to 'the interview'.

Checklist for improving selection interviews

The main lesson to be learnt from many studies of interviewing is that anyone who wants to be good at it, for selection purposes, should:

1 Be clear what work the candidate will have to do, if he is chosen.
2 Study the candidate's application form, and reports available on him, before he sees him, so that he does not waste precious time or destroy the man's confidence by beating about the bush while he gets organized.
3 Listen carefully, prompting, steering and prodding only when it seems necessary.

4 Keep clear of irrelevancies.
5 Explore patiently and thoughtfully the compatibility of the man's abilities and interests with those apparently desirable in the job under consideration.

With these principles and aims, and bearing in mind everything explained above, a trained and experienced interviewer will be able to learn what he needs to know and evaluate what he learns. He will also be able to meet the needs of, and establish a suitable relationship with, those whom he interviews.

References

1 E. L. Kelly and D. W. Fiske, *The Prediction of Performance in Clinical Psychology,* University of Michigan, Ann Arbor, 1951.
2 A. Rodger, 'The worthwhileness of the interview', *Occupational Psychology,* vol. 26, 1952, pp.101–6.
3 M. Reeb, 'Structural interviews for predicting military adjustment', *Occupational Psychology,* vol. 43, 1969, pp.193–9.

Further reading

Dunnette, M. D. and Borman, W. C.: 'Personnel selection and classification systems'. *Annual Review of Psychology,* **30,** 477–525.
Rodger, A. (1974): *The Seven-Point Plan* (with 1968 postscript). National Foundation for Educational Research, on behalf of the National Institute of Industrial Psychology.
Rodger, A. and Cavanagh, P. (1968): 'Personnel selection and vocational guidance', in A. T. Welford *et al.* (Eds) *Society, Psychological Problems and Methods of Study.* London: Routledge and Kegan Paul.
Sneath, F. A., White, G. C. and Randell, G. A. (1966): 'Validating a workshop reporting procedure', *Occupational Psychology,* **40,** 15–29.

13

Group Selection Methods

John Toplis and Bernard Stewart

A short description and discussion of group selection procedures, including an example of a typical programme, appear in Chapter 3. In view of continued interest in such procedures, they are discussed in more detail here.

This chapter deals mainly with those special group methods of selection, such as discussions between the candidates, which can be used only if the candidates meet together in groups. However, it would be unusual to determine suitability solely on the basis of behaviour in a group, and mention is made of other components of selection procedures involving group methods (such as psychological tests and individual interviews) as appropriate: these other techniques are discussed fully elsewhere in this handbook.

Group methods of selection can have considerable appeal. Candidates may believe them to be fairer than other methods of selection, while line managers and others making assessments may enjoy the experience of assessing and any training in assessing that they are given. There can also be administrative advantages in seeing all the candidates in groups. However, while apparent fairness, acceptability and administrative convenience are all important, they have no bearing on the critical point of whether these procedures forecast performance with adequate accuracy.

This chapter will be of the greatest benefit to readers wishing to optimize selection decisions and prepared to spend time and effort doing so. Contents may be particularly relevant to those selecting supervisors, middle management and management trainees. In contrast, readers seeking panaceas will be as disappointed with this chapter as with others in this handbook — successful procedures cannot be instantly assembled from instructions in books!

This chapter contains descriptions of:

Some well-known group selection methods.
Research findings and their implications.
The merits and deficiencies of group selection methods.
Features of potentially successful group selection methods.
Determining the need for group selection methods.
How group selection methods may be introduced.
The need for follow-up.

Some well-known group selection methods

War Office Selection Boards

At the beginning of the second world war, potential officers for the British Army were being selected by interview. A 1942 edition of the magazine *Picture Post* gave further details:

> A man who showed promise in his unit was recommended by the CO for an interview. On the strength of the interviewer's impression in a fifteen-minute talk, a candidate was either rejected or sent on a course at an OCTU (Officer Cadet Training Unit). Stories got round that it was no good putting up for a commission unless you'd won your colours at cricket and rode to hounds.

The same article contained the claim that more than half the candidates recommended for commission had proved unsuitable to become officers when tested in actual training, and went on to extol the virtues of the new War Office Selection Boards (WOSBs) which apparently had been seen as a fairer method of selection than the interviews and had resulted in a doubling of the men applying for commissions.

In setting up the WOSBs, consideration had been given to methods used by the German forces since 1923, but these methods had been rejected in favour of exercises concentrating on the dynamics of interpersonal skills. Garforth[1], a professional soldier involved with the British War Office Selection Boards described the methods finally adopted:

> Tests may vary from the 'group discussion', in which eight or ten candidates sit around in easy chairs and are told to select a subject for discussion and talk about it to each other, to a 'group task' which may involve improvising, with limited materials found on the spot, some method of 'escaping' as a group over a wire entanglement, including electrified wire and alarms. In another form of the test, groups are told to invent their own situations and act on them.

Each candidate was appraised, at the end of a procedure totalling two or three days, by the board's president, visiting member, psychiatrist and military testing officers. Psychologists helped with the training of the board members and with the subsequent evaluation of their work: Garforth describes how board members viewed the tasks done.

> In judging these tests the observer watches above all the interpersonal reactions of the group and the significance of the contributions to direction or execution made by each member of the group. It is by no means always the candidate who talks the loudest or most, or apparently takes the lead, that gets the highest grading.

By the end of the war, information had been built up about individual boards. This information led to a study, reported by Morris[2], involving two boards whose pass rates up to that time had been widely different. When a group of candidates was randomly split between these two boards, pass rates of 23% and 48% resulted. However when the same candidates were seen by the two boards there was 60% agreement between the two boards and only 25% disagreement.

In another study reported by Morris[2] two boards considered to have reached a high standard of assessment independently assessed 200 candidates. Intercorrelations between their judgements varied between .59 and .80, the intercorrelation of .80 being the judgements of the final grade.

So far as validity is concerned Morris reported that 76% of officers selected by War Office Selection Boards gave satisfactory service compared with the 50% failure in training alone under the old method. Such an improvement could, of course, be due to reasons other than the selection method itself: for example, better applicants may have been coming forward, standards may have changed, etc. However it seemed that there had been a considerable improvement over the state of affairs in 1940 when, towards the end of the old method of selection, as many as thirty parliamentary questions a week reflected growing public concern.

Civil Service Selection Boards

At the end of the war, the British Civil Service faced problems in recruiting adequate numbers of academically qualified staff, partly because qualified staff had been killed on active service during the war, and partly because able school-leavers had gone straight into the services and had not gained academic qualifications (Arbous[3]).

Civil Service Selection Boards (CSSBs) were therefore set-up to provide a method of recruiting, to higher appointments, able candidates who lacked the academic qualifications hitherto considered essential.* The procedures were sometimes called Country House Selections after the premises in which some early procedures took place. While psychologists continued to take part in the procedures or help train assessors, there were changes in the methods used in civilian life; for example, wire entanglements were swept away and topics such as 'Is saluting a waste of time?' were abandoned. The CSSBs introduced their own form of 'analogous tests' in which the candidates were presented with situations that might be found in government work; a psychologist (Wilson[4]) described them:

> Each has been built round one item or another of the job analysis of Civil Service or Foreign Service duties and they have been most ingeniously set by our lay colleagues in an imaginary community which is affected by most of the problems, social, political and economic, which afflict British officials today. This setting, about which candidates brief themselves from a bulky memorandum in Civil Service style, undoubtedly lends interest and realism to the examination. The feeling of realism, experienced by candidates and staff alike, is indeed one of the chief advantages of the practical exercises in our omnibus testing programme. They have, that is to say, a high 'face validity' . . . .

Anstey[5] describes the form on which assessments were made. Assessors were required to make a rating of 1–7 against the following characteristics which were all carefully defined on a separate sheet. The characteristics were: penetration, fertility of ideas, judgement, written expression, oral expression, personal contacts, influence, drive and determination, emotional stability and maturity.

In time, follow-up studies were made. For example, Anstey[5] reports that Vernon found correlations of 0.563 and of 0.583 between assessments made at CSSBs and subsequent job performance, and, at this time, it was Anstey's view that the procedure could not be improved by extending it beyond two days. However, later Anstey[6] says that the procedure was 'streamlined from 4 to 3 days'. In the 30 year follow-up of those selected in 1945/48, the correlation coefficient (after correction for selectivity) was found to be 0.660 between the Final Selection Board grading and rank finally obtained[6] after approximately 30 years of service.

When Macrae[7] wrote *Group Selection Procedures* for the National Institute of Industrial Psychology against a background of 'increasing interest' in 1967, he described the War Office Selection Boards and Civil Service Selection Boards and developments and findings since that time; this included work

---

*This issue of academic qualifications is still topical today: it is important that the selection exercises and criteria are demonstrably job-related. If they are not, the procedures may be open to serious challenge as has been seen in the recent cases regarding the Sex and Race Discrimination Acts. It may be appealing to ask for certain qualifications but they cannot be justified on grounds of business convenience alone.

carried out by the NIIP's own staff in an advisory capacity and by psychologists employed by commercial and other organizations. Macrae reported that, in one Australian study, observers had ranked the attributes of candidates on six scales, while scales on which four aspects of personality and six aspects of ability could be rated had been developed by staff of the South African National Institute of Personnel Research. In all cases, there was some evidence of the worth of the procedures but conclusive evidence was lacking because information was subjective (eg procedures were described as 'encouraging') or numbers small. Executive trainees, supervisors and salesmen were among those selected by these methods.

American developments

In recent years a large number of American companies have started to use 'assessment centres', a term used to describe a method or technology for selection or appraisal rather than to denote the place at which the method or technology is used. The centres are normally seen as an additional method for identifying staff development needs and employ multiple assessment techniques including the kinds of special group methods which are the subject of this chapter. Some assessment centres have recently appeared in the United Kingdom[8].

The origins of assessment centres can be traced to the American Telephone and Telegraph Company in which, in the 1950s, Douglas Bray began experimenting with 'multiple assessment methods' to identify the potential of existing staff; this formed part of a study to gain insight into the management development process and to identify the variables related to success.

In 1966, Bray and Grant[9] reported the follow-up of predictions made as to which candidates would reach middle management level; the predictions, which had been made eight years earlier but held in confidence in the interim to avoid 'contamination', appeared convincing. For example, in one part of the study, 48% of those thought able to reach middle management level did so; in contrast, only 11% of those thought below the standard made the grade.

Because of its findings, its business context, the length of follow-up, and the independence of the original assessments and the assessments of performance, the so-called 'A T and T study' is often quoted in support of the principle of assessment centres. Yet the results also suggested caution—for example, the accuracy of prediction varied markedly from year to year, while factor analysis showed the actual number of qualities rated to be far fewer than the number of qualities rated by the assessors. The study was also inconclusive on issues such as the relative importance of professional and non-professional assessors.

Such caution has tended to be forgotten because of the acceptability to management of group selection methods. 'A T and T' now operate fifty centres throughout the United States through which some 10 000 candidates pass annually. The British Institute of Personnel Management report[8] estimated that as many as 150 firms in the United States were using assessment centres in 1973, although only 13 of 360 companies surveyed in the UK were using similar techniques.

However, central to this chapter is the assertion by Mackinnon[10] that 'the procedures which contributed most significantly to the overall staff prediction were group exercises and the in-basket'. It was also considered that group exercises contributed most importantly to the assessment of interpersonal skills.

Research findings and their implications

During group selection methods, it is common practice for assessors to record the performance of each individual in the group. Later, selection judgements are based on what has been recorded. As a result of research, a number of factors have been identified as affecting what is recorded or the judgements which are made. These factors are as follows:

1 Membership of the group.
2 Nature of the task.
3 Training and instructions given to observers.
4 Methods of recording.
5 Decision making.
6 The selection of the assessors.
7 The construction of the procedures.

Membership of the group

The performance of an individual can be affected by the performance of the group members; for example, laboratory experiments by Asch[11] showed that individuals tended to move their judgements towards those of the rest of the group even when their judgements were of relatively objective matters. Other studies of groups have shown that leadership changes according to expertise in the task in hand[12].

Anstey[5] (op. cit.) expressed concern that the reliability of the procedure could be affected by the composition of the group. A candidate tends to be at a disadvantage if the other members of his group are all so strong as to shut him out or so weak as to not stretch him fully.

Individuals may find themselves in a group in which they are at a particular advantage—an individual may be known to some of the other candidates and perceived as an 'expert', as someone with relevant experience, and so on. Indeed, all the other members of the group may feel at a disadvantage from the moment that one well-dressed individual arrives in a large new car.

Pearn[13] also expressed concern regarding the possible disadvantages that can occur for a candidate in these groups, particularly for those candidates from other cultures. He says:

> In our competitive culture we tend to assume that people are automatically motivated to do their best in any task that is set before them. It is perhaps surprising to come across groups who have no sense of personal rivalry, and so no sense of competition with others.

Which is not to say that they are less capable.

It may also be that different standards are set for different groups of candidates especially when stereotype evaluations occur. Hammer *et al.*[14] found strong evidence for differential criterion bias in the evaluation of work samples, especially for high performing black applicants by white assessors. Similarly Arvey[15] indicates that the kinds of standards and criteria used may depend on whether an applicant is male or female.

Thus the contrasts inherent in the random mixing of candidates is of major concern. Wexley *et al.*[16], however, conclude that training can be given to reduce this contrast effect.

Problems do not disappear if group members are of equal status and have similar work experience. In real life each candidate may be expected to deal successfully with people from other backgrounds, and the ability to convince like-minded colleagues may not be a good guide.

It can also be difficult to separate individual and group performance, although research about the benefits of the group to individuals have not yielded consistent results. Argyle[17] reports that, while group membership is likely to be stimulating, (Zajanc and Sales (1966) showed that the sheer presence of other people produces a flow of adrenalin) it can also inhibit the production of new responses and restrain creativity (Zajanc 1965).

Nature of the task

Many possibilities exist, each demanding different behaviour to achieve success. For example, candidates may be given time to prepare, may be given individual roles, may be given a time limit, and may be given a specific objective to reach (as in the exercise for CSSBs described earlier). Conversely, they may be required to tackle a topic at a moment's notice without being clear as to what the assessors are looking for—as when tackling 'select a topic to discuss and argue about it' in which the assessors may be looking for the emergence of a leader and the methods he or she employs to establish the position.

It can be important to brief candidates as to whether cooperative or competitive behaviour is expected of them. In the absence of briefing the procedure will be unreliable because some candidates may be incorrect in their assessment of the styles of behaviour that are expected.

It must also be ensured that, if specific tasks or roles are assigned to each group member, there should be equal opportunity to display appropriate behaviours. Jaffee[18] points out the need to ensure this equality of the various designated positions: 'In other words, does a man have a favoured position simply because he has been given a stronger case to argue'.

Instructions to observers

Without any instructions to observers, acute problems may arise—for example, the names of group members may be confused, individual candidates may not be observed by any of the assessors, and so on. At a more subtle level, a study by Lévy-Leboyer (reported in Macrae's paper[7]) threw light on other possible sources of error; for example, it was found that candidates near the middle of the table in a group discussion tended to be given lower ratings than the candidates at each end; Lévy-Leboyer believed this to be because candidates at the middle of the table were occupying the traditional seats of the leaders and yet were failing to dominate the discussion in the way that seating arrangement suggested they should.

In practice, instructions to observers can become so detailed that the observers are required to attend special training courses where, for example, they may be required to record information about the performance of candidates in a filmed or video-recorded group. The recording of behaviour during the group task and the subsequent rating of performance is often encouraged and can help prevent errors of the kind found by Lévy-Leboyer.

Although there is general agreement about the need for training, opinions are divided as to whether assessors should record the performance of 'whole candidates' or whether they should concentrate on behaviours and tasks that all might display. In so far as personal preferences based on appearance and social values may lead to bias on the parts of some assessors (for example, assessors may be influenced by a candidate's age, sex, ethnic origin, apparent social values and sense of humour), it may be preferable for assessors to watch for particular behaviours in the group as a whole; however, it may then prove difficult for a single observer to record all relevant behaviour when, for example, all group members are talking at once.

However, Spool[19] observed that 'in general there seems to be a lack of concern regarding training programs for observing of behaviour'. Though in his major review of twenty one years of research literature he concluded that 'the results, in general, reveal that training programs are effective in improving accuracy of performance'. Thus, although Schmidt[20] found training was effective in reducing race and sex biases it may not be sufficient solely to lecture assessors. Latham[21] concludes that 'knowledge of these errors alone will not lead others to take effective steps to counteract them'.

Methods of recording

A related issue to that of instructions to observers is the method of recording to be used. Standardized forms are normally provided which encourage assessors to report or rate specific behaviour. Predictions based on rankings of candidates have been fond less successful than those which encourage the separation of recording and judgement.

If the dimensions on which candidates are to be assessed are not made clear, the error called the 'halo-effect' can occur. Borman[22] states that:

> The so called 'halo-effect' is perhaps the most pervasive rater error. Raters succumbing to the halo error assign ratings to individuals by attending to global impressions of each ratee rather than by carefully distinguishing among levels of performance that individual ratees exhibit on different performance dimensions.

It is therefore essential to clarify the dimensions of assessment. Some boards develop this further by restricting the dimensions which each assessor observes and rates: one might assess the intellectual contribution of the candidate whilst another attends only to the social skills and verbal style of the candidate.

Decision making

Decision making is a further related issue. If assessors have each concentrated on a different aspect of the same candidates, their information will need to be combined before judgements can be made. If different assessors have seen different candidates it is important that the candidates' performance is systematically compared rather than judgements based on the personal preferences of the assessors. Successful chairmanship may thus be critical and appropriate training is needed.

Keenan[23] found that: 'Some relationships between individual's personal feelings about candidates and their general evaluations of them suggest that assessors unconsciously adopt personal likeability of the individual as one of the criteria for selection, despite the fact that most assessors agree that this is not a valid criterion.' Perhaps more difficult to deal with is the finding (Forbes[24]) that non-verbal behaviour is significantly associated with the categorisation of accept or reject and that the candidates in an 'accept' group displayed more direct eye gaze, less avoidance of eye contact, more smiling, more nodding, and less static positions. Keenan[25] also found that the assessors' non-verbal behaviour can also influence not only the impression the candidates gain of them but also the candidates' performance.

The selection of assessors

Another often ignored feature is that of the ability of the assessors. The assessment task is a highly complex one which is not to everyone's liking. Spool[19] concludes that:

> of the observer characteristics, the ability level of the observer may be the key to minimising observer error. For the observer to be more accurate in observing he or she must, among other things, be able to recognise the behaviours to be observed, be able to use the systems with ease, and be able to make observations in accordance with some standard of criteria.

The construction of the procedures

Bias may be introduced if, on a number of different exercises, the same assessors rate the same candidates and do not rate the other candidates. Cohen *et al.*[26] concluded that: 'assessor/candidate acquaintance must be minimised so as not to permit biases gained from previous exposure to intrude into evaluations'.

The merits and deficiencies of group selection methods

At their best, group selection methods have been seen as fairer than alternative methods of selction and have thus improved the numbers of applicants. There have also been occasions when they have shown better reliability and validity than the techniques that they have replaced—in other words, they have proved a better method of selection.

Grouping can have other advantages—those involved in the selection process may welcome a one or two day procedure which gets everything over and done with. Also there are savings in, for example, being able to show all the candidates their potential place of work at the same time.

On the negative side, group selection methods are likely to be relatively expensive compared with, for example, the cost of individual interviews. This is because the organization may have to provide overnight and other accommodation for all the candidates and the assessors and because more time is required; there will also be the cost of training the assessors.

It may also prove time consuming to find a date convenient for all the assessors and candidates and such administrative delays may not go down well if a new member of staff is urgently needed. Furthermore some candidates may withdraw because their appearance at a group selection method would mean that their application would be known to the other candidates.

Finally, how good are group selection methods 'on average'? Although it is now some forty years since special group methods were first used in selection, conclusive evidence about their worth is sparse. In particular, there is a lack of replication of many of the studies which have been made, either by psychologists or by line-managers; furthermore the technical quality of the selection procedures on which reported studies are based is likely to be far superior to that in non-research situations, if only because of the extra care taken with work intended for publication. It is likely that, in many day to day situations where candidates meet, assessors pay little attention to behaviour or interaction and are oblivious of the potential use of what is happening.

Features of potentially successful group selection methods

It is unlikely that a group selection method will be successful unless it is carefully designed and executed with particular attention being paid to the points discussed earlier in this chapter.

Some idea of the preparation that will be required can be obtained from considering the list of abilities to be assessed. Below are the list of 12 abilities drawn up by the Management Centre Europe in their programme designed 'to identify an individual's first level supervisory management ability and provides specific evaluations for specific purposes in the following management abilities'.

1 *Functional ability.* Existing successfully in one's environment.
2 *Planning.* Developing a course of action to achieve an objective.
3 *Organizing.* Structuring or arranging resources to accomplish the objective of a plan.
4 *Controlling.* Maintaining adherence to a plan, modifying it if necessary to achieve the desired result.
5 *Oral communication.* Transferring a thought from one person to another by speech, adjusting to audience reaction.
6 *Written communication.* Transferring a thought from one person to another by writing, without the possibility of response to audience reaction.
7 *Company orientation.* Identifying the organization's goals and values as complementing one's own.
8 *Leadership.* Getting people to work towards reaching an objective.
9 *Decision making.* Consciously weighing and selecting one of two or more alternatives.
10 *Creativity.* Developing alternate solutions to problems.
11 *Initiative.* Introducing one's own thought or action into a situation.
12 *Flexibility.* Adjusting to changing internal and external conditions both personal and impersonal.

The MCE package recommends 24–28 hours training, plus 8 hours homework (for the board chairman only). It also suggests that there should be one assessor to each three candidates.

It is unlikely that selection will be based on a group selection method alone, and attention therefore needs to be paid to the rest of the selection procedure including shortlisting, interviewing and, perhaps, testing. In particular, the objectives of the interviews need to be clarified. For instance, if the group selection method is held early in the procedure, assessors can meet and compare notes and parts of the individual interviews can be based on matters arising from the group methods and assessments which are being formed. However, a contrary view would be that the interviews should not be influenced by the group methods, and that the findings from the different stages of selection should be drawn together only at the very end.

Determining the need for group selection methods

In general, it is suggested that group selection methods might be considered as part of a procedure:

1 When applicants are critical of the fairness of existing selection methods.
2 When existing selection methods are not successful.
3 When the qualities likely to be measured by group selection methods appear relevant to the work for which selection is taking place or to which candidates may be promoted in the long term; this might be particularly important if manpower planning suggests that there will be shortages in key areas in the years ahead.

Decisions about whether or not to use group selection methods may, in practice, turn on one or more of the following.

1 The organization's manpower situation. If, for example, a number of top managers are likely to leave an organization because of retirement in the next five years, it may well be appropriate to invest a large amount of effort in the assessment and development of their subordinates, using a variety of techniques including special group methods. In time, the worth of such procedures can be followed up and assessed, and component parts which do not contribute can be dropped. It is probably far better to start with a thorough procedure, and then streamline it, than to start with a short pro-cedure which may prove completely ineffective—there might not then be time to develop and prove a second (hopefully effective) procedure before large numbers of decisions have to be made.
2 A practical consideration may be the availability or otherwise of tasks and simulations on which candidates may be assessed; for example, assessment centre packages are available for supervisory staff but may not be

available for other specialist functions. However, it may be important to investigate the worth of the package, and also how its contents can be kept secure if large numbers both in and outside the organization become familiar with it.

3   Another practical consideration may be the availability of potential assessors and their enthusiasm for the methods: a related issue is that of their willingness to undergo training. In general terms, there is perhaps a danger of the sophistication of the methods outstripping the ability of the assessors to make use of the information available. More complicated procedures involving several days are best reserved for assessors who are willing to be trained for the appropriate amount of time.

How group selection methods may be introduced

Two main options are available. The first is to approach a management consultancy or other organization and 'buy in' a group selection method. This might be done by using an assessment centre package, although it was indicated earlier that only thirteen out of 360 companies surveyed in the UK were using these techniques. Of these UK companies, five were using the Management Centre Europe and the list of twelve 'management abilities' which are assessed when the Centre's package is used as described in the previous section.

However, Ungerson[27] has made a number of serious criticisms of this package and three are now described. First, good practice would normally involve the identification or confirmation of the twelve 'management abilities' by a statistical process known as factor analysis; Ungerson points out that such an analysis had not been carried out on the 'abilities' in this package. Second, Ungerson also reviews three researches quoted in support of the package. 'In the first two "one of the program developers acted as chairman"; in the third research "the program was completely run by each organization's own personnel who were trained for one week". This latter training is longer than in the proposed package, in which the *chairman* only is trained for a week and he, in turn, trains the other assessors in two days (according to the MCE brochure).'

A third criticism made by Ungerson concerns the 'all-important question of validity'. When examining the worth of a procedure psychologists normally look for evidence of predictive validity which can be defined as 'how well do assessments forecast future performance?' Ungerson points out that data about the MCE package available for review did not relate to predictive validity but to concurrent validity in which assessments are made of existing staff and statistically related to aspects of their present performance; no test of prediction had been made.

An alternative to buying in a package is to buy in expertise or to develop it within an organization. This is worth serious consideration because, as explained earlier, there can be no guarantee that group selection methods will be effective and follow-ups should be carried out (see below). An experienced adviser will be able to follow-up the people appointed through the group selection methods and should be able to advise on how the methods can be adapted and modified to give the most relevant information at minimal cost. The adviser should also be able to set up training and documentation, and advise on the alternative topics for discussion that will be required if security is to be maintained. An adviser may also wish to introduce techniques over and above those mentioned so far in this chapter. For example, if candidates are not competing for a single vacancy, it is possible to get them to make assessments on the performance of the other candidates in the group and to look at these assessments as predictors of subsequent performance.

The need for follow-up

The longer such procedures continue, the greater the need for cost and comparative effectiveness to be studied. The IPM report[8] calculates the total cost of assessing 600 employees using an assessment centre package to be £28 275 or roughly £47 per candidate, while Wilson and Tatge[28], also writing in 1973, give an estimate of between $500 and $600 per candidate.

Information on cost effectiveness is virtually non-existent. Nor is information available about benefits to assessors and trainees. However, the cost of recruiting from outside the organization is normally far higher than either of the figures quoted above.

Information about the technical worth of some group selection methods in the widest sense of the word (ie multiple assessment techniques) have produced a range of results; for example, the 'corrected' predictions of the Civil Service Selection Board have given a correlation of 0.6. Studies have also been made of the component parts of group selection procedures; although there are technical complications in so far as performance on each component part will be known to all the assessors and their judgements and assessments may therefore be 'contaminated'.

Nevertheless, such studies are important if the efficiency of a procedure is to be maximized. For example, Bray and Grant[9] found that it was the simulations (group problems and 'in-basket') that played the largest part in the overall assessment; tests of mental ability proved less effective and personality questionnaires less effective still; however, each part contributed independently to the overall assessment made, and none could have been omitted without the loss of important information. In contrast, one study of the predictive value of pencil and paper tests and background information gave a correlation of 0.7 and clearly it is possible that one component of a procedure may be as good a predictor if not better than the summed or even 'weighted' total of the parts.

Conclusions

The main advantage of special group selection methods is that they aid assessment of abilities and characteristics which cannot be studied by other methods. There are also some 'fringe benefits' in terms of the involvement, training and development of the assessors and in the completeness of appraisal of performance of internal candidates if such an appraisal is policy.

The main disadvantage of special group selection methods lies in the lack of evidence about their worth when designed and implemented by untrained staff; hence many would think it prudent either to retain the services of a consultant experienced in this kind of work or to use a proven assessment centre package if one is available for the type of staff to be assessed.

Much may depend on whether manpower planning and forecasting suggests that it will be hard to fill vacancies in the areas in which special group methods of selection have been developed and proven. Without such planning and validation, the sophistication required may be hard to justify.

References

1   F. I. de la P. Garforth, 'War Office Selection Boards (O.C.T.U.)', *Occupational Psychology,* vol.19, 1945, pp.47–108.

2   B. S. Morris, 'Officer Selection in the British Army 1942–1945', *Occupational Psychology,* vol.23, 1949, pp.220–34.

3   Arbous (1953) reported in M. C. Knowles, 'Group assessment and staff selection', *Pers. Pract. Bulletin,* 1963, pp.6–16.

4   N. A. B. Wilson, 'The work of the Civil Service Selection Boards', *Occupational Psychology,* vol.22, 1948, pp.204–12.

5   E. Anstey, 'Assessing managerial potential', (Notes of talk kept in the library of the Institute of Personnel Management).

6   E. Anstey, 'A 30 year follow-up of the CSSB procedure, with lessons for the future', *Occupational Psychology,* vol.50, 1977, pp.149–59.

7   A. Macrae, *Group Selection Procedures.* NIIP Paper Number 5, NIIP, London, 1967.

8   D. Gill, B. Ungerson and M. Thakur, *Performance Appraisal in Perspective.* IPM Information Report 14, Institute of Personnel Management, London, 1973.

9   D. W. Bray and D. L. Grant, 'The assessment centre in the measurement of potential for business management', *Psychological Monographs,* vol.80, 1966.

10   D. W. Mackinnon, *An Overview of Assessment Centres.* Centre for Creative Leadership, Technical Report Number 1, 1975.

11   S. E. Asch, 'Effects of group pressure upon the modification and distortion of judgements' in D. Cartwright and A. Zander (eds), *Group*

Dynamics, Research & Theory, Tavistock Publications, London, 1960.

12　D. Cartwright and A. Zander, *Group Dynamics, Research & Theory,* Tavistock Publications, London, 1960.

13　M. Pearn, *Selection Tests for Immigrants: Some Problems of Administration and Interpretation.* Industrial Training Research Unit, Research Paper SL8.

14　W. C. Hammer, J. S. Kim, L. Baird and W. J. Bigoness, 'Race and sex as determinants of ratings by potential employers in a simulated work sampling task', *Journal of Applied Psychology,* vol.58, 1974, pp.203–11.

15　R. D. Arvey 'Unfair discrimination in the employment interview: legal and psychological aspects'. *Psychological Bulletin,* vol.86, 1979, pp.736–65.

16　K. N. Wexley, R. E. Saunders and G. A. Yuki, 'Training interviewers to eliminate contrast effects in employment interviews', *Journal of Applied Psychology,* vol.57, 1973, pp.233–6.

17　M. Argyle, *Social Interaction,* Methuen, London, 1968.

18　C. L. Jaffee, 'The partial validation of a leaderless group discussion for the selection of supervisory personnel'. *Occupational Psychology,* vol.41, 1967, pp.245–8.

19　M. D. Spool, 'Training programs for observers of behaviour: a review', *Personnel Psychology,* vol.31, 1978, pp.853–88.

20　F. R. Schmidt and R. H. Johnson, 'The effect of race on poor ratings in an industrial situation', *Journal of Applied Psychology,* vol.57, 1973, pp.237–241.

21　G. P. Latham, E. D. Pursell and K. N. Wexley, 'Training managers to minimize rating errors in the observation of behaviour', *Journal of Applied Psychology,* vol.60, 1975, pp.550–5.

22　W. C. Borman, 'Effects of instructions to avoid halo on reliability and validity of performance and evaluation ratings'. *Journal of Applied Psychology,* vol.60, 1975, pp.556–60.

23　A. Keenan, 'Some relationships between individuals' personal feelings about candidates and their general evaluations of them'. *Journal of Occupational Psychology,* vol.50, 1977, pp.275–83.

24　R. J. Forbes and P.R. Jackson, 'Non-verbal behaviour and the outcome of selection interviews,' *Journal of Occupational Psychology,* vol.53, 1980, pp.65–72.

25　A. Keenan, 'Effects of the non-verbal behaviour of interviewers on candidates performance'. *Journal of Occupational Psychology.* vol.49, 1976, pp.171–6.

26　S. L. Cohen and L. Sands, 'The effects of order of exercise presentation on assessment centre performance: one standardisation concern', *Personnel Psychology,* vol.31, 1978, pp.35–46.

27　B. Ungerson, 'Assessment centres — a review of research findings', *Personnel Review,* vol.3, 1974, pp.4–13.

28   J. E. Wilson and W. A. Tatge, 'Assessment centres — further assessment needed?', *Personnel Journal,* vol.52, 1973, pp.172–9.

Further reading

Bass, B. M. (1954): 'The leaderless group discussion', *Psychological Bulletin,* **51,** 465–92.

Korman, A. K. (1968): 'The prediction of managerial performance: a review'. *Personnel Psychology,* **21,** 295–322.

Kraut, A. I. (1973): 'Management assessment in international organizations', *Industrial Relations,* **12,** 172–82.

McConnell, J. J. and Parker, T. C. (1972): 'An assessment centre programme for multi-organizational use', *Training and Development Journal,* **26,** 6–14.

Parry, J. (1959): 'The place of personality appraisal in vocational selection', *Occupational Psychology,* **33,** 149–56.

14

Deciding the Appointment

Leonard J Holman

This chapter deals with the problem of making the final choice (or choices) in a selection procedure—deciding which, out of five or six apparently eminently suitable applicants for an important job, is the most suitable. Or perhaps, with twelve vacancies and only five or six apparently quite suitable applicants, deciding which of the remainder would be satisfactory and which unsatisfactory. Some of the original applicants are, of course, definitely *unsuitable*. The five or six mentioned are quite suitable—but there are many borderline cases. These are always a headache in selection problems, from eleven-plus children at school to ministers for a new government; nevertheless, with the aid of all the evidence collected and deductions therefrom, decisions have to be made.

The intention of this chapter is to provide as much scientific assistance as possible in making the decisions. For pure science, of course, the ideal is 100% mathematical proof; but in the field of selection (as elsewhere) the ideal is unobtainable. The selector has to be satisfied with getting as close to it as possible, using the maximum of scientific evidence and the minimum of subjective assessments, prejudices, hunches and intuition.

As final decisions must be made upon *all* the evidence collected during the previous stages of the selection, the plan is to run through them all in turn, explaining what can be learnt at each stage and how the applicants match up (or not) with requirements. Elimination of the impossibles must take place at every stage to save time and money by obviating useless testing, marking and interviewing, and to avoid confusion in the later stages if possibles only are considered and discussed.

The basis for argument is a particular vacancy with a dozen or so recruits. As this is merely a basis, many digressions will occur in order to illustrate various points. The separate stages considered are as follows:

1   The advertisement (or particulars sent to an employment agency).
2   Sending application forms to most applicants.
3   Studying the returned forms and arranging interviews.
4   Pencil and paper testing, and the scoring thereof.
5   Personal interviews (three or four, perhaps).
6   Discussion and final decisions made by a small group.

Dealing with replies to advertisements

The advertisement might be something like the following. This is not a model, of course. A specific advertisement would be based on careful study of the vacant post, as discussed in earlier chapters:

> Representatives required, age 33–37, preferable married, valid driving licences (cars provided by company), long distances probable, to visit country houses to sell electrically operated gadgets for fuel saving. Almost sells itself, but difficult to explain working to housewives. Some engineering aptitude necessary, though course of instruction given in our workshops. Brash salesmen type not required. Apply . . . .

The process of personnel selection starts with such an advertisement, and all the applications received are attracted by it at either first- or second-hand.

Sending out application forms

Unless an agency is employed, the next step is to send out the company's application forms. Even at this stage, selection through elimination can be exercised. It may be obvious that a certain letter has been sent in by a boy of fifteen, or by an old-age pensioner who could not possibly have the vitality to drive eighty miles, to try to sell the gadget to several people, to drive home again and to do it all again the next day. Or the language used may be so quaint and foreign that the writer could not possibly be expected to explain difficult mechanical and electrical points to a housewife. The person carrying out this preliminary selection must understand these matters yet not be so inflexible as right at the start to lose more possibles than justified.

    The application forms should have been designed as very searching and revealing documents. Not only is an applicant's previous employment record (especially if he is middle-aged) of vital importance, but questions on his sports, games, hobbies and pastimes can also be very revealing. They also make a good leading subject to establish friendly relations at the beginning of an interview. (Why did you drop this and take up that? How good are you at it?) The man with no hobbies whatever should be regarded with reserve. A healthy mind needs some recreation or relaxation.

Calling applicants for interviews

About three times as many applicants should be selected for first interview as there are vacancies in one particular line although, if there is only one important job going, six or even ten might be interviewed. Each candidate must be told that the interview will take from two to three hours, and that he must be prepared to set aside a whole morning or afternoon for the purpose. Twenty minutes or so during his lunch-break is definitely not on.

Conducting the interview

An advanced selection procedure will make use of two or three valid pencil and paper tests before personal interviews. In the present instance, a 'g' test of general ability and a test of mechanical aptitude would be the minimum. Perhaps a personality test may also be included, provided a psychologically trained tester is employed for its evaluation. (Strangely enough, a clerical aptitude test is nearly always worthwhile, even if the job in question includes practically no clerical activities). But all tests require careful scoring, and it is essential that correct scores should be placed in front of the interviewer before the applicant himself appears.

Make-up of selection board

Now the face-to-face interviews may start, and it is to be hoped that the company has progressed beyond the sitting selection board process. Up to the beginning of the last war (and even a bit later) it was thought by the Armed Forces that a good way to select young officers was for them individually to sit facing a long table, broadside on, behind which sat an impressive array of high-ranking officers, all in dazzling uniforms. This was no doubt an excellent method of discovering whether an applicant was embarrassed, scared or just terrified when faced by a tableful of authority (an experience which would never happen again in his forces career). As a method of determining whether he would be likely to choose the best route when leading his platoon to outflank a troublesome enemy machine-gun it left a lot to be desired. True, the uniforms of high-ranking business executives are not (at the moment) as dazzling as those of forces officers, but a lot of this illustration still applies, and the arguments in favour of friendly interviews by one person at a time (possibly with an unobtrusive additional observer) are unanswerable.

This necessitates, of course, each applicant being interviewed (quite shortly) three or four times, and the interviewers getting together occasionally before the decisions board to check that each applicant tells the same story each time. And here it might be stressed that each interviewer must have at least five minutes to study the application form, including the test scores, of each applicant before his interview. It is chaotic if the application form arrives five minutes after the applicant.

Value of interview procedure

The importance of interviews of some kind for applicants must be undoubted. From their point of view, they would not feel satisfied unless they had had at least one personal chat with somebody in the firm; and, from the employer's point of view, it is important to collect personal impressions (however unscientific) of prospective employees who will be contacting the public or even just mixing with fellow employees. An applicant who makes a bad impression on his interviewers is unlikely to make a good one on important visitors or on the public at large. Supposing the poor chap has a badly scarred face which could scare housewives whom he wished to interview; or has to do a lot of walking and turns out to have a deformed leg and needs crutches? These points may well not have been covered in the application form.

Function of decisions board

Now, some sort of decisions board must meet to make the final selections. While decisions are frequently made by a single individual, research has shown that decisions reached by a small group are superior. Each member of the board should have seen all the applicants, and should sit in to give evidence if called upon to do so. A *small* board (three or four) is the ideal; too large, and a deadening sort of committee procedure has to be adopted; too few (one or two), and the opportunities for the distorting effects of error, prejudices, intuition and the like to carry the day are multiplied.

Applying statistical methods

For the most accurate weighting of all the pros and cons for each applicant, the advice of a statistically minded psychologist (or perhaps a psychologically minded statistician), rare birds though they may be, is invaluable. Nevertheless, all the evidence gathered must be weighed by someone, and preferably by someone without personal prejudices who can explain the statistical consequences of different approaches to the various factors concerned. ('Factors' here means variables such as age, test scores, present salary, number of children and so on.)

Amassing criteria for validation purposes

The first thing such an adviser will demand or seek is some criterion for validating each separate factor. It follows that, even if there are no records available on which criteria can be based, a collection must be started immediately, so that the most scientific selection procedure can be introduced without delay. If, however, people have been engaged for similar jobs in the past, it is possible to produce historical facts (records) about each one at the time of his engagement, and subsequently; a present rating score for each man can also be obtained, representing his satisfactoriness or value to the company. Later will come the more difficult process of assessing what effect each factor has upon his general satisfactoriness, and how they should best be combined (weighted) to produce the final result. Although mathematical procedures (*coefficient of correlation* and *multiple regression* techniques) exist for this purpose, quite a lot can be done in practice by what Americans call *guestimating*, provided the simple underlying theory, now to be explained, is clearly grasped.

Reading a regression line

The most important point to be understood—at least, to some extent—is the meaning of a *regression line*, and in Figure 14.1 the most simple case of all is illustrated. A man's value to his employer, running from 0 to 10, is shown on the vertical axis and his age, or perhaps his score on a selection test, along the horizontal axis. As will easily be seen, this is a case of the higher the better. According to this graph, examination of records has shown that the most valuable people were aged 45, or scored 45 on the selection test. (Apparently nobody over 45 is employed and the top score on the test is 45.) People aged 25, or who score only that figure on the test, are useless. It can easily be read from the graph, or calculated, that anyone of age or score 35 is of value 5, etc.

All this is, of course, rather oversimplified. Very seldom is it discovered that the older the better applies to a job; or even the more intelligent the better. For most jobs, some people can be just *too* clever. They can easily become mentally unsatisfied, bored and finally perhaps tricky and unreliable. The best people for such jobs may be those who score 35 on the test; those who score only 25, or the maximum of 45, may alike be useless. Similarly with age: 35 is the optimum, and people become of less value the farther they are removed from this figure.

It is very easy to calculate, and to show on a graph, the case where the optimum and the two points of no value are known, provided these two points are equidistant from the optimum score and the falling-off is proportionate—that is, the same amount each year or test score point. This gives two sloping straight lines joining to form the letter A as shown by the continuous lines on Figure 14.2.

What about the curved line on the graph? This is to illustrate the rather more complicated case where it is felt that an applicant's value decelerates more quickly the farther he is from the optimum; if he is just a mark or two (or a year or two) away, it is almost negligible—which in practice is usually the case. But

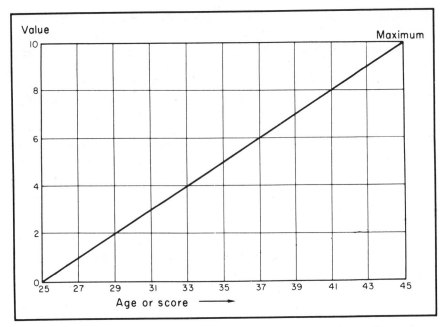

Figure 14.1   Straight-line regression showing maximum score as having highest value

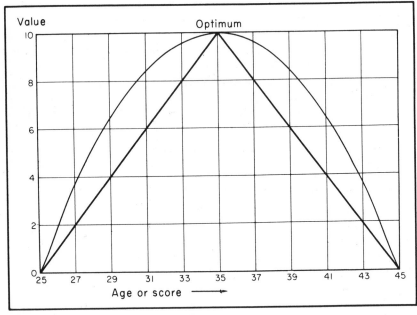

Figure 14.2   Straight-line and curvilinear regressions showing optimum score as having highest value

there is no need to make any calculations; it has all been done for you in Figure 14.3.

Of course, the first column in the table would have to be adjusted to the *actual* optimum age or score (or other variable) decided upon—and the same for the no value points. If these points are not equidistant from the optimum, two value scales are needed: one for below the optimum, and one for above. If, instead of calculations on the basis of recorded data, guestimating procedures are used, great accuracy is unnecessary. Obviously, it will not be found in practice that everybody of age or score 35 rated exactly 10; the value score of each age or test score has to be averaged out.

Rating the job factors required

Before discussing how to *combine* the various factors required in this job, it would perhaps be better to run through the items suggested in the advertisement separately, to consider how each should be treated.

Value to be set on age

Would a man aged 32, or one aged 38 be completely useless? Remember, in a few months the man of 32 will be 33, and the accepted man of 37 will be 38. It might be decided for some cogent reason that anyone under 30 or above 40 is unacceptable, the optimum still being 35. As it is better to keep the optimum value score at 10, the possible ages in the first column of Figure 14.3 would be

Possible age or test score	Divergence from optimum $(=d)$	Values from straight-line regression $(10 - d)$	Values from curvilinear regression $(10 - d^2/10)$
(optimum) 35	0	10	10
34 or 36	1	9	10
33 or 37	2	8	9½
32 or 38	3	7	9
31 or 39	4	6	8½
30 or 40	5	5	7½
29 or 41	6	4	6½
28 or 42	7	3	5
27 or 43	8	2	3½
26 or 44	9	1	2
25 or 45	10	0	0

Figure 14.3   Alternative value scores calculated as divergences from optimum

changed to half-yearly instead of yearly intervals; or, keeping to whole years, alternate lines of the remaining three columns can be used (which implies doubling the actual divergence).

Unfortunately, pension schemes nowadays militate against the employment of men who are no longer very young, which seriously interferes with the strict calculation of their true values to new employers unless they can carry their benefits with them from previous employers.

Marital status

It is difficult to rate this item. Married men are preferred, but how many times married? Obviously a steady, reliable sort of chap is preferred, probably (at that age) with a wife and family to support.

He can be asked how many children he has, how old they are, and what they are doing. He can be expected to have a few children. But if he has none (or nine) it might be decided not to give him full marks.

Driving record

A valid driving licence is required. That seems straightforward enough but there have been cases of applicants saying that they were due to take their driving tests next week or next month. The longer the accident-free driving record of the applicant the safer driver he probably is.

At the other extreme is the classical case of a prospective employee, drinking an informal cup of coffee in the canteen with a person on his own (prospective) level. On being asked whether he liked driving, the applicant proudly produced a newspaper cutting from his wallet with the comment: 'Look. Here's a photo of me rolling over at Brands Hatch!' This sort of thing opens up a lot of questions about the sort of chap really wanted—and, arising out of the whole incident, demonstrates the advantage of sending applicants to drink an informal cup of tea or coffee with some existing employee on their own level. But it should be possible to make *some* value rating for driving ability.

The next item ('long distances probable') suggests that a reasonable state of health is necessary. This perhaps is best discovered by tactful questions about the applicant's medical history, unless the company has an arrangement with a doctor to vet applicants for important jobs. However, a long driving experience could be an effective compensation here to a slightly less than robust physique, and it is difficult to suggest value scores other than 'acceptable', 'dubious' and 'unacceptable'—say 10, 5 and 0.

Intelligence and mechanical aptitude

The next two items to be considered can be regarded as general intelligence and mechanical ability, and it is assumed that pencil and paper tests are used. For intelligence, as has already been indicated, top value scores are given not to the highest scorers, but to the optimum—which means, in practice, to the average score of this test of all those past successful applicants who are now quite satisfactorily performing the job in question.

As for mechanical aptitude—and it has been proved several times that a high score on a pencil and paper test is a valid indicator of this attribute—there is no reason why this should *not* be one of the very few cases of 'the higher the better'. It is difficult to imagine any disadvantages associated with top-scorers in this instance—though your records may suggest otherwise!

Personality and character

The last point made by the advertisement ('Brash salesman type not required') could possibly be assessed by interview, notoriously unreliable though this procedure may be. With reference to this, Arbous[1] remarks (p 34):

> In many real-life situations, the 'gas-bags' get away with too much, and there is a tendency to overestimate a man's capabilities because of his capacity of self-salesmanship.

If that is the sort of man wanted, all right; if not, it is best to use a personality test of some kind. Although the procedure needs a psychologically trained person to elucidate the results to laymen so as to obtain the maximum benefit, it can be so revealing that it is surprising that such tests are not more popular with personnel managers and other selectors in industry and commerce. At the least, they should give scientific support to feelings, hunches and intuitions about applicants and in addition probably show up some facets of their personalities that have been missed; on the other hand, should they in some instances point in the other directon from interviewers' impressions, how interesting it is to keep the records and discover in due course which was right!

The various value scores to be allotted to different personality traits present knotty problems to psychometricians as well as to personnel managers; and, of course, different jobs need diferent traits, which implies different scales of values. However, traits considered (or better, found by experiment) to be immaterial can just be ignored, which to some extent reduces the problem.

Character and personality traits are usually regarded as having two extremes, just as Aristotle regarded a virtue as the mean between two vices; so it has to be decided or discovered just where each person falls on each of the trait scales of, for example, dominance–submission, or extroversion–introversion, or stable–unstable. These are usually illustrated by a set of horizontal bar-charts, one bar for each person, which is called his profile. Of course, other attributes of an applicant which are not, strictly speaking, character and personality traits (for example, age, general intelligence and mechanical aptitude) can also be illustrated by horizontal bars in the same profile.

Combining the job factor ratings

Unless the whole set of charts can be quantified and compared by computer the decisions board has to examine and discuss each one. Psychological advice is really needed here, though the test manual should be studied by each member of the board. In fact, it would be best if each were first given (in confidence, of course) the test himself! However, records will accumulate in the course of a few years, and it should become easier to sort out the more dubious applicants by peculiarities in their profiles in the course of time.

If definite minima can be set, below which you flatly refuse to accept anyone no matter how high he scores on other attributes, on some of the bars, of course the problem becomes that much easier; but there are still the comparisons between the remainder. Unless they are all given some sort of arithmetical interpretation into total value scores, even though this does no more than produce more argument and discussion, very little progress can be made. After all, there is no obligation to offer jobs to the highest scorers!

Weighting particular factors

Now, how are the value scores of each separate attribute, factor, variable, characteristic or whatever else you like to call it transformed into a total value score? It is obvious that some attributes are more important for some jobs and others for others. So how is each one weighted for the particular job in question? It is no use thinking that adding up all the separate scores gives each an equal weight or leaves all unweighted. In every separate selection situation, the weighting of every attribute depends on the dispersion around its own average; which means that, the more the applicants differ from each other in this respect, the more likely the job is to be allocated on the basis of this attribute alone, irrespective of how important it is felt (or known) to be.

To demonstrate this, let us assume that there are six shortlist applicants for three vacancies, and that they have been scored on four attributes; extroversion–introversion, mechanical aptitude, age and driving ability (the last having been scored on number of years of accident-free driving). Their scores are tabulated in Figure 14.4. Perhaps it should be mentioned here that a high score on extroversion–introversion does not mean *for this job* that the man is at one extreme or the other—here he is bang in the middle, it having been decided that his is the type wanted, so that any divergence in either direction gets a lower score.

Name	a (E–I)	b (MA)	c (A)	a+b+c	d (DA)	Total
Brown	9	5	10	24	10	34
Jones	9	6	10	25	8	33
McEwen	9	6	9	24	6	30
O'Reilly	9	5	9	23	6	29
Robinson	9	5	10	24	4	28
Smith	9	6	9	24	2	26

Figure 14.4   Effect of divergence from the average on weighting

The first point to notice from the table is that, as everybody has the same score on the extroversion–introversion scale, it has no weight whatever for comparison purposes in the present selection problem. If everyone had nine subtracted from their total in the last column, nobody's place in the final order would change. Secondly, although there are differences in mechanical aptitude and age, they tend to cancel out, although they do just give the edge to Jones and handicap O'Reilly a point. So this appointment is being decided purely on driving ability! Was that really the idea? It is not assumed that the DA score is the actual number of years of accident-free driving, but is based on a scale derived therefrom. Nevertheless, accidents are, in the main, accidents, frequently with neither side much to blame. Should a representative be chosen on that alone? It might be said that there is nothing else to choose between them. But might there not be?

Should not more weight be given to (say) mechanical aptitude? Smith, a top-scorer in this direction, is slightly out in age (too young? too old?), suffers either from being a recently passed driver or had a recent accident. Was it his fault, to any degree? And if so, is it likely to occur again?

Applying the weight calculation

That brings the matter back into the argument and discussion field again! And so it should; unless there are records, statistics, validities and reliabilities all neatly calculated, coefficients of correlations and intercorrelations all tabulated in a matrix, multiple regressions calculated and beta-weights worked out. (Beta-weights are what separate value scores are multiplied by so as to produce the most mathematically correct answer.)

In this completely imaginary example, it may be decided to revalue for driving ability or to *reduce* its weight by dividing by, say, five (answer to the nearest unit) or even to omit it altogether. That would be just guestimating, of course, but it might be quite justified in the absence of more accurate evidence. Or the MA scores could be multiplied by, say, eight, which would have the effect of giving a bonus of seven points over their present marks to Jones, McEwen and Smith—and giving the jobs to Brown, Jones and McEwen. But it will have to be decided whether the difference between one mark on mechanical aptitude is really so much more important than the large differences between the scores allotted on driving ability. The most important thing is to understand *exactly what is involved—and why*. It is put into figures for the sake of the records and as a basis for future selection problems.

Even when weights are calculated most accurately to several places of decimals, only simple whole-number multiplications or divisions need be used. In practice, multiplying scores by, say, 3.859 does *not* give statistically better results than multiplying by 4.

The publications mentioned below give help with all such calculations. With complicated problems entailing a range of pros and cons, the intellect can deal best with arguments presented in quantified form. The more that problems of recruitment and selection can be expressed in such precise terms, the easier it is to make the right decisions.

Reference

1   A. G. Arbous, *Selection for Industrial Leadership,* Oxford University Press, Oxford (this describes mathematical procedures at work in an experimental project)

Further reading

Anstey, Edgar (1966): *Psychological Tests.* London: Nelson. (bases for tests, with valuable introductory chapters)
Holman, L. J. (1974): *Basic Statistics for Personnel Managers.* London: Institute of Personnel Management. (this explains calculation of correlation coefficients)
Miller, K. M. (1975): *Psychological Tests in Personnel Assessment.* London: Gower (tests and techniques for various appointments)
Rulon, Tiedeman, Tatsuoka and Longmuir (1967): *Multivariate Statistics for Personnel Classification.* New York: John Wiley (comprehensive textbook)
Thomson, Sir Godfrey (1948): *The Factorial Analysis of Human Ability.* London: University of London Press (this includes calculation of multiple regressions)

Part Two

Recruitment of Particular Categories of Employee

15

Recruiting Shop-Floor Personnel

Derek Torrington

Success in recruiting for shop-floor positions depends largely on factors over which the recruiter has no control. The level of local unemployment, the availability of specific skills and the extent to which other firms in the neighbourhood are growing or declining are a few of the factors that influence a recruitment record. The most important factor of all is often the nature of the locality. Those seeking shop-floor employment rarely look outside their immediate residential area, so the recruiter has to draw from a specific, small neighbourhood with all its characteristics and traditions.

Appropriate recruitment strategies will probably vary frequently. This is not because shop-floor recruitment is all a matter of gimmicks, but because the local labour market can change so quickly. The recruiter must know what is happening in that market.

Another factor over which the recruiter has less control than he may wish is the selection decision. As with other aspects of personnel work the necessary approach in recruitment and selection is moving towards that of bargaining rather than unilateral determination. Much traditional thinking has been concerned with how recruiters develop an understanding of candidates in order to predict their potential within the organization as a preliminary to a selection decision by the recruiter. It is becoming increasingly important to consider the selection decision being made by the prospective employee about the potential of the organization to him. The shop-floor recruiter has to concern himself as much about the decisions of candidates as he does about his own decisions.

Importance of local reputation

The recruiter needs to make sure that his position in the local community is a favourable one and is likely to induce appropriate applicants to come through the door of his office. The essential preliminary of all factory recruitment is public relations work in the neighbourhood. The company needs to develop the right sort of reputation, so that prospective employees are predisposed to the idea of working in the organization. This can be done by maintaining a general community presence through the active participation of executives in local affairs. One particular method is to have representatives on the various local committees which deal with such matters as employment, education and youth employment. Another means is the local chamber of commerce and rotary.

Of great importance in the locality is the local newspaper. It will certainly carry news about companies in the vicinity, and it should receive a continuous supply of information about the company, however trivial.

Good PR groundwork in the immediate vicinity can put the local inhabitants in a frame of mind where they want to work for the organization; and for shop-floor vacancies it is clearly advantageous to have recruits from as near to the factory as possible. The PR effort should be designed, however, to give an *accurate* representation of the company. An impression of overindulgent benevolence merely attracts people looking for an easy time with as much money as possible. The aim should be a rounded picture which interests the type of person required.

Recruitment sources

For shop-floor vacancies there are four main sources of recruits:

1   Department of Employment Job Centres.
2   Vacancies lists outside the premises.
3   Press advertisements.
4   Personal recommendation.

The Department of Employment has a very good method of presenting suitably qualified candidates quickly, and this can often be the speediest method of filling a vacancy. The job of the DE, however, is to find work for the *un*employed. The recruiter may well want to appeal to those who are already in work with another employer in the hope that they might change to a new company. Obviously this reservation does not apply when school leavers are required. Then the Local Authority Careers Service is the ideal channel to use.

Vacancies lists by the factory gate produce only a very small number of casual applicants and must be regarded as a minor source.

Advertisements in the press can often produce the largest number of applicants and are an effective method of reaching a wide audience, including those who are already quite happily employed elsewhere. Furthermore each advertisement in the local paper assists the job of maintaining the name and reputation of the company in the locality.

Personal recommendation by other company employees already with the company can often be the way to get some excellent people. It is unlikely that any employee will suggest anyone else for a position, unless he is confident that he will be acceptable. Therefore, providing the person making the recommendation is reliable, it is reasonably certain that the person recommended is worth interviewing. Also the prospective new recruit will be helped to settle because he will already have some contact within the working group. This eases the process of becoming established.

The question of sources can be summarized by saying that personal recommendation is likely to produce the most appropriate people, although perhaps not in large numbers. Press advertising probably produces a wide range of applicants, including many who will be appropriate. The Department of Employment may be the quickest way of filling vacancies, and the vacancies list outside the factory premises is of marginal usefulness.

These are the main sources of external applicants, but vacancies must be advertised inside the company as well. This aids morale and indicates possible openings for friends and relatives who can be recommended. Also it can be a way of turning up forgotten talent and coping with the sort of problems that arise from time to time of there being a surplus of personnel in one department and a shortage in another. If people can be moved around as a result of their own initiative, this is more acceptable and effective than if they have to be drafted.

Dealing with applicants

When dealing with applicants, the first thing to establish is that the task is to employ people. It is dangerous to talk in terms of hiring labour, because this has connotations of people being as indistinguishable from one another as bags of cement; or alternatively that the selection task is no more important and no more individualized than the job of checking passengers on to an aircraft flight.

The essential job in recruiting shop-floor personnel is to find someone to become a member of a working team. Every working team or working group takes on a personality of its own. It is made up of human beings, and those individual human beings fit together rather like the stones in a dry stone wall. They are all different shapes and sizes, but they fit closely together so as to become strong and effective. When one of the stones in the wall has to be replaced, the right stone must be found to fit into the particular space that has been made. For a reasonable chance of success, as many applicants as possible are required.

Reception of applicants is important. The first person to be seen by the applicant is the commissionaire or security man on the gate. He needs to understand clearly the procedure for dealing with applicants, so that they are directed quickly and courteously to the personnel department. As soon as they arrive at the personnel office, they again need to be dealt with courteously and quickly, and in a way which follows a simple comprehensible routine in order to establish a proper selection frame of reference.

When applying for positions many people are doing so by taking time off work, and (unlike most personnel managers) they take time off work at their own expense. If they are kept waiting, they lose money.

For each applicant there will at least need to be an application form, setting down the main data about him, on which later decisions about job offers can be based. All that is required at this stage is information relevant to such decision-making. Details like national insurance number are not needed unless and until the applicant becomes an employee.

Some enquirers may not be able to read and write; some may not be able to cope with English. Provided these skills are not required in the job to be performed, a member of the office staff can complete the form for the applicant.

Four stages of selection

In the job selection process there are four principal stages:

1   Seeing the personnel officer.
2   Seeing the foreman or supervisor of the department in which he will work.
3   Seeing the job.
4   Having the offer of employment in writing.

Seeing the personnel officer

This is to make sure that the applicant is interviewed by somebody who has a professional background, interviewing skill, perception and knowledge of the prevailing job market. These should be among the attributes of any personnel officer because that is how he earns his money from his employer: by being good at deciding whether or not an applicant is appropriate for the particular working environment for which he is being considered.

There is, however, another aspect of this meeting: it helps to make the applicant feel that his application is being thoroughly and seriously dealt with. Any employer wants to avoid people coming to him on a 'suck it and see' basis. Not only do they waste time and cost money if they leave after a short space of time, they also tend to unsettle the other members of the working group into which they move, because those people who stay behind begin to think that either there is something wrong with themselves as a group of people or there is something wrong with the job they are doing, and perhaps they too should be looking elsewhere.

A vital aspect of all selection and recruitment is to make the applicants enthusiastic about wanting to work in the organization. If they are recruited, they then start off their spell of employment with a genuine sense of commitment. If people are unsuccessful in their application and are told frankly why they are being turned down, they are likely to have more respect for the organization than if they are cursorily dealt with.

Within reasonable limits 'playing hard to get' can improve the standard of intake to a company. A reputation for thoroughness and selectivity in employee interviewing builds a good reputation, making the factory one in which a job is prized.

Seeing the foreman or supervisor

This again links with the fact that the job is to select a man to fit into a working group. However skilful the personnel officer may be in selection, the foreman or working superior must participate in the selection so that he too is committed to the applicant being successful in his new appointment. If the foreman just has to accept anybody who is 'sent down from personnel', he may be justifiably sceptical about the adequacy of recruits. If he is given an opportunity to reject candidates he considers unsuitable, then he is committed through his own judgement and choice to the fact that those people who come into the department are basically suitable for the job and acceptable to him as the leader of the working group.

Seeing the job

One aspect of human behaviour is to adopt an optimistic attitude towards a new employment opportunity. If a man is changing his job, he is almost certainly expecting it to be a change for the better. He is also quite likely to build it up in his imagination into something rather greater than in fact it is. The job applicant should have as clear and as unglamorous an understanding as possible of the job he is to do before he starts.

With executive and managerial appointments, this is done by compiling detailed job descriptions. With most shop-floor personnel, job descriptions are not likely to be effective, because they would be found tedious to read. Also a shop-floor employee is greatly concerned with practical and physical aspects of his work, which can be demonstrated much more clearly and effectively by seeing the environment, than by any verbal description.

If the man sees the job, the working conditions and, however fleetingly, the people with whom he will be working, there is less likelihood of his being disillusioned when he starts work.

An example of this is in the battery industry, where lead casting is a job that involves working in high temperatures. If the applicant is asked to stand for four or five minutes next to a lead 'pan' while he is being shown the job, he will get an idea of what to expect. If a man will accept the worst features of a job, he is likely to accept the rest of it.

The offer of employment

It is surprising how often shop-floor personnel are recruited and offered employment without anything in writing to confirm the appointment. Employers who make only word-of-mouth offers are surprised by the large proportion of people who never turn up for work.

This is almost certainly because the applicant is not sure whether he has got the job or not. One recruiter was amazed to hear that his standard statement of: 'Well, I would like to offer you the job', was construed by a large proportion of the people to whom he said it as being a conditional offer, and that he had to obtain some further approval before the offer would become absolute.

Apart from this basic uncertainty in the mind of the applicant, the written offer also confirms details which he might otherwise forget or be uncertain of. After the interview the applicant is very likely to be uncertain about an important piece of information that was discussed in it.

The written offer can also contain the essential instructions of what to do when taking up employment, such as the date and time to arrive and what to bring in the way of government forms, tools, clothes and so on.

The letter of offer should be impressive and show thoroughness in the way the application has been treated. It must build confidence in the organization.

A piece of harmless and potentially useful window-dressing may be to arrange for the letter of appointment to bear the signature of some more senior official than the person the applicant has seen.

Interviewing for shop-floor selection

When the personnel officer carries out his employment interview with the applicant, he needs to maintain a warm, friendly yet professional manner in order to gain the applicant's confidence and to establish rapport with him. The easiest way in which the personnel officer will get the applicant's confidence is by his thorough knowledge of the job that is to be filled, and by his clear explanation of it.

The application form is used as the basis for the interview, because it contains all the information about the candidate that the candidate himself has furnished. The personnel officer's questions are based on this information, seeking additional and clarifactory data about the applicant. At the interview stage the personnel officer needs to eschew quick judgement about the applicant in favour of building up a useful body of evidence on which to make a sound judgement later. Jumping to a conclusion can be inaccurate as well as unethical.

Building an image of the applicant

The information to be sought in the selection interview is data about what the applicant has done previously. This will principally be the jobs he has held. How long has he held them? How much change has there been in career pattern, such as going out of his trade? Has he moved about a great deal geographically? Have his periods of employment been long or short and so forth? There will also be useful information to come from the question of what the man does outside his working hours and at least something about his family background. In days of mass production and much soul-destroying manual work, a better understanding of a man and his potential can often be gleaned from what he does away from work rather than from what he does at it. Also, particularly with younger applicants, the educational record, however thin, gives useful indicators.

Throughout the interview the personnel officer needs to be on the alert for gaps in the story where he needs to probe to see if some important piece of information is being withheld, such as a protracted illness or a spell in prison.

He is building up a picture of the whole man; every man is the sum of what he has done, and what has happened to him throughout his life up to the present. If an applicant is questioned only about what jobs he has done, the picture is like the edges of a jigsaw: the shape and size is known but there is no indication of what it is all about. The main body of the jigsaw puzzle is necessary as well.

Type of information required

Among the matters to be probed in interview are the following:

1 Has working experience been in a factory or a shop, indoor or outdoor?
2 Has it been skilled, semi-skilled or unskilled?
3 Is it work that has required manual dexterity or particular intelligence or is it of a general plodding nature? If the position to be filled requires manual dexterity and there is no evidence of it in the working record, there may be some in spare time activities. For instance, does the applicant play a musical instrument? It is almost impossible to do this without a high degree of manual dexterity.
4 Is the work to which the applicant is accustomed repetitive or varied?

5   Has the tempo of work been continuous, on/off, fast or slow?
6   Has there been any supervisory or clerical experience?
7   What is the attitude to authority?
8   What is the physique and general mental suitability of the applicant?
9   What type of intelligence level can be inferred at interview (a dangerous judgement to make)? Is he quick and articulate in his answers to questions, or does he frequently misunderstand? Does he show sufficient intelligence to be able to adapt quickly to a changed working environment?
10 What type and degree of social skill does the applicant have? Does he demonstrate any strong and intolerant views? Is he loud and aggressive? Is he easy-going, nonradical in his attitudes? All these questions are important clues in establishing how he will fit into a particular working group.
11 Is there indication of his being accident-prone? Has he appropriate union membership or acceptability for future membership?

Not all these matters will be relevant in all situations, but for most vacancies the majority of these questions will need answers.

More questionable are those aspects of the application where the interviewer may be tempted to think that he knows better than the applicant. Is there a realistic assessment of the domestic financial situation, for instance? A man may be thoroughly disenchanted with night work and seeking a move to days at a lower rate of pay. The interviewer may feel that the drop in earnings will be greater than the man can afford, so that he will resign after a few weeks and return to night work. The danger of this type of thinking for other people is that, at best, it will only be right in the majority of situations. An alternative is to discuss the issue with the applicant in order to test how fully it has been thought about. Few applicants are likely to agree, there and then, that they have made a mistake, but if they do accept an offer of employment, their commitment to the new job should be the stronger.

Giving information to the applicant

At the same time as eliciting information from the applicant, the personnel officer needs to remember that a job interview is a two-way business. He must also supply information *to* the applicant, who has to decide if the job is what he wants. Details of the job, working conditons and pay both during and after training are the most important aspects. He should be careful to explain the unattractive as well as the attractive aspects of the job. If somebody is going to be put off by the unattractive aspects at interview stage, then it is much better to prevent him starting work at all than for him to start work under a misapprehension and soon start looking round for a fresh opportunity.

Dealing with the unsuccessful applicant

A personnel officer may feel that he can and should offer constructive advice to unsuccessful applicants, explaining why they are not being offered the position, and perhaps suggesting other types of work for which they would be better suited. If a company gets a reputation in a neighbourhood for turning down unsatisfactory people and for being thorough and selective in its recruitment, then it is likely to establish a good reputation and in the long term to improve the standard of applicants for work with it.

Use of waiting-list

If there is a good prospective employee for whom there is no immediate vacancy, a waiting-list should be kept.

The waiting-list can provide a means of quickly filling a future vacancy, and an applicant who is 'remembered' by an employer some weeks after his interview is again likely to feel that his application for employment has been seriously and thoroughly considered and that the vacancy which now occurs is one for which he will be particularly well suited.

What the applicant looks for

At this point it is worth considering what the applicant is looking for in the prospective employer. There are seven suggested cardinal points of interest in the mind of the applicant for a shop-floor vacancy:

1   A fair deal.
2   Industrial training.
3   A trouble-free atmosphere.
4   Welfare facilities.
5   Job satisfaction.
6   Personal dignity.
7   Level of pay.

A fair deal

Applicants will be interested in organizations that have a reputation for fair dealing in employment matters, where employees are appreciated as being people of common sense and reasonableness. Very few people are looking for a firm that is 'soft'. Not many are really looking for an easy life: they are looking for an opportunity to do something worthwhile and satisfying. Of particular relevance here is the reputation of the firm as a non-discriminator against women, ethnic minorities, the aged or the disabled. The importance of such a reputation is not only in the eyes of those particular groups, but as an indicator of fairness and protection against managerial whim for all employees.

Industrial training

Effective training can increase a person's occupational skills and his own market value. In addition it is an indication of commitment by the employer to the career of the employee. It also boosts the self-confidence of the applicant. Most people feel apprehensive about taking on new and unfamiliar duties. If they feel that thorough training is provided, they are more sure of their ability to succeed.

A trouble-free atmosphere

While industrial action is a regular occurrence in contemporary society, it remains axiomatic that the great majority of people find such activities unsettling, even where necessary. A discordant or unsettled working environment is a discouragement to applicants. A company with a trouble-free industrial relations record is much more likely to interest potential applicants.

Welfare facilities

The expectations of employees about the facilities the employer provides are certainly rising. They are no substitute for payment, but employees partly select organizations in which to work on the basis of the fringe benefits that are offered.

Job satisfaction

Almost all people at work, particularly the more able, are likely to be attracted by a job which provides opportunity for some sense of personal achievement. It would be unwise to believe that those seeking shop-floor positions are looking for the same satisfiers as those applying for managerial positions, because the potential of the two is so different, but some form of satisfaction will nearly always be sought.

Personal dignity

Much of the shop-floor work available in a mass-production economy is mindless and undignified, because the technology demands people simply as extensions to the machinery. This is a part of the very high price that has to be paid for mass production—as well as the technology—and the situation is made worse when managers conduct their dealings with employees as if they were automata. The applicant will be much more interested in a position which supports his sense of his own dignity.

Level of pay

Deliberately at the bottom of this list is the question of remuneration. The post-war development of the social security system means that nobody needs to work in order to have the economic wherewithal for a basic standard of living. Within a few decades work might well become a luxury. Clearly the question of the level of payment is vital in any job, but to most people its importance is as a yardstick of their own personal value to the community, rather than a measure of their own personal purchasing power.

Recruitment policies

A policy for shop-floor recruitment can guide recruiters in avoiding pitfalls and declare the standards by which procedures can be judged. A sample general policy statement could be like this:

It is our policy to recruit the most appropriate person for each vacancy, regardless of race, nationality, colour, religion or sex.

All vacancies will be advertised internally and internal applications will be handled in the same way as those from outside. Anyone being recommended by an existing employee should note the fact on the application form, but this does not give a right to employment. For each vacancy applications will be treated in the order they are received.

Where there are not vacancies immediately available, names will be placed, in order received, on a waiting-list.

No offer of employment will be made until the applicant has seen the department in which he would be working and the job he would be doing.

No offer is valid until the applicant receives it in writing, signed by the Chief Personnel Officer.

Variations would be needed for particular categories of employee, like skilled tradesmen, especially where a union membership agreement is operating.

Dealing with special problems

New problems are constantly occurring in the recruitment of operative staff. For example, there is the increasing incidence of shift-working and the difficulties people have in adjusting physically and psychologically to this pattern of working.

Perhaps the saddest thing about shop-floor recruitment is that it is so often undertaken in a defeatist attitude. Because of the widespread shortages of factory personnel, there is a tendency to adopt the attitude that anybody is better than nobody, and there is no need to bother about selection. Alternatively some recruiting officers feel that the conditions and atmosphere within their factories are so unsatisfactory that there is no point in doing a thorough selection job because anybody going through the factory gates will very soon become surly and uncooperative like everybody else.

Ironically it is precisely when either of these attitudes prevail that selection becomes really important as a first step in overcoming the problems with which the organization is beset.

Shop-floor recruitment has not had yet the close attention it deserves. When it is treated with the same thoroughness as is now applied by some firms to selection for management posts, a more stable and effective industrial society may be achieved.

Further reading

Blair, Jon (1973): 'Opportunity knocks — or does it?', *Personnel Management,* vol.5, No.12, Dec., 34–37, 39.

Dunnette, M. D. (1967): *Personnel Selection and Placement.* London: Tavistock.

Goldthorpe, J. H., *et al.* (1968): *The Affluent Worker: Industrial Attitudes and Behaviour.* Cambridge: Cambridge University Press.

Kornhauser, A. (1965): *Mental Health of the Industrial Worker.* New York: Wiley.

Mayfield, Eugene (1964): 'The selection interview — a re-evaluation of published research', *Personnel Psychology,* vol.17, August 239–60.

Plumbley, Philip (1974): *Recruitment and Selection.* London: Institute of Personnel Management.

Roberts, K. (1968): 'The entry into employment', *Sociological Review,* vol.16, New Series No.2, 165–84.

Torrington, D. P. and Chapman, J. B. (1979): *Personnel Management.* London: Prentice Hall.

Turner, A. N. and Lawrence, P. R. (1965): *Industrial Jobs and the Worker.* Boston: Harvard Graduate School of Business Administration.

16

Recruitment and Selection of Supervisors and Foremen

D J Bunter

Many tears have been shed over supervisory management in the past thirty years, because, one suspects, of the feeling that foremen and supervisors no longer achieve the results that they once were held to achieve. As year succeeds year, additions to the ambiguity of the role emerge. The social and economic environment has changed enormously without necessarily clarifying the position of supervisors or the attitudes of supervised and superiors to them. Those in direct and hour-by-hour contact with those performing and achieving tasks can no longer apply sanctions such as fear, dismissal, suspension or other disciplinary controls, independently. Reconciliation between the aims of senior management and the ability of supervisors and foremen to translate these aims into tangible achievement has resulted in frustrations of extreme complexity.

Definition of a supervisor

In very general and superfluous terms, the alleged decline of the effectiveness and quality of the foreman and supervisor is ascribed to inadequate pay and low status. Both, it can be argued, have led to a serious decline in the number of potentially viable candidates, the field having been depleted by bypassing the category in favour of specialist or functional roles or a considered judgement that the responsibility is just not worth it. Much of the problem has been caused by lack of definition of the role of the supervisor and the foreman—top management assuming one set of criteria and the foreman and supervisor performing to another, the latter being more practicable.

Job titles, as even the most cursory glance at the voluminous pages of appointments advertised in our national Sunday and daily newspapers will reveal, show considerable differences between appointments described, for example, as production managers. In functional or staff appointments both carrying the same job title the differences in job content are quite enormous; so, too, for foremen and supervisors. There is a[1] 'need to avoid assuming that a given title has a given meaning other than in a given context'.

For the purposes of this chapter, the foreman or supervisor is held to be responsible for supervising and organizing the work of people allocated to him to carry out a task or tasks, without himself carrying out the work to be performed (this is the definition given by the Swedish Supervisor's Union). In this connection it is necessary to draw a distinction between foremen and supervisors and working chargehands.

Specification of a supervisor

Much of what has been criticized in foremanship and supervising, certainly in the past years, has arisen because of an attitude that the foreman and supervisor is 'all things to all men'. Genius is rarely found at this level. If it exists it is not there for every long. Drucker[2] paints a somewhat depressing picture of the supervisor and the history of supervision in Chapter 25 of *The Practice of Management* but alleviates the gloom by postulating that the supervisor needs clear objectives for his activity (ie that which is to be achieved), promotional opportunities based on performance, and status. Drucker goes further and seeks to abolish the supervisor's job and to have it recognized as that of manager.

Taken entirely within the context of manufacturing industry, the foremen's and supervisor's responsibilities or obligations to carry out the task include the following:

1   Planning, scheduling and controlling activities of his section so that work flows at an even pace.
2   Provision of the tools, equipment and materials necessary to do the work.
3   An adequate environment for himself and his work force to operate in.
4   An adequate number of employees to perform the work necessary.
5   Motivating his work team.
6   Setting objectives for his team and individual members of it.
7   Training and developing individual members of his work force.

Although this definition is manufacturing oriented, the clauses are applicable to supervisors in other walks of life.

Any definition of the role of the foreman and the supervisor must, for effectiveness, contain only those factors for which he can be held accountable and accepts, those clearly unambiguous and those weightable in importance. Part of the confusion in the past has resulted in reducing the supervisor's team and not the number and range of tasks involved. Small units do not necessarily solve management's and/or the supervisor's dilemma. Many supervisory jobs have grown to impossible proportions, often because of the seniority of certain supervisors and foremen in their roles who have accumulated new tasks year by year without consciously recognizing their order of importance.

This proliferation of jobs expected to be performed by foremen and supervisors has led to exaggerating the importance of the role. Whilst the supervisor and foreman is a manager, he is not management, if we accept that the management of an enterprise is the establishment of objectives, principles and practices. These are all established at levels way above that of the supervisor, although it is uniquely he who can identify the needs of his work force to achieve their best performance.

The foreman and supervisor shares with members of management, who might similarly act in ill-defined roles, a propensity to weight activities by personal preference and prejudice. Whilst it can be argued that self-selection of priorities adds to a feeling of participation and discretion, the dangers of being allowed to drift farther and farther from the real key features of the job inevitably lead to inadequate performance—a judgement which will be made by both superior and supervised. Uncontrolled it is likely that such selection of tasks will veer in favour of those likely to present the fewest problems.

If the objective of the foreman and the supervisor is to supervise and organize the work of people then the priority task must be that of man management. If we ask the supervised to weigh the factors of the foreman's and supervisor's job in order of importance, we are almost certain to find that the human aspects come well before the technical or clerical aspects of the job, however important they might be[3]. These priorities have been recently established as follows:

1 *Consideration.* The extent to which the supervisor makes an effort to understand the feelings of those under him and to take them into account.
2 *Initiating structure.* The extent to which the supervisor initiates and accepts changes.
3 *Quality of work.* The extent and method of criticizing poor work.
4 *Quantity of work.* The supervisor's reaction to what is performed in a good time.

There are two common alternative supervisory styles, either of which might fulfil some, but certainly not all, of the criteria listed. Both lack involvement with the supervised. The first style is all too common—an aggressive, harassing, constantly vigilant, bustling style. This supervisor thinks he knows what is happening every moment of the day, is never short of an answer and is distinguished by his communication one way, down to the supervised. The second supervisor is remote, often widely experienced, but a believer in letting the team get on with their jobs, and available, indeed only visible, when things go wrong and a problem requires solution. Both these examples lead in their different ways to loss of productivity, ie they demotivate.

Groups or teams of supervised are never static. Members leave, change, go sick, get married, acquire new interests, etc, and their motivations individually and corporately change accordingly. One new arrival with strong needs and values ought to alert the man management oriented foreman or supervisor to action that means do exist to satisfy the former. The foreman and supervisor therefore needs to be coached in this whole area of subordinate motivation.

Whilst man relations and motivational awareness might well be the priority activity of the foreman and supervisor, he also has the task of supplying goods or services or of turning materials or components into goods, either finished or as part of a process. It is the reconciliation of the supervised's motives with the foreman's essential control procedures which can lead to conflict. The foreman and supervisor is presumed to understand his own motivation, although few may have actually stood off from themselves and honestly considered the matter. If there is recognition that to do as you would be done by is a cornerstone of the supervisor's reaction to man management, then he will see the need for recognition and appreciation and to these relate job security, adequate financial reward and relationships within the team.

The role of the foreman and supervisor must be thoroughly researched and defined in terms of:

Objectives.

Responsibilities, which must include his activities of organization, personnel, finance, reports and any membership of company committees.

His authority, expressed in terms of his powers of decision and right to use determined resources and any limitations of such authority.

His relationships, particularly to whom he is directly responsible, for his subordinates and his contacts both regular and occasional with other company personnel.

When each and every foreman's and supervisor's job has been analysed in this detail, a specification can be created. The specification should include such personal data as age, sex, home circumstances and marital status (if these are appropriate), a general standard of physique for the task expressed in terms of health, eyesight, hearing, etc, and of speech in terms of its quality, manner, as evidenced by smartness and vigour, and appearance. The job specification should also include educational and technical qualifications and training, both essential and preferred, and finally work and other experience, again essential and preferred, to carry out the task. The specification in these terms is, however, only a skeleton and to be confident that one knows what is being sought it is necessary to put flesh on the bones. This is best expressed as the essential abilities required by competent foremen and supervisors, viz mental abilities (his intelligence, verbal ability in both speech and writing and mathematical ability). The list should also include a statement and judgement about the social role of the job highlighting the gregarious, leadership, persuasive and organizing requirements. Ability will also be required in the general area of initiative and some judgement expressed of the extent of self-starting, ability to work without supervision, administrative and organizing skills needed.

Finally, no checklist of abilities required by foremen and supervisors can omit the requirement for emotional stability expressed in terms of his ability to tolerate stress, of his maturity, or of his motivation in which he must have his own guidelines and objectives and awareness of drive.

As Sidney and Brown[4] say: 'Selection involves measuring an individual's capacity against the requirements of a particular job. But no measurement is possible unless what is to be measured has first been defined.'

Job definitions, job specifications and statements of abilities required are not difficult or laborious documents to prepare so long as all the factors are codified in an easy-to-read fashion and are comprehensive enough to allow for alternatives and weighting. The foregoing applies to any job within an enterprise. The danger is in allowing definitions to remain static and unalterable. Jobs, not least those of the foreman and supervisor, are dynamic and can and do change with some rapidity.

Before, therefore, proceeding to recruitment action, all such documented checklists need to be thoroughly researched. Even with such assurance the recruiter, in order to be confident that he knows precisely what he is looking for, must review the requirements of the job with a clear understanding of the climate of the enterprise.

Finding a supervisor

Where are we likely to find people able to perform in the job as defined, as specified and with the abilities prescribed? The first and obvious area of search is unquestionably within the personnel of the enterprise in which the job arises. Employees at least can be presumed to understand and accept the climate of the enterprise. Further, on the assumption that the enterprise has some form of training, career development, appraisal and self-identification, there should be a ready list of potential candidates. If, however, the enterprise is in an era of change (particularly that of climate) then such a list will be subject to pruning.

There are of course inherent dangers in any policy of making promotions or appointments of foremen and supervisors exclusively from within. The first is that the variation of standards by selectors and recruiters might well reflect the type of persons to whom the selected are responsible and to whom they might defer.

Secondly there is the danger that, unless the highest standards of selection are applied, the new supervisor is placed in an immediate stress situation by pressures from both above and below. As we have seen, management has its expectations as presented in the job definition and job specification. The individual, however, still retains loyalties to and from the people he is required to lead. The stress of identification in these circumstances is much greater than that in higher strata of management where the art of getting things done through other people has already been exercised, often for many years.

The risk can, however, be minimized if the enterprise advertises vacancies for supervisors and foremen internally, thereby allowing natural selection to supplement all other channels of information such as appraisals and *ad hoc* discussions between managers and supervisors concerning men of potential. In this context, natural selection necessarily implies taking into account the opinions of those members of the working group who influence its feelings, attitudes and needs.

From what other sources are candidates likely to arise? There is the admirable Professional and Executive Recruitment (PER) of the Department of Employment. Secondly, the enterprise can advertise its vacancies both locally and nationally. Whilst the appointments advertisements columns of the local, national and trade publications do not usually include any great number of advertisements of this nature, job mobility (temporary difficulties regarding housing not excepted) and individual career planning are such that the field of consideration can and should be widened to include able and qualified outsiders.

Recruitment or executive search consultants are not likely to be very helpful in this category of recruitment but certain professional bodies are willing and able to nominate members who are known to be seeking a change of company for one reason or another.

In addition, most companies receive letters of application from time to time and these can form the basis of a register to be researched when vacancies arise.

Analysis of candidates

Having accumulated a number of nominations and applications, the next requirement is to analyse the data disclosed by candidates or available from records with the criteria listed in the job analysis and specification. If the analysis and specification is accurate, one can be quite ruthless in eliminating from the list of applicants those not possessing the essential qualities for the job.

Recruitment is a lengthy and expensive business and the inclusion of candidates in an interviewing list who can only be classified as 'possibles' ought to be resisted. Selection consultants may well be able to devote time and energy to the interviewing of a wide field but this is often deliberately done in order to build up their own bank of generally viable candidates. A company recruiting for a particular task, having taken the trouble to be specific about defining that task, must be equally vigorous in eliminating those who have no prospect of filling the job to the standard required. The selector must develop skills enabling him to judge something of the personality, motivation, intelligence and behaviour of applicants from what they reveal in their applications, whether these are received by letter, telephone call or appraisal. Those appearing to meet the job specification should then be called for interview.

The selection process

Colonel L.F. Urwick[5] says: 'Selection should always be a group process; it is one of the few things a group does better than an individual'. He then adds some telling factors as to why he believes this to be so. Certainly in the selection of supervisors who are primarily concerned with influencing others, getting on with others and communicating with others, and who face constantly changing problems, selection by several people rather than an individual has its attractions.

Every selection procedure should have participation by a defined group. First by the organization's trained interviewers, secondly by the manager to whom the selected candidate is to report and thirdly by the manager next above who ensures that there is balance in the teams under his control. With such a procedure there is an assumption that each interview will be conducted on a one-to-one basis and that at the end the three interviewers will present their findings and, hopefully, reach a unanimous conclusion.

The use of formal 'group selection' techniques and the techniques of interviewing are discussed elsewhere in this book. Whatever the selection methods adopted, the following characteristics should, for foremen and supervisors, be carefully assessed:

1 Familiarity with, and opinions of, consultation and delegation.
2 Familiarity, including participation, with operator training.
3 Attitudes to staff departments—accounting, industrial engineering, personnel and industrial relations, purchasing, quality control, etc.
4 Company communications—up and down.
5 Opportunity and appropriateness of training and self-development.
6 His understanding of and his actions to prepare himself for the role for which he is being considered.
7 His understanding of and his activities in the exercise of leadership.

8   Past achievements, failures and aspirations—and why.
9   Attitudes to criticism.
10 Contradictions he has observed and envisages.
11 Attitudes and any participation experienced in the setting of objectives.

The relevance of questions depends entirely on the approved job analysis and specification for the appointment concerned and must be framed to elicit how much he knows, what he has done and with what success and what his opinions are.

Follow-up

Both interviewer and interviewee are conscious that the selection process is a subjective one. The former, whether professional or a line manager, being made constantly aware that predictions can be quite seriously in errror. Improvements to selection and recruitment procedures depend entirely on adequate information about the subsequent performance of the successful candidate in the job situation.

No procedure is, therefore, complete until and unless structured checks are made on actual performance, comparing this with the original analysis and specification. Newly appointed supervisors should be appraised one month after appointment, and again at three months, six months and twelve months. Such reports will not necessarily reveal all that is required about the original analysis, specification or selection unless the appraisal itself is structured. A blanket 'is doing all right' is unlikely to be of value if the selected candidate is failing in one or more of the four or five key areas of the job identified by the interviewer, even if the successful candidate is getting on superlatively well with his manager.

References

1 E. F. L. Brech, *Organization—the Framework of Management,* Longmans, London, 1965.
2 Peter F. Drucker, *The Practice of Management,* Heinemann, London, 1955.
3 D. Tscheulin, *Supervisory Behaviour Description Questionnaire, Behavioural Science Report International,* 1974.
4 E. Sidney and M. Brown, *The Skills of Interviewing,* Tavistock, London, 1961.
5 L. F. Urwick, *Sixteen Questions about the Selection and Training of Managers,* Urwick Orr & Partners Limited, London, 1958.

Further reading

Munro Fraser, J. (1966): *A Handbook of Employment Interviewing.* London: Macdonald and Evans.

Plumbley, P. R. (1974): *Recruitment and Selection.* London: Institute of Personnel Management.

Plumbley, P. R. and Williams, P. (1972): *The Person for the Job.* London: BBC Publications.

Rodger, A. (1952): *The Seven-Point Plan.* Paper No. 1. London: National Institute of Industrial Psychology.

Thurley, K. and Wirdenius, H. (1973): *Approaches to Supervisory Development.* London: Institute of Personnel Management.

17

Clerical Staff

J G Knollys

Despite the increasing use of computers and the arrival of the microchip, clerical staff continue to play a vital part in the operations of most companies, either in close association with the data processing departments or, particularly in smaller organizations, in their own right. In the larger 'white-collar' organizations, (banks, insurance companies, etc.) clerical staff remain a major asset, perhaps second only to the property owned by the employer; it is therefore vital that recruitment in this field is not relegated to the level of being a 'chore' to be palmed off on the least competent or least experienced member of the personnel department.

Identifying the clerical staff market

The clerical staff market differs in one major aspect from other traditional labour markets. In mining and many major industrial concerns most, if not all, of those employed come from clearly defined geographical areas in relation to their work place and from a social background which is traditional in relation to the particular type of work. In the clerical field, however, employees are drawn from a far wider geographical area and a wide range of social backgrounds. These have changed over the past half-century as a reasonable level of education has become available to more and more people, particularly to girls. Added to this, many young women who at one time would never have dreamed of setting hand to a pen or typewriter, or any other form of employment now view a clerical job (secretaries are included in this category) as a normal step from classroom to kitchen sink. These factors add to the difficulty of identifying the market when recruiting for a particular kind of clerical job.

Conurbation versus county town

One of the significant factors affecting the recruiting of clerical staff is the geographical location of the employment. In a small- or medium-sized town, even in larger cities where there is no single dominating employer, it is comparatively easy to recruit staff of an acceptable standard, provided that working conditions are comparable with those offered by other employers. There are obvious reasons for this; most of the local population live within half an hour's journey of any part of the town and most of them read the same local newspaper; there are probably only a handful of reputable employment agencies in the centre of the town. As the size of the town and the complexity of its business life increase, so the difficulties increase until, ultimately, they reach the nightmare proportions of London (which deserves separate consideration).

Even in the most peaceful and compact country town, however, the recruiter's life of comparative ease can become a nightmare if a national employer 'relocates' from London or another major conurbation, particularly if he comes armed with such inducements as national pay scales, expensive bonus schemes, subsidized mortgages and free canteen lunches. On the other hand, recruiters whose companies are relocating to these country areas should not be complacent. They may be regarded as 'foreigners' and local loyalties may be stronger than all the free lunches in the world; there may just be not enough people to go round and excessive 'poaching' will not create goodwill with other local employers with whom the company may need to do business.

Recruitment in London

London presents a special challenge to the recruiter of clerical staff for it contains every kind and size of employer competing for the best staff, further complicated by the large number of employment agencies who rely on continuous staff instability or, in the case of temporary staff suppliers, on continuous shortage to make their profits.

In central London it is largely a case of the highest bidder getting the goods, simply because the main reason for clerical staff living in the area or being prepared to put up with the discomforts of commuting is that the money is better than if they work nearer home. Fringe benefits should not be ignored, especially if they add to the value of take-home pay, but it is of little use to rely on them as bait if you cannot compete on salary.

Recruiting in outer London is a far more complex operation, requiring considerable planning, as will be explained later in the chapter.

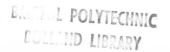

Recruitment strategy

For reasons already stated, there is a need to plan carefully when faced with clerical vacancies. Where do the potential applicants live? How can they most effectively be reached? What is the competition and how can one out-manoeuvre and out-bid it?

The smaller town

In the smaller country town the answer can be obtained easily. Most, if not all, of the town is within a few minutes' travel of the office, so applicants may be obtained from the area as a whole. They can be reached through the main local paper. Better still, there may be a local free paper which is circulated on a house-to-house basis. Being free and compact it will usually be read. There are probably only a few employment agencies and, through personal contact, a reasonable service may be obtained. The competition is easy to assess through local knowledge and there is a good chance that existing members of staff have worked for them or have friends or relatives who still do so.

London and large cities

In the larger cities the task becomes more complex. This is where, as in outer London, in-depth planning is not out of place. Firstly, study a map of the area surrounding the place of employment.If it is in the city centre, is it close to a particular railway station or bus terminus or a particular bus route? This will indicate the most likely sources of applicants.

Having established where they live, how can they best be reached? Is there one local paper giving better coverage than others? Is there a local free paper which is circulated in different areas each week; if so, when will it be effective in the area concerned? Are there any local employment agencies in that area in addition to those in the city centre?

If the place of employment is in a suburban area (this applies particularly to greater London) the planned approach becomes even more vital. In addition to the factors already mentioned there is a vast additional source of staff—commuters in transit. If the office is close to a commuter bus route or railway station there are thousands of clerical staff passing each day, probably in conditions of acute discomfort and at vast and ever-increasing cost. Again, where do they come from? How can they be persuaded to cut their journey (probably the worst part of it) by working in the suburbs? Can they be offered an employment package which will offset any financial advantage of working in the central areas? Are there more central areas from which staff could travel out, against the commuter flood and therefore in greater comfort? The geographical factors apply to many places but, as a classic example, consider Wimbledon in southwest London (Figure 17.1). This is a pleasant area, just far enough from central London to have an identity of its own and with a sufficient variety of good shops to meet the everyday needs of most staff. Even a brief glance at the map will show that it enjoys a number of potentially valuable characteristics. It is midway between two main commuter roads, the A3 and the A24 and easily accessible from either. No fewer than seven railway routes converge on it, mainly carrying large numbers of commuters to central London. It is at the end of a branch of the District Line of the Underground system, on which thousands travel inwards in appalling discomfort and very few travel out from such areas as Putney or Fulham. Enquiries will reveal that it is well served by bus services from several directions. Along these lines of communication are many major residential centres, providing between them more than enough staff for half a dozen large offices, if only they can be persuaded of the advantages of Wimbledon compared with the City or West End.

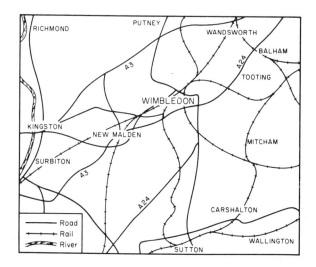

Figure 17.1   Simplified map showing some of the features to be considered when locating staff sources

Reaching the applicant

Having considered the physical factors which help to identify the potential staff market, it is necessary to set about reaching the right people at a reasonable cost. What are the options? Are employment agencies better value than newspaper advertising?

Employment agencies

Opinions on employment agencies differ as much, probably, as on any other matter in the field of personnel management. To some they are the easy option; you give brief details of a vacancy and then sit back and wait for applicants to be provided, paying only when a suitable person is engaged. If the vacancy details are given to enough agencies, sooner or later someone reasonable will turn up, meanwhile one is free to get on with really 'important' work. At the other extreme are those who believe (and this belief is shared by many trades unionists) that agencies are a menace to the business world, encouraging staff turnover and pushing up expected salaries in a 'buyer's' market to ensure a larger fee and thereby adding to the problems of inflation. As with most things, however, the choice is not as simple as that and a closer look at employment agencies is justified.

Many agencies start out with idealistic standards of service but, sooner or later, particularly when, as frequently happens, a larger company takes them over, the ideals are replaced by the need to make a profit. It is very important, therefore, to know the agency before giving it any business; it is equally important to know its terms of business, since to agree to allow it to search for an applicant is construed as acceptance of its terms.

What then should one consider at the outset?

1   *Licence.* Under the Employment Agencies Act 1973[1], every agency must be licensed by a local authority. If there is no evidence that this is to (eg no reference on the agency stationery), keep away.

2   *Fee's structure.* Most agencies, regrettably, base their fees on a percentage of the starting salary to be offered, with increasing percentages for higher salary ranges. If questioned on this the reply is usually either that this is a requirement of the licensing authority or, more frequently, that the higher the salary the more difficult, and therefore more costly, to find candidates. In the case of clerical staff, this is debatable, on the contrary, the higher the salary the more attractive the job and consequently the easier it will be to secure a suitable candidate. In any event, the higher the salary the higher the appointment fee, even if a fixed percentage is charged for all salary levels. Better than this is an arrangement whereby an agreed sum is paid on engagement. All agencies run on business-like lines must cost their operations and must therefore know the estimated cost of filling a vacancy and the profit margin required after allowing for inflation and other factors. If they cannot make such calculation, far better keep them at arm's length; if they can but do not it is always worth haggling; they will sometimes compromise.

There are two other aspects of fees which are worth investigation. If an agency charges a percentage of salary, what is meant by salary? Does it include average estimated overtime, London allowance, bonuses; in other words does it mean 'salary' or 'gross earnings'. It is well to establish this from the start, to avoid acrimonious correspondence and ill-will later. Secondly does the agency charge different fees for different areas? Some of the largest and (at least outwardly) most respectable agencies charge higher percentages for employment near to the centre of London. In such cases, it would seem dishonest to include any element of London allowance as part of the salary on which they base their fees.

Having enquired into the agency's methods of business, the client employer should state his own terms and reach agreement before placing a vacancy. It may sound a long-winded procedure but, with the ever-increasing cost of recruiting staff, it is seldom time wasted.

Although there are, without doubt, agencies who are unscrupulous and seek to profit from situations of staff scarcity or even to create such situations for their own ends, this does not apply to all of them and there are, equally, many who genuinely seek to provide a service. It is, therefore, worth the effort to get to know your agency, preferably by meeting the local manager or a senior representative.

Press advertising

The major alternative to employment agencies is advertising in newspapers or periodicals. Although this may seem obvious and may seem to require little consideration before placing an advertisement, there are many possibilities of wasting money if the matter is treated lightly. Whereas, with agencies, one pays by results, with press advertising one pays in advance and it is therefore important to ensure that the risk of paying for no result is minimized. What is the choice? What is the geographical and numerical circulation of each paper or periodical? How much space does each give to recruitment advertising? How can one compare the results which can be expected of one compared with another? How far in advance of publication must the advertisement be booked and copy submitted? The best way to obtain answers to these questions is to use the services of a reputable advertising agency, preferably one specializing in recruitment advertising or having a recruitment division. Personal recommendation is the best method of choosing an agency but, failing that, one may obtain some idea of its worth by finding out which other employers use it for recruitment advertising. In most cases, agencies are very ready to sell themselves on the basis of their more famous clients. Advertising agencies obtain much of their income from commission paid to them by the media and the only cost to the client, apart from the normal space cost for the advertisement, which would be incurred in any event, is that of production of display advertisements. This aspect of cost will be considered later.

If an agency is used, it will be able to answer the questions above from its knowledge and experience. If it is worth using, it should also be able to write copy and design lay-outs to project the desired image of the employing organization. A good working relationship, based on personal acquaintance with the agency's account executive, is essential if a worthwhile service is to be provided. If no agency is used, the recruiter must do his own groundwork. On the first occasion this will involve considerable effort, studying individual papers, contacting the publishers to establish circulation areas and using a process of elimination to measure cost effectiveness in terms of response. In this situation much basic information may be obtained from the advertiser's 'bible', *British Rate and Data* (BRAD)[2], which includes details of more newspapers and periodicals than most recruiters are ever likely to need.

The advertisement

Job advertising is dealt with in detail in Chapter 5. The general principles apply to clerical staff, with one exception—in the nonspecialist press there are likely to be more advertisements for clerical staff in a given space than for any other staff category. It is therefore important to catch the reader's eye with an aspect of the job which could make it more attractive than the competition. The obvious point is salary. Is it better than the average for the area? Or is the holiday entitlement better? It is difficult in many cases to make effective use of basic terms such as these since most employers try to keep abreast of market trends without incurring excessive staff overheads. The best potential 'carrot' is something the competition cannot offer; for clerical staff this might be such a benefit as flexible working hours, which has many attractions, especially for married women with their dual loyalties as employee and housewife. Many employers do not yet offer flexible hours and it can therefore be used in a prominent way to outbid competitors for the scarce commodity being sought.

Handling job applications

At the beginning of this chapter it was stressed that clerical staff recruitment should not be treated as a 'chore'. It is particularly important to avoid giving such an impression to the applicant, more so if the introduction is through an employment agency. It is useful in this event for the agency to give the applicant details of several employers and for the applicant to have registered with several agencies, if they are available. The situation, especially in London, is very much one of the applicant selecting an employer rather than the reverse. The employer must, therefore, come up to scratch. See the applicant as soon as possible. Be flexible in agreeing the interview time, even if it entails upsetting your lunch hour or staying half an hour late in the evening. Do everything possible to create a good impression of the organization when the applicant arrives; the atmosphere of the reception area and the personnel department can have a critical effect on the outcome of the recruiting exercise even if taken for granted in day-to-day working life.

Whereas, with most clerical vacancies, telephoned applications are usual, when dealing with a senior vacancy, written applications may be required. The first letter to the applicant may be just as critical to the success of the exercise as the applicant's first letter to the potential employer. This applies particularly to senior secretaries; ensure that the letter sent is at least up to the standard to be required in the job.

The interview

A single short interview is a very chancy method of discovering whether an applicant and a job are compatible. However, it may be the only opportunity provided before another employer snatches the applicant from under one's nose. Circumstances are frequently against the interviewer; there may be several applicants to be seen for different vacancies, all wishing to come during the lunch break; individual applicants may be 'at the dentist' and anxious not to be away from the office for too long; the interviewer may have other, urgent duties to perform which seem at the time more important than 'another tiresome interruption'. Despite these factors or, more accurately, because of them, particular care must be taken to ensure that the interview achieves its prime objectives: the exchange of sufficient information between employer and applicant to minimize the risk of later incompatability and to enable both parties to make valid comparisons with the alternatives available. This can seldom be achieved if the interview lasts under half an hour, unless the applicant is clearly unsuitable from the start (allowing for any prejudice on the part of the interviewer).

If possible, the interview should be backed by some form of aptitude test. The most obvious and most widely used is a typing test for typists (with shorthand if applicable) but it can be equally important to assess ability with figures and general neatness of work. Tests for general clerical aptitudes and for specific clerical skills are available (see Chapter 8).

Having satisfied oneself that the applicant fulfils the basic requirements of the job, it is important that a final decision be made by the supervisor or manager of the department concerned. If they are to work together they must feel, from the start, that they *can* do so effectively and happily (since so large a proportion of our working life is spent at work, there is much to be said for the maxim: 'If you are not happy in your job, move'). If at all possible, the final decision should be taken at the applicant's first visit; otherwise a subsequent interviewer may prove more tempting. Even if it is possible, there is a risk of losing out to the competition but, if the selection has been carried out effectively, the applicant's choice will at least be made with all the relevant facts to hand. Having said that, it is, of course, difficult always to make a decision immediately after the interview, especially if there are other applicants to be seen. In this instance it is important, at least, to give a clear indication of when a decision will be made.

The final stages

With any category of staff there is a risk that, even after an offer of employment has been accepted, something more tempting will arise. In the case of senior or specialist staff one is usually informed if, as a result, the acceptance is to be withdrawn. With clerical staff, however, it is common, particularly in London, for the recruit to say nothing, the employer only discovering the truth when the starting date arrives but the employee does not. This can be very irritating, particularly if other passable applicants have been rejected. If the selected applicant has received an offer and has accepted it, whether in writing or verbally, a contract of employment has been struck and failure to stand by it constitutes, in the strict sense, a breach of contract. Few employers, however, are prepared to go to the expense and trouble of suing an applicant in such circumstances; in the rare cases where they do, the damages, if any, are nominal and the publicity for the employer is unlikely to ease recruiting in the future. The point made here is that it pays to start the applicant as soon as possible after the offer is accepted, allowing time to obtain references but ensuring that there are no unavoidable delays.

The recruiting exercise cannot be said to be completed until the new employee is settled into the job. This does not mean that, on the first morning, the new arrival should be unceremoniously planted at a desk and set to work. It may seem nonproductive to do otherwise but a period of induction, however short, is seldom a waste of time. Even the most routine clerical job will become more worthwhile if the employee understands how it is linked to others within the department and, better still, to the activities of the organization as a whole.

References

1   *Employment Agencies Act 1973,* HMSO, London.
2   *British Rate and Data (The National Guide to Media Selection),* 35–39 Maddox Street, London W1R 9PF.

18

Sales Staff

T S Duxfield

The aim of sales management is to sell a company's products in the maximum possible volume at the minimim possible cost in overheads. The means of achieving this aim is more often than not through a sales force which consists partly of men from within the company who have transferred to outside sales from indoor jobs, and partly of men who have been recruited from outside.

Since the cost effectiveness of a selling operation depends not only on the volume of goods sold but also on the cost of the selling, an important element of which is the *quality* of the salesmanship, it follows that enlightened recruitment plays a highly significant part in cost effectiveness.

Essential qualities of sales staff

When transferring a man from an inside job to the outside sales force, it is important to be reasonably certain that he is cut out for a career in salesmanship. He should be temperamentally suited to selling in the ways we shall touch on later. When recruiting from outside, where the applicants are already salesmen, it is important to make as sure as possible that a candidate has genuine interest in the branch of industry or commerce for which he is applying.

Temperament, interest in the products, knowledge and skills are the four cornerstones on which professional salesmanship is based. Given that temperament is an absolute prerequisite, the order of the other three is debatable. The order just given recognizes the fact that if interest is synonymous with enthusiasm, as is frequently the case, it is such a strong motivating force that it will nearly always create knowledge and skill. In this context the word knowledge embraces both product expertise and knowledge of selling principles; skill implies the ability to apply both these facets of knowledge.

The two essential prerequisites for a successful career in salesmanship—that a man should be temperamentally suited to the way of life and that he should be fired by enthusiasm for the particular branch of it that he selects—may sound rather obvious, but it is unfortunately true that far too many men embark on selling careers for the wrong reasons. Even those whose personalities are otherwise suited to selling sometimes take insufficient trouble over finding out to which sector of industry or commerce they are best fitted.

Reasons for becoming a salesman

There are good reasons and bad reasons which motivate a man into salesmanship. The two most commonly heard wrong reasons are probably: 'I like an open-air life and travelling' and 'I like to be my own boss'. In the second of these a man means, of course, that although he has a boss, he is answerable to him only at certain intervals.

There is nothing intrinsically wrong with preferring a relatively open-air life and travelling, so long as these inclinations are regarded as peripheral benefits attached to the job of selling, which ideally should be desired for itself alone. The art of salesmanship has been defined as the ability to persuade other people to do what is wanted of them in such a manner that they actually want to do it. In other words, a salesman must ideally possess a rather special type of personality in which something of the motivational zeal of a missionary is combined with persuasiveness.

Missionary zeal is compounded of two elements—a firm belief in something and a burning desire to pass on that something to other people. This may seem a high-sounding way of trying to define the force which animates the true salesman, but at his best he is very much of a proselyte in the urge he feels to influence people to do what he wants them to do.

Persuasiveness may be defined as the application of selling skills and, although these can mostly be taught, they do require as foundation a personality that is fundamentally acceptable and, if possible, pleasing to other people.

The best reason then for a man wishing to become a salesman is that he should actually enjoy the persuasive presentation of products or services in which he believes and in which he is genuinely interested. As regards possessing an acceptable and pleasing manner, he need not be an out-and-out extrovert but he must be a ready conversationalist and not prone to shyness. Incredible though it may seem, there are men who drift into salesmanship only to find that in different degrees they actually *fear* confrontation with prospective buyers.

It is even possible for a moderately successful salesman to suffer from this disability. The most common pattern in these cases is that a man steels himself at the outset of his selling career to make a circle of good connections and, having slowly and painfully achieved this limited objective, he sits back contentedly and makes no effort to extend his small circle of buyers. His temperament is such that he only likes to call on 'friends', and shies away from unknown faces who may rebuff him.

Interest in the product and the job

Every salesman should therefore try to operate in a field of genuine interest to himself personally. The enthusiasm that follows is then authentic and self-generating. Far too many salesmen work in fields where interest in the product has to be stimulated and to a large extent even simulated as part of the skills of selling. In varying degrees therefore the enthusiasm is forced and sooner or later the quality of the salesmanship suffers. It is a common mistake to think that the skills of selling are in themselves the open sesame to success. True enough, without them a man is always less than fully effective in his efforts, but selling skills themselves are less than fully effective unless they are based on interest and enthusiasm.

Having chosen a selling field that interests him, a salesman should never forget that he is performing a vital and indispensable service in promoting the sale of his company's merchandise or services. He must never fall prey to the suspicion that he is a suppliant whose career consists of touting for business by asking favours. Any salesman harbouring such a notion has succumbed to just about the most negative and dangerous mental attitude of all—the old-fashioned concept of salesmanship as consisting of high-pressure tactics designed to disguise the fact that a salesman is essentially a suppliant.

In short, good salesmen believe beyond all doubt that they are engaged in a worthwhile profession and are additionally motivated by an intrinsic interest in the merchandise or service they are selling. The essence of believing in salesmanship lies in being convinced of its necessity. A revolutionary new product or a significant advance in the properties of an existing one will not attract buyers simply because they are the best of their kind available. Indeed, the structure of industry and commerce has evolved in such a way that buyers in general adopt a passive attitude in the sense that they do not expect to take the initiative until they are activated into making a purchase by either salesmanship or advertising, these being today's chief sales media.

In this connection it is worth remarking that in contrast to the enormous advances that have been made in industry's production methods, and the revolution in administrative systems brought about by the computer, no better method has yet been discovered of actually *selling* goods and services than through the salesman on the road, reinforced where appropriate by advertising. But the cost of supporting salesmen on the road has risen phenomenally in recent years, not least because their *professional* status is receiving ever increasing recognition.

It follows that the very considerable cost to a company of employing sales force misfits of one sort or another ought to be a most compelling reason for following sound and tested guidelines in the selection of sales staff.

Deciding what attributes to look for

Whatever selection process is resorted to, the initial screening should be designed to identify the psychological bents so far discussed. By one means or another it is necessary to select men whose temperaments are favourably predisposed to the business of selling. They should have the kind of personality that not only enjoys meeting people but has the capability of influencing them as well. It is worth exploring these attributes.

Attitude towards other people

It has been said with perhaps an element of truth that the human race can be divided into those who instinctively like their fellow mortals and those who, often unconsciously, subscribe to the saying that: 'The more I see of man, the more I like my dog'. Salesmen must emphatically come from the first group. No matter how much a man in the second category may be subjected to sales training, his limitations in terms of fundamental temperament will seriously militate against his sales effectiveness.

Extrovert–introvert comparisons

Most good salesmen are fundamentally extroverts, but the best of the breed will combine extrovert and introvert characteristics. Conversational ease springing from a warm personality and a genuine pleasure in getting to know new faces are highly desirable qualities in a salesman, but strongly extrovert personalities sometimes exhibit characteristics which are the reverse side of the coin and are by no means conducive to successful selling.

What are the liabilities of the extrovert? At their worst they can include a wide selection of the following: impatience; lack of tact; impulsiveness; ill-considered snap decisions; poor judgement; inability to plan and organize; slipshod attention to paperwork; carelessness over appointments and follow-through on promises; inability to analyse performance and solve problems.

Such a list may well prompt the reply: 'Give me the introvert'. In fact the ideal salesman is someone who, while basically extrovert in temperament, is sufficiently close to the line dividing the two basic categories in human nature that he exhibits few of the worst features of the out-and-out extrovert. To compromise is not necessarily to abandon principles but rather to recognize the realities of life, and in the context of selecting salesmen it has an important factor in its favour—that it is nearly always easier to *train* the extrovert out of the worst limitations of his temperament than it is to do the reverse and to inculcate extrovert behaviour patterns in an introvert.

In practical terms this means that a man will often be employed for his desirable extrovert tendencies in the known likelihood that he is capable of being trained to suppress the liabilities which are the reverse side of his virtues. In short, while it is next to impossible to change a man's innate personality, it is often feasible—and indeed this is one of the several objects of sales training—to subdue or modify most of the liabilities which are the obverse features of his nature, or at any rate to reduce them to acceptable proportions.

Importance of positive attitudes

It is often supposed that good salesmen need to be aggressive, but this is simply not true. In the dictionary sense of the word, aggressiveness implies 'bulldozing' tactics or 'high-pressure' salesmanship designed to obtain orders by different forms of cajolery. Such methods are in fact a negation of true salesmanship, for they violate the definition mentioned earlier, that it is the art of making people *want* to do what is wanted of them in such a manner that they actually want to do it.

Those who regard aggression as a necessary characteristic in salesmen are confusing the word with what can best be described as 'positive attitudes'. These may be defined as the attributes found in the type of person who seeks to impose his own will on the stream of life so that declared objectives are achieved according to a predetermined plan. The opposite type of person, possessed of negative attitudes, thinks first of all of the reasons why something *cannot* be done. His nature is negative because he is content to allow his life to be dictated by the flow of events, without any attempt to influence them to work for his own good and that of his company.

There is more than a small element of the confirmed optimist in a person with positive attitudes—expressed flippantly, but nevertheless with a grain of truth, he is the type who will speak of a glass of beer as being half full rather than half empty!

Positive attitudes are essential prerequisites in a salesman because the nature of his profession makes him something of a 'loner', if only in the sense that he needs in large measure to be self-motivating. It is because positive attitudes are an indispensable ingredient in self-motivation that they form such an important component in a salesman's make-up.

Salesmen are both born and made

Summing up thus far, it can be said that salesmen need to be both born *and* made. This is not begging the question whether they must be the first or can be the second, but rather acknowledging the fact that they need to be both. The true salesman has to be born with certain minimum traits of temperament and character which render him amenable to the stresses inherent in the essential nature of the selling function. But, given that those traits of personality which fulfil this condition are present in a man, he must also be trained in the *skills* of salesmanship.

The job specification and the man profile to fit it

First and foremost among ways for locating applicants is the press advertisement. It is worth emphasizing that advertisements make only a limited, though essential, contribution to the actual process of selection. They do no more than *locate* suitable material, or material that thinks itself suitable. In other words, a well-conceived advertisement should attract only the sort of applicant who is broadly suited to the job in question, so that the interviewer can then use the skills of true selection rather than waste time in having to reject totally unsuitable material.

Therefore, before an advertisement comes to be placed, the copy-writer must have access to the job specification covering the post to be filled. Usually it will already exist, but if the post happens to be a new one then it will need to be written. From an in-depth consideration of the job specification will emerge the man profile delineating the kind of person most likely to fit the specification.

Job specification

The job specification is dealt with in Chapter 4. In addition to the primary features listed in Chapter 4 are secondary considerations applying specifically to sales staff such as the following:

1   The territory to be covered.
2   The outlets to be called on.
3   The range of products the successful applicant will handle.
4   The returns/reports/statistics required of a successful applicant.

Man profile

This term delineates the *type* of person required to fit the job specification. This too is covered more fully in Chapter 4.

The man required must be temperamentally suited to whatever style of selling is involved. The fundamental characteristics of the true salesman have already been dealt with in this chapter, but there are obviously considerable differences between what may loosely be called 'technical' as distinct from 'consumer' selling. Within these two broad categories, the difference in selling styles between one commodity/product/service and another may well have an important bearing on the personal characteristics required.

As one moves up the scale of engineering/scientific knowledge required in technical selling, the old conundrum constantly recurs—which is the more important: technical expertise or the ability to sell? The answer is that both are equally necessary. It is undoubtedly true, however, that the higher one moves up the 'technical' scale, the less likely are sales staff to match their technical competence with selling skills of equal magnitude.

There is a marked tendency, in fact, for this category of sales staff to see themselves too much as technical experts and not enough as salesmen. To exaggerate somewhat, they expect orders to come to them 'on a plate', without being earned through the deployment of selling skills.

This is yet another reason why continuous sales training is so necessary. Industry and commerce in general tend to interpret the word training in terms of 'product knowledge' alone instead of what it should be—product knowledge plus selling expertise.

The high cost of bad sales staff selection

The urgent need to fill a vacancy should rarely if ever persuade a company to appoint the 'best of a bad lot'. It is usually far better to take a hard and critical look at the advertisement copy that produced the bad lot and then to start again.

It is true to say that bad appointments in the case of sales staff are among the most expensive that management can make. Recruitment misjudgements are *all* expensive, but with most staff the loss is confined to wasted salary during the work familiarization period when a man is largely nonproductive. But with outside sales staff, this waste must have added to it the high overheads of a failed salesman being on the road at all. Furthermore, the 'lone wolf' nature of the job often means that it takes longer for mistakes to come to light, and besides the wasted overheads there can often be damage to a company's image.

To sum up, then, urgency should rarely if ever be allowed to blur judgement in the selection of sales staff. Applying principles and procedures discussed elsewhere in this book, the sole yard-stick for measuring an applicant's suitability must be how closely he fits the required man profile. For the appointee's competence in performing the job specification will be very close to a direct reflection of the judgement with which the interviewer brings to bear the principles and techniques discussed elsewhere in this book.

Advertising for sales staff

The place of advertising in the context of recruitment is dealt with in Chapter

5, but it is as well to add a few additional comments in so far as the press is a primary tool in the acquisition of sales staff.

As with other kinds of recruitment, the main objective in writing advertisement copy for sales staff is to attract the maximum number of applicants of the right type. In other words, to aim for quantity and quality, where quality implies that the men who respond will be reasonably in accord with the man profile required to fulfil the job specification.

Within this overall objective, the aim must be to attract not only men who are actively looking for new jobs but also those who had no idea at all of making a change until they saw the advertisement.

Copywriting style

The enormous demand for professional men of all descriptions, which has followed in the train of the post-war business explosion, has given rise to a new style of writing in the English language. This new genre is almost as distinctive as the language used in Victorian play-bills. The following are a few typical examples:

1 'So you're a big shot in . . . , aged 25 to 35, qualified to at least . . . , with a successful track record in the field of . . . . But this is only half the man we need to train as a . . . . For the rest, you must be a man of personality and drive, a self-starter with the ability to communicate freely at the highest levels.'
2 'Our plans are laid—we know where we're going. Like to come with us? What we need are live-wire men with selling in their blood . . . .'
3 'Our continued expansion has created the need for further additions to our staff. Ideal experience would be selling in the food industry but the ability to achieve results is paramount. The men we need will possess . . . .'
4 'Featuring for the first time in the *Chemical Age* Top-Ten Contracts Table, and at No. 3, ... are poised for their next step forward into the £ million contract range. Responsibilities are therefore increasing and there are career possibilities for technical representatives qualified to . . . standard and capable of *creative* selling.'
5 'The laboratory is situated in a particularly pleasant part of Wiltshire. Relocation expenses, company car and generous fringe benefits will be paid to men possessed of . . . . The job content includes . . . .'

All the above examples have one thing in common—maximum *inducement* consistent with a sketchy and sometimes 'gimmicky' attempt to put across the required man profile. Anyone who remembers the situations vacant columns in the immediate prewar years will recall that quite important jobs received no more than a half-inch of column space. Likewise the style of language used was cold and tersely impersonal. These dull and uninviting advertisements reflected the economic climate of the thirties—a decade when in general there were always many more men than there were jobs.

The situation is very different today and the language in which advertisements are couched reflects the fact that over the past two decades or more the overall demand for sales staff has exceeded the supply. Hence the fact that *inducement* is the keynote of most advertisements; sometimes the abbreviated details of job specification and the man profile to fit it suffer in consequence.

Advertisements for sales staff should entice but must never mislead. Their objective is to give the employing company the widest possible choice consistent with the applicants' being reasonably in accord with the man profile required.

Screening and interviewing applicants

After advertising there comes, of course, the business of screening and interviewing applicants, which are fully dealt with elsewhere. It is as well, however, to touch on those aspects that have a special relevance to the recruitment of sales staff.

A well-designed 'application blank' is of first importance. It is the means by which the sheep are graded and the goats discarded. As such it is worth taking trouble over the way application forms are designed and the kind of information they call for. All too many such forms ask for details in an applicant's life history which are quite irrelevant to the selection process. Others are sound, so far as they go, but fail to elicit basic facts which materially affect the business of selection.

If all applicants could be relied on to write good letters then the importance of application forms would be lessened. But good salesmen and good potential salesmen are often poor performers in the art of letter-writing. It is to offset this human failing that application forms are designed. They extract information which otherwise would be withheld, mostly inadvertently, but sometimes with intent.

Application forms are the means for arriving at shortlists, after which they form the basic framework round which the subsequent interview or interviews are structured.

Interviewing, needless to say, is a large subject and is dealt with in Chapter 12. In the context of recruiting sales staff it takes on what almost amounts to an added dimension which makes it more exacting still. For salesmanship is so essentially a matter of personality and temperament as well as qualifications and experience that interviewing techniques must be capable of peeling away even more of the human onion, in order to uncover not only the individual's qualifications but also his innate ability to sustain the unique stresses and strains that sales staff are heir to.

19

Management Trainees in Retailing

J F Jenkins

To achieve the highest possible degree of success in selection for retail management requires much investigation, research and experiment. There is no single golden thread to lead to absolute success.

The difficulty is to select from young men and women who have so very little to offer as proof of their ability and willingness to reach management levels and to accept the responsibilities that go with the positions.

The personal characteristics that will be needed for management of retail stores in the next decade are not easy to predict. The trend is for small shops to be replaced by large department or chain stores and supermarkets.

Competition is rife and sales techniques are improving so quickly that anything that happened last year is now 'old hat'. It is doubtful whether the management job will require the same basic abilities and personality traits in the future as it does today.

Are successful managers born or made? Or to put it another way, is there a management type? It is a fallacy that leadership is the property of the individual—it is far more likely to be acquired than inborn. While it does not follow that any individual can become a successful manager (given the opportunity), it does follow that successful management does not depend on the possession of a set pattern of traits and abilities. It is also likely that management potential is broadly, rather than narrowly, distributed in the general population.

The requirements are different, however, according to the different kinds of management. Sales management, buying and accountancy are all to be found in the retail business but they demand different abilities and skills. They may also be at different levels. Managers successful in one function or at one level are sometimes not successful in another.

These are some of the problems that have to be considered when planning a management trainee recruitment scheme, but a specification for the selection of management trainees for retail trades must also be influenced by other major variables that are likely to affect an applicant's progress.

Factors affecting the success of recruitment

A prospective trainee's effective performance will vary, depending on the following factors.

Personal qualities of applicant

First, there is the question of the personal qualities required in the applicant. What would be the young man's own attitude towards training? Is he willing to learn and to strive to succeed? Has he the ability to adjust to the demands of retail store life?

Most advertisements require applicants for management training to have all the qualities of a tycoon: drive, tenacity, enthusiasm, high intelligence to cope in a fast-moving, quick-changing, highly competitive world. The young man looks at himself in a full-length mirror and says: 'That's me.' Alas, his view of himself is often distorted.

Unfortunately, very few young men are serious when they apply for management training. As recruitment officers know, many applicants go through school, conforming to the educational pattern, taking and often passing their examinations in good order but not *aspiring* to anything outside educational institutions. An increasing tendency for university graduates to enter for higher degree courses similarly indicates the lack of willingness of many young people to set their sights at goals in the open markets of industry and commerce. Eventually the day arrives when such people are unemployed and their thinking goes like this: 'What can I do? I don't want to work in a factory and I am sure I won't like an office or a bank or insurance. The only thing that will suit me is management. Let's look at the ads.'

This stage is not always the awakening of latent aspirations. If the job looks right and the remuneration is below expectations, they turn away. If the money is right, regardless of the job, they apply. If the advertisement is for dynamic personality, on comes the Walter Mitty act. The indolent youth does not investigate, he relies on the company's brochure to tell him about the prospects and promises. No thought is given to the hazards or hurdles, nor to the vocational aspects.

Attitude of management

Rightly or wrongly, managers of today select and create the managers of tomorrow. It is human frailty that managers tend to favour and reward trainees who conform to their own patterns of behaviour and to punish trainees who deviate in any way. The deviant individuals are weeded out, although some of them might have become effective, perhaps outstanding managers. This intuitive like or dislike can happen in selection. The following experiment illustrates the point.

A company decided to engage for management training some applicants who satisfied certain minimum criteria of age, education, intelligence tests results, health and references. Applicants who satisfied these specifications were interviewed for 'personality' approval by a panel of three men consisting of a senior administration officer, a sales superintendent and a recruitment specialist. The panel made majority decisions, recorded as a pass or fail result, but *all* applicants were invited to join the company.

After four and a half years, those trainees who, having played an unwitting part in the experiment, were still with the company, had completed their training and were deputy managers or in their final stages of training as assistant managers. As might be expected, the results were significantly in favour of the panel. Seventy-five per cent of those who remained had been passed by the panel but the other twenty-five per cent had been 'failed'; yet the 'failures' had received favourable merit reports at various times and had proved themselves very suitable for employment in management positions. Under normal selection conditions they would never have had the opportunity of proving themselves.

Attitude of subordinates

The trainee's prospects are affected not only by his own characteristics but also by the attitudes, needs and personal characteristics of his subordinates. It is said that a manager gets the staff he deserves, but the unfortunate trainee manager *inherits* his, and relies upon their immediate acceptance and support. With every transfer to a new department or store, with each promotion, the trainee is vulnerable until he can convince the staff of his effectiveness. Sometimes he is moved and any mistakes or misunderstandings do not have the opportunity of being healed by time.

Nature of tasks

Other variables affecting the result of training include the nature of the tasks to be performed and the speed of assimilation of knowledge at different levels. The needs of the organization determine the length of the training period and its range. The greater the pressure and complexity of training the more precise the qualitative measurement of the applicant needs to be.

Demands of mobility

Many retail organizations are nationwide, with stores dotted round the country like currants in a bun. This presents a mobility problem. A management trainee must work anywhere the company chooses to place him. In a relatively short training course he must gain experience:

1   In varying sizes and shapes of stores. All have their different problems of supervision and security.
2   Of differing customer buying habits. Although fashion influences customers according to their age and pocket, people in the North generally wear heavier clothing, or more of it than those in the South. People in depressed areas have less money to spend and, therefore, are more thrifty than in rich towns.
3   Of the methods used by managers. All the managers are effective in their way and have systems for administration and merchandising within their control. They are experienced in sales promotion and selling techniques and apply other management skills regarding staff and organisation. By observation and discussion, by exposure to the designs and pressures of a selling environment, the management trainee matures. He could learn the trade in one store, but he could not gain all the added experience of being involved in the operations of many managements. To understand the whims of managers is one of the rules of survival.

Mobility presents a serious personal problem to the trainee. If he is married and has children, he has difficulty in providing accommodation and suitable schools, not to mention the cost of removals and setting up house. Even if he is single, the trainee is vulnerable to the fair sex in any part of the country and sooner or later has to make the decision: 'Shall I leave her or settle down to domestic bliss within arm's length of mother-in-law.' Unfortunately sex is often stronger than career in the long run.

Economic and political climate

From time to time this can affect the management trainee's progress. It obviously determines the number of recruits required. If trade trends are rising and more stores are to be built or bought in the years to come, there must be managers to run them. If it takes five years to train a manager, the decision to recruit must be made in proper time.

Writing the job specification

The first practical step is to write an objective specification as a guideline for the selection of management trainees. The aim is to predict or estimate the probabilities of young people's measuring up to the complexities of retail store management. When possible, minimum standards must be specified. There may be a case for discussing maximum standards on occasions but they are harder to justify.

Standards differ according to the complexities of the job, the range of responsibilities for people, merchandise and equipment, the extent to which promotion is attainable, and the range of the company's demands on the manager. The manager sets the standards.

Physical make-up

The store manager must be physically active. Normally he is to be found on the sales floor or in one of the many behind the scenes departments, and a full day on the floor is physically and mentally exhausting. Only a very small part of his time is spent in his office.

The manager must look the part. He should not wear a beard, long hair or way-out clothes. Instead he is neat and well groomed. The manager can always be recognized on the sales floor. So he must be more than five feet six inches tall; to enable him to *stand out* in a crowd! Customers will know him when they see him. He is impressive and looks important, as indeed he is.

The manager is very pleasant and well mannered. He may have a dialect but is clearly understood. He is calm and approachable at all times.

An applicant for training as a retail store manager must satisfy this part of the specification if he is to inspire confidence in his staff and impress the customers. Good first impressions sell merchandise.

A typical physical aspect that must be tested is colour vision. In chain stores, particularly, the sales method is by display and customer selection. Merchandise is displayed by range and by size and colour options. The attractiveness of displays often involves careful colour ranging in pastel variations and contrasts.

Only a small percentage of men (and a much smaller number of women) suffer a colour defect, but it is well spread out in the general population. A red/green blind management trainee in retail is very handicapped. A store manager was once heard to say: 'I don't know what is the matter with Mr X. He is very intelligent and quick on the uptake, and so willing, yet in matters of display and window-dressing he is hopeless.' Mr X was given an Ishihara colour test and found to be a deuteranope. Colour blindness is a hazard in the retail trade.

Age

Most young people leave school at sixteen and are available for training and employment. Girls enter the retail trades at this age but few start with the intention of making a career of sales work.

Boys have a wide field of opportunity in industry and commerce and, unless positive training and financial inducements are offered by retail organizations, few are interested in entering shops and stores. Smart lads are not content to become mere sales assistants.

Young men mature exceptionally quickly in the environment of retail stores. They are exposed to dynamic personalities and have to handle fast-moving merchandise. They become sharp to obey instructions and to carry out work on their own initiative. They attract responsibilities because they give a ready impression that they can accept them—regardless of their age. In such a climate, they grow up very quickly.

Early maturity brings its own problems. Those young men who thrive in their early years feel they are ready for ultimate positions long before they are qualified to fill them. There is no doubt that after two years in the store environment an eighteen-year-old has assimilated a lot of knowledge. He is forward in learning the techniques of sales promotion, anticipating sales and display difficulties. He even acquires a way with young female staff and inspires them with his boyish enthusiasm. He has reached the age where his mental development is said to be complete.

At eighteen the young man is not always very amenable to the advice of the sage, and when his initiative is frustrated he often becomes unsettled and is vulnerable to thoughts of a change of job.

Recruitment of boys under the age of eighteen to a *management* training scheme may not, therefore, be advisable. Their growing-up process should not be rushed. Any training given should be of a basic, practical nature and opportunity should be given the lads to use up part of their daytime on further education. Outward Bound courses and the like. Youthful exuberance must be allowed fair rein before the boys are eventually forced into positions where they must exercise restraint, responsibility and control.

That recruitment for management training at too early an age may be wrong is shown in the following example. A group of eighteen junior management trainees aged sixteen to eighteen was recruited into a very sophisticated scheme. Only one remained after five years. Twelve resigned for other employment, five were deemed unsatisfactory and the remaining young man, who was eighteen at the commencement of training, is now manager of a small store. This turnover repeated itself so that the minimum age of recruitment was eventually increased to eighteen. At this age young men will have had more time to mature in other employments or, as sixth-form students, in passing their GCE 'A' Levels. The older and more developed the personality, the more likely is the trainee to adjust to the demanding forms of store training. The most desirable range is, therefore, eighteen to twenty-eight, with, perhaps, special consideration of a very small number of appropriately qualified older applicants.

Education

With modern emphasis on fast-moving, technical store management training and promotion from within the company, it would seem logical to tap a variety of educational sources: universities, grammar and comprehensive schools, including students from the top 10% of the class, from the middle and from those whose academic achievement was only average because school never really interested them.

As leadership potential is widely spread over the general population, careful analysis of administrative and technical needs, and of the time-scale of training, determines the minimum standard of educational attainment required of trainees. The shorter and more intensive the technical aspect of the work to be learned, the higher should be the academic requirement. If training applies on-the-job techniques only and adopts a 'dead men's shoes' promotion policy, the trainees sought should have a much lower educational standard consistent with good manners and practical aptitude.

In most retail organizations there will always be senior management and administrative positions calling for people with academic honours, who nevertheless will benefit from initial practical on-the-job training. Higher education produces a capacity for future development and for greater appreciation of the complexities of management and occupational control.

There is, however, not much evidence that high academic achievement represents an imperative characteristic for success in retail management. Intellectual achievement may be evidence of motivation and willingness to work—but it is also willingness to conform to the arbitrary controls of the educational system. There is little reason for assuming that high motivation and hard work in school are the best predictors of motivation and effort in later life. Confidence and social poise are relatively independent of intellectual capacity.

One of the major causes of management trainee losses may be the recruitment of young people who have higher educational qualifications than are necessary for contentment in the job. However, the intellectual level of the trainee is not the most important condition for securing happiness in his work. The greatest satisfaction is gained in striving to achieve goals that are difficult to reach; easily attained goals bring only temporary fulfilment.

For management positions in most medium to large retail units, education to the age of sixteen with four 'O' level GCE passes (or their equivalent) should suffice.

Work history

What sort of working background is desirable? If the applicant comes straight from school or college, the only work history he can show is that which he has performed during vacations or at weekends. There is usually no particular pattern of vacation work except the desire to obtain financial benefits, but evidence of physical effort or thought-provoking activities may indicate latent aspirations.

'Saturday work' could give more definite information. In this day and age, Saturday employment most often means service to the public, such as in public transport and the many forms of retail trade. Continuous experience of Saturday work presupposes some interest in service and, if this has been in the retail trade, familiarity with the atmosphere of shop life during peak trading periods affords some assurance that the applicant is aware of the work he wishes to undertake. This experience lessens the prospect of his becoming disenchanted with retail sales work and hours.

Interest in voluntary work projects and good causes such as National Trust and Social Service, or later in Voluntary Service Overseas, gives an insight into a young man's thoughts and attitudes and indicates a social conscience.

As the work history of young people is often so brief, the impression of willingness and conscientiousness, though subjective, can help to sway opinions of their potential.

Apart from those who have already had sound experience in the retail trade, there is no particular background which will predict special suitability in older applicants. Many of these will already have made a false start. They have become frustrated with their jobs, believing that promises have not been fulfilled (or opportunities have ceased because of failed examinations). Will such people have benefited from their mistakes?

It is better not to speculate. It should be assumed only that frequent changes of employment suggest instability and therefore are likely to predict failure in any job requiring firm endeavour.

Intelligence

Intelligence can be measured far more reliably by tests than by recruitment interviews, but the right tests have to be used (see Chapter 8), such as a verbal reasoning test, which measures not only intelligence but also word facility—an essential requirement in oral communication. The NIIP group test 90A is an example, suitable for grammar school leavers and above; tests with less sophisticated content, appropriate to secondary modern and comprehensive needs, would be satisfactory for use when recruiting supervisory and junior management staff.

What should be the minimum level of intelligence for management trainees? If four GCE 'O' levels are considered evidence of sufficient intellectual ability, can the level for management trainees therefore be pitched low on the percentile scale? When using a sophisticated test like the 90A, a fiftieth percentile minimum score will rake in the top half of the grammar school population. Of this group retail's share will be small, perhaps not enough to go round. The cut-off point therefore depends on the number required and the attractiveness of the training scheme. It would be unwise to go below the fortieth percentile when testing grammar school leavers or higher levels. This test is not generally suitable for comprehensive school leavers because the educational range of these schools produces variations of vocabulary levels, affecting assessment of their real intelligence.

Special aptitudes

A test of arithmetical ability is also required. It is surprising how many people are figure blind. Young men, two years out of school, may say: 'It has been a long time since I converted fractions to decimals. I use a slide rule to do my calculations.' The retail trade also makes frequent use of a slide rule but many of its figures are still handled in the old-fashioned way. A figure sense is important.

Interests

There is no evidence that specific interests directly predict success or failure in retail management training, except perhaps in two aspects:

1   A person who has social interests may be better equipped to realise social goals than one who is socially withdrawn.
2   Experience gained in school or extra-mural leadership activities engenders self-assurance and social poise.

There is, however, no proof that these qualities are essential. A person socially insensitive, or even socially withdrawn, may be an efficient merchandiser and expert in sales psychology. Staff may respect him for his knowledge and sense of justice. The stock reason for applying for management training in the retail trade, 'I like meeting people,' may be of very little importance.

Disposition

The ability to predict what personal characteristics will be needed for retail store management in the future has already been questioned. Is it any easier to predict efficiently those who are likely to lead to success at the present time?

In order to succeed, a person must possess ability, and must have and apply fully the energy, drive, initiative and purposefulness required to bring out and develop his talents. It is true that the company can exercise considerable influence over his development but the first responsibility is with the person himself. No amount of positive encouragement by the company can make a manager of a trainee if he is not prepared to participate to the best of his ability.

The right blend of temperamental qualities necessary in a trainee to make success likely can be gleaned in part at least from existing managers. The manager is required to give appraisal reports on his trainees or subordinates at frequent intervals and, although these do not always draw a complete picture of the trainee's assets or limitations, they help outline desirable qualities. However, a manager's reports often reflect bias relationships between the subordinate and himself. Some are highly charged with emotion in favour or against, rather than measuring efficiency or inefficiency. The value of reports is also limited by the manager's power of description and the inadequacy of the report form.

Alas, these traditional subjective reports are somewhat naïve and predictions must be based on facts as well as on judgements. Clearly a more complete and efficient method of assessing a person's character traits is needed. Personality tests can contribute (see Chapter 10).

Using the best of both worlds, the quantitative approach of the personality tests, with the personal expertise of management and recruiter, may be a means of improving the validity of prediction in selection.

How can the personality test be harnessed as a suitable forecaster of success in management training, and therefore as a selector? The followng preliminaries should be followed:

1 All existing managers should complete the test, in normal group test conditions. When the test papers are marked and analysed it may be possible to find a pattern of scores which differentiate this group from the norms of the general adult male population.
2 All existing trainee managers, at all levels of promotion, should complete the test under the same conditions. The results are similarly analysed.
3 Appraisal reports can be used to separate the 'good' from the 'bad' among both trainees and managers. The test scores can then be analysed to find whether they exhibit any marked pattern which correlates with success on the job or in training. Later, further analysis can be based on the drop-out trainees (known early failures).
4 From all this evidence, cut-off scores on the various probability factors can be calculated.
5 As further data accumulate, the cut-off scores can be modified and the validity of selection improved.

When it is evident that the test is discriminating adequately it can be used to eliminate those who are considered not to have a 'sporting chance'. The test can then be used in combination with the judgement of human selectors who are capable of assessing certain factors not readily discernible by a personality test.

External circumstances

In any training scheme a participant needs support and encouragement. Few young people are really independent of society and impervious to the advice or remarks of those whom they respect. There is, however, no evidence that poor home relationships adversely affect a trainee's progress. Deprivation is often a motivator—a spur towards proving something. In the same way, having to move around the country, leaving the family for a time, sometimes has this effect.

Generally speaking, enthusiastic encouragement from home does more good than harm for the young man who wishes to make a mark in the highly competitive activity of retail sales.

Value of an information booklet

One of the main instruments of a good recruitment programme is the job information booklet (enclosing an application form) which can be issued to prospective trainees at the first stage of their application. The booklet should give a brief description on the following lines:

1   A short, interesting history of the origins of the company, its size, business intentions and its aspirations.
2   Chronological details of its initial training programme and broad stages of subsequent training, with a time-scale.
3   Initial salary and the structure at each promotion stage of training—with some indication of future salary prospects.
4   Conditions of training and attendant problems. What the company offers for its part, and what it expects from the trainee.
5   Conditions of emloyment, privileges and rules.

The booklet should have sufficient pictorial matter with clear typographical lay-outs and creative artwork. Apart from being interesting and readable, it must be honest and lack ambiguity. Above all it must be realistic in order to deter applicants who are not serious contenders for training. Inside the back flap of the booklet there should be a post-paid preprinted envelope to carry the returning application form.

Use and control of advertising

Owing to the high cost of press advertising it is important to know how to get the best out of advertisements. It pays to keep careful statistics to enable investigations to be made at any stage of the recruitment programme, and at any time. The example in Figure 19.1 gives *average* figures for advertisements in national daily papers.

These figures show consecutive stages of the recruitment process and the cost per applicant engaged. It is possible to investigate any stage or aspect of

Medium	National press
Size of advertisement	60 column cm
Initial response	370
Booklet and application form sent out	321
Application form returned	127
Attended selection board	95
Offered	23
Accepted	19
Started	15
Cost	£1440
Cost per starter	£96

Figure 19.1   Cost of recruiting by press advertising

the programme. For instance, 321 booklets were sent out but only 127 forms were returned, which shows that the booklet has added value as a deterrent. This ratio has been fairly constant for years, and surveys have confirmed the desire to give realistic information and so eliminate unnecessary applications.

Size of space taken

This proves an interesting study. The prestige papers have many pages of display advertisements, of all sizes and shapes. It is better to seek to dominate by design than to compete by size. If an advertisement can be seen clearly it will attract applicants, whatever its size.

Frequency of appearance

It is not advisable to advertise too often. During an annual recruiting programme it is important to spread the load over a number of acceptable papers to avoid saturation. With the possible exception of papers specializing in prestige recruitment advertising, most newspapers have a fairly constant readership. If an advertisement is reinserted within a short time of the original, the response and its success rate will drop outstandingly. As an example, two identical display advertisements which were placed in one paper within six weeks of each other resulted in a cost per starter of £45 and £112 respectively. If frequent advertising is necessary, the advertisements must vary in style and content.

Determining the media

Young people who seek opportunities of management training in national companies do not expect to find them in local papers.

On the other hand, the competition on the many display pages of prestige papers tends to scare them off. An advertisement for trainees must be most attractively designed to compete against large displays for professional, executive and technical staffs and the armed forces. Why not, therefore, consider the popular dailies? They are often more costly per insertion but sometimes prove economical on a cost per engagement basis.

Getting the message across

If the advertisement is designed to attract young men for management training, it should say so in the title. One advertisement headed *Young men of imagination and high intelligence* ran for years and produced consistently good results. The title speaks to the potential applicant before he reads the copy.

The copy itself can give voluminous detail of the training programme and conditions of work, or it can be sharp and precise. If it can be followed up with a booklet giving full description of training and so on, it is a waste to spend money on unnecessary and costly column inches. The copy must emphasize age and educational qualifications, mobility requirements, commencing salary and long-term prospects, and, of course, it should supply the name and address of the recruitment officer to whom application is to be made.

The whole lay-out must be well designed, clean and clear. Above all it should, like a store manager, stand out in the crowd.

Planned objectives of recruitment department

If the policy is to recruit a given number of trainees throughout the year, it is important to plan the department's load. Recruitment in surges is costly, whereas a smooth flow of applicants can be dealt with economically by a minimum of staff. Panic drives require extra staff in the short term or long periods of underemployment.

There are certain times during the year when the pace of recruiting is normally slow, and it speeds up when people are restless and motivated to seek fresh employment. January and July/August are two peaks and the opportunities they offer for recruitment should not be missed.

The most systematic and logical method of recruitment is to set a monthly target of starters by dividing the total requirements for the year by ten (no recruitment in November and December) and by *reaching* the target each month. Exceeding the target should not induce complacency: the market may dry up at any time. There are many employers wooing the same applicants.

Quick treatment of applications

Young people who apply for jobs want to be considered immediately. They may have other irons in the fire and cannot wait indefinitely. The motto must be: 'Do it today!' As soon as applications come in, they should be considered and the appropriate action taken. Interviews must be arranged for next week, not next month. It gets a little difficult when the response is nationwide and the recruitment officer has to travel to regional centres or universities—but that is no excuse for losing a sense of urgency. Applicants deserve speedy attention and the policy of catching and impressing applicants pays dividends.

Organization of selection boards

Advertisements in national papers may bring applications from anywhere in the country. To bring applicants to head office would be very expensive in fares and hotel accommodation and would cause them to lose more time from work than convenient. It is far better to meet groups of ten to sixteen applicants at a suitable hotel in their home area. It pays to adopt group techniques when dealing with management trainee recruitment.

The panel of selectors should consist of a personnel officer, at least one senior store management representative, a training officer and a receptionist/ test administrator.

All candidates should arrive at the same hour. They are welcomed, given a short description of the day's programme and tested as a group. During a break in the proceedings, refreshments are taken and the time is used effectively by inviting the candidates to ask questions about the company and its training scheme.

This discussion period gives the selecting officers a chance to express essential information on unusual conditions of employment, the main problems of mobility, mode of dress and general appearance. It is not difficult to stimulate discussion on these subjects nor to introduce thoughts on attitude to training. (These matters may be discussed further with individuals in the privacy of the interview room.) A typical selection board would be as folows:

09 00	Welcome and programme details.
09 15 to 10 15	Tests (NIIP test 90A, arithmetic, colour test). Expenses paid for travel, meals, accommodation and so on.
10 15	Break for refreshments and question time. (Test administrator marks tests.)
10 45	Candidates are separated into groups: 1 Those who have failed tests move to another place. 2 The remainder stay in test room.
10 45 (Group 1)	Individual interviews to complete their participation in the selection board.
10 45 to 12 00 (Group 2)	Personality test (16 PF). Candidates break for lunch. Tests marked.
13 15	Individual interviews (30 to 40 minutes each).

The selection board is expected to be completed by 18 00 hours.

Additional selection techniques

The above procedure could be elaborated by adding group discussions and/or lecturettes. These would be for group 2 candidates. The discussions would be preceded by giving the candidates a typical store merchandising problem. The brief is contained in a booklet which has three parts: a glossary of the store jargon used, the problem and the decision made by the man who was originally faced with the problem.

The candidates sit at their separate desks to read the case details and to write down their own solutions to the problem. They are not allowed to discuss the subject at this stage. The papers are collected and marked.

The desks are then arranged in a semicircle facing the panel of selectors, and the candidates are asked to talk out the various aspects of the problem until they come to a group decision. They can adopt any tactics they wish. No leader has been appointed to control their discussion—unless they wish to elect their own chairman.

Each selector notes individual participation in the discussion and sorts the candidates in rank order for clarity and effectiveness of contribution, and for leadership qualities. Many facets of personality show themselves in this form of discussion.

If necessary, a further discussion on a topical current affairs subject could then be started, with the same ranking method, scored by the observers.

When the lecturette procedure is used, each individual candidate is required to speak to the group and observers for three minutes on a prechosen subject (drawn from a hat). He is given thirty seconds to prepare. The order of speaking is determined by the same process as the allocation of the subject so that no candidate has any advantage over the others.

These additional selection techniques could help the panel to know the candidates better. Having seen and heard each of them in discussion, a degree of understanding may have been reached from which could develop a searching conversation about the aims and motives capable of supporting his application. At the same time the candidate is able to observe his interviewers, hear their replies to the questions uppermost in his mind about the company, and establish a greater sense of confidence in his application.

However, selection board frills may not be as helpful in selecting candidates—except as public orators— as one may think, and the time taken may be uneconomical, particularly if more reliable methods of understanding human beings and predicting their behaviour are available. Whatever methods are used, they should be applied systematically and as objectively as possible. The selection board should not be time-wasting, but kept under strict control.

As a matter of general strategy, every selection programme should be tailored specifically to the requirements of the particular company and jobs for which it will be used.

Information required at the interview

Psychometricians believe that interviews are quite unnecessary when a whole range of tests is available. However true this may be, it should be emphasized that at least some information can be gained from personal discussion during an interview that is not easily obtained by other methods. For example, a man's personal appearance can be observed, as can the state of his finger nails (hygiene is a very important matter in the retail business). Grotesque facial disfigurements and mannerisms may inhibit relationships with customers and staff, and indistinct speech can affect good communication.

The interview can indicate what motivated the candidate to apply for training, and if he has done any preliminary research into the company's activities or the training programme. While lack of previous investigation does not mean that the candidate will fail to survive a training course, the interviewer may be impressed by evidence of good intentions. He would reason that a person would not easily become disenchanted if he had previously weighed the pros and cons of the training and the work to be performed.

Of course, honesty and integrity cannot easily be assessed but it is possible to base strong opinions of the candidate's potential effectiveness on his past record. Many an applicant makes the claim that he was misled by his previous employer and that promises were not fulfilled; yet he now accepts a recruitment booklet and statements unquestioningly. Such people do not inspire confidence in the recruiting officer and it is not surprising if their applications are refused.

The interview, at the end of a thorough selection board, is a means of communication. Personal matters can be discussed and private questions answered. The candidate should be assured of the company's good intentions as well as the company of his.

Making the offer of employment

Most of the information has been amassed on each candidate and a decision can now be made regarding his application for training. Without delay he must be informed of his unsuitability or he should be made an offer—subject to satisfactory references and an acceptable medical report.

The offer should include details of conditions of employment as required by the Contracts of Employment Act 1972. Details should include the place of initial training, hours of work, remuneration, financial allowances and all other matters of importance, whether required by the Act or not. Finally, the offer should state a date when such offer will be withdrawn, if not accepted in the meantime.

When a letter of acceptance returns, more details can be passed to the new trainee, such as the name of the training store manager and training instructor, what to do on the first day and where to stay on the first night. He now knows where he stands and it is to be hoped that he will continue to know.

Further reading

Cattell, R. B. (1965): *The Scientific Analysis of Personality.* London: Pelican.
Drucker, Peter F. (1955): *The Practice of Management.* London: Heinemann.
Pigors, P. and Malm, C. T. (1973): *Personnel Administration.* 7th edition, New York: McGraw-Hill.
Ray Maurice (1971): *Practical Job Advertising.* London: Institute of Personnel Management.
Ray Maurice (1971): *Recruitment Advertising: A Handbook of Methods and Procedures.* London: Business Books.
Rodger, A. (1952): *The Seven-Point Plan.* London: National Institute of Industrial Psychology.
Singer, Edwin J. (1974): *Effective Management Coaching.* London: Institute of Personnel Management.
Vernon, P. E. and Parry, J. B. (1949): *Personnel Selection in the British Forces.* London: University of London Press.

20

Staff in Branches of Multiple Unit Organizations

R J Mooney

At least one-third of the UK working population is employed in organizations with a large number of scattered units. It is common for major employers in this sector to have units hundreds of miles apart and it is becoming increasingly vital to maintain uniformly good standards of recruitment. In scattered manufacturing units, measurable skills, certificates and qualifications are nationally supported and recognized in any part of the country. This is becoming increasingly important also throughout Europe.

Methods of recruitment

Too often in a highly competitive labour market, the recruitment officer has to accept whatever candidates he can obtain from Professional and Executive Recruitment or from the local office of the Department of Employment. Planned recruitment must do better than that. There are four main styles of recruitment:

1 Normal recruitment.
2 Specialized recruitment.
3 Saturation recruitment.
4 Campaign recruitment.

Normal recruitment

Most companies can easily cope with many of their everyday recruitment needs by an advertisement in the local paper or by a window poster or board. This is normally the action found to be successful in their locality.

Specialized recruitment

This normally takes the form of notifying vacancies to specialist agencies or placing advertisements in trade papers, such as the *Fruit and Vegetable Trade Journal* and so on, as well as the use of management consultants.

Saturation recruitment

This implies the use of absolutely every possible source of obtaining recruits. It checks on whether all possibilities have been followed up. Regular use and analysis of results, particularly the cost per applicant engaged, will influence or improve the normal, special and campaign methods.

Recruitment campaigns

These are planned series of projects investigating one particular source of labour or a planned series using different sources in conjunction with all or any of the other three main methods.

The best answer to the specific problems of recruitment in any business lies in a simple analogy. Use as many fishing lines as possible with as wide a variety of bait. Indiscriminate or isolated one-line angling does not gain enough fish for either sport or supper.

Training for good selection

It is one matter to attract candidates, another to select those that will be suitable. So many of the skills of staff are personal, such as courtesy of manner, warmth, consideration and thoroughness. Assessments of such qualities are basically subjective or qualitative.

The selection of successful applicants is often also influenced by personal preferences. In the vast majority of cases, selection is performed by the department or branch manager. However, many shops and stores are run by multiple organizations, and many of their units are small. The managers of these units tend to be appointed for their selling, trade and managerial skills—not their recruitment skills. So the classic errors of engagement are repeated: starting staff who never stay for more than three or four months; staff who, at the end of the first month, have walked out with cash from the till; staff who either cannot sell to a customer or cannot total a bill; and so on.

Recruitment training is very necessary. To omit it is a costly error of judgement.

Some people seem to have the knack of becoming good interviewers in a short period of time without any training—but they are very rare indeed. The training method which is the most satisfying and which produces the best results is role-playing recruitment training sessions. Further details of interviewing techniques are discussed elsewhere in this handbook.

Effect of labour turnover on recruitment policy

Establishing thorough labour turnover figures is a priority causing some difficulties in personnel departments and more particularly in the offices of local managements. The simple master plan (see Figure 20.1) is most helpful. A chart like this completed monthly, quarterly or half-yearly gives the following information quickly:

1 Total numbers of workers: increases and decreases.
2 Labour turnover percentage. In the diagram given the figures are approximate for the sake of simplicity.
3 Reasons for leaving. These will probably spotlight difficulties in particular departments as well as in the company as a whole.

Labour turnover and reasons for leaving, as shown in Figure 20.1, highlight the fact that low pay in three divisions and a wish for no Saturday working in one division ought to be taken into account when deciding on recruitment policy.

It is vital to have some kind of exit interview procedure for several reasons. If units are widespread, or there is difficulty in giving a personal interview by a central executive, a form can be used. For example, every worker can be obliged to complete a simple form stating the notice he is giving and the reasons for his resignation. His immediate manager can be required to countersign the form, stating whether he believes the reason given to be a true one and, if it is not, what he believes the real reason to be. The central recruitment or personnel department who extract information for termination procedures and for the labour turnover record can follow up appropriately.

The reasons for leaving may show a disproportionate number of workers leaving because of dissatisfaction with working hours, pay, travelling difficulties and so on, which must alert recruitment officers to the possibility either that policy with regard to terms and conditions must be changed or often, just as important, that the policy is not being fully explained by recruiters at interview. If there is a high figure for leaving because of unsatisfactory state of health, dishonesty or unsatisfactory references, it may well be that interviewers are omitting questions in these areas. If not, then it is probable either that the available manpower in the area is of poor quality or that the level of salary and conditions being offered by the company are such

Labour turnover and reasons for leaving

Division, branch or department	Number in department	Left of own accord 1–27				Dismissed 28–32				Total number	Total department (%)
		More pay	Less hours	No Saturdays	Other reasons	Dis-honesty	Poor references	Poor work	Other reasons		
		1	2	3	4–27	28	29	30	31–35		
management	100	35	1	5	4	1	1	2	1	50	50
marketing and sales	40	1	—	—	1	—	—	—	1	2	5
distribution	80	15	—	—	4	—	—	—	1	20	25
processing and manufacturing	250	40	—	4	1	—	—	5	—	50	20
finance and accounting	30	4	—	—	1	1	—	—	—	6	20
general operations	20	1	—	2	1	—	—	1	—	5	25
number of total	520										
number of total leavers		96	1	11	12	2	1	9	—	133	25
percentage of total leavers		18.6%	—	2%	2%	—	—	1%	—		

Figure 20.1 Labour turnover and reasons for leaving

as to attract only the poor-quality end of the labour market.

It is essential that the information collated from the analysis should influence recruitment policy and it should preferably be brought to the notice of the engagers directly. Sometimes the causes of the 'disease' of labour turnover can be seen immediately on examination of the figures. Some trends will only be seen after keeping records for two or three years or more. Others will be seen immediately after an Industrial Tribunal case against the company—a case of trying to catch the recruit as it were after he has bolted.

Establishing recruitment standards

Manufacturing industries have studied recruitment scientifically to a greater extent than have the retail and distributive industries. They generally have the advantage of very large numbers of employees based at one manufacturing site, allowing more manpower and facilities to be used in the field of aptitude testing and engagement interview follow-up. The following are areas where policies need to be consolidated, adapted or given trial in the retail industry.

Medical examination

This is not yet used as fully as it should be. It should be out of the question to engage staff such as those with varicose veins or suffering from dizzy spells in jobs requiring standing for long periods; people with poor hearts, back or stomach conditions for lifting of merchandise; colour-blind persons to sell clothes or cloth; or food handlers with communicable diseases.

Aptitude tests

Reference should be made here to other chapters on testing and on application forms (which in themselves are a test of intelligence, literacy and clerical facility). Some tests of selling ability now being used in the sales representative field are proving useful, but such tests rarely have the qualities of being thoroughly validated and simple—and it is essential that tests for use should be simple.

The ability to write figures clearly and to add up items of purchase quickly is a key requirement in many establishments. A sales bill test can be a useful recruitment tool in these cases where there is doubt.

The ability to work a cash-accounting, checkout-operating or any other machine can be tested, and tests should be used regularly. They will not be perfect, particularly if made by the company or personnel department without thorough training in testing techniques. The simple test quickly given in an informal atmosphere is a considerable help to the selection of able people. Applicants who resist such obvious tests or who are shown by the tests to be incompetent can be sorted out in the selection process.

Similar tests can be and are used in the better run companies before the engagement of butchers, bacon cutters, demonstrators and so on. Some hold the view that, in the case of butchery and provisions tests, valuable food is wasted when testing. Such waste as there may be must be infinitely less than that caused by having substandard cutters.

Recruitment procedure

The rest of this chapter is intended as a summary of a practical recruitment procedure. It can be used for general interest and reading. It can also be made into a four-page reference booklet for staff supervisors in large stores or shops, the area manager responsible for recruitment, personnel officers travelling around branches or the small unit shop managers.

Recruitment procedure can be summarized under the following main headings:

1 Aims of recruitment procedure.
2 Planning recruitment campaigns.
3 Job and personal specifications.
4 Sources of recruitment.
5 The selection interview.

Aims of recruitment procedure

The main aim of a recruitment procedure is to select a bright, quick, healthy person who has practical intelligence, who answers questions directly and clearly and who will be a reliable, cooperative worker with a pleasant manner to other workers and particularly to customers. Almost equally important is the aim of assessing exactly the type and amount of experience of an applicant in order to fit 'round pegs into round holes'.

If mistakes are made at selection, the recruitment work will have to be done all over again, possibly within a week, a month or two months. To select thoroughly in the first place saves endless time, trouble and cost.

The staffing of almost any business is one of its highest costs. It is therefore very important for every manager to see that the selection, training and general welfare of a new recruit are given thorough planning.

Planning recruitment campaigns

The overall planning of recruitment campaigns and future manpower requirements are normally carried out at the central head offices of a group multiple. It is usual for central and, perhaps, area, specialists to be appointed to see that each branch also plans its recruitment.

Is it really necessary to replace someone who has left?

When an employee leaves, the first thought is, too often, 'put in an advertisement and put up a poster'. A few minutes' thought should be given to the following questions:

1 Is there really a need to recruit and replace the worker who has just left or is about to leave?
2 Are wage costs already too high?
3 Could the vacancy be best filled by a transfer or promotion?
4 Would it be more productive to use a part-timer only at the really busy period?
5 Can the work or its organization or method be reorganized so that no further staff are required?
6 Can a young person or school leaver be adequately trained?
7 Will having three good staff be just as effective as having four, the most troublesome or least productive of whom has just left? This applies equally to executive and managerial positions.

Job and personal specifications

Various forms of job and personal specification can be used. The subject is dealt with in detail in Chapter 4.

Job specification

A job specification is a description of the specific details which a job of work entails. The job should be considered in detail to obtain a clear picture of it under the following eight headings:

1 Department and place of work.
2 Physical background: standing, walking, lifting, painstaking clerical work, physical and mental energy involved.
3 Advantages and disadvantages of the job.
4 Working alone, or with others, frequent contact with customers or not.
5 Pay: exact salary or salary range.
6 Hours: exact hours to be worked; whether a part-timer might be better employed all day on certain days.

7   Responsibilities for specific amounts of manpower, money and materials.
8   Exact experience or skills required.

Those who think they know a job well are often surprised after writing a description, or on going through specific items as above, to find that they have failed to consider a small but vital part of the job.

Personal specification

A personal specification is a description of the specific details of a person most likely to be able to do a specified job. It normally covers the following nine headings:

1   Age range.
2   Physique: height, strength, hand dexterity and so on.
3   Education.
4   Qualifications.
5   Previous experience.
6   Clerical ability: evidence on application form.
7   Temperament: sociable and confident; shy, retiring and quiet.
8   Reliability.
9   Honesty.

Sources of new employees

There are a great many sources of recruitment for retail staff. They can be divided into those incurring mainly indirect costs and those involving direct costs.

Sources involving mainly indirect costs

These can be divided into the following:

1   Contacts with interbranch executives, general managers, area managers, staff managers and so on.
2   Recall of previous similar campaigns or successful sources: where did we get the last first-class manager?
3   Internal contacts, such as recommendations of staff or their relatives. Some companies offer cash bonuses to staff for recommended applicants who join and stay for a period of over six months.
4   Recruitment officer's personal contacts.
5   Customers' contacts.
6   Transfers or promotions from within.

7   Reorganization of work.
8   Imminent redundancies resulting from known closure of a competitor.

Sources involving mainly direct costs

Direct cost sources are as follows:

1   Previous applicants' retained name, address and telephone numbers.
2   Department of Employment notifications, visits to and from them, typed cards for their notice boards.
3   Youth Employment Officers' notifications, visits to and from them, careers literature, careers exhibitions.
4   Careers masters' open evenings, career films.
5   Window posters, permanent boards, newsagents' boards.
6   Advertising in national dailies, national evening, local papers, trade journals, careers journals.
7   Use of specialist recruitment consultancies. These might include register services; advertising agencies; recruitment consultancies or executive search agencies or 'headhunters'.

Selection interview

Arrangement of appointments should be courteous and practical. Time must be planned in order to carry out interviews satisfactorily. The recruitment officer should habitually set aside a time for interviewing external applicants and staff, such as 12 00 to 13 00 daily, or Wednesday or Thursday afternoons.

Applicants must always fill in an application form, preferably before interview, if they appear to be of suitable calibre. Their background and personal details can then be studied and compared with the job and personal specification so that the interview, questions and statements can be prepared. If they are unwilling to complete a form, they will probably be unwilling to do many other things!

Conducting the interview

The job specification and personal specification can be compared with the previous employment of the applicant, particularly in connection with the standard and reputation of the employer he has been with and the length of time he tends to stay in a job. Any applicant who has more than three jobs in twelve months should be viewed with caution.

The applicant should then be given the fullest possible information on the following matters:

1 Exactly what he is required to do (job specification).
2 Advantages and disadvantages of the job.
3 Hours, pay and conditions.
4 Place of work.

Finally, the picture of a probably successful applicant's experience and intelligence should be clarified by going courteously, firmly and patiently through the details of jobs he has given. Has he stated clearly the full name, the full address and clear details of salary, dates of employment and reasons for leaving? Is he vague, unintelligent or simply using the old ruse of making the record better than it is? Careful interviewing here prevents bad selection and speeds the taking up of references.

Naturally, whenever possible several applicants should be seen before a final decision is made. It is a mistake to engage the first person who comes along. When all applicants have been seen, specific arrangements have to be made for offer of employment to, or for reconsideration, reinterview or refusal of specific applicants.

When an applicant has to be turned down he should be thanked courteously for his interest and told tactfully why he is unsuccessful.

When new employees are selected, instructions have to be given with regard to induction, engagement authorizations, training and introduction to the department or shop in which they are to work. The newcomer must also be fully informed with regard to all conditions, rules and amenities and somebody must be delegated as, and be stated to be, the person to whom he should go in the case of his having a grievance. The kind of appointment offered and the way it is stated in contract is vital generally to attract the right candidate and also to comply with industrial relations legislation.

21

Technological Staff

Humphrey Sturt

Technologist is rather a forbidding label which conjures in the mind pictures of white-coated men performing mysterious operations understood only by themselves—the sort of person whom managers or personnel men would rather not know about. Most managers are technologists, however, in the sense that they attempt to apply scientific method to the solution of industrial, commercial or administrative problems. Even occupations like stockbroking, which used to be regarded as a last-resort career for the amateur, have come to use analytical techniques and to depend on numerate people highly skilled in the application of specialist knowledge and methods.

Definition of a knowledge worker

It would be better, therefore, to abandon the word 'technologist' and use the term 'knowledge worker' which seems likely to gain increasing acceptance as a result of Professor Drucker's prophetic work *The Age of Discontinuity*. He points out that thirty years ago semi-skilled machine operators were the centre of the American work force: 'Today the centre is the knowledge worker, the man or woman who applies to productive work ideas, concepts and information rather than skill or brawn.'

So important is this change to industrialized economies and the firms working within them that it is worth quoting extensively from the same chapter.

The man or woman who has once acquired skill on a knowledge foundation has learned to learn. He can acquire rapidly new and different skills. Unlike apprenticeship which prepares for one specific craft and teaches the use of one specific set of tools for one specific purpose, a knowledge foundation enables people to unlearn and relearn. It enables them, in other words, to become technologists who can put knowledge, skills, and tools to work, rather than craftsmen who know how to do one specific task in one specific way. What matters in the 'knowledge economy' is whether knowledge, old or new, is applicable . . . what is relevant in the imagination and skill of whoever applies it, rather than the sophistication or newness of the information. The knowledge worker . . . realizes and rightly so, that the organization . . . depends on him. This hidden conflict between the knowledge worker's view of himself as a professional and the social reality in which he is the upgraded and well-paid successor to the skilled worker of yesterday underlies the disenchantment of so many highly educated young people with the jobs available to them.

What the knowledge worker needs to be positively motivated is achievement. He needs to know that he contributes . . . knowledge workers also require that the demands be made on them by knowledge rather than by bosses, that is, by objectives rather than by people. They require a performance-oriented organization rather than an authority-oriented organization.

An organization that does not have young knowledge workers is an organization that cannot grow, and can only defend yesterday.

One might add that, since management exists to manage change, and this change is dependent on the knowledge worker, the latter's skills in self-expression and communication are of some significance. The successful organization will find it hard to survive with too high a proportion of silent geniuses even in a research capacity. The field of inquiry in this chapter is the knowledge worker, excluding those who are already managers or those who are specifically earmarked as management trainees, the latter being dealt with in Chapters 18, 19 and 22. In passing it may be observed that with the increasing importance and status of the knowledge worker the concept of management trainee may become redundant. Management is largely knowledge work and management ranks are filled from below with knowledge workers. In advanced technological companies like computer manufacturers there are no management trainees. There may be new graduate recruits, but they will be recruited as trainee knowledge workers. In the course of their professional work, management skills will, in many cases, become apparent, and indeed need to be inculcated, in the normal course of projects, where teams of technicians have to be supervised by other technicians.

Recruitment policy

Successful recruiting campaigns for knowledge workers must have a style that will appeal to those with motivation of the kind indicated by Drucker. Furthermore, recruitment itself is not necessarily the end of the story. The organization must retain those that it has recruited long enough for them to make a contribution which at least exceeds in value the cost of their recruitment. The knowledge worker in those skills which are in short supply has the freedom to indulge in a degree of job mobility which most managers regard with concern and which previous generations would have looked upon with horror.

It is prudent to assume, when designing a formula for recruitment of technologists, that the relevant skills are in short supply and will become increasingly scarce as the pattern of demand from employers shifts away from the unskilled to the skilled. The assumption should be made that the employee will not necessarily regard it as a privilege to work for the XYZ Company. The company's attitude must therefore be to sell its jobs with just as much enthusiasm and efficiency as it sells its products, and with at least as much attention to the specification and quality of the items being sold.

The company should identify its place in the market and its objectives and define the role of each employee or category of employee in relation to those objectives. It can then more easily both be, and appear to the potential employee to be, a performance-oriented rather than an authority-orientated organization. Further, the company should be prepared to reflect the increasing pace of technology change by offering career change and retraining to its technologists. In this way it can provide diversity of experience of a kind that may make it unnecessary for the employee to change his employer in order to broaden his experience. Recruiting policy should therefore be geared to obtaining adaptable recruits who can build on experience rather than become its prisoner. All detailed technical knowledge will become obsolete within the working lifetime of any young new recruit, if not indeed within a few years. With employment legislation moving towards a principle of 'once in, never out' it is only sensible for the employer to select for adaptability as well as current competence.

Writing the job specification

The importance of job specifications does not need additional emphasis for those who have read Chapter 4. The knowledge worker is as concerned as anyone else to know the area and limits of his responsibilities, to whom he reports for which function, whom he controls, what his title, relative status and privileges are, and where he may progress at a later date. An organization chart answers many of his questions for him and must be available for inspection by applicants during the recruitment process.

In companies doing advanced development work, many of the technical staff are organized into special project teams and the traditional hierarchical approach to organization may be abandoned. An interesting example of this is the research and consultancy firm of Arthur D. Little, where project leadership varies from one project to another and where the president of the company may serve on a team led by a consultant without permanent management status.

Job specifications must be arrived at by consultation with the technical management concerned and committed to paper. It is not enough to say: 'I can recognize the right man when I see him'. It may be true, but the discipline of thinking of jobs in terms of functions rather than individuals is necessary from time to time. In any case the right man expects the job to have been thought out in advance of his applying for it. Having said this, it can be conceded that individual applicants have sometimes made such an impression that job specifications have been rewritten to suit them and that this may have been of benefit to the organization concerned. This, however, does not make the effort involved in the original specification a waste of time. On the contrary there will be increased attention focused on the functions to be performed and a decreased risk that some of them may go unfulfilled by default.

Factors affecting recruitment / *Problems*

From time to time in the United Kingdom shortages have developed among such people as aircraft designers, chemical engineers, draughtsmen, computer specialists and accountants but, in the long term, supply and demand usually come into balance through the operation of market forces. It is pointless, therefore, to become obsessed with any particular category. It is safer to assume that there will always be an employee's market in one skill or another and the organization must be able to cope accordingly.

Salary structure

However much the operation of supply and demand upon salary levels for particular occupations may be deplored it is better for the employer to ride with the market than to attempt to defeat it. Many organizations take a lot of trouble to devise salary scales which relate equitably the varying occupations of their salaried staff so that no category is paid too much or too little. This, while pleasing to the sense of fair play, may make it impossible for the company to attract any but substandard employees into functions which may be critical for the future success of the business. It is only a partial answer to attempt to train novices internally and keep their salaries in line with internal standards but below those payable outside. This leads to losses of the people trained and, if taken to excess, to a waste of talented technicians' time in training novices to the exclusion of performing their true job of solving the problems of the business. The only way to satisfy the salary aspirations of the categories in short supply and at the same time maintain internal equity is to pay all categories at the highest market level appropriate to the highest paid skill. This is obviously an expensive expedient and the equity so gained may well not be perceived, since the employees with the highly rated skills of the moment may feel that their market differential is more valid than the job evaluation system used by their employer.

Opportunities for added experience

The attitude to staff must be as market-orientated as the attitude to new product development. What does the knowledge worker want as a 'job customer?' Usually the first point on his list is the improvement and enlargement of his knowledge and experience. If he is good, he does not want to do in one company exactly what he did in his previous company. Thus it is a mistake to insist that an applicant who is required to do a, b and c in his new job must have done a, b and c on the same scale in his old job.

In advanced-knowhow businesses the technician seeks to improve by association with firms and individuals who are known for their outstanding work. Bright young university scientists are attracted to where the significant research is being done in their specialities and a similar motivation applies in business. Thus the firm's name can sometimes act as an attraction in a job advertisement. For promotional reasons unconnected with employment, however, companies which have no special reputation may also give their name prominence in publicity material and advertisements. Such companies can fail to attract the right candidates if their activities are not stated in a way that makes it clear that they provide good employment experience.

Decline of company loyalty

For the less ambitious technologists not prepared to uproot themselves in the pursuit of knowhow, salary and location are of primary interest. The behaviour of categories in short supply, such as computer specialists in the sixties, provide an interesting motivational study because of their almost complete freedom to suit their personal predilections. As one would expect, this freedom was used to gain technically interesting and advanced jobs, high pay and a congenial environment at work and outside. Albeit that they are one of the most intelligent and strongly motivated segments of the knowledge workforce their behaviour provides a clue to what we may expect from the other segments.

One factor of significance to employers is the decline of loyalty to the single firm. One is much more likely to find an unskilled man staying with one employer throughout his working lifetime than an accountant. In fact, since the Second World War, accountants in industry and commerce have set an example in mobility and in loyalty to their profession rather than to their first employer and this is being increasingly followed by other knowledge workers. Conversely, as mentioned above, legislation is making it easier for those who so wish to stay with one employer until retirement, even if that employer would prefer them to move on.

Methods of recruitment

Press advertising through national, professional, trade, technical and local journals is used in accordance with accumulated experience on the cost effectiveness of the various media. The relative strengths of the respective journals vary from time to time and formulas evolved in years past should not be adhered to uncritically. Nor should readership of particular journals be taken as indicating the effectiveness of those journals as job advertising media. The cheapest medium is not usually the best and the absolute number of replies not the criterion of merit. There are of course methods other than press advertising. Television is tried from time to time and there are registers and agencies, some of which specialize in certain categories of staff.

Use of executive searcher or 'headhunter'

In the upper salary brackets there may be justification for the use of consultants and 'headhunters'. The additional expense of such methods may be justified by advice on job specification and the superior effectiveness of skilled third-party advertising which enables an almost full disclosure to be made of the job characteristics without any embarrassing revelations linked with a named employer.

As 'headhunting', or executive search, has become more popular in recent years, it is worth examining its appropriateness for the recruitment of knowledge workers. This method is taken to exclude approaches made by consultants to previous applicants ('file search') but refers rather to unsolicited approaches to strangers who may or may not be happily employed in their present positions. My personal view, and some will disagree, is that search consultants often find it difficult to track down a top technician unless he is a figure with a public reputation (which may have been earned many years before and may carry with it an unrealistic salary price-tag) or unless the consultants themselves are specialists in the area concerned in which case the most accessible candidates may be employed by their own clients. It then becomes difficult to maintain a proper professional relationship between the consultant and his client unless a self-denying 'no poaching' ordinance is observed.

What is more likely is that the headhunter will go for one of the large firms who are not clients and who are known to employ the type of technologist required. An approach will be made and a 'marriage' consummated without there being any degree of confidence that a much better (and possibly cheaper) candidate elsewhere has not been scanning the advertisements for just such an opportunity.

Having selected the method of recruitment many firms come to grief through bad planning. The good applicant is an elusive animal: his capture must be scheduled. He will not join a company unless he thinks that it is efficient, that it knows what it is doing, that it can explain it to him in terms that he can understand, that it can decide fairly quickly whether or not it wants him, and having decided that it can let him know quickly. There are thus problems in evaluation, communication and administration.

Evaluation procedure

Evaluation in this context means the assessment of the applicant by the employer in relation to the job specification, and the assessment of the job by the applicant. The best applicants may well wish to decide for themselves whether there is a good fit between themselves and the work offered. In such a case self-selection may be an important adjunct to employer-selection. Effort devoted to good descriptions of the job and the organization will then be rewarded. Time will be saved if applicants are shown these descriptions and put in a position to 'deselect' themselves at an early stage in the recruitment process. The other factor that the applicant will wish to assess is the personality of his boss and this can only be done by a face-to-face meeting. This, to save time, may be deferred to a later stage in the procedure.

Evaluation of the applicant is by written letter and form, by interview, skill or aptitude test and by reference. The letter often contains enough information to determine whether or not a person should be seen but often this decision may have to be deferred until a form has been completed. Care must, of course, be taken not to demand a high degree of literacy from an applicant for a job which requires mainly numerate skills. The letter of application may not do the applicant justice. On the other hand, ineptitude in written communication will normally need to be compensated by oral skill.

Design of application form

The form should be designed for its specific purpose. One for computer specialists is shown in Figure 21.1. Apart from the general items which apply to all applicants and which are covered in Chapter 6 there are specialist boxes dealing with programming and systems analysis and design.

The employer needs to know the programming languages and operating systems covered and the length of time for which they have been used. Recent courses in languages not actually used may nevertheless be of value. In systems work, familiarity of the applicant with problem areas (applications),

APPLICATION FOR EMPLOYMENT

No information on this form will be
disclosed without your permission

Advertisement Ref
Position Applied For
Desired work location

Surname
Christian Names
Address

Date of Birth

Office Tel. No.
(if convenient)

Tel No
(When convenient   )

Do you hold current full UK Driving Licence ?. . . . .

Will you need to obtain a Work Permit ?. . . . .

Have you applied before? If so, at which office ?. . . . .   And when ?. . . . .

How much notice must you give your employer ?. . . . .

EDUCATION (Secondary onwards)

Dates From To	School or other Educ. Establishment	Qualifications Gained	Subjects	Grades

Membership of professional institutions/societies   Foreign languages spoken fluently

Figure 21.1   Personal history form for recruitment of technologists

EMPLOYMENT RECORD

Dates From—To	Name and location of employer	Job Title and duties	Final or present salary

TECHNICAL TRAINING AND EXPERIENCE

Aptitude Tests Taken	Dates	Results (if known)

Courses Attended	Dates	Content

Experience: Give outline of significant experience or projects, giving technical environment (e.g. computer configuration and operating system), own role, programming languages used or other experience that you think could be relevant to your application — Continue overleaf

Dates	Technical or Project Experience	Own Role

Figure 21.1 **(continued)**

ADDITIONAL INFORMATION
Use this space for any additional information that you think could be useful in assessing your application, e.g. significant achievements outside your employment, your reasons for applying or your longer term ambitions

I believe the above statements to be true

Signature   Date

Figure 21.1   (continued)

or with 'real time' or distributed data processing techniques may be relevant. The role of the applicant in the project, whether at the detail, immediate supervisory or remote supervision levels, is also important.

Other boxes are required for different types of job and can be catered for on separate sheets or by a variety of gummed panels. The normal objective is to have enough data from the form and letter to decide whether to call a person for interview; but there may be a need to augment information by a telephone conversation with the applicant. He may, for instance, have omitted his salary or have stated a salary which is likely to make him too expensive for the position he applied for.

Other methods of initial approach

With very volatile categories where other employers are likely to be in simultaneous competition it may be preferable to invite the candidate to make his initial approach by telephone. In this way, provided that the employer has very clearly defined his criteria for deciding whether or not an interview should be granted, much time on the preliminaries can be saved by fixing the interviews by telephone.

Another method sometimes used is to invite all comers to an informal chat at one or more locations, not necessarily the firm's offices—hotels are often employed—and use the occasion as an aid to preliminary screening. The difficulty of this approach is to predict the response and therefore to arrange for the appropriate interviewer strength to be available. It may, however, be tried if standard approaches have already failed and it is necessary to make it easy for the applicant by arranging the interview locally and perhaps outside working hours.

Dangers of excessive reliance on tests

Although tests may have a part to play in determining aptitudes the central feature of the evaluation and decision-making elements in recruitment is the interview. It is here that the candidate's record is examined and the job is 'sold' to him if he is felt to be a serious contendant. However much faith is placed in tests as guides to personality it is doubtful whether it is economic to apply them to the bulk of the technological recruits. Some organizations which have placed excessive reliance on tests have in fact defeated their own interests by making the recruitment process so extended that the better candidates have joined other employers rather than accept the delays which occur while the tests are scheduled and administered.

Apart from this practical consideration personality tests have, in recent years, come under attack from two opposing points of view. If successful they are said to constitute an unwarranted intrusion upon individual privacy. Alternatively it is said that the intelligent applicant can readily determine which answers will make him appear stable or extroverted or whatever characteristic he thinks the potential employer will desire. For an amusing guide on how to complete a personality test see William H. Whyte's book *The Organization Man.*

Tests of performance, as opposed to personality, can sometimes be administered quite quickly and conveniently, both for skilled manual workers and for pencil and paper technicians like computer programmers. They then form a most valuable adjunct to the interview.

Interviewing techniques

No good purpose is served by playing down the difficulty of interviewing knowledge workers. The 'social' type interview can often distinguish the neurotic from the well-adjusted, the shy from the extrovert, the solitary from the gregarious. But what the employer is likely to be most interested in is the level of competence in the job to be done, the suitability for other jobs later, the motivation and perhaps the managerial potential. These generally require very skilled interviewing by someone who knows the job environment very well, preferably through having been in similar employment himself. The interviewer should ideally be both more intelligent and more experienced than the applicant, and must be sufficiently inquisitive, alert, logical and skilled in interviewing to evaluate the employment history and personality as a predictor of the applicant's future progress.

The best interviewer is a technologist with an aptitude for and a training in interviewing. Without this aptitude and training the interview has a slim chance of success. Confront one technologist with another and they often gossip about mutual acquaintances and fence around the subject picking at trivial points of detail and leaving the central experiences of the applicant almost unexamined.

The lone personnel man, on the other hand, is at a disadvantage both with the glib but incompetent and with the competent but uncommunicative technologist. A 'double act' with a good interviewer and a good technical manager representing the employer is a possible solution but has a number of disadvantages: extravagant use of resources, difficulty in pursuing a coherent thread if the separate roles of the two interviewers are not clearly defined and inability in the timid applicant to do himself justice if he feels outnumbered.

The interview itself, of course, is not merely a *pas de deux*, ritual courtship or intellectual fencing match. The time should be invested in fact finding, sifting and evaluating the evidence, much of which should already exist in outline in the employment history form. The more the resulting judgements are fact-based and the less they depend on subjective hunches on the part of the interviewer, the greater the chances of success in selection. For further discussions of the techniques of interviewing, readers are referred to Chapter 12. Suffice it to say that with knowledge workers the fact finding must be two-way, not merely an interrogation of the candidate by XYZ Limited, but also a conversation between two parties who hope to cooperate to their future mutual advantage.

Taking up references

The final means that the employer has of evaluating the applicant is through reference, and by reference is not meant the exchange of formal letters attempting to establish the honesty, sobriety, period of employment, status and salary of the applicant, though this information has its uses. *The ideal reference is the informal conversation with someone who knows the quality of the applicant's work.* Such a reference is best obtained by telephone rather than by letter. Such references must not be taken up without the applicant's knowledge and consent.

Communications and administrative procedures

Many technological recruiting campaigns turn out to be dismal failures, simply because the mechanism of recruitment is geared to a long-past leisured age when employment was a fought-over privilege and the employer could afford to be slow, inefficient and discourteous. Even now there are organizations where applications must be made in duplicate, where the only interviewing is by a panel and where the panel only sits once a month. These tend to go with the fixed salary scales where increments and promotions come by time rather than by merit. Even in commercial organizations it is possible to find inefficient personnel departments which issue letters of offer a week after the decision has been taken to employ a person.

The personnel department in its recruiting capacity is as much in the front line as the sales department and must act accordingly. This implies not merely efficient administration but forward planning. How often are campaigns arranged where candidates can only be approved by Mr Jones and Mr Robinson and Messrs Jones and Robinson depart on a fortnight's holiday just as the shortlist has been assembled?

No great effort, but much space, would be needed to catalogue the administrative inefficiencies found in recruitment. Most of them would be avoided if those responsible put themselves in the position of the applicant and asked themselves the same questions: 'Why should I work for the XYZ Company? In what way are they better than ABC Limited? Is there a future there for *me*? Are they efficient? Are they human?' The future of the firm in the long term depends on the answers given to these questions by the people they really want, the intelligent, productive and highly motivated knowledge workers.

Further reading

'A structural approach to hiring', *Datamation,* May 1974.
Bower, Marvin (1966): *The Will to Manage.* New York: McGraw-Hill.
Drucker, Peter F. (1969): *The Age of Discontinuity.* London: Heinemann.
Fear, Richard A. (1973): *Evaluation Interviewing.* Maidenhead: McGraw-Hill.
Sturt, H. and Yearsley, R. (1969): *Computers for Management.* London: Heinemann.
'The EDP people problem', *Data Processing Digest,* Los Angeles, monthly articles, October 1969–September 1970.
Whitaker, Peter (1973): *Selection Interviewing.* London: Industrial Society.
Whyte, William H. (1960): *The Organization Man.* London: Penguin.

22

Management Trainees in Banking

David McIlvenna

With total employees in excess of 200 000, the United Kingdom clearing banks are, by any standards, major employers. Included in that figure are about 40 000 junior and senior managers and ensuring that there are sufficient people capable of filling these positions presents a recruitment problem of some size and complexity.

The position of the banks in the recruitment market has changed considerably in the years since the Second World War. The expanded availability of advanced education has inevitably produced a constant upgrading of the level of academic attainment of school leavers, so that the school certificate holder of the 1940's, the 'A' level school leaver of the 1960's and the graduate of the 1980's are people of similar level and quality and will have to do the same jobs. The difficulties faced by the banks in reconciling short-term operational demands for staff with rewarding career opportunities for all those with long term aspirations have been exacerbated by the reducing acceptability of lifetime career employment. However, the social needs of the community may well make lifetime employment increasingly valuable in the next generation. The problem has therefore been to recruit young people with management potential, to give them a training of complex technicality and wide variety, necessarily involving some detailed knowledge of the routine procedures of banking and, at the same time, to retain them for this lengthy training period in the face of competition from other employers, some of whom appear to offer larger salaries or greater responsibilities at an earlier age, albeit with perhaps reduced career prospects or security of employment.

In many respects the pattern of recruitment has changed little in fifty years. True, it is now accepted that it is not necessary for every person who joins a bank to be of managerial calibre nor are women automatically considered suitable only for junior clerical or secretarial employment. Yet the concept of a lifetime career with one employer is still a main plank on which the bank's manpower planning is founded. The fact that society has tended in recent years to regard the one company career as less attractive is one of the difficulties facing those responsible for bank recruitment.

Qualities of the ideal banker

Gilbart's *Logic of Banking*, published in 1865, describes in lengthy terms the qualities considered desirable for a banker. As might be expected, they include wisdom, prudence, discretion and decisiveness. Gilbart also considered the ability to economize in the company's time by exercising powers of delegation and keeping interviews with customers as short as possible to be desirable attributes, and he recommended that the banker should normally receive his customers standing so as not to encourage them to stay for too long a conversation! To these excellent and basic qualities may be added a few more, shaped to modern trends and to the language of the modern business world:

1   A standard of general intelligence that can be translated under guidance into technical competence.
2   Social qualities and acceptability that can flourish in many varied human group situations.
3   Willingness to apply self-criticism in a search for improved performance.
4   Ability to communicate lucidly by written or spoken word and to listen.
5   A mental outlook that welcomes change.
6   Continuing vitality and drive in pursuit of a common purpose.
7   A good memory.

In other words a veritable paragon of management virtues is sought and indeed is to be found in considerable numbers.

Gilbart's traditional banker was concerned almost entirely with the acquisition of deposits and their prudent and careful lending to customers so as to produce a lucrative income for his employers with a minimum degree of risk.

His modern counterpart is at the centre of changes in technology and management philosophies which have revolutionized banking in the past twenty years. The computer has brought faster and more accurate information on which to base decisions and control the business. The acknowledgement that marketing has a part to play in banking has meant that the manager must be prepared to offer a range of financial sidelines including such things as credit cards, trustee and income tax services, computer services, insurance and so on. The manager does not have to be an expert on all these services but needs to know how to introduce the customer to them.

The salary rewards in banking have, of course, increased to keep pace with the wider demands made on the bank manager and if money, prestige and the power to help other people are the long term objectives which a young person looks to gain from a career then banking has plenty to offer.

Manpower planning

The rapid expansion of banking activities which took place in the 1920s was met by wholesale recruitment not only from one narrow age group but also from an equally narrow band of academic ability and ambition. As a result the banks found themselves with a large surplus of well qualified staff for whom promotion opportunities were quite inadequate. The resulting frustration and disillusion felt by employees whose talents were not being used to the full made the banks keenly aware of the need for long term manpower planning.

A similar expansion of banking activities followed the end of the last war, but, armed with their earlier experience, the banks have made greater efforts to calculate projections of future staff needs. Precision is not possible, of course, in forecasting the future, but the aim is to equate as nearly as possible the number of recruits with the number of appropriate opportunities expected to arise.

All the normal factors such as wastage trends, staff savings by the introduction of computers and estimated growth of the activities are taken into account in these calculations. The result is that the banks can approach schools, universities, and the employment market in general with a clear idea of the opportunities likely to be available to each new entrant, whether he or she is expected to attain a senior clerical, a supervisory or a managerial position, and whether the expectation is of a five year or a forty year career.

Streaming

As we have seen, at one time the vast majority of entrants into banking had the kind of educational background and other qualities appropriate for future management. Nowadays it is realized that it is necessary to have a mix of recruits with differing expectations and different ability levels. It follows therefore that post entry training and development will involve some system of streaming. Terminology differs from bank to bank but the effect is the same. For the short stay entrant the amount of training and development will be limited and therefore the main impact of streaming is on that group of entrants who are looking for a long term progressive career. By careful methods of selection and appraisal the long-term managerial potential of the young trainee is assessed at around age twenty-two. For the high flyers there are accelerated training systems which project them into a junior managerial appointment at the age of twenty-five or twenty-six, to a submanagement at twenty-eight and to a full management job at thirty. At the other end of the scale are those who take longer to train, develop and mature, and who therefore take longer to reach the first rung of the managerial ladder.

In between these two extremes lies the greater bulk who reach a first appointment in their early or middle thirties and their first management in their late thirties or early forties. If the appraisal methods used are accurate (and all the banks use methods which include cross checks by independent assessors), management trainees should find themselves working in streams and at rates which are comfortably adjusted to their own talents. They have, of course, the opportunity to change streams if this is warranted by the pace of their development.

Entry requirements

Precise minimum educational qualifications are not generally stipulated but as those entrants seeking a progressive long term career will be expected to complete the examinations of the Institute of Bankers, the minimum 4 'O' level requirement for admission to those examinations clarifies the situation. In practice it is probably true to say that 'A' level school leavers provide the main intake of management trainees. There are also opportunities for older people aged up to about twenty-five who have had some previous commercial experience. The numbers recruited in this category are calculated so as to fill the vacancies created by resignations of those who have come in at seventeen or eighteen. In this way the projected plan of management succession can be maintained.

A special feature of banking recruitment in recent years has been the increase in the number of graduates in the annual intake of management trainees. The actual figures vary from bank to bank but the four major clearing banks are now taking over 500 graduates a year between them. At one time all graduate entrants, even those recruited for specialist positions, were expected to demonstrate the potential for eventual senior management or executive status. However there are signs that graduates with a broader range of potential are now being recruited so that whilst the high flyers will still be included there will be a greater proportion of the type of young person who in the past joined after 'O' or 'A' levels.

Available on the labour market in recent years have been the second degree graduates from the Schools of Business Studies and people who have taken a postgraduate course in an allied subject such as Operational Research. Their abilities and their training in business organization and advanced management techniques require their employment in specific vacancies or on specific projects where their knowledge and skills can be fully utilised and their recruitment is restricted accordingly.

In the past the banks have been prepared to consider graduates of any discipline for employment and indeed this is still the case. However an increasing interest is being show in graduates who have taken advantage of the growth of degrees in banking and closely allied subjects. Most of these degrees are four years in duration including a year spent in industry or commerce and those who hold them, together with holders of the Higher National Diploma in Business Studies, form an important group of entrants whose progress will be watched with interest in the future.

Specialist positions

The banks require specialists to fill technical posts in departments such as economic intelligence, market analysis, investment analysis, data processing, premises and insurance. In general they are continuing to follow their usual practice of providing these specialists by internal training (growing their own timber) and this has the in-built advantage of providing diversity of opportunity for staff. However, the need to fill limited vacancies for those specialist areas of work mean that it is sometimes either preferable or necessary to recruit from outside the industry.

The methods by which potential employees and the clearing banks come together have changed over the years. At one time personal introduction through connections was probably the most common way in which applicants came forward for consideration. In the post war years there was a considerable growth in recruitment advertising by the banks. There is still a great deal of activity in this direction with television and commercial radio being used as well as the more traditional newspapers. However, the banks have also seen the need to make the public in general and the world of education in particular aware of the real advantages that can be offered by a career in banking.

The banks spend considerable time and effort in establishing close links with careers teachers in schools and careers officers of local and central government careers and employment services. In large centres of population this work is often carried out by personnel staff with some young men and women employed as full time schools liaison officers. In other parts of the country this function is traditionally performed by the branch manager who may well act as his own recruiting officer. The sort of activities carried on under the general heading of schools liaison include visits to schools to make careers presentations, usually supplemented by some form of audio visual programme. In addition there are courses for school leavers and for careers teachers and careers officers, to acquaint them with the current opportunities available to the young people whom they advise. Apart from the programmes of individual banks the Banking Information Service also provides services to education.

In the field of graduate recruitment the 'milk round' is still the main point of contact for graduates wishing to apply to clearing banks. The advantages of being able to visit universities and interview a number of applicants at the same time are obvious but they are off-set to some extent by the exhausting schedules which are involved at a time (the first three months of the year) when weather conditions are often at their worst. A new development has been the inauguration of summer graduate recruitment fairs on a regional basis which are, in effect, conventions at which employers can set out their stalls and either interview or arrange interviews for graduates who with good reason may have left their career choice until after taking their finals. Several of the banks are taking advantage of this development although it is unlikely that in the foreseeable future the summer exercise will replace the spring 'milk round'.

Operation of recruitment systems

Mention should be made of the system by which the banks operate their recruitment organizations. Some work solely from their head offices whilst others are regionalized or decentralized. In the latter case it is customary for graduate recruitment to be under the care of the head offices while other entrants are recruited locally either through regional offices or by branch managers. Such a variety of entry points means that standardization of interview and appraisal methods has to be attempted. The importance of selection interview training has been recognized and is now available fairly widely. In organizing such courses the services of consultant industrial psychologists are often sought. Apart from the selection interview, group selection techniques, aptitude and other psychometric tests are also used.

Future opportunities in banking

Opinions differ amongst bankers on the likely trend of management trainee recruiting in the future. One school of thought looks to the introduction of two-tier recruitment which would give a clearer separation between clerical and executive training streams. Other banks are equally firmly convinced that this is neither necessary nor desirable. It must be admitted that the situation is governed to a large extent by market factors.

It is generally agreed that the graduates (including, for the moment, the holders of the Higher National Diploma in Business Studies and, of course, the holders of CNAA degrees in Business or Social Studies) must form a larger part of the management trainee entrants in the future. It is also agreed that more care must be taken to ensure that the management trainee's early years are made as interesting and stimulating as possible, whilst at the same time continuing to provide a sound basic grounding.

What clearly can be said, however, is that the present period of modernization, expansion and integration that is taking place in the industry is making career prospects brighter and that these factors form a launching pad for growth and new developments and with them many new style careers. So far as mergers are concerned it is argued that size will give strength and increased world standing for the banks involved; the merged banks can be expected to develop their overseas activities and to play an even larger part in international finance than their constituent predecessors. The introduction of more sophisticated technology will produce changes demanding an even shrewder and more purposeful use of human resources.

The banking world tomorrow, therefore offers wide prospects for talents at many levels and in this context recruiters' tasks are eased by the attraction of the varied careers and management training prospects which are available.

23

Recruitment in Local Government

Derek Gould

Historical perspective prior to 1972

Local government is labour-intensive: payroll accounts for about 60% of its revenue spending. In many parts of the country a local authority is the largest employer within its area. And yet, until reorganization in April 1974 local government lagged behind industry and other sectors of the public sector in recognising and developing the personnel management function.

With the benefit of hindsight it seems remarkable that this should have been so. As long as as 1934 the Hadow Committee, reporting to the Minister of Health on the qualifications, recruitment and training of local government officers, had recommended that every local authority should entrust all questions affecting these personnel matters to one committee of the council—possibly the general purposes committee or the finance committee in smaller authorities, or an establishment committee advised by the Clerk of the Council in larger authorities. On selection the Hadow Committee commented that: 'the method should be carefully calculated to secure the ablest of the candidates who present themselves' and 'must be strictly impartial'.

Many authorities followed the recommendation to appoint an establishment committee and some appointed a specialist establishment officer. This focussed attention on the importance of personnel work, but it did not generally bring about a significant improvement in the methods used to recruit and select staff.

The whole situation came under further scrutiny when another government committee, the Mallaby Committee, examined the staffing of local government and presented its findings in 1967. The committee gave much valuable advice, particularly on new patterns of recruitment and employment and on sources of recruitment. However, what is so incredible is the fact that the committee apparently never sought the advice of professional personnel specialists. Neither the National Institute of Industrial Psychology nor the Institute of Personnel Management, for example, appear in the list of bodies that gave evidence; yet the latter institute has been in existence since 1913 and has run courses in personnel management since the early 1930s, including courses for local government officers in the early 1960s which were discontinued owing to lack of demand.

This oversight possibly explains why some of the text and recommendations of the report fail to give sound advice and for a time even may have inhibited development of a professional approach in local government. All would agree that 'local authorities should ensure that the officer to whom responsibility for establishment work is delegated has the status and capacity to undertake it effectively'. But this is followed by:

At present there is no recognized training or qualification for personnel or establishment officers in local government . . . we are certain that establishment work should not become a specialism in which officers made a career divorced from other duties . . . a knowledge and preferably experience of management should be one of the establishment officer's main attributes and instruction in personnel management should be part of his basic training.

The report discussed three aspects of local government recruitment and selection procedures which required clarification. The committee recommended that the advice of outside assessors should be sought, in addition to that of the clerk or establishment officer, when heads of departments or their deputies were being appointed. They also recommended that the interviewing panels of elected representatives which made these appointments should be small. For posts below the top two tiers the committee were of the opinion that heads of departments should be given responsibility for selecting and appointing staff on behalf of the authority, making full use of specialist advice available in the clerk's department.

Again, the committee's lack of knowledge and appreciation of the professional approach possibly explains the failure to give sound and unambiguous advice. The use of outside assessors on occasion was interpreted as meaning use of the head of a similar department in another authority, rather than borrowing or purchasing professional personnel expertise not available from the internal manpower resources of the appointing authority. Generally the need to use expert advice for top appointments was, and today often still is, unrecognized.

Panel interviewing was rigidly adhered to as the only interviewing method, possibly because the committee made no mention of the value of preliminary one-to-one interviewing by a personnel specialist; or serial one-to-one interviewing by the personnel specialist and the relevant manager or managers. The third of the above recommendations was sound, but no guidance was given on what was to be the recruitment and selection relationship between the appointing head of department and the specialist in the clerk's department.

In March 1970 the writer conducted a survey of procedures then being used in the London boroughs. Response to the questionnaire was poor: only fifteen of the thirty-two boroughs returned forms. Nevertheless, the response provided sufficient information to indicate the continuing unsatisfactory nature of recruitment and selection procedures in the London boroughs. Only two of the fifteen used a systematic approach in interviewing: only one used psychological tests; only three had used outside consultants to assist selection of their chief executive; etc. For the whole of the country the general poor quality of staff advertisements suggested a widespread poverty of sound recruitment expertise, since it was evident that job descriptions and personnel specifications were either inadequate or nonexistent.

The Bains Report and reorganization

Although in 1972 one or two local authories—in particular the London Borough of Lambeth—were well on the way to setting up a professional personnel function, official guidance and encouragement to do so did not come until Bains Report of that year. The study group had been appointed jointly by the Secretary of State for the Environment and the local authority associations to examine management principles and structures in local government at both elected member and officer levels. The report was intended to assist those whose task it would be to determine appropriate management principles and structures within the new authorities to be established at reorganization.

The terms of reference of the study group required them to pay particular attention to 'internal arrangements bearing on efficiency in the use of manpower' and they took this phrase to mean something more than extension of existing processes for examination of claims for additional staff. In the chapter on personnel management they recommended enhanced status for the head of the personnel department (the traditional 'establishment' title to be dropped in favour of the more widely recognised title 'personnel manager') and on recruitment and selection commented:

> We believe there is a real need to examine the traditional processes of selection. The importance of the selection decision requires that local authorities should keep abreast of developing techniques; more attention should be paid to the design of man and job specifications; application

forms should be designed to provide the maximum information relevant to the post to which they relate; interviewing skills should be developed and expanded. The qualified personnel officer may have a particular role to play as a consultant to line departments in this field.

From the number of advertisements for personnel officers that followed reorganization in April 1974 it was evident that many of the new authorities were taking Bains' advice. Unfortunately, in a large number of cases the opportunity to establish a professionally orientated function from the word 'go' was lost, however, partly because officers and members lacked knowledge of both the function and the candidate requirements. Such bodies as Lamsac (Local Authorities Management Services and Computer Committee) and the Local Government Training Board offered a spate of sound advice and training—which authorities will need to accept for years to come—yet advertisements for personnal officers followed the traditional pattern of local government recruitment advertising: little indication of the size of the job or what it entailed; no specification of the qualifications and experience required; no description of the authority and its area (see Figures 23.1 and 23.2).

Woodcut District Council

PERSONNEL OFFICER

Grade P.O.1 (1-5)—(£3690–£4182 per annum plus threshold pay)

Applications for the above post are invited from suitable qualified persons with good experience of personnel work and administration. The post is in the Chief Executive's Department, and the personnel officer will be directly responsible to him for the whole range of personnel work in connection with 170 officers and 150 manual workers.

The officer appointed will be based at Blanktown. Consideration will be given to the provision of housing accommodation and removal expenses will be paid. The post carries an essential user car allowance.

Applications, stating age, qualification, present salary and experience, together with the names and addresses of two referees must reach the Chief Executive, Woodcut District Council, - - - - - etc.

Figure 23.1 **A badly worded local authority recruitment advertisement**

Assistant Town Clerk

(Management Services)

£4965–£5472 per annum inclusive
(Plus car allowance)

Applications are invited from suitably qualified officers, with broad experience in local government, with responsibility particularly to direct the work of the Management Services of the Council.

W town is a go ahead, thriving borough within easy reach of the centre of London and the countryside of Zshire.

Assistance may be granted in appropriate cases to assist the successful candidate to purchase accommodation.

Personal and career details with the names of two referees should be sent to the Town Clerk and Chief Executive Officer, - - - - - etc.

Interesting, Satisfying O and M

X town offers you a chance not only to do thorough and far-reaching conventional O and M work in which original thinking is encouraged and expected, but also to help at the design stage of a major project, where good work now will have lasting value.

We want someone with valid O and M experience, able to work at all levels and to get down to the nitty gritty of really mastering the subject. Excellent conditions of service including special leave. £3028–£4429 (A.P. 4/S.O. 2) depending on experience.

Phone - - - - - , or write Personnel and Management Services Officer, - - - - - for an application form, returnable by - - - - - .

Figure 23.2   Badly worded advertisements from London Boroughs

The London boroughs had been created by the reorganization of London government in April 1964, but they too were affected by the climate of change brought about by Bains. Following the report a number of them vigorously attempted to improve their personnel function and image. By 1974 only one or two continued to produce advertisements that suggested the still primitive state of their recruitment and selection procedures: meaningless wording; only vague specification of the qualifications and experience needed; no offer of further job details to compensate for lack of description in the advertisement. The advertisement for an assistant town clerk in Figure 23.2 is particularly confusing because it is unclear whether legal or management services type qualifications are required.

The present situation

At the time of writing, ten years after Bains, the personnel function still appears to have only a shaky footing in the majority of local authorities. In an article in the *Local Government Chronicle* the Principal Management Services Officer of the London Borough of Tower Hamlets is sceptical of whether the hopes of the Bains Report have been fulfilled. He examines in turn the various sub-functions of personnel management and to justify his criticism of current recruitment and selection procedures he invites readers to turn to the vacancies pages of the magazine. 'Comparing them mentally with the adverts you saw five or six years ago, are they not just the same dreary ads?' he asks. And as for selection procedures, he asserts that anyone who has been on a short-list recently can confirm that, with a few honourable exceptions, little has changed: 'one authority recently interviewed for a chief officer post and allocated each short-listed candidate just twenty minutes!'

Unfortunately the author of the article makes his logic suspect by ending with the words: 'Perhaps Bains got it wrong'. Not only is the argument for the professional approach to personnel management unassailable and in general empirically proved, but the author cannot expect readers to accept his suggestion that maybe the recommendations of the report were wrong when he has used the yardstick of good practice advocated by Bains in order to criticise the present situation. Nevertheless, the author's basic premise that so far the personnel service in local government has failed seems to be correct.

Some indication of the extent to which authorities have taken the advice of Bains can be obtained by again assessing the quality of local government advertisements. Since job descriptions and personnel specifications are key documents in all of the sub-functions of personnel management (recruitment and selection; training; career development; manpower planning; industrial relations; wages and salaries administration), it is reasonably certain that if an authority's advertisements are poor, then the whole of the personnel function is weak. If an authority's advertisements are good, this suggests that at least their recruitment and selection procedures are satisfactory.

Moreover, since one would expect to find vacancies for professional personnel posts at least advertised in *Personnel Management* (the journal of the Institute of Personnel Management), an examination of these advertisements also can provide a general indication of local government progress in setting up a professional function.

For example, during a particular twelve-month period 113 local government posts (excluding those from development corporations and education establishments) were advertised in this magazine, 33 of which came from London boroughs and 23 from counties and regional councils. The relatively high proportion from the London area (even allowing for eight from Lambeth alone) may have been the result of high staff turnover. But another explanation may be that the London boroughs are continuing to be more progressive in this field than authorities in general in the rest of the country.

On the other hand, bearing in mind that in smaller authorities the function tends to be completely centralized, whereas in larger authorities there is a justification for having a departmental as well as a centralized function, then the relatively small number of advertisements coming from the counties and regional councils suggests slower progress than one would expect, considering the greater availability of resources.

Some readers may put a different interpretation on these figures. But what is more certain from closer examination of the data is an apparent reluctance to introduce professional personnel management into the larger departments of the larger authorities.

During the twelve months in question there were only sixteen departmental advertisements (from twelve authorities, including two in London): police (1); education (3); housing (2); engineering (2); social services (7); fire (1). With education accounting for 60% or more of the expenditure of the larger authorities it seems inconceivable, in particular, that only two authorities should advertise posts in education personnel, unless education departments have not yet become aware of the need to manage their staff in a more professional manner.

Unfortunately, the fact that certain authorities advertise in *Personnel Management* does not necessarily mean that these authorities already possess a professional function, or, where they are attempting to adopt a professional approach, that they know how to go about it. Most of the 113 advertisements were poor, giving no clear and useful information about the job and wasting costly space on pointless wording (Figure 23.3).

In particular, many of these authorities clearly did not know what qualifications were needed for the job advertised. Some hid behind vague requirements like 'suitably qualified' or 'appropriate qualifications'. Others made their ignorance more obvious by attaching equal importance to a number of very different qualifications: 'should hold MIPM, DMS, DMA or other appropriate qualification'. A common variation was to ask for a degree

---

Good Listeners
Are Hard to Find . . .
Assistant Personnel Officer
Welfare Services
S.O.I. £5194–£5500 p.a. inc.

Good listeners are hard to find. Simply because their capacity to understand and sympathise with the problems of others necessitates experience of life, and that special kind of selflessness which especially encourages other people towards helping themselves towards working and home-life fulfilment.

The present postholder, well-backed by knowledge of Government welfare provision, local government policies, and the ability to counsel in utmost confidence, is leaving us after establishing the essential elements of this important post.

To maintain our personnel welfare facilities to the present high level, we need someone with proven liaison ability who can communicate with outside agencies such as social workers and doctors; trade union representatives; and advise on pre-retirement courses, and related welfare facilities.

As a member of the Personnel Group, there is a great deal to be done in the welfare area providing true scope for self-motivation and ideas. Previous experience in the personnel welfare field is desirable.

Car allowance and car loan facilities are available. For an informal discussion, ring
Applications from disabled persons will be considered.
Application forms and further details from the Head of Borough Personnel and Secretarial Services,
(24 hour ansaphone). Please quote ref:

Closing date: 8th March 1978.

Figure 23.3 Example of a poor advertisement by a local authority

or IPM qualification, as though any kind of degree could be a suitable alternative in personnel work. One authority stated: 'Applications from desirable persons will be considered'!

Why is it taking local government, a labour-intensive sector of the economy, so long to become professional in its management of staff, and, in particular, in its recruitment and selection methods and procedures? The reason may be partly historical—the wrong-headed advice of the Mallaby Committee. A second reason could be the resistance from people in other professions to allowing, as they see it, invaders on their territory. Perhaps the belief sometimes held by line managers that they are naturally good at judging and managing others is being reinforced by the view that only an educationist can know about education people and education jobs, that only a social worker can know about social workers and social work, etc.

To people who hold such a view it can seem inconceivable that anyone who does not hold a qualification in their particular discipline can possibly bring improvement to the management of their department or staff. Such an attitude might be not only inhibiting departmental development of the function, but also preventing some central personnel units from making an effective contribution to the corporate aspects of manpower management.

The tragedy of this situation is that these attitudes probably derive mainly from lack of understanding on the part of line management of the role of personnel in the organization. And for as long as no attempt is made to develop the function there is no way in which it can gain credibility and break free from the apparently self-fulfilling prophecy that personnel is little more than a costly, window-dressing luxury.

Developing the personnel function

In developing the personnel function, recruitment and selection policies and procedures demand priority attention: always there are vacancies waiting to be filled—by the right candidates—and the job descriptions and personnel specifications that are essential to this purpose also are needed for those other personnel activities that may be introduced as resources become available.

Despite my earlier critical comments about the way personnel officers were recruited, there has been, nevertheless, a marked improvement in much local authority job advertising since reorganization in April1974. More authorities have been producing better advertisements and it has been encouraging to see a number of district councils attaining a reasonable standard, bearing in mind the likely lack of resources for preparing job descriptions in a newly created authority. New Forest District Council has consistently produced better-than-average advertisements since it appointed a personnel manager in January 1974 (see Figure 23.4).

However, the products of many personnel officers show how ill-equipped they are for the job. This is unfortunate not simply because these officers ought to be learning the rudiments of the trade by extensive short-course training. From a background lacking in knowledge and experience of professional personnel practice they need to work out their relationships with line management. For every personnel activity there is a boundary to be defined between the specialist responsibilities of the personnel officer on the one hand and on the other the personnel responsibilities of the line manager. In authorities where the status and role of the personnel function is little understood there is a need for the personnel officer to educate his colleagues on the subject.

The extent of the personnel officer's acceptability and credibility to other heads of departments in large measure depends on how successful he is in demonstrating, by argument and action, that his work is a specialism in its

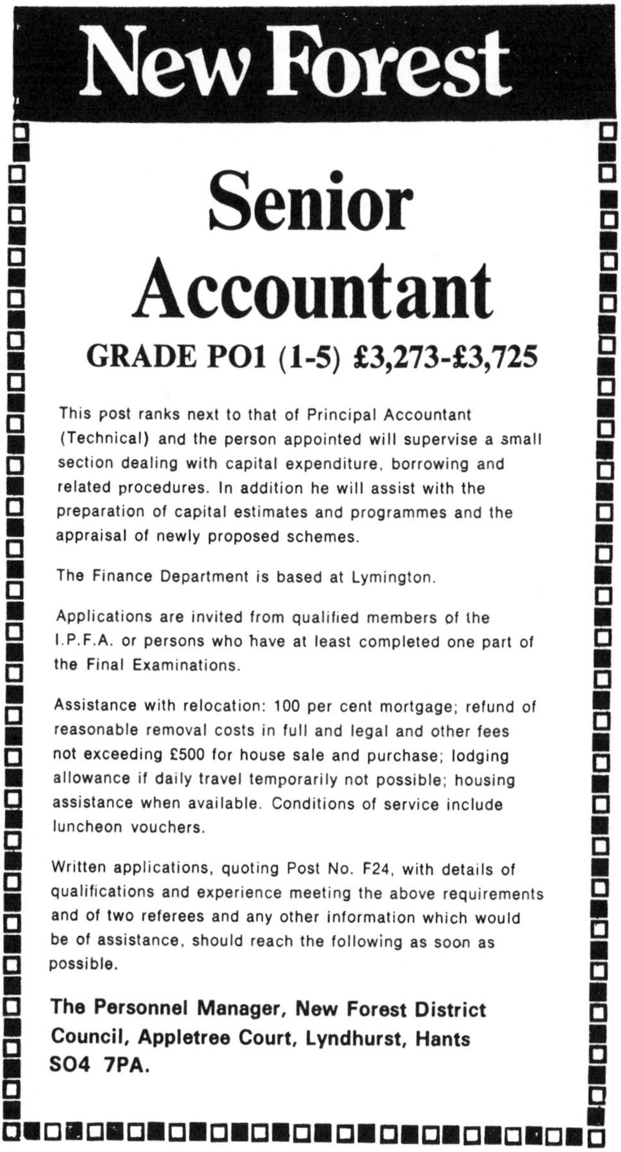

New Forest

Senior Accountant

GRADE PO1 (1-5) £3,273-£3,725

This post ranks next to that of Principal Accountant (Technical) and the person appointed will supervise a small section dealing with capital expenditure, borrowing and related procedures. In addition he will assist with the preparation of capital estimates and programmes and the appraisal of newly proposed schemes.

The Finance Department is based at Lymington.

Applications are invited from qualified members of the I.P.F.A. or persons who have at least completed one part of the Final Examinations.

Assistance with relocation: 100 per cent mortgage; refund of reasonable removal costs in full and legal and other fees not exceeding £500 for house sale and purchase; lodging allowance if daily travel temporarily not possible; housing assistance when available. Conditions of service include luncheon vouchers.

Written applications, quoting Post No. F24, with details of qualifications and experience meeting the above requirements and of two referees and any other information which would be of assistance, should reach the following as soon as possible.

The Personnel Manager, New Forest District Council, Appletree Court, Lyndhurst, Hants SO4 7PA.

Figure 23.4   Example of a good recruitment advertisement by a local authority

own right. Unless he can do this there is no reason why line managers should seek his advice, or allow him to participate in activities which, before his arrival, they carried out alone. Why should he write their advertisements or carry out preliminary screening interviews on their behalf if he cannot prove that his special training and experience enable him to do these tasks better than they can do them? Why should they accept his advice to experiment and change professionally recognized procedures—such as discontinuing the use of application forms for senior appointments, as some personnel officers have done—if he is not even capable of producing an effective advertisement?

In attempting to educate his colleagues the personnel officer may have a singularly difficult task where the recruitment and selection process is concerned. Line managers may be convinced that, solely on the basis of intuition and experience they are quite capable of producing a satisfactory advertisement and of placing it in the right media. They may feel they have never had any problems about knowing what sort of candidate they were seeking at interview and that there are no shortcomings in their interviewing skills. This is why, if resources are available, the personnel officer should arrange familiarization training for line managers in the preparation of job descriptions and in the methods and techniques of selection interviewing. Line managers can thereby learn about the professional approach to recruitment and begin to work with the personnel officer instead of against him.

Some of the misunderstanding about the role of personnel is indicated by the tendency of heads of departments to think that if recruitment is centralized they will be obliged to accept candidates who have been chosen for them by the personnel section or department. This is an example of where definition of the respective roles of personnel and line management can be helpful. What are the respective contributions of the two likely to be in the recruitment and selection process? A possible definition is given below.

Beginning with preparation of the job description, the personnel specialist approaches the task by systematically and objectively collecting facts from such sources as the present post-holder, the supervisor, the head of department, other authorities and training or other literature relevant to the job. He will then sift the information he has collected and summarize it under headings that have been found useful for recruitment and selection purposes. The whole exercise is a collaborative effort between the two departments.

The specialist knows how to interpret items in the job description in terms of the attributes needed by a person if he or she is to undertake the work successfully. He also knows how to prepare this personnel specification in such a way that the task of matching candidates' profiles with the specification is relatively easy. But, as with the job description, the specification is the result of collaboration and agreement between the departments. Only the client department can say, after careful consideration provoked by the specialist, which attributes will or will not be acceptable.

Next the specialist prepares the advertisement—perhaps with the aid and advice of a reputable recruitment advertising agency—and the further job details for sending to potential applicants. The hand of the expert is immediately evident when he has been used to preparing an advertisement and the client department should not interfere with or veto his efforts without justification based on a sound knowledge of the skills and expertise involved. A personnel specialist working closely with a recruitment advertising agency and backed by the records of his department also should have the best information available for deciding the timing and placing of advertisements.

A personnel specification differentiates between essential and desirable attributes. As application forms are received it is, therefore, relatively easy for the specialist to eliminate applicants who do not possess the essential attributes and to rank the remainder according to their possession of the desirable ones. This decides the short list. Since the specification has already been agreed between the departments there is no need for the client department to waste time by being involved.

At the first interview stage the specialist, trained and skilled in one-to-one interviewing, explores the suitability of candidates to discover which of them possess a profile that makes an acceptable match with the specification. Trained in the administration, scoring and interpretation of psychological tests he may also use appropriate tests to obtain supportive information. The client department then conducts a second series of interviews to assess the technical competence of the candidates. After the two sets of interviews have been completed the interviewers discuss their joint findings and the client department—also council members, if they have participated in the second interview stage—make the selection decision.

The procedures described above can help a local authority to create a favourable image in the minds of job seekers. This intent may fail, however, if applications are not acknowledged, interview arrangements are poor, or candidates are kept waiting too long for news of the final decision. Over the years local authorities have been seriously negligent in these matters and the personnel department should assume responsibility for all administrative and clerical procedures so that a high standard is maintained throughout.

In defining the respective roles of personnel and line management the question of one-to-one interviewing still needs to be settled. By tradition the local government candidate has frequently had to face a number of councillors—sometimes a full committee of fifteen or twenty—with appropriate chief and senior officers also present. A disadvantage of this type of interview is the stress the candidate is under, which makes it difficult for rapport to be established with the result that information yield is often reduced. There are also methodological problems, such as who explores which area of the candidate's background, abilities, interests and experience and how can overlap be avoided when a quality like motivation—sampled from a number of areas—is being assessed.

In the past a head of department would sometimes conduct one-to-one interviews before candidates appeared individually before the committee. But on these occasions the majority of chief officers were untrained in methods and techniques of selection interviewing: their questioning skills were poor, they frequently talked more than the candidate and they generally failed to obtain adequate information on which to base a defensible judgement.

It would be a significant step forward if all authorities having a personnel specialist could now adopt one-to-one interviewing, either by introducing serial one-to-one interviews—specialist, followed by selector for the client department—or by at least allowing the specialist to conduct preliminary interviews before officers or members meet as a panel. Fortunately there is reason to hope that increasingly councillors will want to reduce the amount of their participation in selection: generally, the new authorities are larger than the old ones and it is less likely that councillors will be prepared to use valuable time on such relatively minor matters as lower level appointments.

For top appointments it is unlikely, and possibly undesirable, that members should wish to cease taking an active part in selection. However, for these appointments the panel interview—after preliminary one-to-one screening by the specialist (perhaps an outside consultant)—may be of value since it is usually necessary to assess candidates on those qualities that need to be displayed in a committee or working group situation.

At the time of writing continuing economic difficulties are emphasizing the need for local government to develop techniques that will indicate how best use can be made of scarce resources. This should add further impetus to development of the personnel function, since cost-effectiveness is inherent in professional personnel management. In recruitment and selection, for example, an advertisement that cannot be seriously faulted in wording, lay-out and design exemplifies the best use of the media space purchased, while an expert interviewer gathers more relevant and useful information in a given period of time than an unskilled interviewer. Further development—and it is doubtful whether many, or indeed any, local authorities have gone this far to date—would demand records that provide a measure of the cost effectiveness of each advertisement, or that enable the costs and benefits of different selection strategies to be assessed so that it would be possible to determine whether one selection procedure was more economically viable than another.

Further reading

Gould, Derek R. (1970): *Scientific Methods of Staff Selection.* London: Charles Knight & Co.
Gould, Derek R. (1971): 'Advertising for results', *Municipal and Public Services Journal,* 17th December.
Gould, Derek R. (1973): 'Personnel relationships', *Municipal and Public Services Journal,* 9th November.

Gould, Derek R. (1974): 'Perfecting the interview', *Municipal and Public Services Journal*, 15th February.

Gould, Derek R. (1975): 'Personnel specifications', *Municipal and Public Services Journal*, 6th June.

Gould, Derek R. (1976): 'Training for selection', *Municipal and Public Services Journal*, 14th May.

Gould, Derek R. (1979): 'The value of job descriptions', *District Councils' Review*, January.

Local Government Training Board, Training Recommendation No. 8, *Staff Engaged in Personnel Work;* Reorganization Training No. 4, *Personnel Practice — a Training Package.*

Report of the Bains Committee (1972): *The New Local Authorities — Management and Structure.* London: HMSO.

Report of the Mallaby Committee (1967): *Staffing of Local Government.* London: HMSO.

Roman, Eva and Gould, Derek (1974): *Recruitment and Selection of Typists and Secretaries.* London: Business Books Ltd. (sections which refer to local government advertisements, impressions of local government interviews and recruitment procedures in the London Borough of Lambeth).

24

Recruitment of Graduates at the Universities

J S Gough

Anyone who has tried to follow the instructions on a complicated new piece of apparatus knows how different these instructions look when you start to carry them out. The same difficulty appears when the newly trained interviewer sets out to put his teaching into practice with a real candidate. As a matter of fact, the gap never entirely disappears, however skilled you become. You will still, from time to time, suffer those tense moments when the mind seems to seize up, or when the candidate will either refuse to stop talking or reply in monosyllables. Although you have been taught to deal with such difficulties and know all the appropriate countermoves, none of them seem to be working this time. You are aware that you must be relaxed, with a mind like a sponge, but you have come into the office after an unpleasant letter from the bank manager, or after a battle with one of your children, and your mind will not lie down and be quiet.

Of course, the most severe instructions have been given that all candidates' papers must be presented to you to study at least a day in advance and that you are not to be disturbed while the interview is in progress. And yet—well, your secretary went sick at a critical point and the papers are shoved in front of your nose at the same time as the candidate comes unannounced into the room. As soon as the interview gets going the boss decides that he needs you—unpardonable, inefficient and it should never happen. We all know, however, that it does.

This, of course, is not an argument against training or against learning the techniques of interviewing. It is an argument against training which ignores the conditions under which interviewing must quite often be done in real life.

Perhaps the most striking example of the big gap between what is desirable and what happens can be seen in the so-called 'milk-round' at the universities when, over a few weeks, teams of recruiters from hundreds of employers face thousands of individual candidates for jobs. This chapter is concerned with the problems they face and suggests some partial solutions.

Strains of the 'milk-round'

Whoever christened it the 'milk-round' can hardly ever have taken part in it. Anything more unlike the smooth-running electrically driven milk-float as it glides through neat suburban streets is hard to imagine. Call it a gladiatorial contest, a marathon or the gold rush and at least you have something more like the reality.

At some universities each interviewer may have to give up to twelve half-hour interviews a day and the figure has sometimes risen as high as fifteen. He may have to keep this up for days on end. Sometimes he will have received the particulars of the candidate he is to see only minutes before he comes into the interviewing room. This gives him no time to study the application form with the care which is always necessary if the strategy of the interview is to be planned in advance. It gives him no time to take the precautions against drying up—pencilling in a few possible questions to ask—which all practised interviewers use. It gives him no time to try to work out the 'common-link approach' which is another technique found to be useful in breaking the ice between interviewer and candidate as quickly as possible.

Even if he has received all the papers well in advance he will have very little time to write notes on the candidate he has just seen and to wipe the slate of his mind clean before the next one appears.

The strain of seeing so many candidates in quick succession inevitably induces a degree of physical and mental fatigue in the interviewer as the day goes on. This is greatly increased by long train or car journeys in fog, snow or ice and by lack of sleep. Fatigue is a potent enemy of the judgement, ingenuity and concentration which interviewing requires. It sometimes, also, can be the enemy of good manners. This would be true even if the working conditions were ideal.

A few words with anyone who has taken part in this kind of interviewing should be enough to disabuse even the most optimistic of a rosy view of the working conditions. A seasoned hand will tell you of interviews in hotel bedrooms from which the overnight occupant has just been bundled out in time for the nine o'clock interview to begin, of interviews in rooms so hot that both occupants face each other in what appears to be a high fever, or so cold that they cannot sit still. He will speak also of little interviewing rooms like prison cells where he has to sit with his back to the light and face a candidate who is prevented from seeing his interviewer's face because of the glare. He cannot be blamed if he smiles wryly at the thought of his interviewing instruction books which advises comfortable armchairs for both when he feels the hard wooden seat beneath him and spreads his papers on his knees, and watches his candidate balance on a rickety chair with no arms.

To all these discomforts must be added an extra strain. In today's conditions of great change the interviewers must expect to be faced with students who question some of the basic assumptions of the company for which an interviewer is recruiting. This adds a new dimension to the discussion.

All instruction books and courses on interviewing properly stress the two-way aspect of the interviewing process. If the interviewer faces a hard task, what about the candidate? Unfortunately, his position is not much better. He is bombarded for weeks before the interviewers arrive with all manner of high-pressure salesmanship. He is assailed with a huge amount of information—much more than he wants and much of it of dubious value. Where he wants detail he may be given heroic phrases sounding as if they had been issued by Pericles in Athens rather than by the manager of a distribution department at Little Pritheroe. 'Challenge' and 'opportunity' fill the space which should be used to describe what he would actually be doing for his first year at work. Alternatively, at an earlier stage in his thoughts about possible careers he gets given detail when he only wants to know the broad outlines of alternative careers.

At the very time, therefore, when perhaps he is beginning to realize how much work for his degree has been left undone and how near the day of reckoning has come, he is expected suddenly to switch his mind to thoughts of careers and employers. Of course he should have done this much earlier, and University Careers (Advisory) Services* have stressed the importance of doing this and made practical arrangements to assist. But once again practice and precept are often far apart.

It must sometimes seem strange to a student, who has no thought of this from the point of view of the employer, that if he appears for interview without knowing the name of the chairman, the geographical whereabouts of all the main factories and does not carry in his mind a list of all the firm's most profitable products, he is heavily marked down. A moment's thought about the conditions that both parties are subject to should prevent the employer from saying sadly: 'He didn't really seem interested in us'. Perhaps in the throes of a process we call educational, with his mind bulging with other facts. he could not really take very seriously all the niceties of making 'Producta' at the Canal-End factory in Birverhampton.

*Previously known as University Appointments Boards.

Improvement through planning

It will be obvious that the previous paragraphs give an exaggerated picture. The facilities provided by careers services and other accommodation he will arrange for himself are not uniformly unsuitable and uncomfortable. It must be emphasized also that, by and large, careers services make heroic efforts to assist interviewers and often to cover up the mistakes of others. It would be notably unjust not to acknowledge their sustained helpfulness, often at great inconvenience to themselves and their small staffs. But an interviewer who has not been prepared on a number of occasions to meet these kinds of conditions can find himself working far below his real ability. Perhaps worse than this, he may dismiss his previous training as 'academic' and ruefully decide that theory, instead of being the backbone of his practice, is quite unrelated to the job he has to do.

Must it be accepted that university recruiting as we now know it is inevitably a shambles, to be got through somehow, because all one's competitors do it, or because it is just one of those things like overcrowding on the roads? It is certain that it can never be other than a very onerous task to interview huge numbers of students in a few weeks.

Some of the smaller employers of graduates, and even one or two larger ones, are tackling this problem either by visiting only a few selected universities, or even by visiting none and requiring interested students to write direct to their headquarters where interviews for some are later arranged. Those employers who require very large numbers of graduates each year and those who value their relationships with universities, are unlikely to wish to adopt either of these two courses. To refuse to take part at all is slightly reminiscent of the man who, because he cannot stop it raining, decides to stay indoors. There are after all umbrellas which provide a measure of protection!

Some of the protective measures are small and require little more than some personal initiative by the interviewer. For instance, as he will often have no table at which to write, a clip-board for his papers can be a comfort and, as he is unlikely to have a clock on the wall, a wrist watch with a clear face is most helpful. Similarly an instant camera can be used to remind himself later of the candidates he has seen.

Travelling time can be considerably reduced if universities are grouped into geographical circuits and detailed arrangements are made well in advance. Many an interviewer behaves like a fly in a bottle, exhausting himself unnecessarily, when by some careful planning in advance he could greatly reduce the strain of long uncoordinated journeys at impossible times. If hotels have to be used for interviewing, he should come to a *personal* understanding with the management, and that includes the hall porter, well in advance. Problems should be discussed with careers services well in advance and not during the last-minute rush.

Selecting the right type of interviewer

Careful selection of interviewers is of course one of the vital actions an employer has to take if he wants satisfactory recruitment results. If this is poor none of the other measures will be effective. From what has been said so far it is clear that interviewers must have considerable stamina. But there is much more to it than that. That 'pompous little ass' much objected to by a certain university in the past did not lack physical resources! Perhaps the single most important characteristic of the good interviewer for this task is concerned with attitudes. First of all, is he really interested in what modern young men and women are thinking and doing? Even if he disagrees with their views, dislikes their hair style and is put off by their casual dress, has he at least some sympathy with those he is seeking to sum up? Again, has he enough imagination to realize that beneath that untidy hair and slightly hostile, mocking manner may be someone with just those creative gifts his firm will need if it is to survive into the 1990s? With interest, sympathy and imagination, he should at least be free of the criticism still often heard that interviewers are arrogant as well as pompous. This, however, still is not enough. The good interviewer, apart from being trained as an interviewer, to which reference is made later on, needs to be a man of knowledge. He needs to know the answers about pay and prospects, about his firm's attitude to conservation of the environment, about the kind of work done in one's early years; he needs to understand the moral problems involved in selling; the reasons behind the 'small is beautiful' argument and why many candidates are deeply concerned with environmental problems.

Upon two further characteristics, age and qualifications, it is not necessary to be too dogmatic, for to a large extent the previous requirements dictate the answer. The ideal age may well be thirty to thirty-five, by which time the generation gap is not impossibly large and enough knowledge should have been acquired. But some men much older than this have proved excellent interviewers because they have the other characteristics to a higher degree. Ideally too, the scientist should be interviewed by a scientist, and preferably by one whose knowledge lies broadly in the same field. With the growth of new knowledge and mixed courses this is not always easy but a common framework of academic knowledge is obviously a useful point of contact. Sometimes the choice of interviewer lies between an intelligent and flexible nonspecialist and a less tractable specialist. In this case the nonspecialist, provided he does not pretend to greater knowledge than he has, may be the wiser choice.

Emphasis has been placed on the interviewer's attitudes. The firm's attitude to the interviewer is also important. Bearing in mind the crucial importance for its long-term future of the task he undertakes, the interviewer should be deliberately chosen from among a firm's most able younger men—and it should be known that this is the policy.

Training interviewers

Having selected interviewers wisely, it is then necessary to train them specially for this task, for a good training considerably increases their usefulness and tends to reduce fatigue. Other chapters in this book deal thoroughly with this aspect. As part of their training it will have been stressed that they must know what they are looking for. But when seeing, on behalf of large firms, scores, say, of chemists for jobs ranging from research to production or technical sales, how are they to carry this out in practice? A good method of approach is to give the group of trainee interviewers specifications of two or three typical jobs to study and then to ask them to call out in any order the characteristics they think will be required to fill each job in turn. These are written on a blackboard or flip-chart as they are called out. A kind of brainstorming technique is recommended—that is, there must be no criticism of each other's contributions at this first stage. Typically, one may expect to get from, say, fourteen to thirty or even more characteristics produced in this way. The group is then told that these must be reduced to, say, two or three characteristics only.

The argument which follows achieves a number of purposes. It draws attention to the different meanings we all attach to different phrases—this teaches interviewers who are interviewing in pairs that they would be wise to agree on terms they both understand in advance. For instance, what do they both mean by the phrase they will probably both use: 'He isn't very mature?' Does it mean his goals are divorced from reality? Does it simply mean that: 'I, whose education and growth stopped after I took my degree, find this young man who will go on developing all his life rather disturbing? Once they can agree upon terms, they can dispense with the 'I think he's quite a good chap' type of comment and discuss his characteristics with economy in time and effort.

From the exercise outlined above, interviewers can then begin to distil some common characteristics which are the important ones for different types of work. It becomes possible then, to consider a chemist applicant, for instance, in this fashion. Is there evidence of a creative mind (research?), of organizing gifts (production?), of a competitive spirit (sales?) Or when considering say a student reading ancient history, is he really interested in people and what they do and think (personnel?), in logic (computers?), in persuading others (public relations or sales?).

Objectives of the interview

The practical training of an interviewer for this task must include special emphasis upon two points: the limited nature of what he is doing and the necessity of planning the use of his time with the utmost care. It is important for him to appreciate that interviewing at the university is only one of a number of steps which have to be taken before a decision is finally made about an individual, with the exception of those who are so obviously unsuitable for the jobs available that their candidature will end with this first interview. All candidates, who should have first talked to their careers services, should have provided some written evidence, backed in some cases by tutors' reports. The interviewer has to take this written evidence and add to it the candidate's own story, and then make a judgement. This judgement has two elements in it:

1   Is he worth sending on for a further interview, or should he be turned down now?
2   What kind of job is he most suitable for?
He has in addition:
3   To interest the candidate enough in the jobs available, to make him want to go further with his application.
4   To treat each candidate with courtesy and consideration, whether or not he decides at this point to cut his application short.

Quite often, such is the number of candidates wanting to see him, that the interviewer will have half an hour only at his disposal in which to cover all four of these points. Unless he has carefully planned his time a number of things can happen:

(a)   He can spend almost all the time saying what excellent jobs he has to offer and then find that the candidate has hardly said anything—which makes point 1 or 2 a farce and can easily fail to achieve point 4.
(b)   He 'rushes at the candidate' determined to make up his mind on point 1 or 2 and either hopelessly fails to interest the candidate (point 3) and probably doesn't achieve much of point 4.
(c)   He can spend so much time on charming the candidate with his scintillating discourse that although he has achieved point 4, and perhaps thereby a bit of 3, he is quite unable to make judgements on 1 or 2, except in the most superficial fashion.

Suggested interview time-table

The man who has been trained to conduct interviews lasting upwards of three quarters of an hour in ideal conditions, cannot cope with this situation unless he has learnt to discipline himself to a severe time-table which deliberately covers the four points above. For a half-hour interview a rough guide might be as follows:

1   Ice breaking and general courtesies at beginning
     and end.   (3 minutes)
2   Description of firm and jobs available.   (5 minutes)
3   Questions asked by candidate and answered.   (5 minutes)

—which leaves:

4   Interview proper   (17 minutes)

_____

                                                          30 minutes

The order will be varied and the times are approximate only; also the length of each part will be different for different candidates.

Consideration of these four parts of the interview makes it clear that time can be saved on 2 and some part of 3 if means are found of giving candidates as much information as possible in advance of the actual interview. Well-devised booklets with facts straightforwardly displayed are an obvious method. But, because of their multitude and because of the students' own preoccupations with other matters, they provide only a very partial solution. It is perhaps true to say that only those who are very keen to come to a particular firm will have read its literature carefully. Despite a commonly accepted view among employers, these are not necessarily the best people to employ in the long run—particularly when some of the most able students still start off with an aversion to industry.

Value of preceding session

Another method is to provide a speaker or speakers at a presentation session on the previous evening. This can either:

1   Ensure that no one comes the next day for interview—this might save everyone's time.
2   Increase the number of interested candidates.

It should at least ensure that those who do come, come against a much more informed background. Those firms who have not tried this form of presentation should be very clear about their objectives. They should encourage a great deal of open discussion and should cut formal lectures to a minimum. One technique is for the employer to send several managers under a neutral chairman who asks each of them in turn to describe, in not more than two or three minutes, one or two problems which they know will greet them next morning. If this can be done without collusion beforehand it makes its point very much more effectively than by carefully prepared speeches or statements.

Value, and problems, of preselection

There is a further method of reducing the huge numbers of applicants which large employers of graduates generate—a device known as preselection. This essentially is a device for weeding out a number of applicants on paper. Application forms are so devised that they contain a number of questions which, taken in conjunction, can be used to differentiate between those most likely to be of interest and those least likely. By no means all of those now in use have been completely validated. But, provided they are used only to screen out of the system, say, the bottom 25% of large numbers of candidates, they have some attraction. There are, however, a number of dangers, quite apart from the fact that if all employers used them, the students would have even less time to work for their degrees.

The first danger might be called the 'moving goal-post' problem. A system of preselection which is capable of validation must either rely on records of the kinds of people recruited in the past or lean on some clearcut and fixed idea of what kinds of people will be needed in the future. The trouble is that the kinds of people wanted change over quite short periods. It isn't so very long ago, for example, that we were only on the edge of the great expansion in the use of mathematicians. Ten years hence—who knows what kinds of academic and personal skills will be needed? A tested system of preselection makes it more difficult to move the goal posts, though the constant interviewing of samples of rejected candidates and other techniqes can reduce this difficulty to a minimum. But then there is the danger that the effort involved in the constant reassessment of the system needed to keep it up to scratch can be greater than the effort involved in seeing all the candidates! It certainly seems clear that a rush of preselection schemes throughout the country, quickly developed to solve perhaps a short-term problem, might end by finding that they have created for preselection the same low standing as some personality tests in America which have generated a healthy market in half-serious, half-comic books like that of Charles Alex, *How to Beat Personality Tests.*

A further weakness of preselection is that, in the long run, candidates may feel it necessary to play 'preselection games' and to learn how to fiddle their biographies. There are also some uncomfortable moral problems in this. Questions such as: 'Are your parents married or divorced?' may encourage a candidate to lie. If this happens it becomes harder and harder to separate the genuine good candidate from the fake. The net effect would be to add yet another stage to selection in an already complicated business. There are also some other technical difficulties as well. On balance, however, preselection systems can and could be made to work if it were necessary and if there were no other alternatives.

Numbers and the supply of information

The 'numbers' problem facing employers has often been made more severe because so many students apply for jobs for which they are entirely unsuitable—either by temperament or by qualification. Applicants could in the past have argued that this was because they did not have enough information on which to base an application. In recent years, heroic efforts have been made, both by employers and by career services, to fill some of the obvious gaps. Information libraries have been extended, information sheets about a variety of different careers have been commissioned, and new publications abound.

An increased realization of the need to comprehend the real nature of a job and its demands in personal terms is a feature of modern student thinking. This happens to coincide with a revolution in information systems. As one would expect, therefore, the new technologies are being applied with increasing intensity in the field of career choice.

A system, named GRADSCOPE, has been developed by careers services which uses a computer to help students both to narrow their choice of *occupation* (steering them away from those for which they are liable to be unsuitable) and to enlarge their choice (bringing to their attention those they might not otherwise have considered). The system, most commendably, makes no extravagant claims; it aims only to provide a starting point for useful discussion. GRADSCOPE is experimental only, at the time of writing, and is only available for non-technical students. Its scope however may well be extended.

The other big developments rely on the fact that information of all kinds is now becoming available to all who have access to a TV set which has Viewdata facilities. A number of new projects will very shortly provide job-seekers and those with jobs to fill with much more information, far more up-to-date, than was ever possible in the past. Recruiters and their employers would, however, be unwise if they believed that this welter of information will make their own tasks much easier. It may—for those who go well trained and informed. For those not so prepared, it is not difficult to forecast an even more uncomfortable ride!

Further reading

See under Chapter 12 'Interviewing techniques' by Alec Rodger

25

Recruitment of Experienced Managers

George Campbell-Johnston

The recruitment of top management is likely to be one of the most important decisions facing a board of directors. No matter how good its resources, without the right people a company can be left behind in today's competitive world of business and commerce. Recruitment of high-calibre senior executives can mean the difference between success and failure.

Principles of recruitment

The fundamental principles of recruitment for senior management remain the same as for all successful personnel recruitment and are dealt with in depth elsewhere in this book. However, there are a number of significant differences which distinguish recruitment at this level of appointment from that of general manpower. These include:

1 The person sought is likely to be found within a narrow stratum.
2 Maximum inducement is required to attract the right calibre of candidate.
3 The presentation of the organization and the position to be filled are key factors in attracting a suitable field of candidates.
4 Far greater emphasis must be placed on proven ability and past experience, with a corresponding decline in the use of formal measurement techniques.
5 The right choice is far more critical. Faulty selection at this level of appointment will have a more damaging effect with longer-term repercussions and can often cost a company many tens of thousands of pounds.

For all these reasons the choice of method of recruitment and selection is critical.

The recruitment of specialist and senior managers is inevitably expensive in terms of both advertising costs and time needed for the selection process. If the appointment cannot be filled from within the organization or by personal contact and introduction, the choice lies among the following:

1   The company handling the assignment itself (with or without help from an advertising agency in the preparation of the recruitment advertisements).
2   The use of executive search specialists.
3   The use of management recruitment consultants.

The preliminary study

Whichever method is chosen, once a vacancy occurs or a new position is created, certain fundamental matters will have to be considered, such as:

What are the major job objectives, duties and responsibilities?
What are the age and salary parameters?
What probable major difficulties can be foreseen?

A first consideration of these may well lead to deeper study of factors which are, in a sense, preliminary to the recruitment process. There is, first, the question whether the job and the organization are correctly set up—or, indeed, whether the job should exist at all. A job may have been created to meet a particular requirement in the past. The needs of management may vary as the size and importance of the job develops, or in response to the way one particular individual interprets his duties and responsibilities, so that, in time, the job may bear little resemblance to the original concept. When a vacancy occurs, management are presented with the opportunity to rethink the position and to restructure the organization. This can involve redistribution of responsibilities or even the abolition of the job and the introduction of new functions. For example, production and general manager functions might come under one commercial director, or sales director and advertising director combine to become marketing director. Equally, a general management board position might be better broken down in separate financial and technical responsibilities.

Again, at this preliminary stage it is essential to consider and decide whether candidates should be from outside or within—or, perhaps, from both. Far greater emphasis is now placed on the development of second line management with the potential to fill senior vacancies as they occur. Many managements, because of the specialized nature of their operations and markets, prefer to promote from within, while others automatically recruit from outside regardless of existing talent. In either case, there can be a number of reasons why promotion is impossible—vacancies may arise unexpectedly, owing to rapid expansion, the development of new products or the unforeseen loss of a key member of staff, through death,, ill-health or otherwise. Further, it is essential to try to anticipate any likely alterations in company structure or organization which may affect the duties, responsibilities and status of the job. Such changes can be potent causes of dissatisfaction and feelings that promises have been broken.

Another matter to be studied at an early stage is how to attract suitable candidates. The higher up the scale, the more difficult it becomes to induce good people to move. The individual who has reached a senior position will think long and hard before changing jobs. He will be looking at the scope of the job, the prospects for advancement and the financial rewards (including pension)—normally in that order.

It may therefore be necessary to rethink the job in order to attract a strong field of candidates. If it is hoped to recruit a high flier in his thirties but there is insufficient scope for advancement to a board appointment, it is unlikely that suitable candidates will be attracted. Either the job must be upgraded or it will be necessary to go down the age scale and recruit someone who is planning to move on, or to move up the age scale and attract an older, less ambitious but well-experienced man who will appreciate the responsibilities of the job, as they now are.

The job description

Once these preliminary policy decisions have been taken, detailed study of the job must be undertaken and a job description prepared. Without a proper understanding of the job and its purpose within the organizaiton, it is impossible for the process of selection to seek out and match applicants for that position. It is worth remembering that at this level the potential applicant will be skilled at spotting loose or muddled thinking on the part of the recruiters. Chapter 4 deals in full with devising the job description. The more senior the appointment, the more important it is that the existing management team have a clear understanding and are in total agreement about the principal accountabilities, duties and authority of the position before attempting to match the 'man' specification to the job description.

The man specification

The translation of the job description into human terms which will provide a profile of the ideal candidate is described in full in Chapter 4. At the senior level of appointment greater weight must be given to personality characteristics than at middle-management level, because of the close interaction with the rest of the management team. It is essential, however, that this natural tendency to weight desirable personality attributes it not at the expense of other essential characteristics.

A systematic assessment, under the above headings, of the job, the organization and the candidates will ensure the two essential ingredients contributing to a successful placement: the vital criteria against which candidates will be matched and a suitable field of candidates, from which to choose.

Where a personnel manager is represented at board level, the recruitment of senior managers is usually carried out by him. The advantages are several:

1   The insights achieved during the in-depth analysis and assessment of the job specification.
2   The market 'intelligence' gained by interviewing all the relevant prospective candidates. It is possible that far more inadvertent espionage than is commonly realised results from interviews with people from competing organizations.
3   The related job spin-off, whereby a candidate's qualifications, experience and attitude of mind may be recognized as being in line with another simultaneous vacancy within the company.

Unfortunately, too few personnel managers are represented on the boards of companies. The Institute of Personnel Management have for many years pressed for greater representation of personnel managers at board level, but until this is achieved in a greater number of companies, the task of recruiting top management will fall to other top managers.

However, the problems of undertaking a senior recruitment assignment are obvious:

1   The search may stretch over several weeks and occasionally over months, causing serious disruption to a senior manager's time-table.
2   Unless he has acquired considerable experience in interviewing and selection, a nonspecialist may fail to be sufficiently objective. A common failing is to think too often in terms of the man the company would like to employ, rather than the actual job function. This leads, in turn, to an overdependence on rapport with candidates during the early interview stages.
3   It is almost impossible to conduct a search at this level in secrecy, but there will frequently be a number of reasons why it is desirable that an impending appointment is not known to existing staff in advance, particularly if it is controversial. The recruitment process is lengthy and morale may deteriorate during this period, especially amongst those within the company who believe they should have been considered for the position. Counselling with possible internal contenders is therefore important. Any company without a personnel manager sufficiently experienced at top management level should weigh up carefully the

advantages and disadvantages of carrying out its own top management recruitment and be prepared to consider the alternatives available.

Executive search consultancies

The use of headhunters—to use the colloquial term—has become more widespread in recent years, although it has by no means reached the level achieved in America, where there is a greater acceptance of job mobility coupled with the problem of recruiting over an enormous geographical area, without the benefit of newspapers providing national coverage. The method is one of direct approach or file search. The process is expensive—the costs can often equal or exceed that of normal recruitment advertising and selection fees. The main advantage is that it is direct and efficient and makes the minimum demand, in terms of time, on the prospective employer, since the system will produce, in most cases, only one, or possibly two, candidates. There are, however, two major drawbacks to this method of selection: Firstly, it presupposes that the person sought is a 'known' name with an established reputation and thus precludes many potentially suitable candidates, who may exist outside the network of the headhunter; secondly, it should be remembered that the person thus recruited may remain on the headhunter's files and thereafter is vulnerable to further approach, when the agreed expiry date, or agreement between the search organization and the client company not to approach the appointed candidate, has elapsed. This could be at the very time he has reached the peak of his usefulness to his current employer. Although statistics are seldom forthcoming in this area, most top managers, at some time in their career, have been approached in this way and many of them at frequent intervals, sometimes as often as once per month. Whilst flattering initially, this can be disturbing if it happens frequently. At best, it may unsettle the person involved, who otherwise was not contemplating a move; at worst, it can be damaging to his career if it becomes known he is continuously considering headhunters' proposals. The temptation to investigate the approach is nearly always more than most people can resist.

Current thinking, emerging from a study by the Institute of Personnel Management and the British Institute of Management, which included senior management level, shows headhunting to be the least favoured method of recruitment in terms of cost effectiveness and also raises the question of the effectiveness of some headhunters, who have set up on their own in this field with little experience and no qualifications. There is, at present, no clear code of conduct laid down by a professional body in this field.

Management recruitment consultants

The growth in the use of management recruitment consultants has come about simply because this method avoids the disadvantages outlined above and offers a number of positive advantages. The skilled recruitment consultant has the knowledge and expertise to draw up, with the client, a realistic job specification, to evaluate the vacant position within the structure of the organization, to advise on salary levels and the qualities sought in the person to fill the post, and to design a cost-effective recruitment campaign.

The consultant, because he works in depth in a wide variety of fields, can draw on a breadth of experience which is not normally available to the client. This can be of particular value where cross-fertilization of management skills is required. Equally, the consultant will, in most cases, have had experience of recruiting qualified staff in the client's own field, however specialized that may be. Once the job specification has been agreed, the recruitment consultant will select the media to be used, prepare and place the advertisement, process the replies and present a shortlist of suitable applicants within a period which can vary from three to eight weeks—this wide bracket depending on the consultancy used and the geographical location and nature of the appointment. However, this normally proves to be more rapid than recruitment by the client company themselves. The consultant undertakes the specialized job of writing and placing recruitment advertising and the laborious task of processing the replies and interviewing potential candidates. Only when he submits a shortlist of suitable applicants does the client make his choice. In this way, the client is presented with a number of suitably qualified and experienced candidates, who have been briefed in full about the company and the post offered. If two or more are equally matched, he may indulge in the luxury of choosing the one he likes personally, confident that an unbiased and objective assessment of that person's technical suitability has already been made.

In addition, the total exercise can be carried out, up to the moment the shortlist candidates are called for interview with the client, in the strictest confidence. When deciding whether or not to use a management recruitment consultancy, a top manager would be wise to calculate the amount of time he himself, his colleagues and other staff would have to spend on a recruitment campaign, to make an estimate of the overheads involved and to weigh up the cost of what he and they might otherwise have been doing during this time. It will be found that the fees of about 15–20% of annual salary, charged by recruitment consultants, are keenly competitive.

The British Institute of Management maintains a register of consultancies and agencies which it can recommend to employers.

Attracting the right man

Whether recruitment is by the company or by a management recruitment consultant, once the job specification has been agreed, the choice of advertising media and the composition of the advertisement will play a vital role in attracting applicants of suitable calibre with relevant experience.

The general appearance and the wording of the advertisement reflect the image of the company, both as an employer and as a commercial entity. The public relations value of recruitment advertising has long been recognized and it is a short-sighted company indeed which does not make use of one of the many advertising agencies specializing in recruitment advertising.

When it is remembered that the person sought is in all probability happy in his present job and not actively seeking to change his job, it will be appreciated that the positioning of the advertisement, the choice of the media and the wording are all critical factors in gaining his interest and persuading him to apply.

Conducting the interview

It is a paradox that the more senior the appointment the less dependence there usually is on formal systematic selection and assessment techniques. A properly constructed application form will have elicited most of the detailed information required. The application form and curriculum vitae should be studied before the interview. The candidate's time should not be wasted (he is a busy man too) by repeating questions already answered on the form. The interviewer should concentrate on establishing a relaxed and pleasant atmosphere which will enable him to:

1   Assess the suitability of the candidate.
2   Ensure the candidate has sufficient information on which to base his decision about the job.
3   Allow the candidate to demonstrate his ability to evaluate information and relate his experience to the job in question.

It is possible that amongst the candidates there will be some who are the casualties of redundancy programmes. If this is the case, special care must be taken to establish the sequence of events leading to the redundancy and some allowance made for the emotional impact this will have caused. However, it is much more likely that a suitable candidate is happy and successful in his present employment and the potential employer will be as much on trial as he is. The way the interview is conducted will be of paramount importance for both parties if a sound decision is to be reached.

One of the problems a director will encounter is how best to conduct the interview if he is not trained in this skill.

It is important to collate as much information as possible on each candidate—and this is where application forms have particular value, since they extract the information a prospective employer wishes to know. A curriculum vitae will provide in most cases only the information the candidate wishes to release and seldom any important adverse points; a good application form of the type used by leading recruitment consultants, supported by the consultant's report, will go a long way to establishing the strengths and weaknesses of the candidate.

When faced with an appropriately experienced, mature individual who, on paper, measures up closely to the requirements established in the job specification—what should the prospective employer ask?

If not already established by a recruitment consultant in preliminary interview, a check-list of questions, which should normally include the following, adjusted as appropriate to the particular job, can be helpful:

1   When did he last apply for a job? In the main, the better candidates do not make a habit of applying for jobs. A man successful and happy in one place is more likely to be so in another position, than a candidate who has a record of being disgruntled and unhappy in his previous and present work.
2   Why does he want to join the organization? Obviously this is an important step for the company (although many would agree that, whilst it is very important for both parties, it can be even more important for the candidate).
3   What has he found out about the organization? He is likely to be able to comment on such points as profitability figures, return on capital employed, number of employees, range of services or products, new products, share of export market (but bear in mind access to private company information is largely restricted to what can be obtained from Companies House), and what other significant developments have been achieved. Unless, of course, the remarks are uncomplimentary, thank him.

At all times, keep control of the interview and keep the initiative. If you do not receive a satisfactory reply, probe quietly, yet positively, until you do reach the bottom and there is no doubt in your mind that the truth is established.

A word of warning about soliciting confidential information—if it is confidential and he will not divulge it, then this should be accepted. Seldom does a candidate plead confidential protection when it is not genuine. Ask him, from what he already knows about the job—this presupposes he already has a sound grasp of the job requirements—what he feels he can contribute and how his experience relates in his view to your particular company. Ask him what he achieved, what he has actually been responsible for implementing and what he has made as a direct contribution to his present company. Beware of the man who says he was involved in doing so and so—in these situations he was seldom the individual responsible for the innovation or the implementation. Ask him how he overcame opposition to his ideas. Individuals who have been responsible for turning companies round or markedly increasing profits seem often to be able to repeat the exercise when they move to a new organization. Always give the man time to reply, and make sure you do not interrupt him despite any temptation to do so.

It is also important to arrange beforehand that the interview is not interrupted by colleagues, visitors or telephones except in extreme emergency.

Discuss the job description and specification fully with the candidate once you are satisfied you wish to proceed. If you are not satisfied, it is better to thank him for being so cooperative and helpful and say how interesting you have found the 'discussion' (a better turn of phrase than 'interview'). If you can summon up the courage to tell him you are not going further, it is better to do so, especially if it is on technical grounds. If it is on personality, this is not so straightforward, but explain that there are other candidates who are more closely matched to the job specification. Always offer him his travel expenses if he has come, say, more than thirty miles. Surprisingly few candidates at senior level will take this up, as they will have frequently been able to arrange to be in your part of the world in the course of their normal work.

With the candidate, who at this point, is turning out suitable, it is important that, whilst being open, you should not sell him the job. Invite his questions. You can tell a surprising amount of how a man's mind works (or does not work) and thereby establish a better picture of his mental attitude. It is beneficial to ask a candidate what his spouse's reaction is to his joining your company and to the proposed working conditions, and how much interest he or she takes in his or her work. Spouses are very important to a person's success, for it is they who have to put up with late arrivals back from work, awkward domestic hours, telephone calls in the middle of meals and all the havoc and disruption these can cause. They should be the sort of people who can understand the problems, who back their spouse's judgement and who can be used as a sounding board. A spouse's role in business is getting harder—entertaining foreign visitors who may not have a good grasp of English can be helped by a husband or wife who has fluency in the visitor's mother tongue. Such demands are increasing as British industry strives to develop its vital export business—and the overseas visitor, even if unexpected, must be looked after in ways which match the hospitality and treatment which he offers to Britons visiting him in his own country.

There is considerable benefit to be gained from taking the prospective candidate and his or her spouse out to dinner. You will be able to assess how far the spouse will be a good ambassador for your company in the way that he or she supports the candidate.

Overseas positions

Recruitment of senior personnel for overseas posts is inclined to take longer than for posts in this country, as many suitable applicants will be based abroad and a letter may take up to fourteen days to arrive from some parts of the world. Whilst telex is useful, only a few respondents will use this method. As the recruiter, it is vital that an early response is made to applicants' letters, telegrams, telexes etc.

The applicant with the right experience, which has been gained overseas, usually has an advantage over the applicant who has not ventured further than the shores of Europe or undertaken a two week holiday in Morocco. He will have the advantage of understanding indigenous overseas work forces, different cultures and climates and having had to cope effectively with different levels of efficiency.

The husband or wife plays an important role in his or her spouse's success in the job. The fact that he or she has been brought up abroad or has lived abroad recently, is a distinct advantage, particularly if over the age of thirty. It is a big shock to the system for a family to be transported to the far ends of the globe, where they have no friends, are unlikely to speak the local language and everything appears strange and unfamiliar. In the last decade, employers have gone to considerable lengths to explain fully to families the conditions and way of life which they will experience in a country they may never before have visited. This is done at the preliminary interview stage, when they should feel free, and be given ample opportunity, to ask any questions, covering the wide range of housing, schooling, health facilities and local amenities, by means of brochures, slides, maps etc. On arriving in the country, it is important for a representative of the employer to meet the family, show them their new house or flat and be available as a 'guardian angel' to help them settle down happily during the first few traumatic weeks of adjustment.

Homesickness, particularly for a family going to live abroad for the first time, is a very real and disturbing factor. Membership of local clubs can be most helpful, particularly for couples without children; parents of small children soon strike up friendships with other families.

The spouse of a very senior executive, who is used to travelling the world and entertaining, must be regarded as a major asset, who can make a significant contribution to the husband's or wife's success. It is as well to take the spouse out to dinner, before making the appointment, and take careful note of the constructive, or otherwise, attitude he or she has towards their spouse's work. There is a story of a candidate's wife who was taken out to dinner by a prospective employer, and the chairman turned to her afterwards and said 'We think you will fit in very well, so you have no need to worry; it is your husband we're not so sure about!'

The points mentioned on interviewing will be helpful in triggering off other ideas. Remember there are many who will tell you only what they want you to know and not what you want to know. Tackle this subject with the thoroughness and tenacity it deserves. It is never worth cutting corners and this is no exception.

If much of this chapter sounds familiar it is because the job of recruitment to management level follows the same disciplines as any other recruitment. Where it differs is that the stakes are higher and the consequences of an error much greater. Recruitment can never be an exact science but careful consideration of the factors influencing the recruitment and selection of senior managers can do much to reduce the element of risk. The costs of faulty recruitment will continue to rise as employment legislation in the UK moves closer to continental systems with stringent controls on recruitment methods, in which appointments and dismissals can occur only on quarter days and in which compensation to dismissed executives can be very substantial by comparison with present British standards.

Expert advice on recruitment provided by the many firms specializing in this field can lighten considerably the exacting task of recruitment and selection for any company or organization which has to select experienced senior management.

26

Selection Within
the Law

Nancy Seear and Michael Pearn

In the United Kingdom there is a long and strong tradition of voluntarism in
the regulation of relations between employer and employed. Voluntary
agreements between unions and employers and employers' associations have
laid down the basic terms and conditions of employment, but have not had the
force of law. The only legally enforceable contract is the individual contract of
employment between the employer and the individual employee. For over a
century the only statute laws impinging on the individual's actual terms and
conditions of employment were the various Factories Acts, though the 1960's
saw the introduction of a number of laws extending the legal obligations of
employers and the legal rights of employees. Until the 1968 Race Relations
Act it had been taken for granted that, subject only to collective agreements,
the employer was free to choose whom he would recruit. The only exception to
this was the Disabled Persons (Employment Act) 1944 with subsequent
amending Acts or regulations.

The 1968 Race Relations Act, the Sex Discrimination Act 1975 and the Race
Relations Act 1976 (which replaces the 1968 Act) represent a break with this
tradition. By these laws, an employer's freedom of action in the field of
employment is modified in order to remove inequality of opportunity in
employment on grounds of sex or marriage, or of colour, race, nationality or
ethnic or national origin. These Acts, which are an assertion of human rights
and a response to social pressures, lay obligations on employers which are of a
different order from obligations arising from earlier legislation aimed at
improving the rights and working conditions of employees.

The legislation on sex equality, but not on racial equality, is reinforced by

European Economic Community Directives. In amplification of Article 119 of the Treaty of Rome, the EEC has issued a Directive (75/117) which requires member states to implement the principle of equal pay for equal work. The meaning of 'equal pay for equal work' has been amplified in a later Directive to include the concept of equal pay for work of equal value. In addition, the EEC has also laid down in Directive 76/207 that there shall be equal treatment for men and women, and that 'there shall be no discrimination whatsoever on grounds of sex either directly or indirectly'.

The meaning of discrimination

In one sense, all selection involves discrimination. Selection involves the attempt to discriminate between those more likely to succeed in a job and those less likely to succeed. It is not the intention of the legislation to interfere with such fair discrimination. What the legislation requires is not the abolition of discrimination as such, but the abolition of discrimination on grounds, defined in the Acts, which have no bearing on suitability for the job.

Under both the Sex Discrimination Act and the Race Relations Act there are two different types of discrimination, which it has become customary to refer to as 'direct discrimination' and 'indirect discrimination', although these terms are not in fact used in the Acts.

Direct discrimination occurs when a person treats someone 'less favourably than he treats or would treat other persons' on racial grounds or on grounds of sex or married status. Such discrimination has commonly occurred for example, when an employer has not been prepared to consider an application from a fully qualified woman engineer, solely because the post in the past had always been held by a man.

It would be a mistake to assume that direct discrimination is a rare occurrence, though its actual incidence is difficult to gauge. However, some years ago a survey was conducted to assess the extent of discrimination against black workers.[1] Black and white actors who claimed the same qualifications and experience applied for real jobs. The results were dramatic (see Figure 26.1). From these and similar findings it must be assumed that the incidence of discrimination is very high. Most acts of direct discrimination occur covertly without even the victim suspecting that it is happening. Consequently an employer cannot safely assume that there is no discrimination merely because no complaints are made.

Indirect discrimination is a less familiar and more complicated concept. It can occur when a job is ostensibly open to both men and women and to members of any ethnic group, but when, in fact, a requirement or condition is attached to the job with which a considerable proportion of one sex or a particular ethnic group is unable to comply. This situation is sometimes referred to as 'adverse impact'. The mere fact that they are unable to comply

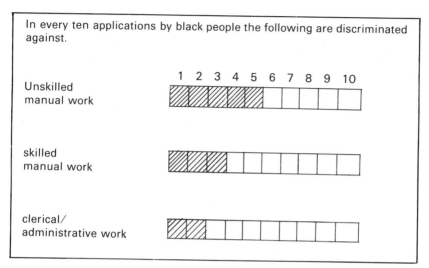

Figure 26.1   Chances of being discriminated against

does not in itself create indirect discrimination. Two other factors affect the position. The person unable to comply has to be able to show that he or she has 'suffered a detriment' because of the condition. Even this, once established, is not in itself sufficient. Neither in British legislation, nor in American legislation where the concept originated, is the employer required to run his business inefficiently in order to create equal opportunity. The employer is free to continue to insist on the requirement or condition if he can show that it is 'justifiable'. An employer may for example lay down that only applicants six feet tall will be considered for a particular job. This clearly rules out the great majority of women and almost all Ghurkas. Women and Ghurkas may find no difficulty in establishing that they suffer a 'detriment' because they are unable to apply for the job in question. If, however, the employer can show that the job really cannot be done by people shorter than six feet, then that is the end of the matter. But the employer does have to establish his case realistically: a preference for tall people reflecting tradition in a certain occupation would not be sufficient grounds.

Unfortunately, the law does not provide any guidance on what constitutes justification of a condition or requirement which results in an adverse impact against women or ethnic minority groups. Our understanding of justification will evolve on a case-by-case basis as complaints are heard by the industrial tribunals. The best guidance we currently have comes from two Employment Appeal Tribunal (EAT) cases. In the first case, under the Sex Discrimination Act, the appeal tribunal expounded the 'business-necessity formula', and listed the main considerations to be taken into account when deciding whether a condition or requirement which results in adverse impact, is justifiable.[2]

First, the condition or requirement should be genuinely necessary, and not merely convenient. The need for the condition or requirement should be weighed against the discriminatory effects. All the circumstances should be considered, and the question should be raised whether there is a non- or less-discriminatory way of achieving the same end. In short, justifiability is not something that can be judged according to a few rules-of-thumb. A later EAT case has toned down the business-necessity formula by saying it should be applied with reasonableness and common-sense.[3] Later cases will add to and refine our understanding of indirect discrimination.

For the personnel specialist the first point to note is that indirect discrimination is a broad, rather than narrow, concept. It will apply to any condition or requirement which results in adverse impact against a racial or sex group. Where there is no adverse impact the law has no application, however arbitrary, capricious or unjustified the selection yardsticks or procedures might be. Educational qualifications, experience requirements, selection tests, and age, strength, or height requirements are potentially sources of unlawful indirect discrimination, unless the employer can show them to be justified. Selective advertising, word-of-mouth recruitment and selection criteria in general fall potentially within the scope of indirect discrimination. The second important point to bear in mind is that much of the justification for a given condition or requirement rests on demonstrating its job-relatedness. This is essentially the process of validation and is discussed separately below.

The selection process

Both Acts clearly lay down that it is unlawful to discriminate:
1   In the arrangements for determining who should be offered employment.
2   In the terms on which employment is offered.
3   By refusing or deliberately omitting to offer employment.
The "arrangements" require consideration. For example, to arrange interviews at times or in places which make the attendance at the interview more difficult for one group than for others could constitute unlawful discrimination.

The details of the actual conduct of the selection process are dealt with below and are not therefore discussed here. When the process is over and an offer of appointment is made, the terms and conditions of employment offered must not include discriminatory elements. For ethnic minorities, this requirement is contained in the Race Relations Act 1976, but in relation to sex the law governing terms and conditions of employment is to be found in the Equal Pay Act 1970. The intention, however, in both Acts is identical.

When charges of discrimination are brought against an employer he may be required to show that the individual was treated fairly. In order to operate selection procedures smoothly and efficiently it is necessary to maintain adequate records. More detailed records may be necessary to permit evaluation of the effectiveness of the process, and to enable improvements to be made. These records are likely to include details of assessments of candidates and, where appropriate, the reasons for rejection. This information is essential to the evaluation and validation of selection. It could also provide the basis of a defence before a tribunal (given that candidates are properly assessed according to job-relevant criteria).

Responsibility for complying with the law lies with both the company and the responsible agent of the company. This means that both the company and the agent, eg the personnel officer or other executive responsible for the actual selection process, can be held liable for a discriminatory act. The fact that the employer did not know that his agent was acting illegally is no defence. The employer is relieved of the responsibility only if he can show that the agent's discriminatory act was not carried out in the course of his employment, or that the employer had taken such steps as were reasonably practicable to make sure that the agent acted legally. It is clear that 'taking reasonable steps' requires something much more far-reaching than the posting of a notice, or claiming to have an equal opportunity policy when nothing is done to implement and monitor it in practice.

Avoiding unlawful discrimination in selection

Discrimination on grounds of race or sex is unlawful, whereas discrimination on job-relevant grounds is clearly desirable. What must an employer do, or not do, in order to ensure that selection is efficient and at the same time free of unlawful discrimination?

Specifying requirements

There are some jobs where the only selection requirement is that the person can breathe and stand up! In most jobs, however, a variety of skills, knowledge and other attributes are required. Unfortunately the essential requirements are rarely specified and, where they are, they are sometimes the result of arbitrary decisions made a long time ago. Job requirements are often retained because no one has thought of changing them, rather than because they genuinely reflect the needs of the organization. In many cases applicants are sized up against those who have previously done the job, on the assumption that if they match existing or past employees they will be able to do the job. The problem that arises here is that the previous job incumbents may not have done the job very well, and the employer could perpetuate a problem by employing mediocre staff, while rejecting talented or more suitable applicants. In addition, the previous or existing employees might have been only, or predominantly, white and male so that women or blacks would have very little chance of being recruited. This could constitute unlawful indirect discrimination. It would also be inefficient.

In order to select efficiently an employer needs to have a very clear idea of what skills, knowledge or other attributes a person should possess (or be capable of acquiring) in order to do a job. To know this the job/s should be analysed, preferably following a systematic procedure. Failure to do this could result in unrealistically high or irrelevant standards being imposed. Once the job has been carefully analysed to determine exactly what it involves, it is then possible to specify the required skills, knowledge and attributes, which can then be embodied in an employee specification. For example, to insist on unnecessarily high educational qualifications, or a particular kind of experience which is not essential to adequate job performance, may result in unlawful indirect discrimination, if the requirement results in an adverse impact on women and/or blacks.

Advertising the job

All advertisements must be free of discrimination on grounds of race, sex or marriage. The use of words indicating a preference for either sex should where possible be avoided, but if there is no unisex word to describe an occupation eg waiter/waitress, then it should be made clear in the advertisement that the job is in fact open to persons of both sexes. Requirements and conditions specified in an advertisement should be checked to ensure that they are in fact 'justifiable'.

If a job is advertised through a Job Centre or employment agency, a word spoken on a telephone or in face-to-face conversation can be as discriminatory as a written word in an advertisement. Employment agencies are subject to the law, and an 'understanding' between the employer and the agency that, for example, only men or only Europeans will be considered for a job is an unlawful discriminatory practice.

When the employer recruits direct from schools or colleges it is necessary to ensure that both sexes and ethnic minority groups are reached by the recruitment process. Exclusive concentration on schools which are predominantly white or male could mean that girls and blacks may have less opportunity to hear about job opportunities offered by the employer. Similarly, advertisements in the press should be placed so that all categories of applicant have a chance to see them.

Receiving applications and short-listing

A number of tribunal cases have arisen where a gateman or a telephone operator or secretary has been responsible for discriminatory acts. Where this could occur staff should be given strict instructions not to turn applicants away, and the employer should take steps to ensure that the instructions are being complied with.

The criteria used for short-listing should be clearly specified in advance, and the reasons for rejecting candidates should be recorded. This enables the employer to ensure that relevant and appropriate standards are being consistently applied. In addition the keeping of records enables him to evaluate the efficiency of the selection process by means of a follow-up study. Selection decisions by individuals, in the absence of records or some form of checking or accountability, constitute a major hazard to fairness, since unfair discrimination could occur without the employer being aware that it was taking place.

Assessing candidates

The application form

Most job applications entail the completion of a form requesting information from the candidates. As with all forms of assessment, the application form cannot in itself be discriminatory; it is the use to which it is put which may be discriminatory in a way which contravenes the law. It is highly desirable that the application form should not be used for a purpose for which it is neither suited nor designed. It should not, for example, be used as a language test for those who speak English as a second language. The skills of understanding and completing the form may be quite different from those necessary for satisfactorily performing the job. If the skills embodied in the application form are, say, in excess of those required for the job, then unlawful indirect discrimination may result. The assessment of language and communication ability, whether it is to diagnose a training need, or the ability to do a job, is a specialized skill and should not be undertaken without either careful analysis of the jobs or professional help. The analysis and construction of an appropriate tool for assessing language and communication ability is best left to experts. (See list of further reading for a more detailed discussion of language testing and indirect discrimination.)

Application forms are usually the sole basis of short-listing and should be designed to elicit the information which will permit valid decisions to be made.

A problem of concern to many employers is whether or not it is unlawful to ask for information about colour or ethnic origin, or the candidate's marital status and dependents. In simple terms, it is not discriminatory to seek such information. Again, what matters is the use to which the information is put. The draft Code of Practice, issued by the Commission for Racial Equality, recommends ethnic record keeping, as this is the only way in which an employer can ensure that discrimination is not occurring, and that its policy and practices are operating according to genuine (rather than presumed) equality of opportunity.

Many application forms ask whether or not the applicant is married. Some forms state that this information is necessary for pension purposes, though the employer does not need this information until someone is actually appointed. It may be simpler, in order to prevent the possibility of misunderstanding, to request this information *after* an appointment is made, rather than to ask all applicants. However, the benefit of such a procedure has to be weighed against the additional administrative complexity.

When applicants are asked for details of ethnic origin it is essential to explain, on the form or otherwise, why this information is being requested. Some employers enclose an extract from their equal opportunity policy statement and stress that the information is necessary to ensure that the policy is working effectively. The information can be obtained on a detachable sheet so that it can be separated from the individual's personal records. The information can be coded and analysed on that basis so that anonymity can be preserved.

The interview

The interview is usually regarded as the universal and indispensible form of assessment. It has been extensively researched, and much of the research has focussed on the unreliability of the interview and its proneness to bias and distortion. The interview is essentially an encounter between people in which the interviewer attempts to obtain evidence of the candidate's suitability for a job. The assessment should focus on determining the candidate's skills, knowledge and other attributes which have been shown to be necessary for satisfactory performance of the job.

In terms of discrimination the following points apply:

The interview should be properly conducted. This speaks for itself and is justified on the argument that selection should be effective and assessment should be efficient. However the practical implications for discrimination become clearer if the point is put negatively. A badly conducted interview, lacking structure, respect or courtesy could lead to charges of discrimination if the candidate fails to get the job. It may be unwise but it is not unlawful to interview badly. It would of course be unlawful if only women or only black candidates tended to receive badly conducted interviews. A number of recent tribunal cases have taken into account the fact that an interview was poorly conducted when judging whether or not an act of discrimination had occurred.

Interviewers should be trained. One of the reliable findings of interview research is that when interviewers are trained there is less disagreement in their assessment of candidates. There are many different courses now available and this is not the place to examine them in detail. However, it should be stressed that, in the absence of training, it is most unlikely that candidates will be fully and systematically assessed. Ideally the training should include an examination of the nature of discrimination, as well as the practical meaning of the law. In addition, the training should cover the skills of interviewing people from different cultures, and the ways in which cultural assumptions and stereotypes may unconsciously influence the interviewers' judgements. This could be manifested in false assumptions (which are not tested because of the operation of the stereotype) or alternatively, the stereotype may mislead the interviewer into failing to provide a systematic and comprehensive assessment of the candidate.

It is unlikely that attitudes and stereotyped thinking can be altered through training, but, if the focus of the training is to place emphasis on the core skills of interviewing, then attitudes and stereotypes will have less room to operate. If the core skill (to which everything else is secondary) is seen as the systematic search for reliable evidence of job-relevant attributes, skills and/or knowledge, which is then recorded, stereotypes will be less influential. This would be particularly so if one aim of the training was to make the trainees aware of how stereotypes can operate without their awareness, and how powerful cultural and sexist assumptions can be in influencing the way we think or interpret what is before us.

The interview should be as objective as possible.   Objectivity in this context has two distinct meanings. First, all the interviews for a given job should be broadly similar in structure, length and the manner in which they are conducted. Here objectivity is equated with systematic assessment irrespective of the sex or race of the candidates. Consistency is a feature of the properly conducted interview. The second meaning applies to the selection criteria which are applied. The point has already been made that an analysis of the job will enable an employee specification to be drawn up. To the extent that this can be done in terms of attributes which can be clearly specified, eg the actual skills used in performing certain tasks, the assessment can be reasonably objective. The problem arises where less tangible characteristics are specified, or if not specified, are used in the selection decision. These criteria are often considered by interviewers to be very important and are often used to choose between candidates who possess the minimum job qualifications. A survey of managers' use of selection criteria when interviewing, revealed four clusters of what the researchers called non-ability criteria.[4] The four clusters, and representative examples are given in Figure 26.2. The percentages show how frequently the criteria were quoted by the managers.

An advantage of the interview is that it enables the prospective employer to take a look at the candidates. However, this is also its greatest weakness, as it allows almost unrestricted use of the non-ability criteria. This is sometimes expressed in terms of a candidate having 'a good personality' or the 'ability to fit in'. There is a danger that these yardsticks can, consciously or unconsciously, exclude women and ethnic minorities. The interview is

I   SOCIAL CREDENTIALS   71%
    eg Social background

II   IMAGE OF SOLID RESPECTABILITY
    eg Married   45%
      Public-spirited   88%

III   SUPERFICIAL PRESENTABILITY
    eg Pleasant personality   99%
      'Looks like a manager'   69%
      Clean-cut appearance   98%

IV   RELATIONS WITH CO-WORKERS
    eg Co-operative   100%
      Self-control   100%

Figure 26.2   Four clusters of non-ability criteria

notoriously unreliable as a means of assessing non-ability criteria, and it is easy, for example, to confuse liking the candidate in the interview with the assumption that he or she is skilled at getting on with people in general.

Subjective factors cannot be eliminated from the interview, but the risks of unlawful discrimination arising from undue weight being attached to non-ability criteria can be reduced by deliberately shifting the balance towards the assessment of concretely specified job-relevant abilities.

Ideally, the interview should not be used to assess abilities which are more directly and more accurately assessed by other means.   The interview is not the best means of assessing whether someone has the ability to undergo training, whether he or she can work quickly and accurately, can present an argument cogently in a group, or is able to plan and organize his or her work effectively and establish realistic priorities, or whether he or she has the potential to develop as a manager. These things can be assessed in an interview by inference from the candidate's description of his or her past, but it becomes inceasingly unreliable if the candidate has not had relevant experience, or is asked only hypothetical questions. A lack of relevant experience is likely to be common among black candidates or women, who, for a variety of reasons, (including discrimination against them and the lack of equal opportunity) may not have had the chance to build up experience and skills which would make assessment by interview a reasonable proposition. Their skills, knowledge and other attributes can be assessed only through other forms of assessments, such as trainability tests (see Chapter 9), psychometric tests, group exercises, in-tray exercises, etc. Ideally these techniques should, where appropriate, be used for all candidates, as they represent a more direct form of assessment than the interview. When comparing the performance of women and ethnic minorities the assessor would need to make allowance for the fact that some skills develop only if the individual has had the opportunity to do certain jobs, though the skills are quite easily acquired in the job.

Pencil and paper tests

Tests come in a variety of forms and serve a variety of purposes, (see Chapter 8). Properly used, tests provide an objective assessment of candidates' abilities, aptitudes, interests, attainments or personality characteristics. The assessment is objective in the sense that each candidate is assessed in exactly the same way, under the same conditions, and the scoring follows a laid down procedure. If a test has been chosen following a careful job analysis, and is interpreted in the light of a thorough validation study, then the test will enable the employer, on the basis of the test scores, to separate those candidates likely to do well on the job from those less likely to do well.

In terms of the law on discrimination it is not in itself unlawful to use a test in the absence of any validation. However, it may be unlawful if a disproportionate number of women or ethnic minorities are rejected on the basis of their test scores. This is usually referred to as 'adverse impact'. Once a candidate has been able to satisfy an industrial tribunal that the use of the test has an adverse impact against women or ethnic minorities, the definition of indirect discrimination, in both the Sex Discrimination Act 1975 and the Race Relations Act 1976, then requires the employer to justify whatever is causing the adverse impact, ie the use of the test. Normally the justification of the use of a test is a validation study. Validation is a basic requirement of good practice irrespective of the law on discrimination. It should be clear that, if the use of a test results in adverse impact, an employer would not be in a position to justify the use of that test in the absence of validation data. The whole issue of validity and the nature of justification is discussed separately below.

It is probably no exaggeration to assert that most tests in this country are not supported by full or even partial practical validation studies.[5] The situation was similar in the United States when the Civil Rights Act 1964 first came into operation. In the USA, tests were very unpopular, especially among blacks, because they were regarded as arbitrary barriers to employment. Blacks tended to do less well on written tests, owing mainly to their relative socio-economic disadvantage by comparison with whites. Complaints were brought against employers using tests, and many, though by no means all tests, were declared unlawful, either because validation was entirely lacking or because the tests were being improperly used. The effect of the court proceedings was to scare employers away from using tests, and there was a dramatic reduction in their use. However, in recent years there has been a growth in the use of tests, but few employers would attempt to misuse tests in quite the same way as was common in the past. Federal regulations now lay down strict standards for the use and validation of tests and tests are being used on a firmer and more professional basis than ever before. Indeed many employers believe that the proper use of validated tests is one way of removing discriminatory barriers. If the standards embodied in the tests are job-related, and the assessment is systematic, then avoidable bias against women and ethnic minorities can be reduced. If the alternative is reliance on subjective assessments by interviewers, then the increased use of validated tests would be one way of reducing the risk of unfair discrimination.[6]

Some employers are concerned that the content of a test may be biased against women because of previous unequal opportunities to obtain jobs or to undergo training, or because of biases against women in their upbringing and education. As a result, a test score may not give as accurate an assessment of a woman as of a man. Similarly, some members of ethnic minority groups may be at a disadvantage, by comparison with others, when being tested. This could arise because of unfamiliarity with the process of being tested, or because of assumptions, implicit in the test content, which adversely affect people who were not born in, or who are not completely familiar with, the culture in which the test was devised.

In practical terms the employer needs to ask: are the inferences made about women testees and ethnic minority testees on the basis of their test scores as valid and reliable as inferences made about men and whites in general? To find the answer the user may need to conduct a separate validation analysis for women and minority groups. It is possible to have validation data which show that the test is valid in use overall, but when the data on women or ethnic minorities are analysed separately it is found that the test is less valid or not valid at all for the sub-groups. This situation is known as differential validity and may require separate calculations for predicting the likelihood of being successful on the job when women and ethnic minorities are being tested. In this way, optimal accuracy in predicting future performance can be attained for any sub-group which emerges. Differential validity is a complex concept, and it is essential that an expert on testing be used in the design and execution of the study.

An instant solution which, at first glance, appears to have attractions for employers is the use of so-called culture-fair tests. They are described here as 'so-called' because it is a myth that any test can be culture-fair or culture-free. All tests are designed in a cultural context, and will be used in a specific culture. It is not always clear what a culture-fair test is supposed to be measuring. Although they may be useful for research purposes when a common basis may be required for comparing people from different cultures, it is unlikely that a culture-fair test will resolve the problem of discrimination against specific groups. The best strategy is to use conventional tests and interpret the test scores in such a way that the accuracy of prediction is optimal for any given group. The critical criterion is whether the interpretation put on test scores can be justified. Only a validation study can provide such justification.

In some cases candidates may obtain lower scores on a test than they are capable of achieving. This could be caused by sheer unfamiliarity with being tested (as some candidates may never have seen a test before) or by excessive anxiety before and during the test. Pre-testing orientation exercises have been developed and used in the United States to overcome a lack of what is known as 'test sophistication', and to prepare socially disadvantaged individuals in order that they are set to perform at their best. Pre-testing packages do not exist in this country, and there is a strong case to be made for regular users of tests to prepare their own, though this would require careful validation. Practice items at the beginning of tests are designed, to some extent, to overcome the effects of unfamiliarity and excessive anxiety. They are unlikely to be adequately effective with recent immigrants, and those who have never been tested before, or who are particularly worried about being tested.

Other forms of assessment

It was noted earlier that the interview is not always the most effective and direct means of assessing candidates' suitability for employment. It is surprising, in view of the high cost of labour, the importance of recruiting capable workers, the restrictions on dismissing employees, and the need to comply with the law on discrimination, how few resources (in time and money) are devoted to ensuring that selection is efficient. There is no law on unfair selection which parallels the law on unfair dismissal but, whenever a selection practice results in adverse impact, the employer may be required, if a complaint is brought, to justify the procedure. One strategy, and it is the one that makes most sense, is to ensure that all selection practices are valid, not only in an overall sense, but for any sub-group that emerges in the analysis, especially women and ethnic minorities. Regardless of the law this can usually be justified on a cost-effective basis alone. An alternative strategy is to avoid any practice or requirement which could result in an adverse impact. In this way systematic biases during the interview could be concealed, but this would be counter-productive as the employer has no way of telling whether suitable candidates are being turned away and less suitable individuals are being recruited.

Some forms of assessment may be less prone to causing adverse impact, and therefore would not require justification in law. Self-report inventories, biographical questionnaires, trainability assessments, in-tray exercises, and other group tasks which frequently form the components of assessment centres may or may not be free of adverse impact. It would therefore be unwise for any employer to embark on these forms of assessment without a validation study.

The problem of validation

For many years the basic principles of validation, and the main types of validation strategy have been expounded by selection experts and professional bodies. In the light of the legislation, validation studies will increasingly be scrutinized by industrial tribunals. As in the United States, the professional experts had become complacent and uncritical in attitudes towards validation, and the law may well stimulate a renewed examination of old ideas. The most powerful form of validation is predictive validation, which studies the correlation between the selection process, either as a whole or in parts, and a reliable criterion of performance in training or on the job. However, this procedure is time-consuming and frequently technically impossible. The criterion-related concurrent model (in which the selection process is validated against the performance of existing workers) is less difficult to use but is weaker and has an inherent problem because it could lead to the perpetuation of past discrimination being based on existing employees, who may be all white and/or male. A procedure may be 'valid' in terms of a concurrent model, but the employers would have no way of knowing whether suitable women or ethnic minorities were being disproportionately rejected by the selection procedure. It is a matter for tribunals to decide whether any evidence of validity, however small, will automatically be taken to mean 'justifiable' in terms of the law, or whether some evidence of practical benefit will also be required. In practical terms, the employer should decide whether to rest content with any form of validation evidence or whether to seek evidence to show that the procedures are as effective and as efficient as possible. For example, it may be possible to use an alternative form of assessment which is as valid as another, but in which the resultant adverse impact is considerably less, ie equal validity but less adverse impact.

Other methods of validation (eg the so-called 'content validation') are, for technical reasons, less satisfactory. In fact, the traditional models of validation are not always adequate, and new innovative research and development is required. To some extent this is already underway, and one of the most promising developments is synthetic validity in which the key element is a formal and thorough job analysis. (For a more detailed discussion see the report, *Discriminating Fairly*, in the list of further reading.)

Effective application of the law: genuine equality or token gestures?

The law lays down the employer's statutory obligations. It does not spell out the actions that an employer should take to make sure that he is in fact complying with the law. Still less does it specify what needs to be done if the intention of the legislation is to be achieved, as distinct from a minimum compliance with legal obligations. It is for the employer to work out the implications of the legislation for personnel policy and practice in his own enterprise and locality.

To help in this process, the Commission for Racial Equality has issued a Code of Practice for the elimination of racial discrimination and the promotion of equal opportunity in employment. As with all codes of practice, the CRE code does not have the force of law but is admissible in evidence in any proceedings under the Race Relations Act 1976 before an industrial tribunal, and compliance with the code is taken into account by the tribunal. Moreover, as the code adds, if employers 'take the steps which the Commission for Racial Equality recommends to prevent employees from doing acts of unlawful discrimination they may avoid liability for such acts in any legal proceedings brought against them.

The code recommends the publication of an equal opportunity policy, advising that this policy should be confirmed in writing to all staff. It is made clear however, that this is only the beginning. Indeed, a statement of policy which is not accompanied by a plan of action can lead to a sense of complacency and an untested assumption that nothing more needs to be done. The code stresses the need for responsibility for the policy to be clearly allocated to a senior member of management and urges discussions with trade unions or employee representatives, together with training and guidance for all supervisory staff and other relevant decision makers. Specially relevant in relation to recruitment is the stress laid on training 'personnel and line managers, foremen, gatekeepers and receptionists to ensure that they understand their responsibilities under the law and under company policy'. The code also stresses the need 'to examine and review regularly existing procedures and criteria and, where they find that they are actually or potentially discriminatory, they must change them'.

Any organization that takes equal opportunity seriously clearly needs to take steps to ensure appropriate behaviour at all key points. Officially, trade union support for equal opportunity is absolute. As the code points out, the TUC has recommended a model equal opportunity clause for inclusion in collective agreements. This does not mean however that such policies are universally accepted by trade union membership and it is therefore essential to discuss the policy and its implications in practice very fully with local trade union officers and shop stewards. Supervisors and shop stewards need training in the reasons for a policy and what it means for them. This should of course include a clear statement of legal obligations but even more important is the opportunity a training programme provides to bring to the surface anticipated problems and to explore some of the assumptions on which prejudice is based.

Such discussions and training are an essential foundation for the implementation of an equal opportunity policy. There is also much detailed work which needs to be done to ensure that personnel management practices are in line with the policy.

References

1   N. McIntosh and D. Smith, 'The extent of racial discrimination', *Political and Economic Planning,* Vol. XL, Broadsheet no. 547, 1974.
2   *Industrial Relations Law Reports,* 288, 1977.
3   *Industrial Relations Law Reports,* 199, 1979.
4   R. P. Quinn, J. M. Tabor and L. K. Gordan, *The Decision to Discriminate.* The Institute for Social Research, Ann Arbor, 1968.
5   C. J. Brotherton 'Paradigms of selection validation: Some comments in the light of British Equal Opportunities Legislation', *Journal of Occupational Psychology,* vol. 51, no.1, 1980, pp 73–9.
6   M. A. Pearn, *Employment Testing and the Goal of Equal Opportunity.* The Runnymede Trust, London, 1978.

Further reading

(1978): *Towards Fairer Selection: A Code for Non-Discrimination.* London: Institute of Personnel Management.

(1980): *Discriminating Fairly: A Guide to Fair Selection.* London: Published jointly by the British Psychological Society and the Runnymede Trust.

Pearn, M. A. (1979): *The Fair Use of Tests.* Windsor: NFER Publishing Company.

Pearn, M. A. (1977): *Selecting and Training Coloured Workers. Training Information Paper No. 10.* London: HMSO.

Seear, N. S. (1980): *The Management of Equal Opportunity.* London: The Runnymede Trust.

(1979): *Language Testing and Indirect Discrimination: Lessons of the British Steel Case.* London: The Runnymede Trust.

Index